D0513859

THE
STORIES
BEHIND THE
LABELS

THE

STORIES

BEHIND THE

LABELS

THE HISTORY,

ROMANCE

& CHARACTERS

OF THE WORLD

OF WINE

AND DRINK

andrew jones

CRAWFORD HOUSE PUBLISHING

BATHURST

A CHP Production

Produced and published by
Crawford House Publishing Pty Ltd
PO Box 1484
Bathurst NSW 2795 Australia

Distributed by
Pegasus Distribution Ltd
Unit 5B, Causeway Park
Wilderspool Causeway
Warrington
Cheshire WA4 6QE
United Kingdom

Designed by David H. Barrett
Cover design by Kylie Ledger

National Library of Australia Cataloguing-in-Publication entry
Jones, Andrew, 1942-
The stories behind the labels.

Bibliography.
Includes index.
ISBN 1 86333 116 6.

1. Wine labels. 2. Wine and winemaking.
3. Distilling industries. 4. Liquors –
Packaging. I. Title.

641.22

Printed in Italy by Amilcare Pizzi s.p.a.

10 9 8 7 6 5 4 3 2 1

CONTENTS

CONVERSIONS FOR COMMON MEASUREMENTS

Because this book encompasses stories from around the world and from different historical periods, it is impossible to convert measurements into any one system. The following table is therefore pro-vided to enable basic conversions to be made between the major systems of measurement which occur in the book.

LENGTH

Metric	Imperial and US
1 millimetre = 0.04 inches	1 inch = 25.4 millimetres
1 centimetre = 0.39 inches	1 inch = 2.54 centimetres
1 metre = 3.3 feet	1 foot = 0.3 metres
1 metre = 1.1 yards	1 yard = 0.9 metres
1 kilometre = 0.6 miles	1 mile = 1.6 kilometres

AREA

Metric	Imperial and US
1 square centimetre = 0.16 square inches	1 square inch = 6.45 square centimetres
1 square metre = 10.8 square feet	1 square foot = 0.09 square metres
1 hectare = 2.5 acres	1 acre = 0.4 hectares

CAPACITY

Metric	Imperial and US
1 litre = 35.2 UK fluid ounces	1 UK fluid ounce = 0.0284 litres
1 litre = 33.8 US fluid ounces	1 US fluid ounce = 0.0296 litres
1 litre = 1.76 UK pints	1 UK pint = 0.57 litres
1 litre = 2.11 US pints	1 US pint = 0.47 litres
1 litre = 0.88 UK quarts	1 UK quart = 1.14 litres
1 litre = 1.06 US quarts	1 US quart = 0.95 litres
1 litre = 0.22 UK gallons	1 UK gallon = 4.55 litres
1 litre = 0.26 US gallons	1 US gallon = 3.78 litres

WEIGHT

Metric	Imperial and US
1 gram = 0.04 ounces	1 ounce = 28.3 grams
1 kilogram = 2.2 pounds	1 pound = 0.45 kilograms
1 tonne = 0.98 UK tons	1 UK ton = 1.02 tonnes
1 tonne = 1.1 US tons	1 US ton = 0.91 tonnes

FOREWORD

I first met Andrew Jones in Boston in 1983. He was taking a break from filming the "Ten Green Bottles" television series and he was very excited about an interview a few days earlier with the octogenarian daughter of the private secretary of the last Russian Tsarina. He was carrying bundles of notes and files and speaking into the inevitable cassette machine. Later, over a glass of Chardonnay, Andrew told me of his idea for a collection of writings about pioneer vintners and their famous products. His passion for history was clear.

Since then, my wife Anthea and I have seen Andrew in action on various occasions as he recorded his experiences for British, fans. Most memorable was the time in Baltimore when he vainly tried to persuade a table of diners to order an Alsace Riesling instead of their customary ice-cold draught beer to accompany their native speciality, hot, peppery, steamed crabs. Famous Olde O'Bryckis will never be the same again.

In pursuit of his dream, Andrew has spent twelve years tracing the heritage of a truly ancient trade. His quest has taken him through graveyards, archives and libraries in just about every major wine-producing country in the world. *The Stories Behind the Labels* is the result.

Professor Bert Smith, MA, BFA
University of Baltimore (Publications Design)

PREFACE

Throughout my career as a wine journalist I have been intrigued by the history and personalities connected with wine and drink across the globe, and it seems that in the course of my broadcasting I have aroused my audience's interest also. So to satisfy the demands of viewers and listeners, particularly in the UK, the USA and Australia, here it is at last – *The Stories Behind the Labels*. I do not claim that these stories have any literary merit, but they do represent years of experience and research in vineyards and distilleries great and small, humble and renowned. Neither am I a professional historian, but in all instances I have made a serious attempt to uncover the truth, be it through written records or oral tradition. In some cases the information gleaned has been given anonymously or in confidence, and on the odd, rare occasion I have resorted to deduction and conjecture. None of this detracts from the validity of the stories as stories and their power to illuminate and entertain.

No preface would be complete without some acknowledgements but if I were to thank all the people who have contributed to this book the list would be endless. Having made that statement, however, I must express my gratitude to several people. First, I would like to thank the two women who have devoted their time and energy to supporting me, namely my assistant, Michelle Menari, for her painstaking diligence in organising photographs, labels, and so on, and my wife, Branwen, for her efforts to translate my jumbled thoughts into some form of coherent English via the keyboard. I would also like to thank the following:

Mildred Howie, writer and old friend, Geyserville, California; Father Gerald McKevitt, University of Santa Clara, California; Clyde Arbuckle, local historian, San Jose, California; Dixie Hibbs, local historian, Bardstown, Kentucky; various officers of the Russian and Ukrainian Orthodox churches, Hartford, Connecticut; Dante Vaghi and the late Carlo Vaghi, Bethel, Connecticut; Colonel Francois Bonal, author and retired Secretary, CIVC Epernay, France; Dr Vittorio Scotti Douglas, Milan, Italy; the late David de Jongh, London, England; Craig Smith, the Australian Wine Centre, London, England. Thanks to the reference librarians in Savannah, Georgia; Greensboro, North Carolina; San Jose, California; Louisville, Kentucky; Tulsa, Oklahoma; the Harold Washinton Library, Chicago, Illinois; Melbourne, Victoria; Cardiff, Wales; the Guildhall library, London; the archivist at the Royal Opera House, Covent Garden, London; the National Maritime Museum, Greenwich, England; and many others who have provided helpful and speedy support. Finally, I must thank the various anonymous hotel, restaurant and retail staff and journalists who, under the seal of confidentiality, provided most of the information for the chapter "Presidents, Royals and the Famous".

As someone who is fortunate enough to combine his occupation with the subject dearest to his heart, I hope that I have conveyed my enthusiasm and love of wine to readers in such a way that they will be inspired to share my delight in the grape and the part it has played in history worldwide.

1. CREATIVE MEN

ACTIONS SPEAK LOUDER THAN WORDS
Champagne Mercier, France

Champagne Mercier is the smaller sister of the huge Moët et Chandon house and occupies the adjacent premises on the Avenue de Champagne in Epernay. In its 18 kilometres of cellars one finds the breathtaking sight of a gargantuan Champagne barrel. It is a 20-tonne monster that the founder of the house ordered to be constructed for the 1889 Paris Exhibition to celebrate the centennial of the French Revolution.

Eugène Mercier realised that many other Champagne houses would be exhibiting at Paris and therefore prepared his publicity plans a generation in advance. According to Mercier records, the mammoth cask "took 20 years to build, using 250 hundred year old oaks". The wood was imported from Hungary and when the cask was completed, the Remois sculptor Navlet was commissioned to decorate it.

The greatest obstacle was the eight-day journey from Epernay to Paris, for which the cask was mounted on four enormous wheels and drawn by a team of twenty-four oxen. Yet on some hills even

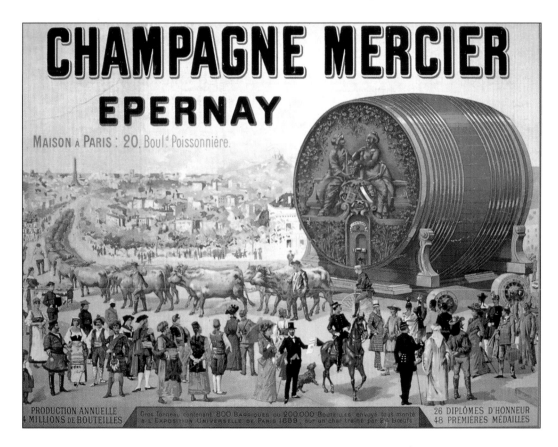

Historic Mercier publicity, from 1889, celebrating the epic journey of Eugène Mercier's 20-tonne champagne barrel

at an alarming rate. Sixteen hours later the balloon, with its bewildered occupants, landed intact in an forest in Alsace, then under German annexation. The police arrived and Champagne Mercier was threatened with prosecution for illegal immigration. The case, it was soon discovered, could not be justified and only a minor charge proceeded. Mercier was fined 20 crowns for failing to declare six untouched Champagne bottles that were found on board the balloon.

The story made headlines in newspapers around the world and Eugène Mercier claimed it was the cheapest publicity they had ever gained, costing "less than a centime a line".

the strength of the oxen proved inadequate and they had to be supplemented by eighteen horses. Complications arose in crossing three different bridges and it became necessary for Eugène Mercier to negotiate the purchase of a number of small houses to demolish them before the gigantic convoy could move forward. Finally, permission had to be requested from the Minister of State for War for the very gates of Paris to be removed for the oak monster to gain access to the city.

The entire undertaking cost Eugène a small fortune and he had good cause to be reticent in admitting the true cost but he did revel in the wealth of exposure and publicity gained. This tempted him to follow the first promotion with another, but far less expensive, activity in the French capital. On this occasion he hired a hot-air balloon with a pilot and secured it in the Champ de Mars. Inquisitive passers-by were invited to clamber aboard and taste the Mercier Champagne. After several successful days of calm weather a sudden squall arose and the moorings of the balloon broke. Nine astonished passengers, a waiter and a pilot skimmed the rooftops of Paris as they hurtled east

THE BARON OF BULLY HILL
Bully Hill Vineyards, USA

What can one say about a man who has been married and divorced four times; has battled in court with the Coca-Cola Company; who, since a 1990 motor accident, has been classed as a "respirator-dependent quadriplegic"; and who paints each of his wine label designs by holding the brush in his mouth? He is the same man who before his devastating collision said of himself: "I've been thrown out of the Californian Wine Industry, the New York Wine Industry, my local club and even the Hammondsport Episcopalian Church." He continued to rail: "Everybody in my family, except my father, my ten year old son and my winemaker, deserted me. The community completely rejected me and treated me like a dog. Why? Because I wanted honesty and integrity in the wine business."

This man was described by *Space World* in July 1988 as "the decidedly immodest Walter Stephen Taylor, the self-styled Baron of Bully Hill".

Having read that account many a reader will wish to take a sharp breath, something the unfortunate Walter Taylor is unable to do, for he who was a source of great vigour, determination and abundant energy now has to struggle for his fresh-air supply with a ventilator.

To begin to reconcile all these extremes one has to search back to the foundation of the Taylor winery by his grandfather, also Walter Taylor, who in 1878 chose a pretty site that overlooked Keuka Lake, in Steuben County. There, in the Finger Lakes region of upstate New York, he set the Taylor Winery on what was then a humble path to success. Over the next forty or so years the family business grew at a steady rate and then Prohibition struck. The Taylor family, however, were circumspect, and turned that position to their advantage by transforming their trade from wine production to grape juice. Within a few years they had established themselves as a major national and inter-

T*he Mercier Barrel, now housed at Champagne Mercier, Épernay, France*

national shipper of that product and continued to reap their rewards.

The repeal of Prohibition found the previously strong New York State wine industry virtually nonexistent but the Taylor Wine Company was in the finest fettle and continued to expand at a healthy pace, outdistancing the economic fluctuations of the 1930s and World War II, and moving from strength to strength as the 1950s arrived. It was then that Walter S. Taylor, a member of the family and a senior of the executive, struck and it was a savage blow. Walter argued fervently against the continuing use of American *labrusca* grape varieties and in favour of the French hybrids, which were beginning to produce some promising results. Additionally he openly voiced his criticism of both his own company and New York wine generally, for its use of additives, and for "watering down its wines". He began to campaign on these issues and his volleys proved to be an irritation to his family and colleagues, and many of his neighbouring producers. Yet nothing happened and the additives, the dilution and the *labrusca* vines persisted. Then Walter took a new tack.

He consistently argued that winemaking should be a completely natural matter. One day in 1970 he overstepped the limits of reason and discretion in the sight of his fellows. He was a guest speaker in San Francisco, at a wine wholesalers' convention, where he launched a dramatic attack upon those practices in the New York wine industry. His own Taylor Wine Company fired him and Walter, never a man to be crestfallen, decided to revive the old founding Taylor property with its 150 acres of vineyards on Bully Hill, near Hammondsport, New York. He called his new wine Bully Hill Vineyards and, quite fairly in the eyes of many, added his own name, Walter S. Taylor.

In 1977 the large Taylor Wine Company sold out to the Coca-Cola Company, during the soft-drink empire's six-year involvement in the wine industry, an involvement which some might call "unhappy". The Atlanta-based giant assumed they had purchased the name Taylor with the transaction and sued Walter to prevent him using his own surname. Coca-Cola was just too powerful for Walter to wage war against in court and he had to accept the initial court decision against him but Walter was made of sterner stuff.

He cleverly turned the court decision to his own advantage with a brilliant marketing campaign. He continued with his very same labels but had the name Taylor blacked out on them and even did the same with the name over the winery. Next he had the wicked idea to picket Coca-Cola with his pet goat tethered alongside him bearing the name Taylor. Coca-Cola sent him and the goat packing

"They have my name & heritage, but they didn't get my goat"

©1993, BHV, Inc.

and Walter coined a campaign phrase which had New Yorkers roaring with laughter at the fizzy-drinks conglomerate. "They've taken my name but they can't take my goat," he protested and then created several "goat" wine labels which heaped fuel on the fire. The most popular was a wine named Love My Goat Red Wine, described by no less a paper than the *Houston Chronicle* as "a touch off-dry, a good starter for those who don't like the oaky, more austere styles of red wines". The Coca-Cola lawyers pursued Walter to a federal judge, who ordered him to stop mocking the earlier court order and instructed him to "turn over all objectionable labels and advertising". Walter responded in typical fashion, taking two trips to deliver the labels. On one he arrived in a muck spreader and tipped a load of manure containing tens of thousands of labels, and on the other organised a 100-car motorcade that included trucks-full of employees yelling, "We love Bully Hill." Once again the publicity rolled and Walter, the Baron of Bully Hill, was seen as the champion of little men against impersonal giants.

In 1983, Coca-Cola, apparently frustrated by their wine-industry experiences, sold out all their wines to the greatly experienced Joseph E. Seagram Company, which proceeded with their work without even an obvious side glance.

Then there was the NASA confrontation, which dates back to 1981 when the iconoclastic wine man first ventured into his part-time career as an artist. Being Walter Taylor, he had to make a lofty start.

He suggested to NASA that he should make an official painting of the first launch of the space shuttle. NASA agreed, invited him to Florida and purchased the picture, which later was hung in the National Air and Space Museum in Washington, DC. Walter then put the drawing on a wine label and filed an entry with the US Patent and Trademark office for the right to use "space shuttle" as a trademark. To his annoyance, NASA filed an objection and the matter went to court. NASA argued three points:

> The term "space shuttle" on wine confuses the public about the source of the product; there is a false suggestion of a connection of the wine with NASA and the term "space shuttle" constitutes a national symbol.

On 21 May 1987, Walter finally won on all counts. Once more the ebullient Mr Taylor was in the news, visitors came flocking to the winery and sales again increased at a healthy rate.

Of course Bully Hill is a quieter place since the accident but the publicity continues to flow at a steady rate, boosted by one of the most remarkable selections of labels one is ever likely to see, a veritable vintitulist's dream.

Whether the vineyard's style of hybrid wines will survive more than another twenty or so years one will have to wait and see, but in the next century the memory of the Baron of Bully Hill will provide a colourful fund of stories, not just for local people, but for wine and other journalists, who will no doubt tell them for many generations.

THE CRAZY COMIC OF SANTA CRUZ
Bonny Doon, USA

Some amateur wine lovers rate him the most amusing character on the American wine scene, whilst in the view of some professional wine marketeers he is the most astute member of their species operating in California. Whichever assessment is most accurate, Randall Grahm of Bonny Doon Vineyard stimulates much debate, as well as

selling a not inconsiderable volume of wine.

Grahm, a major extrovert in a state full of extroverts, has set the US wine stores alive with laughter as the uninitiated read his labels for the first time. His witty presentations include such labels as Ca' del Solo, which features a moggy trapped at the top of a tree, Le Cigare Volant, which is apparently an allusion to some flying saucer incidents at Chateauneuf-du-Pape, and his classic Clos de Gilroy. The latter features "Le Gil des Rois/Le Roi des Gils" and bears a Victorian-style photo of the brilliantined poet laureate of the Santa Cruz mountains, taken some years ago, and an amusing earthquake reference. Under the vintage, 1989, he has printed the jumbled words "cuvée tremblent de terre", the winery being precariously positioned near the San Andreas fault.

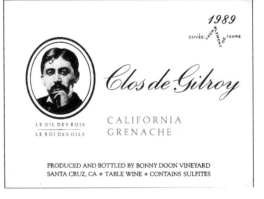

Many wine journalists and feature writers have written about this middle-aged creative comic, who is surely not as crazy as he makes out. But as I cannot hope to match his gargantuan genius, I prefer to leave his labels to speak for themselves and an extract from one of his more infamous parodies for the edification of all:

From "The Love Song of J. Alfred Rootstock"

Let us go then you and I
When the soucoupes and cigares volants hover

peaceably in the night-time sky
Like a tea-service upon a table.
Let us excavate through heavily rummaged bargain bins
The radically reduced, everything must go, red-tagged wholesale outlet tins
Of dented canned goods rising like armor-plated Ziggurats
And deeply discounted lees-filtered [Just say no to dregs] ends of vats
Emerald aisles giving on to architectonic floor-stacks
Smudged shelf-talkers artlessly affixed with thumb tacks.
Oh, do not ask, "Is this Cab fruity, floral or weedy?"
Tais-toi and drink up, sweetie.

Readers may be assured that his wines finish better than his poetry.

THE DANGER OF A PUBLIC COLLECTION
Benedictine, France

One of the most entertaining and illuminating distillery visits that one can make is to the home of Benedictine in Fécamp. Once the secret recipe of the Benedictine Abbey there, the liqueur was first created in 1510 by Dom Bernardo Vincelli, and for over two and a half centuries was used by the monks as a medicine for the sick and poor of the neighbourhood. The liqueur's monastic ownership came to an end when the monks were forced to flee France during the French Revolution.

At the time, the recipe was presumed lost to posterity but it came to light in 1863 as a result of the hobby of a Fécamp wine and spirit merchant called Alexandre le Grand. He was known among his family as a slightly eccentric collector of antique books and curios, over which he would muse for endless hours. He was the father of nineteen

W*eighing the plants (above) which comprise some of the ingredients of Benedictine*

I*nfusion of herbs (left), Benedictine, 1983*

surviving children and one of his great-grandsons, Bruno, told the tale in 1984 of one particular Christmas, probably 1861, when a relative had given Alexandre a large set of volumes which had been found gathering dust in an old shop. They had obviously come from the ancient library belonging to the former Benedictine Abbey and his great-grandfather had been delighted with the gift. Each page had been meticulously inspected until Alexandre, quite by chance, stumbled upon a small booklet. At first glance he was rather puzzled by the papers but he speedily concluded that they contained a recipe of some sort. A year later he was sufficiently enlightened to resume production of the liqueur, which he called Benedictine, and acknowledged the monks' production and use of it by using the initials D.O.M. on each bottle, standing for *Deo Optimo Maximo* (To God, the Most High). However on this occasion the production was a commercial enterprise and the liqueur was being sold for profit, not given away.

In a very few years Alexandre le Grand had made a fortune and decided to reinvest it by combining his work with his hobby and making all his antique curios available for the general public to view. It was an ambitious plan and served to enhance further the fame of the liqueur. He built an imposing Palais Benedictine alongside the distillery and furnished it with his antiquarian collection, allowing visitors to learn of past generations and observe the production of Benedictine on the same trip. His family successors complained that while he did invest a substantial sum in the Palais, it took another generation to repay the cost of the undertaking.

In contrast with most of his competitors, who refused to allow consumers across the threshold, Alexandre le Grand initiated a policy of openness and even presented a special display of the twenty-seven ingredients used in Benedictine by placing them in large wooden chests, where their pungent aromas would attract inquisitive tourists who had previously rarely seen anything more than the odd spice or herb used in the preparation of a liqueur. Each ingredient was identified together with a brief description of its characteristics, such as:

> cardamom: a plant from South-East Asia; the seeds have a peppery flavour;
> cloves: originally from an Indonesian tree, cloves are used as a spice; and
> myrrh: an aromatic and medicinal resin, from an Arabic tree.

Distillery tours were organised and detailed information about the processes of making Benedictine was given. Thousands flocked to Fécamp, its popularity aided by the fact that it was a seaside town accessible to Parisians. In due course visitors from countries throughout Europe began to arrive, some of whom were no doubt professional drink-makers, and the questions tour guides were asked became more and more technical. Then, the inevitable happened – attempts were made to copy the liqueur. A generation later, Benedictine opened a new exhibit, a shelf full of counterfeit bottles from a strange assortment of origins. The cost of litigation became prohibitive but Le Grand believed he should fight every case because he was convinced that when consumers tasted fake bottles of Benedictine the contents were likely to be inferior and could lead to the reputation of the original drink falling into disrepute.

By 1983 the counterfeit bottle collection totalled more than 500 exhibits from thirty-eight countries, including Bendix from Hamburg, Bonidine from Belgium, Bendicta from Spain, Bendetto from Estonia and Benedictus from Italy. Probably the most blatant attempt to copy the liqueur came from Sofia in Bulgaria, where a company called Kotcheff Brothers had renamed themselves Kotcheff Frères, produced an almost perfect replica of the original and labelled it "Veritable or Genuine Benedictine". The most audacious attempt is a bottle from Russia. When its producers were challenged by Benedictine's lawyers, they replied that they had no need to cooperate as they had been given exclusivity to produce Benedictine "by Rome".

A small part of Benedictine's counterfeit-bottle collection

THE LITTLE INVENTOR
Schweppes; Switzerland, England, Germany and USA

For many of us there exists a mental dividing line which separates flesh-and-blood figures from those whom we envisage as mere historical characters from the past. It is a division which particularly affects writers and researchers. For me the invisible barrier exists some time around 1850. After that date I can identify with such emotions as anger, jubilation and satisfaction, as displayed by the very people about whom I am writing. But before that date, I admit to my chagrin, I tend to consider people more or less as facts and statistics that have existed but are difficult to realise. It is as if my brain dehumanises them.

I first became aware of the problem when I began researching the story of "the Little Inventor", when the pathos of the dreadful plight experienced by a poor German family, moved me to tears.

The Little Inventor, as I term him, was always of physically small stature, but from childhood onwards he obviously grew substantially in intelligence, talent and ambition. Jean Jacob Schweppe was born in 1740 into an abjectly impoverished family, where the parents battled desperately to glean a living from their overworked smallholding. By the time he had reached the age of eleven, in 1751, means were so restricted that his mother and father approached a local tinker and offered their under-developed boy to him. The tinker, who made his living by calling from door to door, sharpening knives and blades and repairing cooking utensils, was told that Jacob would work hard all day in return for board and lodging.

To fully appreciate the situation it is necessary to form a picture of the quaint little town of Witzen-hausen, which lies amid wooded slopes in the peaceful, sheltered valley of the River Werra in the Hesse region of Germany. Visiting it today is like stepping back in time, for the narrow streets lined with picturesque wooden gabled houses have changed little, as somehow Witzenhausen has succeeded in staying off the beaten track. There is an air of sleepiness about the place where life continues at an altogether slower pace than is normal in the modern world. Remove electricity, gas and the telephone and all its associated commu-nications, together with every form of motorised vehicle and machine, and a few other trappings of contemporary life, and conditions in Witzenhausen would be largely as they were in 1751, with one exception – prosperity.

In 1751, Germany did not even exist and Witzenhausen was part of the Holy Roman Empire, with both French and German being spoken. The vast majority of the population were peasants, who, like Conrad Schweppe had inherited their small plots and were taxed on their production. They were, as some are today, trapped in a world where they lived on a day-to-day, hand-to-mouth basis, never earning sufficient money to break the mould of their lifestyles. In these circumstances Conrad Schweppe and his wife came to the conclusion that they would have to give their son away if he and they were to survive.

Yet what began as a tragic act by his parents succeeded in enabling Jacob to free himself from that seemingly never-ending chain of poverty. Concluding that their son was too frail to endure the rigours of a farming life, the Schweppes made

their proposition to the tinker. It must have cost them much agonising and distress to make their decision in the realisation that they could not afford to feed and clothe their own child. In the act of giving him up to the care of someone else they were at least hopeful that he would be provided for.

At this juncture the story takes a remarkable turn and highlights the honesty and integrity of the citizens of Witzenhausen. After a few short weeks the tinker returned the eleven-year-old boy to his parents, claiming that it would be a waste of Jacob's intelligence and talents to pursue such an occupa-tion. Astonished but grateful for his advice, Conrad Schweppe took Jacob to a local silversmith but the result was the same. In no time the silversmith too brought the clever young lad back to his parents, arguing that his brain should not be wasted. Either of these two men could have used young Jacob's intelligence to serve their own ends but demon-strated by their actions a disinterested concern for his welfare and future.

Subsequently his father found him a further and more demanding apprenticeship, this time to a *maître-bijoutier,* or master jeweller. Jacob was delighted with what was, at the age of eleven, his third apprenticeship. As far as we know he spent the next fourteen years of his life working at that craft within the confines of his home town, perpet-ually seeking to advance his knowledge and edu-cation. During these years he developed the hungry ambition that was to inspire him to success in later life.

Fortunately a considerable body of facts is record-ed about his early days, due largely to the work of the Protestant Deacon of Witzenhausen, Chris-topher Backmann, and Douglas Simmons, the former Schweppes Company Secretary and author of that company's outstanding book, *Schweppes, the First 200 Years.* These records offer an intriguing insight into that period of Jacob's life, and further research brings to light the fact that he was quite an active scholar in his formative years. In addition to his native German, it appears that he learned at least two other languages, French and English, with a view to widening his reading. In this manner he was able to purchase a variety of pamphlets and works on numerous topics, covering the general subject of mechanical engineering, which was of particular interest to him. It was a period when a *maître-bijoutier* would have been making and repairing the most intricate machinery in the most complicated of clocks and watches and in the stimulating new assortment of musical boxes which were gaining such popularity. It is likely that this delicate mechanical engineering became the chief influence in Jacob's quest to improve his skills. The

Geneva at the time of Jacob Schweppe

more he read, the more he sought to broaden his knowledge.

It has been suggested that among some of the papers Jacob read were certain hypotheses of the English inventor, Priestley, who affirmed on at least one occasion that it was feasible that in the not too distant future a satisfactory method of producing a continuous supply of aerated water would be discovered. Priestley, however, appears not to have been interested in pursuing that line of scientific enquiry.

As Jacob absorbed the theories of great minds and became quite fluent in their languages, his desire to travel grew. The result was that he headed for the thriving city of Geneva, which now, as then, is the pre-eminent world centre for fine jewellery and watch craft. It was probably in 1765 that he set out on his 600-mile journey of adventure to the city that was not part of any country but was a self-governing canton.

At this stage Jacob was deeply interested in three subjects: jewellery, mechanical engineering and chemistry. Clearly, at twenty-five, he was a serious young man, whose life revolved around his work, study and Christianity. In Geneva he sought to live and work in the closest possible proximity to a Protestant church, an action which he repeated later in London. He became an active member of the Church of St Gervais in Geneva and it was possibly through some church connection that he met and fell in love with Eleonore Roget, whom he married in her neighbouring church, the Temple de la Madeleine, on 4 October 1767.

His first employment in Geneva was as a *maître-bijoutier* for Jean-Louis Dunant, but by 1777 that was exchanged for a partnership with Dunant's son, which lasted nine years. Throughout this period, Jacob continued his studies in his scant leisure time with persistent vigour. Part of his study time was spent putting many of Priestley's theories into practice and no doubt these experiments had considerable bearing on Jacob's invention, some time in 1783, of the Geneva water pump. He created a machine, the first of its type in the world, which was capable of providing a continuous supply of aerated water. It was a machine that was to have worldwide repercussions. Without Jacob Schweppe's invention and its further development we would never have had Coca-Cola, Pepsi Cola, Seven Up, Dr Pepper, any of the sparkling diet drinks or any of the Schweppes range of sparkling drinks that are so readily available today. Yet Jacob referred to himself in correspondence of the day as "an enthusiastic amateur scientist".

In 1790 Schweppe signed a partnership agreement with two particularly talented engineers, Jacques and Nicolas Paul, a father-and-son team which was well thought of in Geneva. But at times the relationship was to prove quite disastrous, as each man jealously guarded his reputation, and if there were any disagreements, not unnaturally the father and son took each other's part against Jacob. The trio were later joined by another local engineer, Henri Albert Gosse but this did not guarantee that matters would run smoothly, and consequently Jacob's thoughts began to take another direction.

The partnership was convinced that the sparkling Seltzer and soda waters they were now producing would have international appeal and meetings would regularly include serious discussions on the topic of further markets. A decision was eventually agreed upon to open a branch of the business in London and the help of an English doctor called Belcome, who lived in Geneva, was enlisted for the purpose of arranging the rental of suitable accommodation. Jacob Schweppe, by now fifty years old, agreed to be the partner who would travel to the English capital.

Behind the decision to leave Geneva were the unhappy circumstances of Jacob and Eleonore's marriage. We do not know a great deal about Eleonore but her experiences as a mother had been nothing but tragic. Of nine children, seven died either at birth or shortly afterwards. Two girls, Louise and Colette, survived, but Louise was stricken with smallpox and died at the age of eight, leaving Colette as the sole comforter of Eleonore's maternal grief. Yet she was to lose that daughter also, and one can only feel compassion for Eleonore in her loneliness.

When the New Year of 1792 arrived, Jacob left for London without his wife and he never saw her again. In July of that year he wrote to his partners in Geneva stating that business was not progressing as anticipated and they must urge Eleonore to send Colette to support him. Imagine Eleonore's anguish when she had to agree to send their slight, fifteen-year-old daughter on a potentially hazardous journey across a revolution-torn continent. Her only comfort was lost to her.

In London, Schweppe began trading under the partnership name of Schweppe, Paul and Gosse, from rather dingy, run-down premises at 141 Drury Lane, situated opposite an old Protestant chapel in Broad Court. For the first year life was a struggle, until the arrival of Colette raised his spirits as much as it must have dampened those of her mother. Ironically a situation in which his Geneva-based partners were urging him to persist reversed, and they began to lose faith in the London operation just as Jacob was beginning to gain hope. In 1793 squabbles arose about the expenses involved and by the following year matters had come to a head. Jacob began legal action to dissolve the partnership and the two locations proceeded to manage their affairs as two entirely separate businesses.

Upon his arrival in London, Jacob realised that he had no serious opposition although for many years pharmacists had known how to produce sparkling water in single bottles. But the Little Inventor alone was able to develop a system whereby a continuous flow of bottles of aerated water could be produced by the thousand. At this point Jacob played a master card. He began to use water from various highly reputable sources that had excellent reputations for being beneficial to the health. Soon the business of J. Schweppe was offering among its products such items as aerated Spa and Pyrmont waters; Pyrmont was of particular attraction to him as it was situated some 50 miles from his birthplace, Witzenhausen.

In an environment where drinking water often posed a threat, the presence of Schweppe's sparkling waters on the market was greeted as a great boon by many a leading doctor. Soon provision shops and pharmacists all over London were stocking what amounted to the latest aid to good health, – the aerated waters of J. Schweppe. They appealed first and foremost to the upper classes, who did much to spread their reputation. In 1795 a journal entitled the *Register of Arts* contained an article by one Thomas Green Fessenden, which carried the heading "Slurp Schweppe and Live". In it Fessenden referred to the "artificial mineral waters which contain a large proportion of carbonick acid, or fixed air", and he went on to state:

> That it is highly beneficial as a drink in the evening, to take off the acid, apt to be produced in the stomach after wine and full meals, to dilute the fluids, when containing too much irritating matter, to carry off such stimulating matter, and to strengthen the stomach. It may be justly reckoned the greatest improvement to diet of the present age.

It was the finest publicity possible and such credit was not uncommon. In his book *Schweppes, the First 200 Years*, Douglas Simmons recalls the testimony of Sir Joseph Andrews, who in 1796 wrote in his memoranda book, housed nowadays in the Berkshire County Archives:

> April 23rd. 1796 – Took advice of Dr Pearson for stone and gravel. Ordered six bottles of soda water – double – of Mr Schweppe to be particularly well corked. To take a pint at least per diem.
> April 24th. 1796 – Passed a small red stone easily after the first taking of the Soda Water recommended and prescribed by Dr Pearson.

The word "prescribed" demonstrates that in the space of four years Jacob Schweppe had won the respect and approval of the medical profession, who were perfectly happy to recommend his sparkling waters for the consumption of their patients.

The waters were sold in stone bottles and had firm, deep corks which were probably sealed by a binding. The success of the London venture had meant that as early as 1794 the Drury Lane premises were too small and Jacob moved to Number 8, King Street, an address which no longer exists. But once more his choice was determined by the proximity of a Protestant church, this time one of England's oldest surviving places of worship, St Giles in the Fields.

By then Jacob's business was increasing rapidly and he must have been astonished to find that his second headquarters also were too small for his purposes within just one short year of his occupying them. Again he moved, this time to Margaret Street, just behind Oxford Street, and his neighbouring Protestant church on this occasion was known as the Margaret Chapel and stood on the site of the current All Saints Church. Each time he moved his choice of address rose in distinction as well as in size of building. By 1795, Jacob was ensconced in his third business premises, had been trading in London for three years and was being hailed as a great innovator, a man who was responsible for new benefits to good health. He was also beginning to amass a considerable fortune.

As expansion continued he acquired further property in Margaret Street and remained manufacturing and trading there until his retirement in 1798, when he sold three-quarters of the business and returned to Geneva. He had been in London for slightly less than six and a half years, during which time he had become extremely wealthy and gained an unique reputation for his aerated waters.

Initially, both in Geneva and in London, much secrecy had been maintained regarding the aerating process and outsiders had been kept well away from the apparatus involved. In fact, when Jacob Schweppe signed the first partnership agreement with Nicolas Paul and his father in Geneva, he had refused to allow the two men to see the formula until the partnership's legal formalities were concluded. Security of this intensity became a problem as the London business outstripped the Geneva firm. Added to this, as Jacob found it necessary to move premises the equipment had to be dismantled and rebuilt. Being a small, frail man, other engineers had to be hired for these purposes and secrecy was difficult to maintain. Understandably this resulted in a number of rival operations being founded and ultimately in the spread of his methods throughout the civilised world.

Nothing however could detract from the fact that Jacob invented the system, developed it further in the Geneva partnership and then exploited it to considerable commercial advantage in London. It is his name that will be remembered as the founder of the soft-drinks industry.

His decision to return to Geneva at the age of fifty-eight may seem premature, but he still considered himself "an amateur scientist" and longed to carry out other experiments at his own leisure – something which he did for years to come.

Also he was not a man of expensive tastes, as the fact that he returned to the same village house in the Geneva suburb of Bouchet testifies. He and Colette are believed to have taken a long return journey home via Hamburg, perhaps to visit Witzenhausen, before reaching Geneva, where Colette would encounter a new lifestyle. At the age of nineteen she was the daughter of a wealthy man and while she was reportedly no beauty, she soon married a Genevese citizen of some means, Henri-Louis Maunoir. Jacob was left alone in his retirement.

Jacob's wife Eleonore had died during his time in England, in April 1796 to be exact, but Jacob did not attend her funeral, maybe because of the risk involved in travelling across a battle-ravaged Europe. Whatever their differences, it is a sad fact that Eleonore died a lonely woman without even the comfort of her sole surviving child.

Jacob Schweppe himself lived to a grand eighty-one years of age and died in his Bouchet home in 1821, where he passed his later years enjoying himself amid his experiments. Three years later, in 1824, Colette sold the remaining quarter of the partnership in London. This action severed the last Schweppe family link with a business that was to become celebrated around the globe. Furthermore, with no male successor the name Schweppe was never to appear again in the official records of Geneva.

But the name was not entirely lost, nor its talent, because back in Hesse other members of the wider Schweppe family were on the move. Around that time there are records of various Schweppes emigrating to the United States on twelve separate occasions. Today there is even an annual Schweppe Reunion organised by the honorary secretary, a position currently held by James W. Schweppe of Las Vegas. Distant relatives fly from all over the continent to an agreed location. Possibly the best-known of the contemporary members of the Schweppe family is Earl J. Schweppe, Professor of Computer Science at the University of Kansas at Lawrence. An inheritor of the brilliant Schweppe brain as well as facial features, this fascinating man has served his country well both in his major area of expertise, where he was a member of the initial government panel that drafted the original plans for the teaching of computer science, and in the field of security matters, where great discretion is required. Judge Egbert Schweppe became an eminent Texan lawyer in the 1950s, the Reverend Harvey Schweppe is a retired Methodist minister in Madison, Wisconsin, and another Harvey Schweppe is a prosperous oil and real-estate developer in California. There is even a tiny Schweppe & Co. Realtors in Upper Montclair,

New Jersey. Also in the United States one finds the inevitable case of the occasional Schweppe being a lawyer: Alfred J. Schweppe of the delightfully named Schweppe, Doolittle, Krug, Tausend & Beezer in Seattle is one notable example.

The other success story for the name of Schweppe in the United States concerns the company which is nowadays a division of the Cadbury Schweppes Corporation. Even this story has not been without incident and the success of Schweppes in North America today can largely be credited to the motivation of three outstanding characters: Walter Hawksford, Edward Whitehead and John Carson. If you are wondering whether the last of these could possibly be an entertainer, then read on.

Walter Hawksford had been a senior executive of the Schweppe company in England for some years before being appointed the first worldwide export manager. In his new capacity the board of directors decided in 1912 to send him to the United States, in an attempt to revive what was at the time a rather uninspiring market.

It is difficult to tell just how excited this apparently unexcitable man would have been upon receiving his reservation for a first-class cabin on the maiden voyage of the SS *Titanic*, the new luxury liner that had been basking in the glow of so much publicity. The booking cost was in excess of $2 500.

Walter Hawksford's name can be found on page 45 of the official report into the *Titanic* disaster, where it simply reads among the list of first-class passengers: "Hawksford, Mr W J (saved)". His letter to his wife in England, only four days after the great liner sank, is a masterpiece of understatement and a classic example of concise, informative correspondence. The precision of its content is a great compliment to his clarity of mind and it remains one of the most moving documents I have ever read. Its description of his rescue is particularly vivid:

When it came to the last boat but one I was told to man the boat with about four others and the rest women, we were lowered a distance of 90 feet to the water, and rowed about half a mile from the ship. It was very cold but a beautiful night, starry and the sea as smooth as glass. We watched her bow gradually getting lower and lower and then about two o'clock all the lights went out, her stern rose in the air and she slowly glided away. We took off our caps and bowed our heads and nobody spoke for some minutes. We remained in that boat for five hours and you cannot imagine the strange feeling of being in mid-Atlantic in a small rowing boat; just as it was getting daylight we saw a rocket go up on the horizon and knew it would not be long before we were on another ship. We watched her slowly

appear and then stop, you guess we did not wait any longer, it was the hardest and most difficult bit of rowing I ever did. We rowed about two or three miles and arrived on board at 5.45. They treated us royally on the Carpathia.

And so Walter lived to revive the North American business. Schweppes has been trading in the United States since 1884, when they opened a production factory in Brooklyn. They believed it would be more practical to produce and bottle waters on the eastern seaboard, in the midst of the main market they sought. The plan however proved to be a disaster and after eight years it was decided to abandon the plant, with the entire machinery and material stock being written off as loss.

Despite the Brooklyn failure Schweppes continued their trade by importing their sparkling waters and after a short time, in 1903, there was sufficient improvement in sales to justify serious consideration by the London headquarters of the possibility of setting up a new Schweppes marketing company for their United States trade. After reports that various American soft-drinks companies were finding conditions difficult the idea was abandoned.

In 1912, when Walter Hawksford was sent, Schweppes was still being handled by a number of importers based in various major cities, and Hawksford's aim was to re-energise these agencies.

In the meantime, business grew very quietly and the name Schweppes was becoming more widespread. It was not until the mid-1950s that the range of soft drinks had become sophisticated enough for the company to once more put some major investment into the US market. This they did by the appointment of the colourful and eccentric Commander Edward Whitehead as the new overseas director, with special responsibility for North America, and by agreeing to undertake a major advertising program.

The following events, in advertising and publicity terms, are legendary. From seven advertising-

Schweppe & Co. Realtors, Montclair, New Jersey – named for a Schweppe descendant

agency applicants, Commander Whitehead selected Ogilvy, Benson and Mather, but only after the most careful personal consideration. David Ogilvy, regarded by many as one of the true advertising geniuses of the postwar era, had won the commission by one of the most daring pitches. The moment David caught sight of the elegant and imposing figure of the former naval officer, with his auburn hair and beard, he was so impressed by the substantial presence of the man that he was convinced of the unique commercial possibility of the English executive. Ogilvy succeeded in persuading Commander Whitehead that not only was there no-one as ideal to promote Schweppes products but that he would have enormous appeal to American consumers.

David Ogilvy was right, and an initial series of advertisements featuring Commander Whitehead and printed in the *New Yorker* magazine proved an instant success. It was quickly followed by a Commander Whitehead campaign based on nationwide television commercials and newspaper and magazine advertising which attracted huge attention. The colourful and mysterious Englishman became such a focus of attention that he was invited to appear on "The Tonight Show" with Johnny Carson, where he intrigued both his host and his audience so much that he was invited back time and again. Over the next couple of years he became such a regular guest that complaints were made by other soft drinks rivals to the effect that Schweppes were gaining an unfair amount of exposure and that run of good fortune came to an abrupt halt. But by then Commander Whitehead had become such a popular celebrity that he was being invited to appear on television and radio programs nationwide and to give interviews from San Francisco to Miami.

The commander was a great lover of outdoor life and Ogilvy realised that he would be at his most natural when in surroundings he enjoyed. Subsequently commercials were filmed of him sailing his yacht, exploring the Rockies and horse-riding in rural Connecticut. In between his new-found episodes of dramatic publicity, the energetic commander had to run the business within the USA and would spend many hours toiling deep into the night, dealing with the day-to-day affairs of a rapidly growing Schweppes turnover. In recognition of his efforts, Commander Whitehead was officially confirmed the first President of Schweppes USA Ltd.

Today, Schweppes USA is run from the selfsame desk by another energetic Englishman, whose name, by coincidence, is John Carson. He has recently been the motivating force behind the introduction of many new lines with exotic flavours. Not only does this dynamic leader head the extensive North American operation, but he also regularly crosses the Atlantic to London, where he heads the British management team. All of this he achieves while living in Connecticut, not far from the legendary Commander Whitehead's old home, where that extraordinary gentleman actually rode and filmed many of his commercials.

Nowadays Schweppes is frequently known as the alternative English bubbly, a title which is completely justified since the business has been based in England for some 200 years. But we should not forget its earliest days in Geneva, where it is believed aerated waters made by Schweppe's Geneva Water Pump were first sold in 1783. Nor should we lose sight of the story of Conrad Schweppe and his wife in Witzenhausen in 1751, giving away their son to a tinker because they were too poor to feed and clothe him, and how that child became the Little Inventor whose work was to change the drinking habits of the world.

MR CHARDONNAY
Wente, USA

One warm March day in 1989 a youthful Jean Trimbach stood up to face an audience of some 120 wine distributors and sales people at a large conference organised by the Seagram Chateau & Estate Wines Company, in the magnificent setting of the Ritz-Carlton Hotel at the opulent resort of Naples on Florida's Gulf Coast. It was 8 o'clock in the morning and Jean, representing his illustrious Alsace family house of F.E. Trimbach, was the first speaker of the day. Within minutes he had stunned his audience with the words "Gucci, Gucci", which he used with reference to the rapidly developing trend for using the Chardonnay grape; Gucci was to *haute couture* what the Chardonnay was to the world of wine, the epitome of elegance and quality. Although at the time I did not wholly concur, I admired his boldness in challenging the very barons of the US wine trade about the pattern of trade they were supporting.

Waiting in the wings to make the next presentation, I wondered whether he was not prone to hyperbole but time was to prove my doubts ill-founded and Jean's predictions accurate, for Chardonnay has become the fashionable variety of the 1990s. The very name Chardonnay, in the minds of the vast majority, evokes an image of a dry, fruity white wine but in truth this ubiquitous variety produces wines of varying degrees of sweetness, from practically bone dry to verging on the medium-sweet. Chardonnay has become the word on the label that to most wine consumers is easy to understand and, more importantly, synonymous with easy to drink. That is not to suggest that all wines labelled Chardonnay are simpletons; quite the contrary. From Burgess Cellars Triere Vineyard to New Zealand's Cloudy Bay, there is a plethora of wines that announce the name Chardonnay and have true finesse, not to mention those truly great French offerings such as Puligny Montrachet and the Chablis Grand Crus, which traditionally choose not to mention the name.

Who started it all, one might ask? Who originally labelled a wine Chardonnay? It is a question I have pondered in several countries. Rumours, which briefly aroused excitement, of a 1907 Chardonnay from a Yarra Valley, Victoria, vineyard near Lilydale, have so far proved totally unfounded. It appears that Tyrrells, the prestigious Hunter Valley winery, was the first with an Australian Chardonnay in the early 1960s. The real answer is a name that is recognised by many as offering some, if not the finest, Chardonnay values of all – the Wente family, with their giant estate vineyards at Livermore and Arroya Seco in California. In 1913, Ernest Wente, the third generation of the family, was a member of the first graduation class of the Wine School at the University of California, Davis. The previous year he had developed a friendship with one of his professors, a lecturer from Montpellier University in France, which already had a longstanding reputation for its wine department. Professor Bonnet advised Ernest that he believed California could provide ideal microclimates and locations for what was then referred to as the Pinot Chardonnay. Professor Bonnet also recommended the potential of the Ugni Blanc, a strange choice, since it has seldom caused excitement wherever it has been planted.

With his teacher's support, Ernest Wente pressed his father, generally known as C.H. Wente, to import both varieties. The Ugni Blanc was never to shine but the Montpellier Pinot Chardonnay did, along with other Pinot Chardonnay cuttings acquired from another grower in Pleasantown, just a few miles away. It should be understood that in no way is a claim being made that Wente were the first winery to grow Chardonnay in America, but that they were the first to sell it as a specifically named varietal. The first grower may well have been a man appropriately named Jean-Louis Vignes, who failed in an attempt to grow a number of noble French varieties at Los Angeles in the 1830s.

It was a century later, in 1936, that Ernest Wente claimed the title Mr Chardonnay when he became the first to sell Pinot Chardonnay as a varietal. Ernest had nurtured the idea of developing Pinot Chardonnay as a variety and undertook a continuous program of selecting the healthiest rootstocks, taking cuttings from them and grafting them onto other vines. Carl Wente, the founder of the family house, had possibly purchased some Chardonnay

cuttings before 1890, as the neighbouring vineyard in Livermore of Cresta Blanca was owned by Charles Wetmore, a formidable Californian viticultural pioneer, who had purchased stocks from the Burgundy region of France. Wente already had other thriving noble varieties such as Sauvignon Blanc and Semillon, whose origin was in the great Chateau d'Yquem vineyard in Sauternes, home, most experts would agree, of the finest sweet white wine in the world. It is recorded that in 1938 the then Marquis de Lur-Saluces visited the Wente property in Livermore to observe the progress of the descendants of those early stocks.

What emerges from all this is that the Wente family were clearly exciting pioneers in their attitudes to varietals and Ernest, by his 1936 decision, instigated the move to such widespread and popular use of Chardonnay that it literally became a fashion.

The Wente Chardonnay soon proved a success and their lead, followed by a handful of others, is

Ernest Wente, Mr Chardonnay

history, but the followers were just a handful, because as records reveal, in 1960 only 230 acres of Chardonnay existed across the entire state of California. Yet thirty years later, Chardonnay occupied twenty-five times that area, covering more than 56 000 acres. Today, wherever one travels across the mainland vineyards of the USA, plantings of what has become officially known as the Wente clone of Chardonnay are abundantly evident. The Wente clone is popular because it is an earlier ripener than most Chardonnays and will often add complexity to the blend. Ernest did, however, have a stubborn streak. Shortly after the label was introduced he was advised by the Wine Department at Davis that they had discovered that the Chardonnay was not a Pinot variety at all and should in future be called simply Chardonnay. "You're not changing that while I'm alive," came the spirited reply and Ernest continued as if no communication had ever occurred.

In the postwar years the use of the name Pinot Chardonnay began to spread across the New World countries and gradually, as winemakers developed modern skills, attractive results were achieved. The 1960s and 1970s saw the disappearance of the word Pinot from the Chardonnay labels and the fashion for big, mouth-filling wines began to emerge, but in general they lacked finesse. Even as late as 1984, when I visited Eric Wente at Livermore, the Wente Chardonnay was somewhat unexciting but upon my return in 1989, five years later, it was obvious that a dramatic change had occurred and by 1990 the entire range of Wente Chardonnays were so pleasing that when Princess Diana's father, the late Earl Spencer admitted to me that he had never tasted an American wine, I immediately introduced him to what I was convinced was the best value-for-money Chardonnay one could buy in America. Some might be surprised at my recommendation of an outstanding value rather than choosing the finest example I knew regardless of price, but the reason was quite straightforward. Earl Spencer had explained to me that he was holding a program of banquets for paying guests, a fairly high proportion of whom were American. He had stressed that he had to work to a careful budget and I in my turn tried to offer the most delicious Chardonnay for a realistic price. A little later that choice was endorsed when the *Wine Spectator*, on several occasions, saw fit to name various Wente Chardonnays at the top of their lists for truly outstanding value.

The French, in truth, gained Chardonnay its reputation for finesse with their White Burgundies and might well try to claim that the Emperor Charlemagne was first, with a small vineyard at Corton Charlemagne in the 8th century. While

that is true, he never bottled the wine, sold it, labelled it or used the varietal name. Instead he referred to the grape by its local name and probably drank the majority of the wine with his court.

DISTILLER TO THE TSAR
Smirnoff Vodka; Russia, France, Poland, USA, England and Scotland

For centuries Paris was a favourite venue of the Russian aristocracy, who became such Francophiles that they even adopted the French tongue as the official language of the Tsarist court. The gaiety and allure of the French capital drew Imperial Russians in their hundreds to flaunt and enjoy their wealth. Their fascination with Paris was to prove a crucial factor in this tale of not two, but three cities: Moscow, Paris and Hartford, Connecticut.

The story has its origins in Moscow, the city of golden domes, where it begins to unfold in the year 1818. In the next century the Russian Revolution takes our story across central Europe, first to Lvov in Poland and then on to Paris in 1932. From there the narrative crosses the Atlantic to its final resting place, which it reached in 1939 and where it still resides today – amid more golden domes. For our tale comes to rest in Hartford, the state capital of Connecticut, some 100 miles north-east of New York.

Our history involves some Russian secrets, which travelled thousands of miles between the three capitals, and also sheds light upon how a Russian surname, Smirnoff, as common in Russia as Smith is elsewhere, became a household name in countries all over the world. The Smirnoff family, who are the subject of our attention, possessed the secrets for the formulae of thirteen different vodkas, one of which was to become the world's largest-selling spirit, a distinction it already enjoyed when it was originally being made in Moscow.

The man responsible for smuggling the secrets out of Russia was Vladimir Smirnoff, a singular character, who was born into one of the richest families in the world yet was buried in a pauper's grave. It was his personal love of France, particularly Paris and the casinos of Nice and Monte Carlo, that was to compel him to return there time and again, and it was in that country that poverty eventually drove him to sell the family secrets. Vladimir's life could only be described as reckless and dissolute; he married three times and had at least two mistresses. He gambled, he drank and he was ultimately a lover of the gay life. He sold the formula for the family vodka to a man of quite opposite character, a humble, relatively reserved man who led a strictly Christian life and who finally gave away the majority of his personal wealth to the World Council of

Churches, the Russian Orthodox Church and various other charitable causes. His name – Rudolph Kunett. Kunett was short for Kunertorski, though it appears that sometimes he was referred to as Kunetchansky. He left Russia prior to the Revolution and emigrated to the United States. He hailed originally from Ukraine, where his family were grain producers and he was acquainted with Vladimir Smirnoff through the business meetings held between the two families in Moscow.

Not that Vladimir was inclined to work of any kind. In fact by his early twenties he already had an established reputation as a playboy. He first became notorious in his teens when he ran off with a band of Romanies and fell in love with one of the girls. During this affair he gained experience which would serve him well in the stormy years ahead; he learned to sing, dance and make people laugh, for the gipsies were entertainers and as such earned their livelihood. After this escapade the disgraced young Vladimir was packed off by his father to work with some relatives in China and hopefully stay out of trouble. However, as later events in this story will prove, trouble was something for which Vladimir had a magnetic attraction.

The Smirnoff family was a respected and prosperous family, who were innovators and experimenters in the vodka-production field. They had realised that grain rather than potatoes produced a finer vodka and they purchased most of their stocks from Ukraine, still today known by many as the Breadbasket of the Soviet Union. With experimentation, the family discovered that there were distinct variations in the style of the vodka, depending on the substances used for filtering it. Eventually they were satisfied that a combination of the carbon of certain hardwoods would give them the cleanest results.

Their introduction of distilling grain and filtering with hardwood charcoals gave them a commercial advantage over their smaller rivals, who were still using more traditional methods. One paid the odd kopeck more for Smirnoff vodka, but as the consumer soon learned, one received far better value.

The family's experimentation did not end there, as they began using various metals in the construction of their filter containers and stills and it was not long before they discovered something the French and the Scottish had already learned, namely that copper was the most suitable material. In this manner, in a matter of a couple of generations, a growing family business had been founded, which had taken all the basic steps to providing what could well be described as the world's first major brand of liquor.

The original Smirnoff, at least as far as the famous vodka name is concerned, was called Arseyni. It

Tsar Nicolas I, Emperor of Russia at the foundation of Smirnoff Vodka

was he who founded the house in 1818, just six years after Napoleon attacked Moscow and burned its bridges. Arseyni observed that just one bridge, the great old iron one, survived the torches of the French invaders, and learning from history, he chose to build the first family vodka plant as close to the iron bridge as possible. Fortunately it proved to be an unnecessary precaution.

Upon Arseyni's demise, his son Piotr Arsenievich, took charge of the small business, which at that time had just nine employees. To Piotr's delight his new-found prosperity enabled him to penetrate the outer fringes of the Russian nobility. Subsequently he allowed himself to be persuaded to show Smirnoff vodka at a number of exhibitions which were taking place in great cities such as St Petersburg, Kiev and Samarkand. The 1850s and 1860s were a time of increasing prosperity and economic growth, particularly for the middle and upper classes, and one cannot but wonder what the outcome would have been if this development had been allowed to continue uninterrupted.

As in much of Europe, there was a population trend away from the country towards the cities and urban development grew at a sometimes alarming pace. Each city was determined to display its influence and the craze for exhibitions in Russia rose to giddy heights. Almost every other year a major city would announce an exhibition of Olympian proportions as each new exhibition strove to outdo the former.

It was to one such giant exhibition, held in the city of Nijni Novgrod in 1868, that Tsar Alexander II, decided to pay a visit. He had heard of the success of the Smirnoff company and made a beeline for their stand. He left little doubt that he was delighted with his tasting, which he confirmed by placing the first royal order for Smirnoff. This action launched the Smirnoff company on a series of exhibition successes as it determined to establish itself as a major international brand. In 1873, in Vienna, the distillery was awarded the highest honour, the honorary diploma. In 1876, when the company exhibited at the Philadelphia Centennial, an exhibition held to celebrate 100 years of the Union, the grand jury awarded Smirnoff the ultimate Medal of Honour. And to crown it all, in 1877, the tsarist government granted the company its highest citation, the Imperial State Emblem, in recognition of the company's achievements. In 1878, Smirnoff showed their vodka in Paris and won two gold medals. In 1882, the all-Russia exhibition was held in Moscow, attended by virtually every known liquor producer in the country. It was on this occasion that the new tsar, Alexander III, saw fit to bestow his personal Gold Medal with the ribbon of St Andrew on a triumphant Pierre Smirnoff.

Notice the change from Piotr to Pierre. It was accepted practice among the Russian nobility to adopt the French language, hence as Piotr Smirnoff crossed the borders of social and financial success, so his name changed to Pierre. To the present day, Smirnoff bottles carry his French name and even the few remaining bottles from the imperial period carry the name Pierre, not Piotr.

Smirnoff vodka went from strength to strength, with a series of international successes culminating in 1888 with yet another gold medal, this time

from Barcelona. It was at this stage that Alexander III saw fit to appoint Pierre his personal commercial advisor.

In the meantime, the Smirnoff company had not lost its impulse towards innovation and experimentation. In 1889 the company travelled to another international exhibition in Paris to launch a new product aimed at the world market. This product was known as ashberry brandy and at that time was unique, although poor imitations flooded the market within a few years of its launch. Ashberry brandy proved an instant success. This liqueur, made by blending ashberry juice and authentic Cognac imported from France, was, in a few years, in such demand that production had risen to 2 000 barrels a year. Sadly it was just one of the many Smirnoff products that was destined to disappear with the Russian Revolution.

The royal seal of approval saved the Smirnoff company from catastrophe in 1894 when the imperial government nationalised all major vodka plants. By then the company had an extensive sales structure, with travellers covering a domestic market that stretched north as far as Arctic Siberia, east to the Pacific and south to the Crimea. They also exported to China and Japan, and to Russian emigrant communities on both sides of the Atlantic. On reflection it is odd to consider that Smirnoff vodka was consumed in the United States over 100 years ago, by so few people from rather self-contained communities, that its presence was hardly observable.

Pierre Smirnoff died in 1898 and the ownership of the then giant company passed to his three sons, the eldest, also called Pierre, Nicholai and Vladimir. The two elder sons took control and continued to expand the business, following in their father's footsteps, while Vladimir preferred to pursue his life of abandonment and merrymaking.

Records, believed to have been written at some time around 1896, paint a remarkable picture of the massive Smirnoff operation. Turnover volume was 17 million roubles a year, out of which 9 million, or about 53 per cent, went to the imperial exchequer in excise taxes. It was far from being just a vodka plant, with numerous fruit liqueurs being produced, and it also had an immense wine business.

The vodka plant was using 240 000 tons of hardwood charcoal per year and had a set of steam engines to supply much of its power, which came from six boilers. It produced 150 000 bottles per day, and some years later there was an unconfirmed report that by 1900 Smirnoff had, on some days, reached a peak figure of 1 million. This may appear rather unlikely on the face of it, but if all their other products and wines are included in this figure, then

Forefather of the Russian vodka industry, Pierre (Piotr Arsenievich) Smirnoff. In 19th-century Moscow, his firm's vodka gained international distinction, with the P.A. Smirnoff Company reportedly producing more than 1 million bottles of vodka per day

it is not inconceivable that volume could have risen to this astonishing level.

In all, there were 1 500 employees and the enormous demand for bottles was supplied by seven glassworks. Labelling and other requirements kept four independent printers in full-time occupation. Smirnoff had 200 horse-drawn delivery wagons and claimed to use only "the best horses Europe can offer". At harvest time 700 peasants were engaged on picking the ashberries alone, which were then immediately washed in purified water to prevent the wild yeasts from causing unwanted fermentation.

In total it was claimed that:

> 25,000 people comprise the entire operation, taking into account all the employees and workers at the distillery, drivers, packers, the bottle factory workers mentioned above, printers, crate-makers, the surrounding populace that produces the berries etc.

Wine production was on a major scale, with an output of 45 million bottles a year. At that time, when most consumers in France, Germany and Italy had to purchase their wine in bulk, Russians had the good fortune of the Smirnoff family acting as the largest known wine merchant in the world, offering them the luxury of a wide range of bottled wines. These were Russian grape wines, of which 15 000 casks could be found in the company's cellars at any one time. The wines were supplied to markets all over the country and were especially popular in the Crimea, Bessarabia and the Caucasus.

The ever-hungry tsarist exchequer, however, was not always totally confident that the royal purveyor was paying all its dues and so on one occasion the company received the indignity of a visit from the chief inspector of the department of unassessed taxes, who described the company's cellars in a detailed report:

> The cellars are immaculately maintained and in exemplary order, with a constant temperature of 12 degrees. To give a more vivid impression of their size, suffice it to say that on the day of my visit there were 14,237 barrels. If one were to measure the length of a barrel as $1\frac{1}{2}$ arshin [42 inches] and place all these barrels bottom to bottom in one row, he would discover the distance to be over 14 verst [8.3 miles]. What immediately amazes a visitor to these cellars is the enormous supply of wine stored in barrels. At the time of my visit to P.A. Smirnoff, 546,947 buckets of wine were stored in such a fashion.

Presumably the word translated as "buckets" refers to smaller casks of varying kinds and descriptions.

Close to the cellars the company constructed a large stone building in which the majority of direct employees lived. It was no doubt one of the largest apartment blocks of its generation. It also housed a casualty ward and a pharmacy, which were manned by a doctor and two assistants.

The relationship between the Smirnoff family and the Kunertorski, or Kunnetchansky, family was a simple but important one. The Kunertorskis owned extensive plantations in Ukraine, where they produced grain and distilled it into a pure grain spirit which they then sold to Smirnoff, who filtered it into vodka at their plant. Even today many are surprised that any alcoholic spirit can be used as a base for vodka, though now, as then, it has to be said that it is believed that Smirnoff have only ever used the cleanest grain spirit.

It is sometimes claimed that as the new century arrived, Russia possessed the two wealthiest families in the world, a statement which it is impossible to prove. The richest were the Romanovs, who claimed the throne among their other multifaceted possessions. The second was allegedly the Smirnoffs. Just how wealthy that meant we cannot know but it was perhaps understandable that when the political tide turned the family was high on the executioner's list.

The storm clouds were still gathering after the rumblings of European discontent had burst into World War I. Following generations of poverty the Russian peasants had been leaving the land for the city in the belief that the development of industry would bring prosperity. But as the peasants soon discovered, the industrialists were just another breed of landlord and it was not long before the murmurings of discontent swelled into threats of violence. Political figures such as Trotsky and Lenin were beginning to emerge and their ideals were having an impact upon a nation disillusioned and tired of poverty, hunger and prejudice.

In October 1917 the Revolution brought a wave of terror running through the established ranks as reports of uprisings and wholesale massacres reached them. Hundreds of thousands fled as the Revolution gained momentum but not all escaped the menace and similar numbers were arrested and executed. Reports state that all the Smirnoffs, with the exception of Vladimir, perished but it seems that Nicholai may also have survived, as later information will demonstrate. Vladimir, albeit a reckless fool, had the intelligence to realise that the end of an era had come and hastily prepared to escape the growing tide of hatred. In his flight he had the wisdom to secure many of the company's most important documents, including the vodka formula, which in reality could not have been more than design instructions for the size and number of copper filters, the details of the hardwood carbon mix for filtering and the time involved in

Tsar Alexander II, who granted the royal warrant to Smirnoff Vodka

the process. However, with these safely hidden he fled south, managing to escape detection by continuously moving from place to place.

In 1919, Valdimir was living with Valentina Piontkovska, a Polish baroness from Lvov, with whom he had been involved for several years. To date they had been able to survive on the outskirts of Moscow, but decided that matters were becoming too risky and that it would be wiser to move to the country. They headed in a southerly direction and had to take care to avoid roving detachments of Red soldiers. The troops had a reputation for rounding up anyone whom they suspected of belonging to the ruling classes on the basis that hands which showed no sign of manual work constituted sufficient evidence to justify arrest.

One hair-raising incident found Vladimir and Valentina spending the night in a tree to avoid detection and, like the incurable old-fashioned romantic that he was, Vladimir told Valentina that it was no way for the aristocracy to live and that he could not put her life in danger any longer. He insisted that she should return to Poland and he to Moscow to face reality. With deep regret, Valentina obeyed and returned to Poland, taking with her not just Vladimir's heart but some extremely valuable jewels which he had presented to her, and which later were to be responsible for the survival of Smirnoff vodka.

Within days of parting with his mistress, the luckless Vladimir was arrested and incarcerated in

a town called Pyatigorsk, which lay in the foothills of the Caucusus Mountains between the Caspian Sea and the Black Sea. Here, his skills as an entertainer, acquired during his time with the gipsies, saved his life. With execution staring him in the face, Vladimir played his trump card. Using all his worldly charm he persuaded his peasant captors that he should entertain them each evening with a little cabaret, something thay had never before witnessed. His singing, dancing and show-manship were of such a high standard that in no time he became their favourite prisoner as he relieved the monotony of their lives. But his relationship with his captors was a tenuous one and they devised their own form of macabre and sadistic entertainment, with Vladimir as their audience. For six consecutive mornings, Vladimir was hauled from his bed to face a firing squad, who at the command to fire did nothing. On each occasion they informed him that his skills as an entertainer had saved him – they preferred him alive. One can barely imagine the state of Vladimir's mind by the sixth morning, but survive he did and his luck was to improve further.

Suddenly a White Russian advance under General Schkowso encircled the Red position and Pyatigorsk was liberated. The prison doors were flung open and Vladimir was released.

Carefully guarding the few documents still in his possession, he decided to travel to Lvov to join Baroness Valentina, but in the chaos that existed side by side with the poverty and suspicion that followed in the wake of World War I, making a journey of several hundred kilometres was far from easy. Almost against his will Vladimir was absorbed into a large band of refugees heading south. Realising it was safer to travel incognito than to strike out across country on his own, Vladimir found himself months later travelling through Turkey to the shores of the Sea of Marmara, which lies between the Dardanelles and the Bosporus at the western entrance to the Black Sea. His desired destination, Lvov, lay thousands of kilometres to the north. In these circumstances he headed for a group of four islands, which had been commandeered by the United States, France, Italy and Great Britain for the purpose of clearing immigrants, in the Sea of Marmara. He quickly made it clear, however, that he had no desire to enter any of the countries concerned and was permitted to resume his attempt to reach Poland.

His movements from here on are uncertain, but it seems he made for Sofia, where he had some trusted friends, and then moved on to Lvov. A year must have elapsed since he and Valentina had gone their separate ways and imagine his misery when upon finding her he discovered that she was already embarked upon a fresh affair with a Polish aristocrat named Ladislas Baronowski.

Despite his wounded pride, Vladimir soon enlisted Valentina's support. Valentina sold the elegant jewels that Vladimir had previously given her and with the proceeds, plus assistance from two further investors, one being Baronowski, they set up a new Pierre Smirnoff company in Lvov to produce vodka using the Smirnoff formula.

The few remaining records of this company raise a mysterious question. The directors were listed as Vladimir Smirnoff, Nicolas Smirnoff, Leonide Ivanow, Valentina Piontkovska and Ladislas Baronowski. If Nicolas (Nicholai) was killed in the aftermath of the October Revolution, as has always been reported, why should his name have been registered as a director? Or was the question of survival still unclear at the time, and did Vladimir seek his inclusion in the light of optimism that one day his brother might escape and join them? Certainly no existing record mentions the name of Nicolas as being involved in any activity after the Revolution and it seems extremely dubious that he reached Poland.

As time wore on, Vladimir's persuasive charm began to win his mistress back and in due course he suggested to Valentina that she should visit Paris with him. Vladimir's passion for France and the French nobility's style of life were in no way dimmed by the Revolution, and he adored recounting tales of great escapades he had enjoyed after taking the famous Blue Train from Moscow to the Côte d'Azur. Vladimir simply loved the excesses of life, especially those that he could find in the nightclubs and casinos of France; the gaming tables held enormous attraction for him.

Wining and dining Valentina in Paris, Vladimir battled to convince her that Paris, not Lvov, was the ideal site for a vodka company. Vladimir's tenacity bore fruit as their affair grew in strength, and Valentina, who was a great lover of the Parisian lifestyle, was won over. They could leave Ladislas Baronowski to take control of the day-to-day running of the company in Lvov and could establish another one here in Paris. But Baronowski was not so pliable and was not going to allow both his passion and his financial interests to be so easily thwarted. His response was swift and direct. No, they could not just set up another Smirnoff company in Paris without satisfactory arrangements to protect the interests of himself and his co-director, Leonide Ivanow. He insisted that the rights to the formula were held by the Lvov company and the only way that Smirnoff vodka could be produced in Paris was under licence from the Polish business.

In the meantime, Vladimir had made the acquaintance of a White Russian called Ter-Asarieff,

who was one of the many thousands of his fellow countrymen who had settled in Paris. He had some capital and was prepared to invest in the proposed Parisian company on the strength that he was to be its manager. The idea appealed greatly to Vladimir, who had limited knowledge of working for a living and also conjectured that if Ter-Asarieff worked in the company on a daily basis then that would provide additional security, for his direct involvement would be likely to protect their mutual investment. In due course Baronowski and Ivanow agreed to the proposition and the new Paris-based Pierre Smirnoff et Cie began production. There was, however, a condition concerning the labels; they had to acknowledge that the French-based Smirnoff company was operating under licence from Pierre Smirnoff et Fils in Lvov, who were successors to the Moscow company who possessed the warrant, granted in 1886, to the Imperial Russian Court.

This move, however, proved to be only the first step in a complicated chapter of romance and intrigue which lasted a further ten years.

In Lvov, Ladislas Baronowski grew restless without Valentina and arrived in Paris to challenge Vladimir for her affections. Exactly what happened next remains uncertain, but his arrival seems to have swayed Valentina completely, for she decided to leave Vladimir for Baronowski. Utterly disillusioned by his loss, Vladimir took the familiar path south to Nice, declaring that Paris was now detestable to him and swearing to open a Smirnoff plant in the south. This enterprise did commence trading but failed miserably, since Vladimir had no idea of the commercial world.

At the age of fifty-two Vladimir began to drink heavily and all his old weaknesses began to reassert themselves. He was gambling and spending so rapidly that his funds were diminishing at an alarming pace. Realising that he was on the brink of financial ruin, he made one last effort to put his life in some semblance of order. Vladimir recalled the talents as an entertainer that he had acquired during his time with the gipsies and how those skills had once saved his life. Perhaps they could perform the same office again.

He began to obtain employment in the hotels and nightclubs of Nice as a song-and-dance man, at which he became tolerably successful for a while. Here, as in Paris, there was a community of White Russians, who pursued a life of leisure which meant that there was a steady demand for such acts. Many Russian entertainers tended to work together and move on from show to show. On one such occasion Vladimir was introduced to a thirty-five-year-old light-opera singer named Tatiana Mack-cheef, and within two weeks they were married.

The year was 1925, and Vladimir continued to work the Nice circuit until the early 1930s.

As was normal in Vladimir's post-Revolution experience, he discovered he was yet again short of cash, so when he heard that Prohibition was about to end in the United States he decided to see whether he could take advantage of the situation. Ladislas Baronowski and Valentina had returned to Lvov to concentrate on Smirnoff production there, and Ter-Asarieff was none too happy running the Parisian operation on his own. Perhaps the time had come for sorting matters in Europe out. Vladimir's first move was to trace his old friend Rudolph Kunett, who at the time was working as the sales manager for Helena Rubenstein from an impressive office in Madison Avenue, New York. The proposal to begin production of Smirnoff vodka in the United States certainly appealed to Rudolph, although he was also sympathetic about Vladimir's fall from prosperity. Hopefully the proposed deal would alleviate Vladimir's financial straits. The negotiations affected three men: Vladimir, Rudolph Kunett and Ter-Asarieff. A price was agreed of 40 000 francs, the equivalent of $2 500 at the time, out of which Vladimir received, after expenses, 20 000 francs. The subject of the sale was the Smirnoff vodka formula and some dozen similar formulas or the production of other drinks, and of course the sole right to Smirnoff production in the United States.

Vladimir must have had an inkling that the money would not last long, and he also suspected

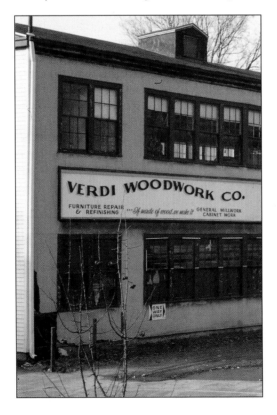

*V*erdi Woodworking Co., formerly Vaghi; the top floor of this building was the world production centre of Smirnoff vodka between 1933 and 1940

that he did not have long to live. On his return to Nice he and Tatiana moved from their rented house at 52 rue Lamartine to a rather more fashionable abode at No. 105 Promenade des Anglais, where they spent their last twelve months together. Vladimir took one last journey to Paris, where he died in 1933, aged sixty, reportedly of cancer of the liver, although some have suggested, without any medical evidence, that it was sclerosis due to his constant excessive drinking. Whatever the cause, he tragically died virtually penniless, a man who had been born into one of the richest families in the world.

But the Smirnoff story does not end with Vladimir's demise; it continues with Rudolph Kunett in the United States. Among the areas Rudolph visited during his work with the cosmetics trade were the small towns of Danbury and Bethel in Connecticutt, where he came across a good number of Russian and Ukrainian immigrants. In Danbury in particular there was a fairly large community of Russian felt-makers who specialised in making hats for the New York market. It was, after all, a period when nearly every man, woman and child wore a hat, and New York, just a couple of hours' train ride away, was the centre of the clothing trade. Understandably, immigrant workers grouped together wherever they could service their major market easily but the cost of living was more attractive than in Brooklyn or Queens. Here too they established their Orthodox churches, a field which had always interest Rudolph Kunett. As a result Rudolph became a well-known figure in these communities when he visited them from his sales office in Manhattan. He appreciated how they missed some of the goods they had been able to purchase in their homelands and this was the decisive factor in influencing him to set up Smirnoff vodka production in the area.

Many a time, seated in the old steam train as it chugged through the level crossing in the centre of Bethel, Rudolph had noticed the narrow two-storey building bearing the name Vaghi Woodwork Company, which stood on the left-hand side of the track if one faced a northerly direction. Most of us at some time will have taken regular train or coach journeys and become accustomed to the sight of those familiar houses, offices, gardens, factories and schools. From the train it was easy to see that the first floor of the Vaghi building had never been occupied. It might be, Rudolph thought, the ideal site for his Smirnoff plant. He realised that he could purchase fine-quality grain spirit and deliver it by train right alongside the building, so if business boomed the situation would prove just right. It was a strong enough lead to begin making enquiries.

Joe Vaghi, a large, amiable Italian-American,

was a gentle but persistent ideas man, who dreamed of becoming a great inventor. As a person he was much respected by his community and greatly loved by his family. But when it came to business matters Joe had something of a *laissez-faire* attitude. He was more concerned with his efforts to create such items as the Vaghi Folding Seatable and Sunshade, which was designed for outdoor use yet could be folded small enough to be stowed away on the running board of a car. Or take his amphibious car, for example. On one occasion Joe had amazed the townsfolk by taking his family on an outing to the Bronx Zoo in this bizarre vehicle. The sight of the Vaghi expedition surging down the East River must have been quite sensational. Yet when it came to commerce Joe was not too worried. As long as he could make a reasonable living building and repairing furniture for local people and this gave him enough time to indulge his ambitions as an inventor, all was satisfactory. So when Rudolph Kunett and his friend Donald McAlpin approached him to make an offer to rent the entire first floor, Joe was rather taken aback and even more surprised by their intentions, but the offer was like manna from heaven and he gladly accepted.

In the summer of 1932 a plumber named Paul Rockwell was hired to construct the filtration system so that it would be ready in time for the eagerly anticipated repeal of Prohibition, which was finally declared in 1933. Then and only then could the first US Smirnoff production work begin. Once again the labels were obliged to show that production was permitted under licence from the Lvov Smirnoff company and to display the warrant of the old Russian Imperial Court.

To his regret, Rudolph had read the market incorrectly. His Russian and Ukrainian friends preferred to drink Kentucky Bourbon and other whiskies; they seemed to have lost interest in vodka. Business was proving an uphill struggle and after a couple of years they were only making and selling 4 000 cases, not enough to break even. Cash problems began to arise and Rudolph set about tackling the situation. Until then he had continued to work for Helena Rubenstein and had only taken a part-time interest in the vodka plant, leaving the daily operation of the business to McAlpin and a chemist called Clifford Evers, but he came to the conclusion that the vodka business needed a more serious commitment.

Rudolph had read that some of the states were setting up their own liquor control boards to regulate the trade in alcohol within their own territories. One such board existed in Pennsylvania and Rudolph decided to approach them in an attempt to gain an approved listing for Smirnoff vodka. He believed an approval of this kind would

lead to a run of orders and so he travelled to Harrisburg, the state capital, to make his application. To his delight it was granted but to his dismay he learned that the licence would cost $1 600, a sum the company was not in a position to raise. The following events remain some of the most fairytale-like stories that one is ever liable to encounter in the American business world.

One of the next visitors to the Pennsylvania State Liquor Board was Jack Martin, the youthful president of the famous Heublein company from Hartford, Connecticut. The chairman of the Liquor Board, apparently touched by Rudolph Kunett's problem, asked Jack Martin if he would consider doing a good turn and proceeded to explain the Smirnoff situation. If Jack Martin handled Smirnoff as an agency product, then since Heublein already possessed a licence, Smirnoff could be offered in the state without the little company having to pay. Jack Martin told the story many times; he agreed to do it and yet he never knew just why. He even declined to accept the $1 per case commission that Heublein were entitled to because in his heart he did not believe that Smirnoff "had any chance of sales amounting to more than 5 or 10 cases a year".

The 1930s moved on and the Bethel-based vodka company's sales crept up to a peak of 6 000 cases, but it was still not enough and money began to run out. Once more Jack Martin, otherwise known for his toughness in business, showed a peculiar kindness towards Smirnoff and Rudolph Kunett. After an approach to the diminutive Ukrainian, who had long since given up his position with Helena Rubenstein, Jack Martin made an executive decision to purchase the company for $14 000, with the promise of a job for Kunett and a royalty for each case sold for a number of years in the future. His co-directors thought he had taken leave of his senses, but Jack Martin's reasoning convinced them.

At that time, in 1939, the Smirnoff company was selling its 6 000 cases at $6 each, which represented a turnover of $36 000. Surely there was every chance that Heublein could do better. Also, the entire plant could be relocated from Bethel to their spacious headquarters in Hartford, thus ending the need for rental and effectively reducing the cost of production. It was also the end of rental income for the Vaghi Woodwork Company at 77 South Street, Bethel, as the first floor was never re-occupied before 'their 1991 sale to the similarly named Verdi Woodwork Company, where a few plumbing relics of the Smirnoff company remain. Twice in the 1980s, Dante Vaghi, the eldest of Joe's two sons, proudly showed me the remainder of the piping which once flowed with Smirnoff vodka, and the odd bottle that Rudolph Kunett had given his father, reminders of the tsarist days when Smirnoff was the world's largest-selling drink yet was distributed in a single market.

Ironically, however, if it could have feelings, Smirnoff vodka should have felt at home in its new setting in Hartford, a city where the skyline is decorated with a scattering of golden domes, vaguely reminiscent of Moscow. Rudolph Kunett, who was appointed president of the new company, must have found his new surroundings a little familiar as he drove past the massive Colt firearms factory, or the State Capitol, or a number of other downtown buildings with their gleaming rooftops. He must have felt at home too amid Hartford's Russian and Ukrainian communities and their flourishing churches.

The Societe Smirnoff Fils Inc., as the new Hartford company was initially called, immediately had what can be termed a lucky break. Jack Martin had stipulated that prior to the removal of the equipment from Bethel, 3 000 cases of Smirnoff vodka should be produced as initial stock for all Heublein's sales areas. The vodka was prepared but when it came to bottling, to his horror, Rudolph Kunett discovered that they had run out of white screw caps. He was rescued by recalling an idea that had never been put into practice. In the past they had thought to make another product and they had many screw caps remaining from that abandoned

idea. The intended new liquor had been Smirnoff White Whisky, so these tops were used for the bottles and a paper over-strip printed to cover the old name with the words "Smirnoff Vodka".

While Rudolph was busily preparing the 3 000 cases of vodka, Jack Martin undertook a rather strange journey, and it speaks greatly of the man's foresight that he anticipated the need for such action then. After sailing the Atlantic to Europe, he crossed the continent by rail to Lvov to reach the parent company. If one day Smirnoff vodka became a major brand, then Heublein would want exclusive world rights. The Heublein president was probably aware that the Smirnoff company in Lvov was struggling to exist and felt that he would be on fairly strong ground, but he was surprised to find the parent company in its death throes. Baronowski had died and Valentina Piontkovska and Leonide Ivanow were facing increasing difficulties in the battle to survive. The case confronting them was the reluctance of Polish consumers to pay a little more for finer vodka. The Polish-made Smirnoff was just too expensive for its market and there was nothing they could do to correct matters.

"It cost me about as much again to buy the worldwide rights, but we had to do it," Jack Martin announced. But the sale was not without the usual conditions. The future labels had to carry the authority of the Lvov company and the warrant of the tsarist court, something which is still observed to this day.

Upon his return, despite his position as president, Jack Martin felt obliged to take to the road and demonstrate to his half-hearted colleages that their new product could be sold. As many of us would do in a similar situation, he went to an old friend, a wholesaler in South Carolina, and begged for his cooperation. The wholesaler agreed to purchase twenty-five cases "out of pure friendship", but warned Martin that if they failed to sell he expected Heublein to take them back. Shortly afterwards he reordered and this time the quantity was fifty cases. A few weeks later 100 were requested, and a curious Jack Martin could not resist enquiring about the reason for the sudden success.

This was the tale that unfolded. Heublein's regional sales manager responsible for South Carolina, after reading the memo from head office about this new product, Smirnoff vodka, naturally decided to taste it for himself. He sent for three sample bottles. When they arrived and he opened one, the paper over-strip which Kunett had used to cover the screw cap fell off revealing the identification "Smirnoff White Whisky". Learning of the first order from South Carolina, he made up a number of display streamers which announced: "Smirnoff White Whisky, no taste, no smell".

Being that far south, a fair proportion of the male population found the idea of a liquor which could not be detected on one's breath very appealing. South Carolina alone disposed of a large portion of the so-called White Whisky, but World War II was declared and interrupted this trend, and Smirnoff vodka was taken out of production, along with many other liquors. It did not reappear until 1946.

When Smirnoff did resurface it was in a wholly different manner and its success was brought about by Jack Martin, aided and abetted by an old school pal, Jack Morgan, and his girlfriend, Osalind. Jack Morgan had settled in Los Angeles, where among other things he owned a fashionable cocktail bar and restaurant known as the Cock 'n Bull. In school he had a penchant for drinking ginger beer, very much a favourite drink during the earlier part of the century. He had made an arrangement with a local soft-drink producer to make thousands of cans of Cock 'n Bull Ginger Beer, envisaging the launch of a new product. All his attempts failed miserably and the backyard of the Cock 'n Bull became a dumping ground for unwanted cans. At the same time, Jack had a girlfriend, Osalind Schmidt, who had achieved some fame as the girl star in *The Blue Lagoon*. One evening Osalind confided in him that she had come into a rather unusual inheritance, a small pottery that specialised in pots with a copper glaze finish. Among its output were 20 000 copper mugs in the design of a mule. Did Jack have any idea what she could do with them? They were pondering this unlikely problem when Jack Martin paid a visit in search of a refreshing cocktail, as the Heublein president himself was feeling somewhat depressed by the failure of his sales staff to make any progress with Smirnoff vodka. He had told them rather forcibly that if they could not sell it he would go back on the road to show them how it was done. It was in the light of this statement that he had come to Los Angeles, because consumers there were known to be intrepid experimenters with new products and ideas. But he was out of luck so far.

The three sat together bemoaning their respective fates when inspiration dawned. Jack Morgan gloomily placed one of his ginger beer cans on the table alongside a mule mug that Osalind had brought. Quick as a flash, Jack Martin seized a bottle of Smirnoff, poured some in the mule and topped it with the Cock 'n Bull Ginger Beer and ice. And in this manner the Moscow Mule, the cocktail with a kick in it, was born.

Jack Martin's confidence was restored and ideas rapidly flooded his brain. He had seen advertisements for the astonishing new Polaroid camera and promptly bought one. Armed with the camera and the ingredients for the Moscow Mule, he entered another Los Angeles bar and showed the bartender how to make the new cocktail. Having accomplished that he took two photographs of the bartender with the cocktail and the Smirnoff bottle, made a gift of one to the delighted bartender and kept the other to display at the next bar he visited. This procedure was repeated again and again, and as the Moscow Mule began to sweep Los Angeles the future looked increasingly bright. Soon the drink was in great demand throughout California and within months the craze had swept the nation. At that point it ran into a hiccup.

It was the height of the Cold War and the New York Bartenders Guild took exception to what they in their ignorance believed to be a Russian drink. They felt strongly enough to hold a large demonstration against its sale. Only when Jack Martin publicly protested that it was completely American and produced in Hartford was the day saved. The reaction swung in the right direction for Smirnoff and Hubelein, and suddenly everyone was asking to try this new white spirit that did not smell and did not taste.

The sales of Smirnoff exploded at a time when the cocktail craze was undergoing a revival and vodka was often the ideal base. Nowadays, notices in bars and lounges in cities all over the United States display a great variety of cocktails at realistic

In March 1994, this became the first Smirnoff vodka distilled in Russia since 1917

prices, and among them is still frequently seen the Moscow Mule. Yet one must pause to wonder just how many customers, even in the middle of Hartford, realise just what happened in their immediate neighbourhood.

Smirnoff sales have risen to such an extent that there are now more than thirty licensed plants worldwide, but for all of them there is one strict rule. They must purchase their carbon for filtering from what Americans might call "home base". The sales from these plants have put the name Smirnoff onto the bars and shelves of just about every country – that is, with the notable exception of Russia until 1994.

By the early 1980s the American market alone reached a peak, with more than 400 different vodkas being produced, a figure achieved over a period of just fifty years. In light of this it is all the more surprising that its success can really be attributed to four men: Pierre Smirnoff, Vladimir Smirnoff, who brought the secrets to the West, Rudolph Kunett, who had the belief that vodka could sell in America, and Jack Martin, who actually proved it. Yet even today's sales do not match the massive consumption that the Smirnoffs obtained in Russia in their heyday. Through a story of romance, mystery and intrigue, the much loved, pure, clean spirit of the tsars has become a favourite drink not just of Americans but of nations worldwide. Perhaps such popularity would never have been gained if it was not for the gift of so many dazzling jewels from an errant Russian noble to his young Polish lover.

The final chapter of the Smirnoff story began to unfold in 1988, when the giant British public company Grand Metropolitan purchased Heublein, and Smirnoff with it. The Russian formula that had been first put to use in Moscow in 1818, then travelled to Poland, and afterwards headed south to Paris before crossing the Atlantic to two new homes in Connecticut, then returned across the ocean, this time to distilleries in England and Scotland. Finally, following the demise of the USSR, an attempt was made to register Smirnoff vodka in Russia once more. Initially the move appeared to be too late, as a Russian citizen called Smirnoff had acted first, for Smirnoff is an extremely common name in that country. Fortunately the problem has been addressed satisfactorily, for in Moscow, in the spring of 1994, Smirnoff distilled Black Label, its first Russian vodka since 1917.

SCARED OF THE DEVIL
Concha y Toro, Chile

Legendary wine figure Marqués de Casa Concha founded his Conch y Toro winery in 1883. He was best-known as one of the leaders of a group of Chilean growers who travelled to Bordeaux at the end of the 19th century to purchase ungrafted pre-phylloxera vines from several Grand Cru Classé chateaux.

Upon his return to Chile he was faced with another problem. In the main Concha y Toro cellars he had allocated one particular cave for his personal use, for storing his own private reserve of wines, which understandably included some of the finest in his production.

Unfortunately, during the marqués's absence, some of his employees had taken a fancy to the contents and begun helping themselves on a regular basis. In the marqués's view there was little to be gained from moving his wine to another section of the cellars because sooner or later someone would recognise his private stock and the thefts would resume. Instead, he decided to take advantage of the local tendency to superstition. He deliberately circulated rumours that the devil lived in that particular cave and to make the story convincing he even spent several nights among his wines, throwing bottles haphazardly, smashing them to pieces and making a great deal of noise. As a result a local myth evolved which terrified the cellar workers so much that no-one other than the Marques was prepared to go near the area.

In due course that section of the cellar became known as *Casillero del Diablo,* or "the cellar where the devil lives", and subsequently the name was given to a special reserve of wine, sold under that label with a small devil hanging from the neck of the bottle. Even to this day it is reported that cellar workers at Concha y Toro will never enter the cave at night.

SCHNEIDER AND SCHNEIDER
Vacu-Vin and Rapid Ice, the Netherlands

A good friend of mine once described Schneider and Schneider as the Lennon and McCartney of the wine world, a statement which might set some readers racking their brains to think of one notable Schneider, let alone two, with any involvement in wine. My friend's allusion to the highly talented musical partnership was his own tribute to the manner in which these two wine men, Bernd and John Schneider, operate alongside one another with mutual understanding and cooperation. They seem to exhibit a sixth sense when working together and yet their respective talents are quite distinct. These brothers are, of course, the world's leading inventors of wine accessories, the men of drive and initiative who have given us Vacu-Vin, the wine-saver pump, and Rapid Ice, the silver sleeve which

Schneider and Schneider – John (left) and Bernd

chills one's white wine to perfection in around five minutes.

Their dramatic success as the owners of Vacu-Products has arisen since 1985, when the laconic John one day invited his wine-importer brother to a party at his house. During the course of the evening he presented the eccentric Bernd with a half-consumed bottle of red Bordeaux, which he recommended Bernd should purchase in his whole-sale and import wine business. As Bernd nosed the wine his suspicions were aroused and when he tasted the contents of his glass he spat them out with more than usual vigour, as they were completely oxidised and quite unpalatable. John asked Bernd to explain why wine oxidised and if anything could be done to prevent it. When Bernd told him how atrocious a problem it was and that the time was ripe for someone to invent a wine accessory that would overcome it, John offered to do anything he could to help.

Throughout the following weeks Bernd searched constantly for opportunities to develop some basic ideas. He examined the vats that he used for some French wines which he imported and bottled, and then he scrutinised the tank's structure and noted how its level lowered as wine was drawn from it for bottling. This gave him his first inkling of how a pump could be developed but he soon concluded that this was, at least in part, a matter of mechanics and that he needed to ask his brother John, who was a skilled engineer, for assistance.

Bernd pondered the causes of oxidation and came to the conclusion that the root problem was that the air contains oxygen which decomposes wine when it is exposed to it. Therefore his decision was straightforward; he had to devise a method of removing the air from a partly-consumed bottle of wine and prevent it from getting back in. The answer, as he foresaw it, was some kind of vacuum pump. Bernd, the man of ideas, naturally

went to John, the technician, to provide the mechanical answer. Their project was now truly under way, and over a two-year period it developed the lightweight wine-saver pumps that are now so visible and popular in every wine-loving nation.

Their research was not without its hitches however. Their first effort was a brass Vacu-Vin which proved to be somewhat inefficient and expensive. A little later Bernd had the idea of producing the pumps in their local blue delft pottery and a small trial quantity was actually made. This experiment was short-lived and the items were merely used as gifts and souvenirs. Finally Schneider and Schneider followed a more serious vein and realised that they needed an unbreakable substance. This was provided in the form of a light polymer, a by-product of North Sea oil.

Along with the pump, Bernd had evolved a basic idea for a stopper, which would be airtight when fitted into the neck of a part-used bottle of wine and yet which would allow the air in the bottle to be withdrawn. Once again the engineer needed to refine the inventor's initial idea. John avoided the use of rubber because of its smell and went in search of inert rubber, previously only used for medical purposes. In this way, Vacu-Vin, the creation of Schneider and Schneider, was born. But before it could be sold Bernd sensibly sought some academic advice.

He called upon the expertise of an experienced professor of economics to guide them regarding the number of units they should manufacture on the first occasion. The advice was 20 000 but Bernd, being farsighted, decided this figure was too cautious and ordered an initial quantity of double that number. Within twelve months that figure appeared derisory as they passed the 1 million unit sales mark and now they have sold around 12 million wine savers in fifty different countries. From an initial test market in the Netherlands, Vacu-Vin swept over the water to Britain, across the Atlantic to the United States, and from there reached around the world to the Antipodes. Millions of consumers became aware that someone had invented a wine accessory that would save them wine and money, and so the idea which was prompted by a mouthful of bad wine grew into a global success. Schneider and Schneider had literally made something out of nothing, a fortune out of a vacuum.

Now there was no stopping Schneider and Schneider as they scoured the world for further ideas. The next item to arrive was a light plastic wine rack called Clik-Clack, but while it has been a consistent performer it has never attracted the widespread attention that Vacu-Vin did. Then the

The second great invention of Schneider and Schneider – the Rapid Ice wine-chilling sleeve

bottle and held in position with velcro. A prototype was constructed but a major problem was straightaway revealed and the experiment was quickly concluded.

Gradually one problem after another was surmounted and, as previously, Bernd's initial concepts were put into effect by John's technical skill. Other considerations, raised by the Schneiders' close but growing circle of confidantes, were also taken into account. One of these was suitability for outdoor use for picnics and barbecues.

Here Schneider and Schneider demonstrated their ingenuity once more by employing a shiny silver surface which reflects the sun's rays away from the bottle. Following the top-secret acquisition of a suitable gel they were ready for production and in November 1992 the first Rapid Ice wine-chilling sleeves were launched on the market, in response to a worldwide demand for an item that previously did not exist.

All one can add is thanks to those two Dutch inventors for their practical ingenuity, and one wonders just what will they invent next.

SUCCESS BY ACCIDENT
Craigmoor, Australia

In the bountiful vintage of 1933 the abundance of the New South Wales crop precipitated a minor crisis among winegrowers, who were suddenly faced with the realisation that they simply did not have the storage capacity for the new wine. This led to a desperate search for old casks and tanks of any kind or description that could be cleaned and reused.

At the Craigmoor winery, on the outskirts of Mudgee, the local port maker, Jack Roth, was racking his brains trying to recollect where he had seen some old barrels somewhere in the little town. Deciding that it was preferable to begin searching

brothers were slightly sidetracked by the request to design an instant pineapple slicer for the American Williams-Sonoma chain.

Other similar requests were received but Bernd was still seeking further wine-accessory projects. In 1990, Bernd and Vacu-Products International Manager, Alan Green, were visiting a European trade fair when Bernd suggested they started looking at all the chilling and cooling devices for wine, as that might be the next direction to follow. Having examined numerous accessories that did not appeal to him, Bernd sat down, took out his notebook and began sketching the outline of a basic wine cooler, and within minutes the concept of Rapid Ice was born.

This time the brothers had their previous experience to guide them and so immediately began to consider the practical application of the basic necessity of chilling a bottle of wine to the correct temperature in a short space of time. They were aware, naturally, of the use of freezer blocks in cooler boxes for picnics, but these were unsuitable for chilling wine as they froze as solid bricks. Yet Bernd felt that they represented the starting point for what they required. However, instead of a single section that solidified, Bernd planned to have several sections that could be wrapped around a bottle and would contain a gel that remained flexible when frozen. One of his initial thoughts was to make a sleeve consisting of several panels that could be wrapped around a

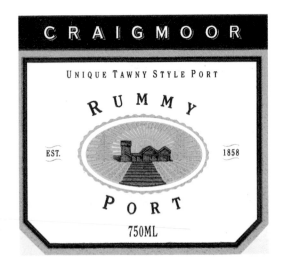

he drove the few miles to the centre of Mudgee to make initial enquiries.

Like most local wine producers he was well-known among the hotel and café owners and he commenced his enquiries with them, asking if anyone could sell him any barrels or tanks. For some while his search was fruitless, until he arrived at the Paragon Hotel, where he was told that some old rum casks were gathering dust in their cellars. After a few minutes of ferreting through a dark, dusty cellar, he suddenly lighted upon a cask with the name Inner Circle on it, and others followed. Though quite uncertain what effect the rum would have on the port as it aged, Jack decided to take the risk and purchased them.

Twelve months later, when the time arrived to sample the contents of his newly acquired casks, Jack was both surprised and pleased. The wine had taken on a most unusual character, with a rum-like flavour that he found most attractive. All he felt was needed was a little more maturity and so a couple

Craigmoor winery, Mudgee, NSW

of years later it was bottled and sold as Craigmoor Rummy Port, hence inadvertently providing the first rummy port of all. It was a style that quickly proved popular and soon found many imitators.

Lovers of rummy port should always bear in mind that the origin of their favourite drink lies in the quite exceptional 1933 vintage and Jack Roth's fortuitous discovery of the old, discarded rum barrels.

2.   ACROSS THE OCEANS

ANYTHING BUT GOLD

Charles Lefranc, Paul Masson and Pierre Mirassou;
France and USA

The Californian gold rush of 1849 began with that lucky strike at Sutter's Mill, which sent waves of excitement rippling around the world. In no time at all tales of new-found wealth – some true, some exaggerated – were being announced in banner headlines in numerous languages. This publicity had a magnetic effect, causing thousands and thousands of hopeful prospectors to embark upon journeys which often took them across the great oceans as they headed for the new El Dorado. Among the multitudes who trekked across the American continent or sailed around the Horn were some 20 000 eager young Frenchmen, few of whom would ever set eyes on a single particle of gold dust, but a handful of whom were destined to become the founders of a large proportion of the Californian vineyards, which are nowadays producing some of the finest and most attractive wines available.

One of these young Frenchman, Charles Lefranc, came from the Parisian suburb of Passy. At that time Paris was surrounded by a substantial number of vineyards, where he may well have gained the experience which was to make him, more than any other man, the true Father of Californian Wines, although that is a much-disputed title.

Along with practically all his contemporaries, Charles failed to make an overnight fortune and concluded that he must seek other employment or starve. Yet in spite of the competition among so many fit, able-bodied young men to secure work, Charles achieved some measure of success when he was hired as a travelling sales assistant by his friend and countryman, Paul Verdier, the selfsame Paul Verdier who later became famous for his City of Paris department store in San Francisco.

It was Charles's task to accompany Paul on his excursions into the surrounding valleys to sell fabrics and clothing. On one such trip they visited the Santa Clara Valley and the entrancingly titled Blossom Hill Road. Here, Charles fell in love with Marie-Adele, the daughter of a French fruit farmer, Etienne Thée. Thée persuaded Charles that he was more suited to a rural life than one in selling, and hired his services to help him run the family vineyard and fruit farm, which lay on the banks of the little Guadelupe River in the shadows of the Santa Cruz mountains running to its south. Etienne Thée had called his property the New Almaden Vineyard, naming it after a large cinnabar mine nearby. Eventually, after a long courtship, Charles and Marie-Adele married and Charles became his father-in-law's partner. The younger Frenchman had entertained misgivings for some while about the quality of the Spanish Mission grapes they were growing and so he took advantage of his new

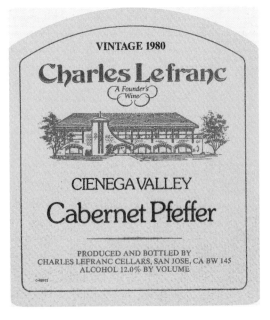

station to import several noble varieties from France. It was then that Charles took the course of action which justifies his being recognised as the Father of Californian Wine. He had often observed the wild native vines, the *Vitis californica*, growing on the banks of the Guadalupe immediately below their vineyard and so he began to cut and graft them with his new French varieties. In a relatively short period of time this enabled him to provide sufficient stocks to advertise French grapevine cuttings for sale to other vineyard owners, something he did in the *San Jose Tribune* in May 1858. The cuttings were purchased by growers for many miles around and were a major step in the improvement of Californian wines.

There is another strange thread to this story which is not strictly connected with gold. As the century progressed the world began to learn more and more about what was being widely called the Golden State, a title which reflected not just the mineral wealth that had come to light but also the climate which offered paradise to farmers' of all descriptions. Such a bountiful land prompted a steady stream of men and women from France seeking a new, healthy and prosperous life.

This second wave of immigrants included a beefy young Burgundian, Paul Masson, who came to San José to work for Almaden. His energy and enthusiasm made him a popular figure and he was treated as one of the family. Not only did he work assiduously but he also studied at the new University of the Pacific in San José. Masson was to become an expert in the development of the *méthode champenoise* and while in the employ of the Lefranc family, he carried out many fascinating experiments with it in the basement cellar of a San José Hotel.

Unfortunately Charles Lefranc met a premature end while attempting to halt some runaway horses and so Paul took over much of the business, which otherwise would have been in danger of collapsing. He married Charles' daughter, Louise, and with her brother, Henri, formed a partnership. In due course, however, the partnership was dissolved and Henri and Paul went their separate ways, each taking a share of the New Almaden business.

Today, as a result of that original association, both producers, Almaden with their Charles Lefranc label and Paul Masson, claim to have started in 1852. Yes, that's right, 1852. But why, when Etienne Thée planted his first mission vines in 1851? Somehow, at some stage, Almaden estimated the year incorrectly and because of the red tape concerned have since been reluctant to change it. And Paul Masson simply followed the date claimed for the Almaden foundation. Surviving court records can quite clearly prove 1851 to be the accurate date.

Charles Lefranc, the true father of Californian wine

The truth is that family links no longer exist for either producer and the original vineyard has been abandoned, but both are justified in claiming the same origin, since 1851 was the year of the foundation of the vineyard that was to be named New Almaden. And the Almaden business would never have survived without the efforts of Paul Masson.

Just a few miles away from the New Almaden Vineyard another Frenchman called Pellier was operating a similar fruit farm and vineyard. Pierre Pellier was a native of La Rochelle, which lies just within the confines of the official Cognac region in western France, and he settled near San José in 1854. His name is long since forgotten, in contrast with that of his son-in-law, Pierre Mirassou, who is remembered by many. Pellier had been one of the forty-niners, but like Lefranc had failed to find any gold and so after some while, along with a number of other French farmers, he settled in the Santa Clara Valley, an area which seemed ideally situated for grapes and soft fruit. Pellier was best-known for his early work grafting pears but the story of his vineyard, later known as Mirassou Vineyards after his son-in-law, has parallels with the Thée-Lefranc partnership.

Pierre Mirassou did not arrive on the scene until 1880, following his emigration from the Jurançon region in the foothills of the Pyrenees. The lean young Frenchman came from a family of general farmers who lived near the Jurançon vineyards but never grew any grapes themselves. It is probable that Pierre Mirassou had learnt a little about vines from distant cousins, some of whom produced a little wine. What is definitely known is that he knew the differences between good and poor wine from his experiences with the plentiful supplies available in his home locality. Mirassou, albeit not involved in the gold rush or subsequent emigrations, should always be remembered for one unusual story, and because Mirassou Vineyards today remains America's oldest continuous family winery since 1854. The story, which is amply documented by others, tells that after Pierre Mirassou married Pellier's daughter he felt that they needed a better standard of vine. With that in mind he sailed back to his native France, where he purchased several thousand vine cuttings and took them with him on the long and arduous return journey around Cape Horn, then the only sea route from Europe to the western coast of the United States. For several weeks the voyage proceeded without incident until it reached its latter stages, when the Pacific Ocean lived up to its name and the ship was becalmed. The result was that the captain imposed a water ration, declaring that all available fresh water was to be used for drinking purposes only.

At this stage Pierre Mirassou displayed a touch of pure genius in his desperation to save his vines. Approaching the captain he offered to buy the ship's entire stock of potatoes, which was agreed. Taking his pocketknife, he made an incision in each potato and inserted a vine cutting, thus enabling the vines to draw vital moisture from the flesh of the potatoes. It must have been an onerous and exasperating task, but for a man who had risked mountainous seas and travelled many miles to achieve his goal it was a worthwhile occupation. To Pierre's relief every vine survived.

In the 1850s, gold must have been the most desirable commodity in the eyes of the majority of the population, but to Count Agoston Haraszthy, founder of the Buena Vista Winery in Sonoma, it was most unwelcome.

Haraszthy was, by birth, an Hungarian nobleman who became an entrepreneur of certain acclaim. His many talents included some expertise in the refinement of gold, an attribute which led to his appointment as gold assayer, melter and refiner at the San Francisco Mint between the years of 1855 and 1857, during which time more than $100 million worth of gold was processed. Unfortunately auditors discovered that a small proportion of the gold was unaccounted for, having seemingly vanished into thin air, and accordingly Haraszthy was charged with embezzling gold to the value of $151 000. Bail was granted but only on condition that the Magyar Count provided as security his entire estate and property.

The San Francisco press and business community held divided opinions regarding the Count's conduct. Some declared him "a reckless experimenter", while others saw him as "a man of vision". The case was a constant topic of conver-

Charles Krug, Napa's oldest continuously operating winery

sation and investigations stretched over three long years before an astonishing discovery proved the Hungarian's innocence.

It came to light that the smelting and refining techniques at the mint had acquired certain defects and gold had literally gone up in smoke, escaping up the furnace chimneys. When scrapings were taken from the rooftops of the surrounding buildings they showed, on analysis, among the soot and the grime, "an extremely high proportion of gold".

There must be a lesson to be learnt from all these experiences. Gold can be discovered in more than one form; it may be the liquid variety rather than the precious ore. After all, that was true for Charles Lefranc, Paul Masson, Pierre Pellier, Pierre Mirassou, and probably a host of others whose names we will never know. And no doubt the vineyards of the Golden State will prove in the generations ahead that they will continue to be worth their weight in gold.

CHARLES KRUG
Charles Krug Winery, USA

The Charles Krug winery, near St Helena in the Napa Valley, can justifiably claim to be the oldest continuous wine producer in that area. It was founded in 1861 by a Prussian of many talents who had made the bold decision to forgo his active life in San Francisco for a new challenge clearing the virgin forest of the fertile valley. He had originally come to the USA from Trendelburg in Prussia, where he had been imprisoned for his political beliefs. At twenty-two he left his homeland seeking pastures new and eventually arrived in Philadelphia.

Later, Charles Krug moved to San Francisco and in the aftermath of the gold strike, earned his living as a schoolteacher before he became the editor of *Staats Zeitung*, the only German newspaper ever printed on the west coast of the USA. When his journalistic duties came to an end with the paper's demise, he chose a completely contrasting lifestyle and with his limited funds moved north.

In the second half of the 19th century he developed his winery into a major commercial success

and encouraged others to introduce the best vineyard practices and disciplines. Frona Eunice Watt, when writing of him in her 1889 publication *Wines and Vines of California*, identified him as:

> Charles Krug, the pioneer wine-maker of the valley: a man whose name has been associated with every venture for the promotion of the industry throughout the state, from its inception to the present, giving a lifetime and a fortune to the work.

Among his early trainees was another young Prussian who had jumped ship in San Francisco; his name was Karl Wente. He later moved south to Livermore, where he founded Wente Vineyards. Other fellow countrymen whom he taught included the Beringer Brothers, and Jacob Schram, the founder of Schramsberg.

For many years Charles Krug has been owned by the Mondavi family, headed by Peter, the younger brother of Robert Mondavi, but it is run quite independently of the elder brother's affairs.

THE JOURNEY OF A LIFETIME
Orlando Jacob's Creek, Australia

In 1837 an illiterate and impecunious seventeen-year-old farm labourer left his home village in Bavaria, little knowing the enormity of the adventure he was about to undertake, nor the huge influence he would exert upon the beginnings of the Australian wine industry. His name was Johann Grampp and he was born on 28 August 1819 in Aichig, a hamlet within the jurisdiction of the small town of Kulmbach. He was the third son of an impoverished smallholder in a community whose life centred on the Lutheran Church. When his eighteenth birthday arrived he found himself, quite unexpectedly, a passenger on a barquentine called the *Solway*, bound for the colony of South Australia.

The Lutheran Church was the prevailing influence on two occasions in Johann's life. It appears likely that his initial intention was to go to sea, but as he was a complete stranger when he arrived in Hamburg, the church was his sole point of contact, and it was there that his lifelong friendship with Wilhelm Milde, a baker, began. Milde, at thirty-eight, was more than twice Johann's age, and planned to emigrate with his wife and child. He exhorted Grampp to join them on a journey that would last some four months.

Milde was no ordinary baker but a man of literary talent who recorded the epic passage in a poem of thirty-one verses entitled "My Sea-Voyage", which is not a diarised account but one which highlights their experiences as they sailed the 12 000 miles to their barely known destination. For that poem we remain indebted, as it provides an unique and independent first-hand account.

On board ship the two men developed a lasting relationship with a third Lutheran, Friedrich Wilhelm Kleemann, also thirty-eight years old, who appears to have been a farmhand but with additional skills. For Kleemann the journey was to be one of personal tragedy, as he lost his wife and one of his four children. All three men were to eventually settle in South Australia's Barossa Valley but much was to happen between their departure from Hamburg and their arrival in Australia, which exemplifies the trials and tribulations suffered by so many early migrants to the land of the Southern Cross.

The 337-ton, three-masted *Solway* was to be their home from 2 June, when they boarded, until 16 October 1837, when they docked at Kangaroo Island. The small ship, under the command of a Captain Pearson, had been chartered by the South Australian Company to carry contracted workers and their families to Australia and upon arrival the vessel was to join the company's whaling fleet. The ship was registered in London under the ownership of Graham Bros and measured a mere 103·feet by 27 feet by 9 feet 6 inches. As in many similar instances, the number of passengers and crew on board at the time of departure was not necessarily the same as the number on board upon disembarkation, because of births and deaths during the four-month journey. In this case, the *Solway* departed

Hamburg with fifty-four passengers and fourteen crew, the total upon arrival being reduced by two, due to the Kleemann deaths. Of these fifty-four passengers, twenty-eight men were described as breadwinners, eight of the men had wives and two were accompanied by sisters, and there were sixteen children.

The twenty-eight men had all signed complex contracts with the South Australian Company, fortunately for them an organisation headed by George Fife Angas, a character of high moral standing. His co-director, John Pirie, was also a man of integrity. The emigrants accepted the terms in good faith while being completely ignorant of the conditions that awaited them and of the possibility that had Angas and Pirie been rogues, then their immediate lives would not just have been miserable but at risk.

The contracts committed them to work for the South Australian Company as required for three years from the day they set foot in the colony. The payment varied, depending upon the skills demanded, but under a typical contract, the employee would receive 20 shillings per week in the first year, 21 shillings in the second and 22 shillings in the third, and arrangements were made for the deduction of the cost of the one-way passage. Surviving records show that Milde paid £36 for his wife, three-year-old child and himself, which suggests that a single man such as Johann Grampp would have paid around £14 or £15. In addition the contracts allocated half an acre of land rent-free and permitted "the Colonial Manager to retain the sum of 2 shillings weekly from the wages, to be paid on expiration of the term of service". In spite

of the promises of the documents and the hopes for the years after the contracts were completed, none of the men could have had any idea of the conditions that would greet them, and their trust in the company and its agent had to be absolute.

To some degree their travelling arrangements were protected by the British government. Aware that unscrupulous shipping companies were abusing the movement of emigrants to the United States, the government had intervened to ensure that similar practices did not occur with emigrants to Australia, since it was a British colony. Controls were brought into force which meant each ship had to be registered and inspected as well as carry a ship's surgeon. At the time, 25 per cent of the emigrant traffic consisted of Germanic people, who were mostly Prussians, but occasionally Bavarians and a few from the Palatinate. The British insisted that these sailed in British ships and called at English ports for inspection both of the vessels and of the documentation. A surgeon was also taken on board when the ships docked. Most of this shipping originated in Hamburg or in the Rhine, and the boats called at London, Gravesend, Deal, Dover or another of the Kent ports. It was such a stop at Deal that was to provide the catalyst for Johann Grampp's eventual decision to plant the first commercial vineyard in the Barossa Valley, for there he was considerably impressed by a clergyman whose influence would attract the young Bavarian to the future wine region.

It appears that the South Australian Company had the intention of supplementing the overall cost of the trip by carrying some independent paying passengers, and advertised in the *Times* offering poop cabins at £40, with the invitation to enquire at their offices at 19 Bishopsgate Street in the City of London. In the case of the *Solway*, no additional ticket was sold and the passenger list remained entirely Germanic in origin. It might well have been that more prosperous emigrants, who could afford to select their vessel, considered the barquentine too frail for the journey, an opinion borne out by the fact that fifty-three days after its arrival in South Australia, the *Solway* was wrecked upon rocks in Encounter Bay while carrying a load of whale oil.

The new company recruits began to board the *Solway* seven days before their departure on 9 June 1837 and Milde's poem, translated by Pastor J.E. Materne, relates that although it was small the ship was taken up the Elbe estuary by a pilot who left on another boat once they reached the open North Sea. It was indeed an emotional moment as the hard reality that most would never see their friends and families again was taken to heart and tears of grief flowed:

Johann Gramp, founder of Jacob's Creek

Then the open sea we entered
And soon there was much lamentation.

A few days later they arrived at the Kentish coast:

At Deal in England we arrived
To enjoy four days of calm.

And it was during those four days that documents were verified, fresh bread, biscuits and beer were purchased and a Lutheran pastor called Kavel went on board:

Soon he began a sermon
That God may protect us
From shipwreck and such like;
Admonished all to diligently pray
And tracts he did present.

It was an experience that Grampp and his friends, all devout Lutherans, were never to forget and it seems that Pastor Kavel told them of his intentions to travel to South Australia to build Lutheran settlements there, where their persecuted people could live and worship in peace.

Pastor Kavel was a native of the province of Brandenburg in Prussia, where the Lutherans had been experiencing considerable religious intolerance. He was a minister in a town called Klemzig and had been negotiating with George Fife Angas to move his entire flock the lengthy distance from Eastern Europe to South Australia. Angas, who was keen to encourage people of good character and conduct to settle there, supported religious freedom and offered such conditions to those intent on making the journey. Apparently Kavel had sailed to England to negotiate matters and may well have gone to Deal on that date by pure chance, as his intention was probably just to inspect the arrangements. No doubt when he heard of fellow Lutherans emigrating he felt prompted to address them.

Shortly after leaving Deal the *Solway* passed some fishing smacks in the Straits of Dover and Milde bought some fish from one. Then it was onward into the vast Atlantic Ocean and unusually fine weather all the way to the equator. Some readers may find the route they pursued at this stage rather illogical, but there was a reason. They passed the island of Madeira to its west but close enough to catch sight of it before sailing past the Canaries and across the South Atlantic to the Brazilian coast, which they hugged until they berthed at Rio de Janeiro.

For Johann Grampp and his fellow passengers, arrival at Rio de Janeiro must have been eye-opening. Even then Rio was a hectic port where people of numerous races and nationalities thronged, a colourful city with an unique and imposing landscape, yet one where bountiful wealth rubbed shoulders with abject poverty. Into these surroundings came this diverse contingent of Germanic peoples, few of whom could speak more than the odd word of English, and probably none of whom knew a single word of the Portuguese language used in Rio. Furthermore the temperature and humidity in August were greater than that to which any of them had previously been exposed and it must be a fair conjecture that by then the travellers were weary and bewildered.

Having loaded fresh stocks of food and water the *Solway* then crossed the South Atlantic for a second time to South Africa's Cape, where they were nearly swamped in a tempestuous storm:

The storm did rage fiercely
And wave after wave did rise
Like mountains followed by mountains.

A breaker as it is called
Came with the tempest and the weather.
It rushed upon our doctor
And cast him through the boards,
That he did not know what happened
And the captain alongside
Nearly drowned in his bed.

The following day the weather was a little calmer and the sun shone brightly but they were still carried along by a powerful wind. Yet conditions were safe enough for all the passengers to be asked to assist with clearing the debris from the deck and repairing the damage. The fowl sheds were discovered to be flattened and all the birds dead, which meant the end of their supply of poultry and eggs. This, Milde recorded:

Brought distress to the captain,
Henceforth he had to eat salted meat.

Strangely they did not dock at the Cape, a regular port of call for early migrant ships.

For several years there had been some debate over the best route from England to South Australia and at the time the most popular theory was that the path from North Africa to Rio and back to the Cape was the most efficient route, bearing in mind the elliptical shape of the globe and the most favourable trade winds. Later the consensus changed and sailors reverted to following the coastline of Africa.

From the Cape the immense space of the Indian Ocean lay ahead of the travellers and for weeks they sailed without sight of any land until the island of Amsterdam was spotted. This indicated that there were only some 3 000 miles remaining to their destination, and they knew that if the weather provided them with reasonable fortune they would

only have to endure three more weeks on board.

With just two days of the voyage remaining, tragedy struck with the unexpected death of Mrs Kleemann, who had been seriously ill for some time. A decision was made not to carry out a burial at sea as they were so near their destination. Accordingly the ship's carpenter built a coffin so that Mrs Kleemann could be buried on land when they arrived. Her death, with the voyage's end so close, must have been sad and heart-rending, and an experience often undergone on lengthy emigrant journeys. Yet one must remember that the *Solway*'s seaboard conditions were quite tolerable for that era and though its passengers must have been anxious to step on dry land, their trip had certainly been blessed. As Pastor Kavel had prayed at Deal, God had protected them from shipwreck, a fact that became clear to them when they learned two months later of the *Solway*'s destruction.

On 16 October 1837 the *Solway* approached the shore of Kingscote on Kangaroo Island, just south of the site of the proposed city of Adelaide. They were greeted by a motley flotilla of tiny vessels led by David McClaren, the unofficial head of the community and manager of the South Australian Company's base there. Otherwise there was no form of immigration control or customs. All such formalities had been completed more than four months earlier in Deal.

The exact population of Kangaroo Island is not known but it probably had slightly fewer than 300 inhabitants. These comprised four main factions: seal hunters, escaped prisoners, Aboriginal women who had become the common law wives of some of the escapees, and recruits of the South Australian Company, who were of British and German extraction.

When the colonisation of Australia was planned originally, it had been proposed that three of the colonies, namely New South Wales, Queensland and Victoria, were to be prisoner colonies, while South Australia was always intended to be a free territory, where land grants and purchases would be the order of the day. However, over time, this created a situation where prisoners who fled to South Australia were likely to retain their freedom. No doubt the relative isolation of Kangaroo Island added to their sense of security. Subsequently when any previously unknown ship was sighted its arrival was observed with considerable care.

McClaren may not have ostensibly supported the ex-prisoners, but he had been sent to the island to bring matters under control after problems of drunkenness and violence had broken out involving both the company's employees and members of the ex-prison population. His instructions had been to restore peace and discipline and to this end he had found it necessary to assume an overall leadership role. With this status he attracted the trust of all the islanders. Milde described him as "a gaunt person with thin hair" and identified him by name.

The first request made to McClaren was for a plot to bury Mrs Kleemann, which was made the prime objective the next day upon landing. Near the lone grave, Friedrich Kleemann planted a symbolic mulberry tree, which some claim to be the oldest surviving fruit tree in the state today. It was an especially poignant gesture in memory of the fact that his wife, and many others, had been greatly encouraged on the voyage when, upon reaching the tropics, the fruit-tree cuttings they had brought with them had burst into bloom.

Indeed the landing and the burial must have been a time of conflicting emotions, for these normally disciplined folk allowed themselves to relax for a while and after the funeral headed for the local blacksmith. His must have been one of the most unusual and original bars ever visited and he sold them brandy, rum and wine by the glass, which was partaken in such copious quantities that some of the party failed to return to an agreed assembly on the shore at 5.00 p.m. and remained instead to sleep off the effects of overindulgence.

Two days after arrival, they removed all their belongings from the *Solway* and searched for a shaded spot where they could await the delivery of the tents which the company provided as initial accommodation. Since these did not arrive immediately, some of the group slept in the hollow trunks of gum trees. Fortunately, October weather conditions in South Australia were springlike and clement and so they were not troubled by any extremes of temperature.

There is much confusion regarding the early days of Kangaroo Island and the construction of the spacious, purpose-built city of Adelaide. The situation was complicated by the role of the new state's governor, William Hindmarsh. The intention had been for Hindmarsh to take charge of the building of Adelaide but he fell out with the British government and eventually resigned his post, leaving a clear field for the South Australian Company to take over the project. It was at this juncture that the majority of the labour force which had been steadily expanding on Kangaroo Island was moved into the area planned for Adelaide, to begin the task of developing the city.

Gradually, during the time spent on the island, life had evolved a certain pattern and structure. Gramp had now lost the second "p" of his surname, probably through a company spelling error, while his friendship with the unfortunate Freidrich Kleemann and Wilhelm Milde grew from strength to strength. There is no doubt that Gramp and Milde proved a great support to their newly widowed friend and slowly the sun began to shine on the horizon of Kleemann's life. He made an arrangement to leave his four children with the sister of another emigrant while he was at work. Her name was Friedricke Christian and she was engaged to a fellow emigrant, Wilhelm Hauser. The Germans were nothing if not practical, for Hauser volunteered to rescind his engagement to the twenty-eight-year-old woman so that she could marry Kleemann and look after his children permanently. Early in 1838, just a few months after the death of his first wife, Kleemann married Friedricke and in the following year a child was born of the new union.

The three men were industrious by nature and quick to find a way of supplementing their basic income. They cleared a small parcel of land and planted some wheat and barley, which after harvesting they ground for porridge and bread. In addition they fished and hunted, albeit on a small scale, and what they did not eat themselves they sold. At this time, Gramp learned to bake bread, a profession he was later encouraged by Milde to adopt. Eventually, when the time came for Gramp and Milde to move to the mainland for the building of Port Adelaide, Kleemann and his wife remained behind and produced another child, although all three men were later reunited in the Barossa Valley.

When the South Australian Company transferred its headquarters from Kangaroo Island to Adelaide early in 1839, Gramp worked as a labourer on the preparation of Port Adelaide and Milde as a baker for the company and its employees. Kleemann remained on Kangaroo Island until 1842, when he joined his friends in the Lutheran village of Klemzig, named after the town in Brandenburg from which Pastor Kavel had brought so many families to settle.

Meanwhile, Gramp continued to work out his three-year contract by completing his work at Port Adelaide. He collected his final payment and moved to Currie Street in central Adelaide where he became a baker, employed by two fellow *Solway* emigrants, Bremer and Bauer.

In 1838, George Fife Angas, the principal director and shareholder of the South Australian Company and a man who actively promoted religious freedom, had supported the emigration of Pastor Kavel and his flock and had provided them with a site on the banks of the River Torrens about 4 miles from the centre of Adelaide, and which they named after their former home town. On 1 May 1839 the *Southern Australian* carried an article which complimented the industrious activity at Klemzig:

> Four or five months only have elapsed since the hand of man began to efface the features of the wilderness, yet nearly thirty houses have already been erected. All are neat, clean and comfortable. They are built mostly of pise, or of unburnt bricks which have been hardened by the sun.

As increasing numbers of German immigrants arrived in South Australia, many settled in Klemzig. These were not just from Brandenburg but also from Silesia, other parts of Prussia, and Saxony, and most had in common the fact that they were Lutherans. In 1843, aged twenty-three, Johann married a seventeen-year-old Prussian girl, Johanne Eleonore Nitschke. They appear to have acquired some land in Hope Valley and moved there quickly, for in September of the following year their first child, Louisa, was born there. She was followed by another daughter, Anna, and a son, Johann Friedrich, who died when six years old. Shortly after the birth of the ill-fated son on 4 May 1847, the Gramp family, attracted by another Lutheran settlement in the Barossa Valley called Langmeil, moved to that vicinity. Reports of vines being planted in the area for sacramental purposes have an oral tradition and H.G. Burgess, in his 1909 *Cyclopaedia of South Australia*, refers to vine planting and to Bethany

(the village bordering Langmeil) first being settled in 1842. His suggestion is that cultivation was on a tiny scale, "possibly these were not sufficient area to be classified as vineyards". This is not surprising as most of the Prussians and other Germanic emigrants came from beer-producing communities in Europe, where it was too far north to grow healthy vines. As for Johann Gramp, the only Bavarian settler in the early days of the Barossa Valley, he also hailed from a village where hops, not vines, were grown.

Nevertheless, the belief was prevalent that South Australia offered ideal climatic conditions for wine production, particularly as the colonies of New South Wales were already achieving some promising results. I maintain it was this factor and the belief that Pastor Kavel planted vines for eucharistic purposes at Langmeil or Bethany, that influenced Johann Gramp to plant a vineyard. Time has since shown how vines thrive in the Barossa Valley and how its climate regularly provides the ripest and fullest-flavoured grapes. No doubt when Gramp saw his pastor's vines he foresaw the potential for growing grapes in the region. Subsequently he acquired land near a tiny stream called Jacob's Creek and there in the latter part of 1847 he planted 4 acres of vines amid what was to become a mixed farm. In 1850, Johann Gramp pressed his first grapes by hand, making just 1 octave – that is around 15 gallons – of a hock-style white wine. It seems that even with his first vintage he began a Jacob's Creek tradition of providing consumers with what they wanted, for Johann made a style of fragrant, medium-dry wine that would have been instantly recognisable to his fellow Germans.

Alongside Jacob's Creek he constructed a small winery of ironstone and then excavated a cellar below. The little building still remains but has since been converted into a private residence. At its peak, Gramp's Jacob Creek winery produced 2 500 gallons and there can be no doubt that Jacob's Creek was the first commercial Barossa winery and Johann Gramp the pioneer vigneron there.

As to the christening of Jacob's Creek, the little tributary of the Para River was named, as was often the custom, by one of the land surveyors responsible for allocating land grants, called William Jacob. It seems he chose what appeared to be the most attractive spot in the Barossa Valley and identified it with his own name.

In 1874, when Johann Gramp's son Gustav married, Johann gave him, as a wedding present, 40 acres of land he had purchased earlier at Rowland Flat. Three years later the main wine business was transferred to that site, where in due course it traded as Orlando Vineyards. The same name still identifies the giant Orlando Wyndham wine group

and appears on the Jacob's Creek label. The name Orlando came about in a rather unusual way when, before World War II, Hugo Gramp, one of Johann's grandsons, acquired a F.W. Thieme's German-English dictionary and discovered in it that Orlando was the German equivalent of the name Rowland.

Johann Gramp died, aged eighty-three, on 9 August 1903 at Jacob's Creek. When he left this world he was prosperous, literate and proud of the Jacob's Creek wine business that he had founded and his son, Gustav, had expanded at the nearby Rowland Flat. The portly Bavarian would have been even prouder if he could have seen the international popularity that his label has achieved since.

A LITTLE SICILIAN ESPIONAGE
Florio Marsala; Sicily and USA

In the 1830s a wine trade war, waged in the Trápani province of Sicily, had far-reaching repercussions on the production and sale of Marsala, the fortified wine of the region. It also led to the owner of a small Sicilian fishing fleet pitting his wits against two English-owned Marsala houses.

The wine of Marsala already had a long history, dating back to 800 BC when the Phoenicians were believed to have brought vines to Sicily from Crete and planted them in the clay and limestone soil. These vines they pruned as short, stubby plants, using a method known as *alberello*. At that time, and for many centuries afterwards, these stubby vines produced nothing more than everyday red and white wines for early consumption. Fortification was not to be introduced until the late 18th century, when John Woodhouse, an English merchant, first made an attempt to emulate sherry. The name Marsala is accredited to the Roman leader, Claudius Marcellus, who was victorious at

the battle of Syracuse on the eastern side of the island of Sicily and who, so legend relates, became a landowner in the western vineyard area.

In the 15th century the cultivation of olives in the dry local microclimate began to attract many small farmers and interest in wine production waned. It was a further three centuries before Woodhouse, a wealthy English merchant from Liverpool, stimulated a revival by shipping the first major consignment of some seventy pipes of Marsala to Britain. Apparently it was sold immediately and most profitably and so Woodhouse returned to Sicily on his brigantine, the *Elisabeth*, to construct cellars in the port of Marsala and organise the purchase of supplies on a regular basis.

For thirty-three years Woodhouse monopolised the Marsala trade and it is only right and proper that he should be credited with taking the first steps in transforming it. Later, in 1806, a young wine merchant from the city of York, Benjamin Ingham, travelled to the Sicilian port and established himself in direct competition with the older man. Presumably Ingham noted that the entire stock of Marsala available in Britain bore a single name and deduced that there was an opening for some opposition. Marsala had been enjoying a substantial boom in popularity, which had brought great prosperity to John Woodhouse and an increase in the number of growers on the island.

The British Navy itself had no small influence on the popularity of the drink through the heroism of none other that Admiral Horatio Nelson. Under an ancient alliance it behoved George III to defend the Kingdom of the Two Sicilies, comprising Naples and the island of Sicily. To protect the kingdom against the empirical forces of Napoleon, George III despatched Admiral Nelson and his fleet, who succeeded in defeating the French Navy in 1798 at Aboukir Bay, in what became known as the Battle of the Nile. Nelson was also given the task of safeguarding the Sicilian royal family, a responsibility that resulted in his being rewarded by King Ferdinand and Queen Carolina, after his evacuation of the royal household from the threat of the oncoming Napoleonic forces. Nelson's prize was a vineyard in the Marsala region, which initially did not receive much attention from him as he was too preoccupied with the Naples-based Lady Hamilton.

Later, however, demonstrating some astute business acumen, Nelson persuaded George III that the British naval fleet should be supplied with a generous annual stock of 500 pipes of Marsala, the equivalent today of 282 000 bottles. No doubt the admiral made a worthwhile profit from the transaction and it also further stimulated the Marsala economy, a fact noted by the young Ingham. For

Nelson the wine was to play an ironic part in his destiny, for when he won the Battle of Trafalgar in 1805, despite the loss of his life, the Navy's success was celebrated with what was termed Marsala Victory Wine, some of which came from Nelson's own vineyard.

Twenty-eight years later the most significant figure in the history of Marsala appeared on the scene. He was a prominent industrialist, merchant and entrepreneur called Vincenzo Florio. He already owned a shipping line the size of a small navy, a major fishing fleet, various mining interests and factories for items as disparate as silk and ceramic tiles, and he and his family lived in some splendour, with three imposing villas in Palermo alone. Vincenzo felt that the time had come for Sicilians to reap the major profits from the Marsala trade, rather than the Englishmen who had developed a duopoly market in the British Isles. When he took the decision to build his cellars on the waterfront in Marsala, he encountered an almost comic situation which he turned to his advantage.

Woodhouse was now dead, but Ingham was prospering and Woodhouse's successors were occupied with meeting the ever-increasing demands for the popular wine. The two houses, however, ever since the moment Ingham had established himself in competition to Woodhouse, would have nothing to do with each other. The position was such that in maintaining a policy of secrecy, Ingham had taken great care to build his cellars within sight but not sound of the Woodhouse property. Between them on the harbour side lay a great open space of land upon which neither house was permitted to build. Florio simply purchased this land and constructed his cellars between the two English companies. From this site, probably to

Horation Nelson, owner of a profitable Marsala vineyard

Florio Marsala, circa 1910

He sought a market where he could ship the wine under the most favourable circumstances and discovered the answer in the United States of America. Following the War of Independence, items of British origin were not popular in the US and wines with British associations, such as port, sherry and Madeira, were often in short supply. Florio's little fleet set sail and Marsala arrived in America for the first time, to be used both for drinking and for culinary purposes. One other factor in Florio's favour was that other fortified wines depended on all manner of cargo shipping, whereas he could guarantee promptness with his own shipping service. His name soon became synonymous with Marsala across the American continent, a state of affairs which resumed when Prohibition was repealed and which continues to this day.

In the course of time the Florio company absorbed both of its rivals and clandestine activity on the waterfront ceased, and the flourishing trade came to realise that not only Florio, but also Woodhouse and Ingham, had done much to develop the economy of the island vineyards. The result is that nowadays there are over 3 000 Marsala growers in Sicily, producing some 50 million bottles per year, and Marsala is sipped and sizzled around the globe.

the secret delight of the local populace, Florio developed something akin to a mini-intelligence service to discover both houses' methods of production and their costs. He soon acquired the information that a pipe of Marsala cost Woodhouse 265 ducats and Ingham just 200. Florio examined their techniques and succeeded in producing equally fine Marsala at 143 ducats per pipe.

To further his research, Florio visited England and painstakingly tracked down his opponents' trading arrangements. Over a short period of time he made several trips to England and learned much, including the fact that his competitors had a firm grip on the market. This latter conclusion meant that he had to contemplate other export markets, where Marsala was unknown, and in so doing achieved his greatest success. He had invested 200 000 ducats in his new business and many of his fishing boats had been exchanged for brigantines.

LIVERPUDLIAN WINE
Morris of Rutherglen, Australia

Early in 1993, while on a visit to Victoria, Gerry Amdor, Britain's best-known importer of Australian wine, presented Mick Morris with the Muscat Trophy from the 1992 International Wine Challenge. The occasion could have been interpreted as

Florio Marsala range in the 1920s and 1930s, including a bottle of tonic (centre) for use during US Prohibition

the old country congratulating its viticultural roots in the new. Without doubt the Morris dynasty deserved such international and public recognition, for apart from achieving fame in the current generation for their dessert wines, they could lay claim to G.F. Morris, one of the most colourful pioneer wine figures in Australia.

At the presentation, Mick, a shy man who seldom smiles unless someone is sipping a glass of Morris Muscat, reluctantly agreed to have his photograph taken but appeared a little more at ease when he was told the picture would be published in England. Mick Morris is perhaps a quieter reflection of his illustrious ancestor George Francis Morris, who in the late 19th century became a major figure on the international wine scene and the man who made Rutherglen famous.

G.F. Morris, as he was generally known, is a story in himself. Born in 1834 in Warrington, Cheshire, he was the son of William Greg Morris, a draper who originated from Bristol. The family, who were Quakers, moved to Liverpool, where they were active members of the Hunter Street Meeting House, which came under the auspices of the Hardshore West Division of the Friends. Unfortunately for all, William Greg Morris committed some unpardonable offence which resulted in the extremely rare circumstance of his being officially disowned, not only by the Hunter Street Meeting House of some 300 Friends, but also by the Hardshore West Division. Though the cause of this action has never been publicly revealed, it appears to have had a distressing effect on the family, and in 1852, aged eighteen, George Francis Morris came to the conclusion that Liverpool was no longer congenial to him and emigrated to Australia.

Upon landing in Melbourne later that year, he chose to join the gold rush at Ovens River. He immediately began prospecting at a spot known as Reid's Creek, but preferred to use his brain rather than his brawn and saved his earnings carefully to invest in a partnership in a wholesale supply business called Scott & Co., at Beechworth. As gold fever reached its climax the store's turnover multiplied,

bringing excellent profits. Business was so good that a mere six years later G.F. Morris was able to sell out his share and return to England a wealthy man, accompanied by his young wife and two children. He was reunited with his parents before setting off to Europe on the Grand Tour, and came back to England early in 1859 when his wife, Sarah Anne, gave birth to Charles Hugh Morris, the third of their seventeen children. Later in the same year they sailed for Australia, where the family travelled to Browns Plains in north-east Victoria. Here G.F. Morris purchased 220 acres of land and later added various further parcels to form the impressive Fairfield property, named after a district in Liverpool where he had spent much of his early life. Originally Fairfield was a general farm, but in 1864 Morris planted 10 acres of vines using a team of twenty-eight bullocks. A decade later he added another 40 acres, but his winemaking ambitions were curbed when he found that even his finest wine would sell for only 10 pence per gallon on the wholesale market. Instead he concentrated on his other crops and a new interest in farm machinery. In this area he was able to increase his not inconsiderable fortune as he became one of the founders of the agricultural plant-hire industry by investing in new equipment and renting it to farmers in Victoria and New South Wales.

Evidently G.F. Morris was a man of drive, determination and ambition. The *Rutherglen Sun* once wrote of him: "He never did anything by halves when he went for it." The truth of this statement was demonstrated in his actions when wine prices showed a healthy increase in the late 1870s and early 1880s. Employing Chinese coolie labour in addition to modern machinery, he rapidly

Gerry Amdor (left) presenting Mick Morris with the Muscat Trophy

George Francis Morris (1834-1910), the winemaking king of Rutherglen

increased his vineyard plantings. It was at this stage that circumstances led to him becoming a player on the world stage. Phylloxera had wreaked havoc on the vineyards of France, and much of the British trade in French wine had been supplanted by New World vines from its Empire vineyards in South Africa and Australia. However, phylloxera was beginning to harm South African supplies, giving Australian wines some real opportunity. Morris was quick to see the opening and became a most successful exporter to the land of his birth.

In 1886 he was appointed Wine Commissioner for the Colonial and Indian Exhibition in London. As a result he sold huge volumes of wine to Gilbey & Co. and W.W. Pownall. For G.F. Morris and his family, life became one of ease and affluence. Two of his sons were sent to France to study wine production and an imposing mansion called Fairfield House was constructed. In 1894, "Vagabond", a Melbourne columnist, described it as "one of the most charming mansions in Australia", and referred to its ballroom and tennis court, its carriage drive, bordered by orange and lemon trees, and its cellars, some 300 feet long by 150 feet wide. G.F. Morris showed the journalist more than 300 prizes won at competitions worldwide. During this time he had more than 700 acres planted with vines and was planning to purchase a further 1 250 acres.

Then the politicians interfered and the boom relapsed into a recession. In the late 1880s, the Victorian government decided to adopt a policy of encouraging the growth of various successful agricultural activities, one of which was the production of wine. Incentives were offered for increased acreage, and in 1889-90 the total surface area of vines in the state doubled to more than 30 000 acres. In just a few years the result of this expansion proved disastrous, for the home market was flooded with cheap, low-quality wine from young vines. The wine was not suitable for export, which

created a large surplus in Victoria, and prices crashed bringing about the collapse of much of the wine industry. Later, in 1905 and 1906, phylloxera caused chaos in the Victorian vineyards, and the ageing figure of G.F. Morris saw his once immense fortune seeping away.

On 8 January 1910, at the age of seventy-five, the Liverpool-born wine king died, and Rutherglen lost the man who first made its wine famous. He had planned his will with foresight and left a comfortable inheritance for his then third wife, Ellen, who unusually for that day and age was described as a banker and accountant. Just eighteen months later the Rutherglen community was shocked to read advertisements announcing the sale of Fairfield mansion with its 1 220 acres of land, of which only 210 acres remained as vineyards. In a short space of time the Morris winery was nothing but a memory, although fortunately it was to be revived by later generations.

A MIXED WELCOME
Cooks Hawkes Bay, New Zealand

When, in the name of his monarch, George III, Captain James Cook claimed New Zealand, he received a rather mixed reception. On 15 October 1769, in clement springlike conditions, Cook's ship the *Endeavour* sailed south, passed the Mahia Peninsula and reached a wide sweeping bay on the east coast of the North Island. This bay he named Hawkes Bay after Sir Edward Hawke, the First Lord of the Admiralty. Hawke was a popular English hero, having defeated the French Navy in a memorable victory at Quiberon on the coast of Brittany just ten years earlier. As Cook approached

Admiral Lord Hawke, after whom Captain James Cook named Hawkes Bay

the shoreline a veritable armada of canoes emerged, heading for the *Endeavour* at a rapid rate. Many of them were trading vessels hoping to exchange fish for other goods but some were war canoes, with one monster vessel being described as "capable of carrying up to 100 men". The war canoes performed a war dance called a *heiva,* which was a warning to potential enemies to keep a good distance.

In a later generation, the "potential enemy" landed at Hawkes Bay and established a community which prospered and attracted fame for two disparate reasons. Vines were planted and the microclimate was found to be ideal for a surprisingly wide range of varieties, including Sauvignon Blanc, Chenin Blanc, Merlot and Cabernet Sauvignon, from which wines were made to welcome any visitors. On the other hand, the settlers formed the renowned Hawkes Bay Rugby Club, where opponents receive the rudest of greetings, known as a *haka,* which is a war dance performed on land. A true welcome does not take place until after the visiting team have lost. Only then does the best-known local wine, Cooks Hawkes Bay, begin to flow, and usually only the minimum of blood will have been shed.

PUSSER'S RUM
UK and Jamaica

In 1655, when Admiral William Penn captured Jamaica, the British Navy found the answer to a perennial problem in the quantities of rum that abounded there.

In European waters it had long been the practice for the Navy to issue seamen with a daily ration of beer, which was more than appreciated while it was fresh and palatable. But lengthy transatlantic

Grog' – Pusser's Rum & water – being issued from the grog tub on board HMS ENDYMION in 1905.

A *photograph from the early-20th century showing Pusser's Rum being issued as the grog ration aboard a Royal Navy ship, HMS* Endymion

voyages, particularly those forays which took the Navy into tropical waters, caused the beer to deteriorate to the point where it was no longer fit for consumption. Rum, on the other hand, would not be affected by such conditions and provided the ideal replacement. The word "rum" is an abbreviated form of *succarum,* the Latin for sugar. No doubt Admiral Penn became a popular leader when he instructed that every man in his fleet should have a daily allowance of half a pint of rum.

However, nearly a century later in 1740, another British Naval commander, Vice-Admiral Edward Vernon took a somewhat dim view of this generous allowance and decided that the rum issue should be subject to tighter controls. Dismayed by the drunkenness prevalent among the members of his crew, he introduced what became known as "grog". He declared a new regulation that "Rum be no longer served in species (i.e. neat)", and instructed that it should be diluted by mixing a quart of water with half a pint of rum. The word grog came into being from Admiral Vernon's nickname, Old Grogram, which was applied to him on account of his attachment to wearing a coarse grogram cloth cloak. The actual term grogram was derived from the French for coarse cloth, which is *gros grain.*

The person responsible for the rum stocks on board ship was the purser, hence the name Purser's or Pusser's Rum. The brand known as Pusser's British Navy Rum only became available to the public after 31 July 1970, known as Black Tot Day. On this auspicious day, tea replaced rum among the British naval rations, with mixed feelings from the seamen. Following this momentous occasion, a company was formed to market the same mature, high-strength blend of Caribbean rums. Later, in 1979, the British Admiralty gave its official approval to the blend and the use of the British Navy's name on the label of Pusser's Rum.

With the termination of the rum ration came the end of an era, but that era is recalled today on Admiral Nelson's flagship, the HMS *Victory,* which

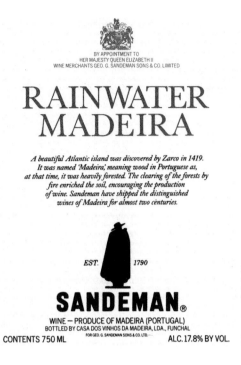

for all 192 years of its service issued the daily ration of half a pint of rum. Visitors to the famous ship, now a tourist attraction in Portsmouth, are always offered a tot of rum when on board.

RAINWATER MADEIRA
Sandeman and Welsh Brothers; Madeira and USA

William Habersham, a 19th-century shipper of Madeira into Savannah, Georgia, has often been credited with the creation of the Rainwater style of the drink. Some ten years ago, in 1983, I was given by the Madeira Wine Association in Funchal a written explanation of the derivation of the name, which read in part: "This delightfully named wine owes its origin to an American gentleman, Mr Habisham, resident in Savannah, Georgia in the mid-18th century." This information proved inaccurate both in date and substance.

William Neyle Habisham was a fascinating and eccentric character, who was indubitably the most important overseas influence on the transatlantic

shipping of the range of fortified wines that comes from the island of Madeira, 300 miles west of the coast of Morocco in North Africa. While it is certain that he did trade in Rainwater Madeira to a considerable degree, there is incontrovertible evidence that the Rainwater style was shipped into the more northerly colony of Virginia more than half a century before he was born.

The city of Savannah, on the south bank of the deep river estuary of that name, happens to lie just south of latitude 30°, a bearing almost parallel to the island of Madeira. So with the assistance of favourable trade winds it is not surprising that the busiest New World port for Madeira wines was this delightful city of fine squares, majestic houses, old oaks and hanging Spanish moss. This trade became well established in colonial days and it is widespread knowledge that both George Washington and Thomas Jefferson had a fondness for Madeira wine.

Habersham was indeed fortunate to find himself born into a wealthy shipping family who sent him at a fairly early age to Yale. Upon his return, at the age of nineteen, the able and talented young man joined the family business and was not behindhand in indicating his interest in one of the goods they shipped with regularity, namely Madeira. In particular he was intrigued by the cellaring and ageing of the wine, and he singled out for specific attention a style called Rainwater, which his family had never handled and did not seem able to acquire. It was a stage when the method of naming Madeira was undergoing change. Previously it had been the common practice to name the wine by identifying the vessel on which it had been shipped.

Now the names of producers and shippers were becoming more prominent along with more specific identification of the grape varieties.

As a matter of course most Madeiras were sold as shipped, without any blending of any kind, though there were no fixed rules forbidding such a practice. It was also not uncommon to find Madeiras that were between fifty and 100 years old. Therefore when William Habersham came across the Rainwater Madeira from Virginia that was approaching its centenary he must have been surprised at its unusual style, for without knowing its true and very simple origin, he seems to have planned with meticulous care to emulate it, in the hope that it would permit him to offer Habersham Rainwater Madeira.

Over a number of years William concentrated on increasing the family's trading in Madeira and gradually obtained large stocks of wines both for sale and for maturing. With Savannah's notoriety for mosquitos he probably imported one style that had quinine dissolved in it and which was reputed to be a cure-all for infected bites and even for malaria. In no time the warehouse space proved inadequate and he took advantage of the situation to put into practice a rather unconventional notion.

He decided to purchase a new and fairly large wooden mansion for his family and himself, and to house a vast quantity of his beloved Madeira. The property had to be sufficiently spacious to provide not merely for their personal accommodation but also for a revolutionary new cellar which would hold a substantial stock of his favourite wine.

Habersham, after whom a Savannah street, a wine store and a shopping village are named, acquired a commodious residence at 206 Harris Street West, less than a mile from the harbour side. There he proceeded to remove a large section of the rear roof on the third floor, which he replaced with a glass solarium. Next he disposed of the floors in between, creating a vast space that varied dramatically in temperature depending on the time of day, the season and the weather. In this area he aged an ever-increasing stock of Madeiras in a variety of butts, demijohns and bottles. At one stage an Atlanta newspaper reported that he had "as many as 3,000" items there. Some verbal accounts have intimated that eventually William's long-suffering wife, Josephine, decided that matters had come to a head and ordered him to reduce the stock by placing some of the butts in their backyard, where a thunderstorm unleashed torrential rain which seeped into the wine and provided its title. Such an explanation of Rainwater Madeira can only be described as fanciful. Much more accurate is the theory that William Habersham aged some of the wine in a similar manner to tawny port, another

George Washington, a great patron of Madeira wine

fortified wine which would have been familiar to him. He aged his Madeira by exposing it to daylight for varying periods, a practice which would have made it paler.

Whatever the truth, Habersham did succeed in producing an attractive style of wine which he sold as Habersham's Rainwater Madeira and claimed to be made by a secret process.

When he died at the age of eighty-two, there was a most flattering obituary in the evening paper, the *Savannah Press*, which eulogised his qualities as a gentleman but strangely failed to mention Madeira and merely noted that "he had quiet and simple tastes". Either it was an ignorant piece of journalism or a reflection of the temperance movement that was taking hold of Georgia in the year of 1899.

The fact of the matter, as far as the original naming of Madeira is concerned, is exactly as rendered by Noel Cossart, a former partner of the highly reputed shippers Cossart and Gordon, in his Christie's publication *Madeira*. The book is an

Traditional aging of Madeira in a roof space

invaluable work and has provided the writer with much edifying and helpful background material and is clearly well researched. Noel Cossart attributes the name Rainwater to the Newton Brothers, who shipped Madeira between the vineyard island and Virginia in the mid-19th century. Francis operated on Madeira and Andrew in Virginia, where he distributed and sold the wines. The island of Madeira was not blessed with natural harbours and loading ships was a tricky procedure. There were one or two pebbly shores which provided for some forms of loading arrangements but with wine it still posed a problem. The practice was that men would swim out to boats which were lying in deeper water, pushing half-filled barrels in front of them. Once the barrels were raised on board they would be topped up with the contents of other half-filled casks, and the empty barrels would be returned to shore. Noel Cossart recalls how Francis Newton on one occasion left some pipes on the beach to await loading the next morning, "and by mistake they were unbunged". It rained and some rainwater seeped into the shipment, which, however, still went ahead. In Virginia, Andrew particularly liked the new style, which he described as soft as rainwater. He requested that his brother send more of the new style, which was shipped with five letters stencilled on each cask. These were RWMAP, which signified Rainwater Madeira with Aqua Pura.

It was without doubt the Newton Rainwater Madeira that Habersham would have seen so many years later but one can be fairly convinced that he never knew how it was produced. Today Rainwater Madeira is still in evidence but in limited quantities and sadly is often preferred as a cooking ingredient rather than as a well deserved, chilled aperitif, which is when it is best enjoyed. Nowadays Sandeman is probably the only Rainwater Madeira label

widely found on the eastern seaboard of the United States, where it was once so very much the fashion.

Over the years one of the most successful producers of Rainwater Madeira has been the nowadays little-seen label of Welsh Brothers, who at one time had extensive markets in the United States. Today it is part of the Madeira Wine Association, which involves a host of brands in a joint production arrangement. Also, it is one of the older Madeira firms, having been founded in 1794. This author, as a Welshman, which means coming from a land reputed for its excessively wet climate, has always found the image of Welsh Rainwater Madeira amusing, and especially the knowledge that such a label was a great favourite in the heady days of the last century in Imperial Russia.

One further unusual association of rainwater with Madeira is that it seldom rains in some of the vineyards, which means that they have to be irrigated. This is done by a system of narrow trenches which drain water from the cloud that regularly covers the mountain top. Water simply runs down the island by gravity.

RHINELAND HERITAGE
Stein's Wines and Helm's Wines, Australia

The influence of the Rhineland in the development of Australian wine can be seen through two small proprietor-owned wineries in New South Wales. Stein's Wines, at its delightful address of Sandal Park Estate, Pipeclay Lane, Mudgee, has the oldest heritage, dating to Johann Stein in 1838, and Helm's Wines at Murrumbateman, just outside Canberra, claims an Australian winemaking tradition that began in 1851 with Johann Peter Fraunfelder. In contrast with the large numbers of highly successful major Australian brands, many of which are considered elsewhere in this book, these small

producers and the growing band of their fellow viticulturists offer the consumer the opportunity to purchase the produce of small farmers. Also it is interesting to note that unlike the majority of the large brands, which usually had Protestant founders of British or North Germanic extraction, a number of the smaller producers, of whom Helm's and Stein's are examples, have come from a Rhineland Catholic tradition.

In the case of Stein's Wines it is obligatory that they have some Rhine Riesling in their vineyards, for their ancestor Johann Stein was the man who brought the very first Riesling cuttings from the Rhine to Australia in 1838. He came from the highly rated Rheingau wine village of Erbach, famous for its Markobrunn vineyard, and appears to have been born into a family with a long viticultural tradition. His tiny home there still stands at 23 Erbacher Strasse. He sailed on the *Kinnear* with his Riesling vines, following the signing of a contract with Edward Macarthur on 9 October 1837 in the neighbouring village of Hattenheim. The agreement covered the emigration of six vignerons to work for Macarthur in New South Wales. Macarthur's father, John, had been the owner of what was only the second private vineyard in Australia (the earliest attempts to grow vines having been carried out by the authorities). Bob Stein, head of the family enterprise, relates, with understandable pride, how the wreck of the *Kinnear* has been recovered from the

waters of Sydney Harbour and is therefore a little piece of viticultural history.

Johann Stein was joined by his brother Jacob four years later in 1842 and they both became superintendents at the large Camden Park Estate, owned by the Macarthur family. In 1847 another younger brother, Joseph, arrived and also worked at the property. Jacob Stein was the more ambitious of the brothers and in 1848 he acquired land at Prospect Creek and planted his own vineyard, which he called Sandhill Farm, a name that some while later he amended to Sandal Farm, after which the Mudgee property, purchased in 1976, is named. Sadly it seems the original vineyard was yet another victim of phylloxera around 1870.

At their Mudgee property, Bob Stein, with his wife, Lorna Margaret, and their family, has revived their winemaking tradition in one of the prettiest winery locations you could ask to see. There they have Shiraz, Chardonnay, Rhine Riesling, Traminer, Semillon, Cabernet Sauvignon and Black Muscat on some 18 acres out of an overall estate of 75 acres. The Chardonnay was my preference and was a most attractive wine. Bob admits to having made "a small fortune in construction" which he then invested to spend the rest of his life doing what he most wanted to do. He is sufficiently adventurous that in 1993 he sent his son, Andrew Stein, to London with a party of Mudgee producers, to the London Wine Trade Fair at Olympia, which is where I first met Andrew and gained an inkling of their story.

I met Ken Helm in altogether different circumstances, shortly after broadcasting on ABC Radio in Canberra. As I was leaving the station the receptionist asked me if I would take a call from a listener, something I believe one should always do unless one's travelling schedule is under severe pressure. The caller said he was interested in what I had been saying about phylloxera and that if I wanted to know the truth about the subject I should call and visit him in his winery. I explained

Jacob and Anna Maria Stein in their later days

Stein's Mudgee Winery in winter

that we had to drive to Bathurst but he said that was no excuse, as we had to drive right past his place, which was only about a mile from the main road. He gave precise instructions and said he expected to see my road manager, Dave Hollyman, and me in about half an hour. I accepted the invitation as he had implied that his was a very small winery and at that stage my experience extended to only the major ones in Australia.

It would not be inaccurate to describe a midwinter visit to Helm's Wines at Murrumbateman as akin to a journey back in time. Upon leaving the main highway we followed a narrow, winding lane called Butts Road, not unlike many small country roads found in Britain, and it was quite navigable until we reached the ford. We were indeed lucky, as recent rainfall had been lower than average for the season and we splashed through without too much trouble, but we were well aware of certain markings alongside the water which indicated various depths that might trap one's vehicle, submerge the occupants or wash one away.

I could not help but warm to Ken Helm who, together with his family, admits that winery life can be an uphill struggle but still an enjoyable one. As an occasional indulger in tongue-in-cheek humour, I was kept amused trying to fathom when Ken was teasing and when he was being serious. But as he entertained us with one or two colourful stories about those who had been stuck in the creek I quickly concluded that the vineyard must also be subject to flooding, and so they could never produce anything truly exceptional. In fairness, they have won a number of medals and awards and the samples I tasted were acceptable without being exciting, the Cabernet Merlot being the best.

As Ken showed us around his tiny cellar, I could see that it was certainly well organised, if fairly basic. In many ways it was like visiting a small producer in the Loire Valley twenty years ago, except that there was no tuffeau cave and the owner spoke not French, but English of a strange sort. The best was still to come, for I was about to be put in my place on the subject of phylloxera. While I tasted the first sample, Ken Helm placed in my hands a printed document entitled "Phylloxera and Vitis: An Experimentally Testable Coevolutionary Hypothesis, by A.J. Wapshere and K.F. Helm", followed by another, "Phylloxera: political or pest? by K.F. Helm", and yet another, "The Effect of Drought on Populations of Phylloxera in Australian Vineyards, by K.F. Helm, J.L. Readshaw and B. Cambourne, CSIRO, Division of Entomology", and even more. It was enough to make any taster swallow or indeed gulp. "I think perhaps there's a little too much to read now," I proposed.

"Don't worry about that. Take them with you.

They're yours and do make sure you read them before you do your next broadcast on the subject."

I hastily picked up the second sample to taste and between sips explained that I had a little more experience in the history of wine than in phylloxera.

"Then you couldn't have come to a better place. My ancestor was one of the great early wine characters of Australia called John Peter Fraunfelder. You're so lucky because I've got lots of papers on him in the house next door."

Five minutes later I was deluged with my kind of literature and as we left I assured Ken that I would read as much as possible in the car on the journey ahead. Possible it was not, for when we left Murrumbateman the metalled road was good but about an hour and a half later, as we headed for Bathurst, we discovered our first unmade Australian road and poring over small old print had to be abandoned in a hurry.

The documents gave an accurate account, which I have since been able to verify, of the voyage of Johann Peter Fraunfelder, a Rhineland Catholic who in 1848 sailed from Rotterdam to London and on to Sydney aboard the barque *Beulah*. He had been born in 1800 in Großsachen, a tiny vineyard village in the northern extreme of Baden, near Heidelberg, overlooking the River Necker, a tributary of the Rhine. He brought with him his second wife and seven of his eight children by his first marriage. Some have written of Fraunfelder as being one of a party of "Catholic Rhinelanders fleeing to Australia", suggesting religious persecution. In his case, however, there does not appear to be any specific evidence to indicate that the decision was made for other than personal and family reasons. Johann, later John Peter Fraunfelder, had been raised in Großsachen and had inherited a small vineyard. In 1826 he had married Barbara Kolb, from the same community, and they had lived there happily with their growing family. In 1843, Barbara had died prematurely, leaving Johann with the double burden of his work and the need to look after his eight children. It seems he was quite heartbroken and decided that he could not live in the village any longer than was absolutely necessary. In 1846 he sold his property and moved to another wine village called Hainstadt, where he purchased 20 acres, which was quite a substantial holding at that time. There he met Margaret Pfohler, a widow five years younger than him, whom he married on 1 October 1848. Other than one nineteen-year-old daughter, Margaret was free of commitments. Seven weeks later the Fraunfelder party travelled down the Rhine to Rotterdam where they joined the *Beulah* on 1 December. It certainly seems true that the entire passenger list of that ship comprised Catholics, but perhaps that was

HELM'S

Cabernet Merlot
1989

Canberra District Wine

not surprising as the emigrants came from a variety of towns and villages in the Rhineland where Roman Catholicism was particularly strong. It is illuminating to observe a major difference between the educational standards of the Catholic emigrants and the Lutherans, who travelled from further north in the Germanic states, mostly to South Australia. The majority of the latter had limited or virtually no education and many were illiterate, while the Catholics had often received teaching from the Church and Catholic-supported schools, so that when the *Beulah* docked only one of its passengers could not read and write.

The obligatory short crossing to England for such vessels was made to ensure all documentation was in order and for a ship's surgeon to be taken on board. The departure from London occurred just five days later and the barque entered Sydney Harbour on 3 April 1849, four months later. Just before the Rhinelanders disembarked on the following day, they received a special visitor on board. He was Roman Catholic Archbishop Polding who, speaking through an interpreter, invited them to attend the Easter celebrations at the Sydney Catholic cathedral. The Fraunfelder family were happy to accept and later wrote home, praising "the quality of the singing of the Latin Mass and the friendliness with which they were ushered to seats reserved for them near the organ".

One puzzling aspect of the family history is that immediately prior to departing, Johann Fraunfelder had sold his 20 acres to travel to Australia under a contract for a two-year term he had signed "to work at the property of Mr William Walker to attend to a vineyard of about 4 acres". It somehow did not make sense that a man should sell 20 acres of his own to journey to another country on the other side of the world to become an employee in a much smaller vineyard. What evidence exists leads one to believe that Johann Peter Fraunfelder's land purchase at Hainstadt had been unsuccessful and his early years in Australia, which were carefully chronicled by one of his sons, related details of their circumstances which indicated the most basic living standards.

After completing the two-year contract with William Walker at Kyeema the family moved on with some fellow emigrants with whom they had become acquainted. They headed for Albury, where in 1851 Johann Peter Fraunfelder, in partnership with two other *Beulah* shipmates, called Rau and Schubach, leased 9 acres. There his son, also Johann, recorded in his account:

> We fell to a-building huts of mud or more properly speaking wattle and clay, clearing and trenching for vines and got about ¼ of an acre of vines in.

Albury proved a happy new home for many German Catholics on a smaller scale but in a similar manner to the Lutheran settlements in South Australia's Barossa Valley. Jenny Paterson, a Catholic historian, wrote:

> The German attendance at the Sunday Mass had become so great by 1857, that the newly appointed parish priest, Rev. Cornelius Twomey, decided he ought to learn German – for those times, a most unusual gesture in multiculturalism.

Johann Peter Fraunfelder and his partners planted the first vines in what was to become known as the Riverina and which today is one of the largest reservoirs of everyday wines for popularly priced Australian brands. In 1860, his son, aged twenty-four and known as John Fraunfelder, was hired as manager of a major new winery development called Fallon's Murray Valley Vineyards, which subtitled itself "the Garden of the Riverina". He was still there fifty-three years later, aged seventy-seven, when a journalist from the *Albury Daily News* wrote a review on "Fallon's Albury Wines", which then had 400 000 vines planted. The company had its own sales force which, unusually, sold their wines direct to consumers and had two distribution bases, one in Albury and another major centre at 93 York Street, Sydney.

Ken Helm had provided an insight into the early days of one of the less romantic areas of Australia's wine story, but nonetheless one which plays a significant and much needed role. He and his fellow small producers in that country may not receive the exposure that they would in the United States but they will grow in strength and numbers if they market themselves carefully and do not just expect their wine to sell itself to passing customers. If I found Helm and Stein without too much difficulty, how many others must there be who own an important part of Australia's wine heritage? Let us hope that we will soon begin to hear of them.

THE SS *WALRUS*
Stubbs Queensland Dry White Rum, Australia

Some experts suggest that Stubbs Queensland Dry White Rum is the purest in the world. Produced at Australia's oldest surviving distillery at Beenleigh, just south of Brisbane, it is not made from molasses like most other rums, but from the virgin juice crushed from sugar cane that many say is the finest grown. In contrast the story behind it is not quite as pure and provides one of the more colourful episodes of early distillation.

While today Australian rum production has dropped to a relatively modest level, in the early

The SS Walrus *with its floating distillery*

years of settlement, in the late-18th and early-19th centuries, it played a crucial part in everyday life. It was used in many places as currency to purchase the staple requirements of life, such as food, clothing and various goods, and even, on some occasions, convict labour.

During that period there were dire problems with currency. The British, who constituted the majority of the population, understandably expected their new colonies to use sterling currency but completely failed to arrange for sufficient coinage to be available. It was not until 1850 that the Sydney Mint was opened.

Next to the British in numbers were the Germanic peoples, who were from a diverse assortment of dukedoms and states, such as Silesia, Prussia, the Rhineland and Bavaria. Most, though not all of these, were relatively poor, but they too brought their savings and few wished to exchange them. A third, but influential group, were the sea-traders, the adventurous dealers and merchants of the day, who were attempting to supply the material demands of the colonists that Australia could not meet. They shipped everything from Oregon timber to Chinese silk, and often would only deal in Spanish dollars and, to some extent, the satisfying rum which was being distilled in small but ever-increasing quantities.

The general lack of security speedily infected the early settlers, who realised the necessity of currency to trade and for simple domestic survival. Even today the majority are apprehensive about accepting unknown currencies and will sympathise with the suspicion of those hardy, early immigrants, whose thinking can so easily be understood. The result was that commodities were traded and rum was an abundant commodity. Virtually everyone knew the price of a flagon of rum and so it soon became an acceptable form of exchange; as it could be transported without difficulty, it gradually developed into one of the most popular forms of currency.

Across the Australian colonies small stills were being constructed, often in a rather crude fashion and at a fairly rapid rate. Drunkenness began to prevail alongside the various trading economies that excluded the revenue men. Another complication of the general situation was the involvement of the New South Wales Corps of the British Army. This corps had sailed from England in 1790 to replace the marines who had arrived with the First Fleet. Its principal duty was to enforce law and order, but it soon became corruptly involved in the production and distribution of rum, a practice that attracted its nickname, the Rum Corps.

In 1808 matters came to a head in New South Wales, when Governor William Bligh, of HMS *Bounty* fame, tried to prohibit both the distillation and importation of rum and all other spirits. Bligh's intention horrified the officers of the Rum Corps, who realised that their illicit wealth was at risk. This resulted in an uprising known as the Rum Rebellion. On 26 January 1808 the corps, led by Major George Johnston, inflicted a humiliating and historic second mutiny on the unfortunate Bligh, who was later "virtually exonerated" of all responsibility for the matter.

Aware that a search was under way, Governor Bligh hid under his bed but was soon found, placed initially under house arrest and then expelled from the colony. With his English superiors being eight months' return journey away, his official status had proved worthless.

Nonetheless, as the 19th century progressed, the licensing of distilleries gradually spread as the authorities began to gain control. This was until the issue of licence number 567 on 14 April 1869 to James Stewart, to distil rum from his pot on his rickety old boat, the SS *Walrus*, which plied its trade on the Albert and Logan rivers. In all likelihood this was the only such licence ever granted, probably because it was soon found to be impossible to implement one strict condition of the licence which stated that "an inspector was on board at the time of distillation". Having traded illegally for many years, James Stewart found it difficult to comprehend the necessity for this rule and continued to play cat and mouse with the excise man. The 1870 records show that he declared 14 224 proof gallons of his heavy dark rum, yet the following year, with business thriving, he declared only 4 151 proof gallons. A year later, he so frustrated the excise men that they deregistered his licence and intended to confiscate his still. But the cunning Queenslander slipped quietly away before they could locate him and for the next thirteen years cruised the creeks and deltas of the colony, always managing to evade arrest and yet profit from his unusual operation by selling rum to merchants and storekeepers up and down the Queensland coast. In 1883 the SS *Walrus* ran aground in the Albert River, leaving Stewart with the pressing need to sell his still. This he did to two English gentlemen farmers called John Davy and Francis Gooding, who owned a sugar plantation on the banks nearby and which they had called Beenleigh after their old family estate in Devon.

Gooding was a well-respected character and in the following year, 1884, had no problem obtaining a fresh licence to use the old copper pot-still. James Stewart sailed around the creeks and rivers for a few more years, until the battered old SS *Walrus* began to leak and very slowly sink to the muddy bottom of the Albert River, where it still rests, quietly rotting away. As for James Stewart, legal distiller and then bootlegger, how amused he would have been to know that his old still was used for another three years until 1887, when a devastating flood hit the Queensland coast, swept up the river, and washed the still and much of the distillery away. But his tradition lives on in a pure white rum called Stubbs, which is sold across the seven seas.

TEN YEARS APART
Hardy's, Australia

A number of Australian wine pioneers had their roots in the west of England, mostly among the gentry, a class which generally founded its business on healthy inherited fortunes. One rare exception was a young Devonian of staunch character called Thomas Hardy. In 1850, at about twenty years of age, Thomas arrived in South Australia with his cousin Johanna, his life savings of some £50, a single box of belongings and a seemingly inexhaustible supply of energy. In dramatic contrast

with the wealth he later accumulated, he was first employed as a lowly cowherd by a farmer named John Reynell, who hired him for just 7 shillings a week. Three years later, the Forest Creek gold rush would transform Thomas's basic capital into sufficient funds to purchase the land on which he founded the business that eventually became the giant BRL Hardy Company of today.

By coincidence, Thomas Hardy was baptised with the same names as the famed Dorset writer and poet, Thomas Hardy, renowned for such classics as *Far From the Madding Crowd*, *Jude the Obscure* and *Tess of the D'Urbervilles*. The coincidences regarding the two literary men extend even further, for they were born just ten years and 50 miles apart. The word "literary" is used deliberately, for Thomas Hardy, the wine producer, proved his literary ability in a memorable way. Born in 1830, the son of a yeoman farmer, he was noted in the ship's papers as an emigrant labourer, not a particularly accurate description of a man of his standing and experience. At the age of fifteen he had moved from his peaceful home village to the established Somerset County town of Bridgewater, where he had been indentured as an apprentice to a grocer by the name of Horsey. It is evident that Hardy took some trouble to improve his education during his apprenticeship, for when he came to emigrate he was able to write a lucid and comprehensive account of his "long journey" to Australia and of his earliest days there.

Unfortunately the first couple of pages of his personal story are missing, but at the point where

ESTABLISHED 1838

CHATEAU REYNELLA

Stony Hill

1989

SHIRAZ

McLAREN VALE

This bottle is No 27596 *of the vintage*

750ML PRODUCT OF AUSTRALIA 13.5% ALC/VOL

the papers begin, Hardy is reflecting upon his five-year period of apprenticeship in terms which any employer would be proud to read. He noted that under Mr Horsey's roof: "I spent five of the happiest years of my life-time", and he continued by referring to the grocer as having "more to do with forming my character than perhaps either he or I am aware of". Such a comment is one of many which reveal the mature insight of the young man. Indeed his literary ability can be seen in his accounts of his journey from the day that he and his cousin boarded the barquentine the *British Empire* in Plymouth. He recorded the transformation on board, from chaos into order, in simple but graphic terms:

> We are divided into messes of eight. We have some very agreeable fellows in our mess. I marked all the mess utensils with a graver. We had beef and potatoes for dinner. Johanna complained to me that she is put into a mess with a lot of Irish girls, I spoke to the steward, he promised to speak to the doctor under whose care we are … wrote a letter to my dear parents … also wrote one for E. Wilcox [an illiterate fellow passenger].

Hardy goes on to reveal his meticulously careful planning. Apparently the passenger's chief belongings, clothes and so on, were stowed away for the duration of the journey, but they were allowed to take one small bag or box to their berths. Thomas Hardy's choice had been "my little box". He wrote:

> I find my small box very useful. I do not think of a single thing that I have forgotten to bring from home. We are getting more regular in our management. Our captain fetches all the allowances

and I divide it equally among us all and they all seem satisfied. We got a weeks supply of treacle, sugar, tea, cocoa, mustard, pickles and pepper.

His accuracy and observation give us a record of some historical significance.

On Thursday, 9 May 1850, ten days after they had set sail from Plymouth, his entry reads:

> A notice was put up to say all who wished for the office of teacher must apply in writing to N. Colhurst Esq. I have had a great wish to have the office. I therefore wrote the following letter and gave it to the surgeon. "I have been advised to apply for the office of teacher. I therefore beg to offer my services in that capacity. Should you consider me a fit and competent person for the situation I will use my utmost endeavours to give satisfaction."

Two days later the Captain approached him and asked if he had any teaching experience. When the reply he received was negative, he compromised by sharing the role between Hardy and an older man called Walker. A fee of £2 each was fixed, payable at the end of the voyage if the job had been completed satisfactorily. The sexes were segregated, the girls being taken under the wing of the ship's matron, and Thomas and Walker being left in charge of the education of twenty-five boys.

The task was not straightforward and by 19 June, as Hardy reported in his diary:

> The Matron told me this morning that she should not teach any more, the girls are so dirty and ill-behaved. I told her I should bring them on as well as I could. I take care never to get into any rows and to mind my company.

Hardy was true to his word and seems to have possessed an innate ability to cope with troublesome human problems. Even when he heard that his colleague Walker was also quitting, he persevered, and his diary entry illustrates his integrity:

> Walker has heard that we shall have to wait some time for our money in Adelaide. He does not care anything about the children now. I do not intend to follow his example. I promised to do my best to instruct the children and I will not break my promise if my employers do. I do not think that shows any principle in Walker.

On Sunday, 14 July, the *British Empire* had reached latitude 38.40 south and longitude 52.47 east, a point far from any land, in the vastness of the southern sector of the Indian Ocean. Here Hardy recorded what would have been a typical day for him, in his usual sparse and lucid style:

> This is the only leisure time I have for writing. My time is so occupied. I get up about $\frac{1}{2}$ past 6 (it is not

HARDYS

Jeremy Boot   1 9 9 0   *Red-Browed Finch*

SHIRAZ
DRY RED WINE—VIN ROUGE SEC
13.0% alc./vol.

PRODUCT OF AUSTRALIA PRODUIT D'AUSTRALIE 750mL

light before 7), wash and dress, make our pudding, get breakfast which consists of oatmeal porridge. We are very fond of this, although but few of the English use it. A Scotchman in the next mess showed me how to make it. I got a sieve and sifted the fine from the coarse. The coarse is much the best. We often have a dish of preserved potatoes besides. We always have a plenty ... I often get a piece of meat from one of the sailors. I get all the oatmeal from the mess my cousin is in. This I give to the Irish chaps for potatoes and flour. I don't think any single chaps in the ship fare better than Wilcox and myself. As soon as breakfast is over I manage to write for about half an hour, which is all the time I can spare. At 12 I come down but can scarcely begin to write, it is dinner time. After dinner I have an hour or scarcely so much to spare. After school hours, 4 o'clock, there is seldom light enough to write below. After supper I go above and smoke a pipe or two for an hour then below and read or cipher by the lamp until near 9 o'clock when I turn in.

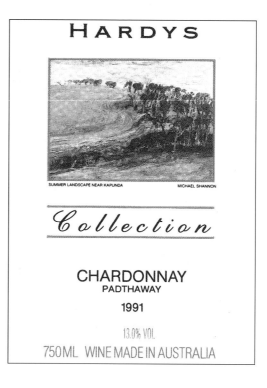

On Sunday, 18 August, the barque arrived at Port Adelaide. Johanna had decided to accept an offer to travel to Rapid Bay, some distance south of Adelaide, to work for a sheep farmer by the name of Burrows, at wages of £20 a year, plus board and lodging. Having first made enquiries with the captain and the ship's surgeon to ascertain the good character of Burrows, Hardy advised Johanna to accept. Thus discharging all that could be expected of a young man after a voyage of four months, Hardy felt he could "let his hair down", and in his own words, "went ashore in the afternoon in my shirt sleeves. Drank some ale first."

The following Friday, after several frustrated attempts, he found his first employment. He had journeyed slightly south of Adelaide, into the hills, where he was hired at Reynella Farm as a cowherd for 7 shillings a week. He preferred to earn this lowly sum than encroach upon his hard-earned savings, particularly in view of the fact that employment at the time was scarce. His living conditions as a cowherd were a rude awakening, as testified by his diary:

Got to my masters just as they were going to bed, had supper and turned in along with Paddy the shepherd boy into his watchbox, where I could not sleep a wink all night for the swarms of fleas.

After the qualities of leadership he had displayed on board the *British Empire,* his first experience of work in Australia brought home the harsher realities of life. Hardy's "master", a bearded giant of a fellow-Englishman called John Reynell, led him into the hills to instruct him in his responsibilities

as a cowherd, an occupation which brought Hardy into some difficulties:

About dinner time I had lost sight of my cattle. I hunted high and low for them. About 4 I went home and found they had been there 3 hours before me.

Fortunately his new employer was a kindly man who served his community well and who had experienced times of great personal hardship, and there were only words of sympathy for Hardy. So the resilient young Devonian looked to his laurels and determined to improve matters. He found better sleeping quarters but two days later suffered the same indignity when he once more lost the cattle. Upon discussion with Reynell the problem was solved by tying some bells onto the animals.

Apart from his contretemps with the cattle, Hardy proved himself a good worker and gradually his responsibilities were increased. Early on he was given the task "to cut and dock 20 lambs". He began to take note of the vineyard work being carried out and during his time with Reynell he was able to watch the pruning of the vines as well as the ageing process of the wine. On Sunday, 6 October, he was summoned to his master who said that "he was very well pleased with me". But Hardy was already saving and planning ahead, as witnessed by his diary entry on 9 September, almost a month earlier: "I hope in two years to be in a business of my own."

At Christmas 1850, at the height of a sticky Australian summer, Hardy left John Reynell's service, having notified him of his intentions some time in advance. He travelled about 20 miles further south to Wattle Flat, where he was hired by a farmer named Heathcote at Cudlatiyunga Station for almost double his previous pay. Hardy's move, however, was influenced by factors other than money. Since his arrival in Australia he had been leading an essentially solitary life, separated from those with whom he had been familiar, and during that time his almost brotherly love for Johanna had undergone a transformation into a deeper affection. His move to Cudlatiyunga Station meant that he was only 14 miles from Rapid Bay where Johanna was employed and from the station he could visit her by coach. Also, all the mail to and from Rapid Bay passed through the mail office at Cudlatiyunga and so they could correspond regularly. At this point Hardy had ceased to keep his journal and probably had more time as well as the desire to write to his cousin. The romance blossomed and was crowned by marriage in 1853.

During the intervening years the gold rush began and there was a series of strikes at Clunes, Ballarat, Castlemaine, Forest Creek and other spots, but it was to the last of these that Hardy made his way and immediately found himself in trouble with the law. He was arrested for digging without a licence, imprisoned overnight and fined £1 for his trouble. For Thomas Hardy it was a turning point in his career, as it made him assess the hardships the miners endured and the risks they ran with their investments, when so much effort often resulted in little or no return. Instead he looked for an area where he could provide a service to the miners, and which might be of profit to himself. He quickly realised that miners had large appetites which were not being satisfied, particularly where supplies of fresh meat were concerned. Hardy, as was his wont, considered his plan carefully and then set off to Adelaide to withdraw a major portion of his funds. He returned to Cudlatiyunga Station and made arrangements for the regular purchase of cattle from his erstwhile employer. With the benefit of his chequered experience as a cowherd, he drove the cattle across the country to the Forest Creek Gold Strike and sold them at an extremely substantial profit. He repeated the exercise for eighteen months until he had banked sufficient funds for his long-term purposes.

In 1853, Thomas and Johanna bought a large block of land alongside the banks of the Torrens River, 3 miles west of the centre of Adelaide. They called the property Bankside. The astute Devonian formulated a twenty-year plan and in 1854 set about putting it into effect. He planted $\frac{3}{4}$ acre, chiefly with Shiraz and Grenache vines, but also with a variety of fruit trees, and during the succeeding years he increased the amount of land under cultivation at a steady rate. In 1857 he made his first wine and sent two hogsheads to England. Two years later, undaunted at the prospect of the lengthy return journey, Hardy was affluent enough to be able to travel to England, taking some samples of his 1858 Bankside wine with him.

In 1866 an Adelaide publication, the *Observer*, carried a report of a visit to Bankside by one of its staff, who painted a glowing picture of industry and application:

> The trees in the oldest part of the orchard are now in magnificent order. The same remark applies with even greater force to the vines, which have made splendid growth. Leading up to the house is an avenue of olives. The orange trees which have been propagated from seed are in flourishing condition. Wine is his mainstay and his experience has enabled him to turn out a very credible article. The mill and the stalker can handle 1,000 gallons a day. There are two wine presses, one very powerful, being modelled after a press in Lewis's Printing Office in Hindley Street. There is underground accommodation for 20,000 gallons of wine. Mr Hardy has casks of oak and oregon with a capacity of 850 gallons and there is also a gigantic one of red gum holding 1,500 gallons.

In fact records show that Thomas Hardy produced 14 000 gallons from the previous vintage in 1865.

Hardy's business enterprises prospered, but tragedy struck in his domestic life when Johanna died giving birth to their sixth child, Eliza, in 1868. Curiously Hardy later married Johanna's younger sister, also called Eliza, making him one of the very few men who have married two of his own first cousins. His second wife also died prematurely, in 1886, at the age of fifty-two.

By 1875 the Hardy production had risen to a noteworthy 53 000 gallons and his fruit business was also reaping major profits. The next year he decided the time was right to expand and so purchased the Tintara Vineyard in McClaren Vale, about 18 miles to the south. It had been the subject of an ill-fated investment scheme called the Tintara Vineyards Company, which had been a spectacular failure, and Hardy, who knew the area well, was convinced of its potential. In the following years Hardy made it a weekly practice to drive his own horse and buggy between Bankside and Tintara to supervise the development of the latter. He had acquired a semi-derelict inn near Tintara called the Clifton Hotel, which he restored and then used for his overnight visits.

At this stage Hardy was shipping large quantities of wine to London but was encountering problems with rogue importers there, who would buy in bulk and then blend his fine South Australian wines with the cheapest European stock they could find. Thomas Hardy was keenly aware of the damage being done, not just to the reputation of his wines but to that of Australia, and took action to stop the practice. When his efforts were thwarted he simply refused to sell to the majority of shippers in England and announced the opening of his own London Wine Depot.

His Tintara Claret continued to be supplied to Burgoyne's, a large and reputable English merchant who took a lively interest in Australian wines, especially since at this time Bordeaux was facing the ravages of phylloxera. Tintara Claret was exhibited and praised in London and soon attracted attention. At Tintara Vineyards much of the winemaking was under the direction of a distant relative, Thomas Hardy Nottage, after whom the highly successful Nottage Hill brand is named.

By 1885, following further vineyard purchases, Hardy had accumulated more than 1 500 acres of vines and made more than 100 000 gallons of wine. He was the king of the wine industry in the colony, at least in terms of volume, and there was certainly no shortage of favourable comments on the quality of his wines.

In 1887, Thomas Hardy felt the time was ripe to formalise his affairs and so formed the company Thomas Hardy and Sons Ltd, which included his sons, James, Thomas and Robert. Many other wineries made fortified wines but practically all the Hardy stock consisted of red table wine, aimed primarily at the British market. Just seven years later the Hardy accounts show that their volume exceeded the 300 000-gallon mark for the first time. Awards and medals came from all over Australia, from Paris and, amusingly, from the 1876 American Centennial Exhibition at Philadelphia, which granted medals to Hardy's for its dried fruit, wine and jam.

Just once more, in 1884, Thomas Hardy was to put his literary talent to effect. He sailed for Europe with his second wife, Eliza, and youngest son, Robert. They travelled through Spain, Portugal, France and Germany, observing the vintages, which start earlier in the south and are usually at their latest in Germany. He had been commissioned by the Adelaide newspaper the *Register* to write forty separate articles of 2 000 words each. For a man who had hardly picked up a pen for thirty years it was a mammoth task and one which he relished.

The new century brought him two separate tragedies. In 1901 his son James, who had moved to Sydney to open a branch of the business there, collapsed and died of a heart attack and in 1905 the cellars at his beloved Bankside were all but razed by a fire. It was a cruel blow for a man of seventy-five. His son's life was irreplaceable and the cost of the

Bankside damage was estimated at £25 000. The subsequent decision was not to rebuild there. Undaunted, Hardy and his son Robert made another trip to Europe the following year. It was the first of a succession of trips that took him to every major continent.

In 1911, he suffered another blow when his second son, Thomas Nathaniel Hardy died prematurely, aged forty-nine. When Thomas Hardy himself died on 10 January 1912, aged eighty-one, he had outlived two wives and two sons. Only Robert Hardy remained. In a fitting tribute, the *Register* wrote:

> Generally regarded as the father of the wine industry in South Australia, he was a grand pioneer who came to South Australia as a young man and by his unbounded energy built up a business which is known in both hemispheres and which has played an important part in winning for the central state such pre-eminence as the producer of wine.

So when any shopper in downtown Philadelphia, spacious Adelaide or historic York spies the beautiful Hardy's Bird label by the nature artist Jeremy Bird, or even a bottle of Chateau Reynella Stony Hill, he or she should not reflect on the recent boom in Australian wines, but should remember that Hardy's were winning medals and exporting wines across the oceans more than a century ago. Indeed, how delighted Thomas Hardy would have been to see the size of the empire which he established and which now includes vineyards in Victoria, fine

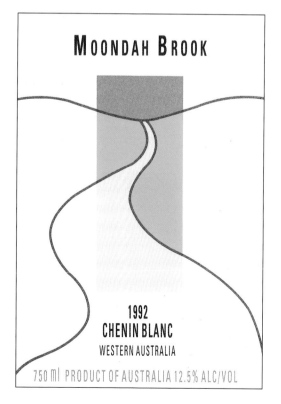

estates like Houghton in Western Australia, and even the rising star of Chais Baumière in southern France.

He would surely have approved of the Hardy company's acquisition in 1983 of Chateau Reynella as their headquarters. Named after John Reynell, it is the property where Hardy found his first place of employment in Australia and where on his first night he "could not sleep a wink for the swarms of fleas".

THAT FAMILY SACRIFICE
Babich, New Zealand

In these latter days of the 20th century, education is commonly regarded as a right, but in the last century the reverse was true and it was a privilege that only a few enjoyed. It is to the credit of the Austrian Army that during the years 1880 to 1883 it so increased the knowledge and ambition of an illiterate Dalmatian private called Petar Babich that he was able to pass on that education to his offspring. His children acquired a literacy that is immortalised in the family signature, which can still be seen today, displayed on the labels of their successful New Zealand wines.

Petar was born in Runovic, in the Imotski region, in 1860, and was a member of what could best be described as the Babich clan, who lived in a cluster of impoverished houses perched on the mountainside above the little farming town. His story, and that of his descended family, is typical of many large, humble families of a century or so ago, yet that does not diminish its power to move.

One day, while in a Podgora coffee shop, Petar encountered Ivan Vela, with whom he was only vaguely acquainted but who was to become instrumental in the destiny of the Babich family.

Ivan appeared to be a prosperous small dealer in dry goods and he invited Petar to accompany him on an overnight buying trip to Makarska to purchase such goods as rice and macaroni. Petar readily accepted the offer as a brief respite from his humdrum existence.

Ivan Vela had just returned to Dalmatia (then in Austria-Hungary) from a ten-year period in New Zealand, where he had lived at a settlement known as Sweetwater. He enlarged to Petar on the life he had experienced there and of the affluence he had enjoyed. The picture he painted was in stark contrast to the life of continuous struggle that Petar, the peasant farmer, endured and Ivan persuaded him that his sons too would have a brighter future in New Zealand.

The year was 1904 and Petar had seven sons whose ages ranged from four to eighteen years. Three of these boys were by his first wife, Matija, who had died in childbirth, and four were by his second wife, Iva. Until the previous year they had occupied a house with Petar's brother Nikola's family, with as many as four adults and eleven children sharing the accommodation. The situation had improved when his brother built another small house nearby but Petar knew that despite this small boon, life in Runovic would always be a battle for survival.

The following night, upon his return home, Petar called his family together and broached his decision to send his sons to "this country called Nova Zelanda", where they would have a greater opportunity to make a good living. To his young wife, Iva, his words must have brought much distress, which in time was tempered by her love for her sons and her hopes for a brighter future. Ivan Vela had spoken of gum that could be dug out of the soil and sold. With this in mind, on one cold February day in 1904, Jakov, the eldest son, began his journey and became the first of five brothers to undertake that emigration. It is believed that the cost of the journey, then about £14, was raised by the village priest and later refunded from New Zealand. The priest also helped to make all the arrangements and explained the intricacies to Petar and Jakov.

Six years later, in 1910, the last Babich sons to leave Runovic, Josip, fourteen, and Stipan, seventeen, set off in their brothers' footsteps. Again the money was borrowed but on this occasion from a friendly Italian landowner who had considerable holdings just outside the Babich village. At that time such travel was a dramatic improvement on the exhausting, perilous and seemingly never-ending voyages endured by the earliest Antipodean settlers in the first half of the 19th century. In 1910 the Suez Canal was open and the quality of shipping had very much benefited from the access it gave to the Southern Hemisphere. Nevertheless the experience of travelling such an immense distance would have been a shock to the system for most of us.

Leaving their mother behind with their two youngest brothers, Pero and Luka, the hopeful Josip and Stipan walked away from a life of tending sheep and goats and cultivating their somewhat inconsistent vines, and turned their faces towards an unknown future. It was a wintry morning as they were accompanied by their father, Petar, and his brother, Nikola, travelling on foot with a small group of young men to Makarska. The two older men each led horses carrying their meagre baggage, and the foursome must have made a sorry sight to their grief-stricken mother. She had raised three stepsons as her own and they had already left; now she was to lose her own two eldest boys. She realised that she would probably never see them again. Ironically her supposition was to prove untrue, but that would only be the source of more grief to herself and her husband.

The rest of Stipan's and Josip's party consisted of a relative, Vid, a friend, Marko Buljan, and their cousin Ivan Babich. When the group arrived in Makarska they rested for a few days and acquired further provisions for their journey. The second stage of their trip was on board the 1 000-ton *Bosna*, which sailed to Trieste, where they remained overnight before travelling by train across the border to Rome. From Rome they took another train to Naples.

Italy was their first experience of a foreign country and none of them spoke a single word of the Italian language but no doubt they collected one or two from their brief passage. They remained one more night in Naples before boarding the *Orsova* of the Orion line, which was making its maiden voyage. It sailed via the Suez Canal to Colombo, before traversing the breadth of the Indian Ocean to Fremantle. Hugging the Australian coast, the liner made for Sydney. The party was not allowed to disembark there and perforce spent the night on board before transferring to a third vessel, the *Maheno*, and continuing their voyage for a further four days to Auckland.

The main part of the journey had lasted about a month, and there to greet them in Auckland was their brother Jakov, who by that time had become relatively fluent in English. After a brief stay in Auckland they boarded yet another boat, the 500-ton *Apanui*, which sailed to Awanui in the far north of the North Island. This voyage took two days, and a further two days were spent travelling overland before they reached their final destination, Waipapakauri, where Jakov and Mate, another

The five Babich brothers (left to right): Josip and Stephan (standing), Ivan, Jakov and Mate

brother who had joined Jakov in 1906, had a 50-acre farm. Later, Josip stated that he was surprised at the good quality of its house.

For two years Josip and Stipan worked with Mate, their elder brother, digging white gum, which they sold for £4 per hundredweight to Jakov, who ran a store at Waihara as a wholesale dealer in gum. The copal gum, as it was named, came from the fossilised remains of ancient forests of the kauri pine. It was used in the manufacture of furniture oils, varnishes, paints and linoleum, and was claimed to be greatly superior to fresh gum. At that time it accounted for nearly 5 per cent of all New Zealand's export earnings.

The hardworking brothers prospered and sent home to Runovic excited accounts of their new-found successes. Occasionally they moved to a different plot of land in search of further reserves of gum. At one stage, in early 1914, this took them to Kaikino, about 8 miles north of Awanui, on the last finger of land leading to Cape Reinga, at the very top of New Zealand's North Island.

In June of that year, World War I erupted and Austria declared hostilities against Italy. As the eldest brother, Jakov, then twenty-eight, felt it was his duty to volunteer to serve in the Austrian Army and so returned to Europe. It would have been with conflicting emotions that his father and stepmother greeted his return to home soil, painfully aware that Jakov would soon be risking his life in action. For ten years he had lived in New Zealand, and he probably had just enough time to relate the progress of each of the brothers to his

*B*abich Brothers winery,
Kaikano, 1916 (top); the only
gum-field winery ever known

*W*inemaking paraphernalia
(bottom) at the Babich Brothers
Kaikano winery, 1916

vineyard and winery at Kaikino. Records imply that he had planted the vines a couple of years earlier, because they were soon able to begin trading, which they did from the sadly-lamented Jakov's old store. From this base they sold the wines in cask and bottle under the name Babich Brothers. From the very beginning Josip had always signed the name Babich in longhand on their casks and labels and it is this signature which is still found on their bottles nearly a century later.

Josip, now twenty, was evidently in charge, but soon his efforts were to lead him into trouble and cause him to move location to the site which is the home of the Babich winery today. He was a bright young man and the education his father had given him in Runovic stood him in good stead. He was not only completely literate but was competent in mathematics and so able to carry out the Babich Brothers' administration without problems. His only oversight was studying the intricacies of the New Zealand licensing laws. As a result he was prosecuted for selling just two bottles of wine to a Maori customer, when amazingly the law required a minimum sale of 2 gallons.

Joe, as he was fast becoming known, valued his integrity and good reputation and hired an up-and-coming lawyer called H.H. Ostler (later Sir Hubert Ostler, Judge of the New Zealand Supreme Court) to defend him. Aided by an incompetent police witness, Ostler succeeded in having the case dismissed. Afterwards he advised Joe Babich that he should move nearer the city of Auckland, where he would find life more rewarding. "You want to get away from this place. There's no future for a winemaker up here," the lawyer told him. Later, Ostler followed his own advice and moved south.

In 1919, Joe decided that the move was crucial and sold all his possessions, including his prized Edison phonograph and sixty-five cylinders for

eager parents before enlisting to fight on the Italian front.

Initially Jakov was radiantly happy, for upon his return from his first period of service, he married his stepmother's daughter, Mara Karlusich, with whom he had been raised since he was four and she was three. Within months she was pregnant and he anticipated fatherhood with joy. But he was fated never to know his son Marijan, for he lost his life a few months later. Early in 1915 he was wounded at the Piava river, and despite being repatriated to Zagreb, he died of his wounds while in hospital there. His widow and child must have often wondered whether, if he had survived, he would have taken them south or remained in their homeland.

In the meantime, many miles away across the globe, the lessons Petar had taught his son Josip were beginning to bear fruit. Not content to spend his adult life merely digging gum, his thoughts began to turn in other directions. By 1916 the brothers in New Zealand had agreed to diversify and Josip, encouraged by the others, planted a small

£8. He then headed for the Henderson Valley, where he built a new winery on the land that is still occupied by the family today. Later, in 1930, he married Mara Grgic and together they raised five children, two of whom, Joseph and Peter, joined the family business.

In 1983, aged eighty-seven years, a greatly respected Josip Babich breathed his last, leaving a successful winery with an outstanding reputation. His death, for many, signalled the end of an era of pioneering winemakers who had crossed half the world to reach their destination. He had returned home just once, in 1954, some forty-four years after his departure. His father Petar had died eight years previously and his mother in 1940, but he found many of the Babich clan still occupying the cluster of houses above Runovic, Imotski, living in a conglomerate country called Yugoslavia, where communism ruled and suppressed the initiative of those who wished to achieve any personal ambitions. It was at that point that he was ultimately convinced of the true value of the loving sacrifice Petar and Iva Babich made when they took the fateful decision in 1904 to send their sons to New Zealand.

The adversities for those who remained in Runovic are exemplified in the plight of the valiant Pero, Josip's younger brother, who was left to share his childhood with Luka, two years his junior.

Luka, as a young man, emigrated to South America, leaving Pero as the only young adult male breadwinner. It was a role that brought with it grave responsibility, especially when, in his middle age, World War II broke out. It was his duty for the duration of the war and for the years immediately afterwards to provide food for sixteen people, at a time when many in the area were starving. It was not unusual for members of the Babich family to survive without any nourishment for two or three days. Pero would set out in search of food and yet he would always return with as least some of the basic necessities for everyone.

Joe Babich, when he visited his home town in 1954, knew how indebted he was to his father for the education given to him and his brothers, without which they would have remained, like many, illiterate peasants, often in desperate circumstances. Instead he had prospered as his parents had dreamed. His winery had flourished, his vineyards had expanded, his name was attracting custom from countries in every continent and now he had his own sons to work alongside him and share the rewards of "that family sacrifice".

WHISKY AND THE WITCH
Cutty Sark; Scotland and USA

London, 1922: the stirring of the city was blurred by damp fog as a lamplit taxicab stopped to collect a smartly dressed gentleman from one of the capital's finest hotels.

"Number 3, Saint James's Street, and I want you to wait for me there. I'll be about half an hour and then I want to go to London Docks, and I've got a handful of these for you if you cooperate."

"Pleasure, squire." The cabby gave a wry grin, as he touched his cap. He would do just about anything for a fistful of money.

The cab chugged to a halt at the bottom of St James's Street and the man alighted and passed into a building, which gave the impression of not having changed its appearance in over 200 years. Inside, a sombre-suited, side-whiskered clerk raised his eyes and gazed over his pince-nez at the visitor, enquiring politely if he could be of any assistance.

"Sure thing, bud. Just tell Mr Francis Berry that Mr Diamond has arrived. I telephoned and made an appointment yesterday."

The information that an American gentleman had arrived for his appointment with Mr Francis Berry was duly conveyed and presently a young male secretary appeared and ushered the American into a quaintly appointed boardroom at the front of the first floor. Excusing himself with the statement that Mr Francis Berry would be along shortly, the young man turned to quit the room but was detained by the visitor.

"Say, tell me, do you really sell the King of England his Scotch and his other booze?"

Joe (left) and Peter Babich, 1993

The home of Cutty Sark – 3 St James's St, London

The merest flicker of amused surprise crossed the secretary's face.

"I'm sure Mr Francis will be able to confirm that. Whilst details of our arrangements with the royal palaces must remain confidential, it would not be improper to divulge that we do provide His Majesty, King George the Fifth, with some Scotch whisky and also some extremely fine wines."

Further conversation was precluded by the entrance of a strikingly tall and aristocratic gentleman, who approached with hand extended.

"Ah, good morning! You must be Diamond. My name's Berry, Francis Berry."

The American came straight to the point after the hand-shaking introductions were concluded.

"It's very simple. I've a cab outside your door and want to buy thirty cases right now of your best Scotch whisky, just like you send to the King."

"Well, Diamond, it may be one of the less usual demands we receive but I'm sure we can oblige. Perhaps you would care for a coffee, whilst the cab is loaded and the papers prepared," smiled Francis.

"Papers!" was the sharp response. "There ain't no need for papers. I'm fixing all the shipping myself."

For the first time the gentlemanly facade slipped and the gruff New York accent asserted itself.

"Ah, let me see, you must be the from the great city of New York," suggested the Englishman easily.

"Not bad, not bad, Mr Berry, but then if I pay you with these I don't suppose you'll mind where the hell I'm from."

Legs Diamond placed a large bundle of crinkly white £5 notes on the polished table in front of them.

"There's more than enough there," he quipped.

Bemused, Francis Berry gazed at the man and the money. He had never before been acquainted with quite such a character, though his business introductions had been impeccable, and he had met one or two Americans previously who were not exactly top drawer.

The streetlamps were gleaming through the thickening fog as later that evening Francis Berry sipped a small glass of port in the warmth and comfort of his club. Leaning across the table to his cousin David, he mentioned the morning's experience.

"It was really remiss of me," he confided. "But at the time I completely forgot about this new Volstead Act, or Prohibition as our newspapers are calling it. On the face of it, one has to presume that Mr Diamond is intending to smuggle the Scotch into the United States. But surely if he knew what he was about he would have asked for it free of duty?"

During the following weeks, Francis pondered the transaction in his mind, wondering whether there was not a golden opportunity to make a great deal of money – legally, of course legally. A couple of months later he was on board the *Lauretania* on his way to New York. His mind was made up.

Once in New York, Francis spent some time summing up the situation before taking the night train to Florida. A day's recuperation in Florida and he was again on the move, this time on the old ferry to Nassau, where he booked into the Carlton. His search had begun in earnest.

All the evidence pointed to the majority of rum-running being organised from Nassau, and Francis had come with the intention of changing a good proportion of rum-running into whisky-running. The name he heard most frequently associated with the venture was that of Captain Bill McCoy, an experienced seafarer operating a well-organised business from his fast schooner *Henry L. Marshall*.

Rising a little later than was his practice and after breakfasting to the sound of surf on sand, Francis set out to track down Captain Bill McCoy. By unwritten international custom, the placing of a reasonably generous tip in the hand of the head porter was a sound investment, and Francis Berry left the Carlton with a short list of liquid establishments likely to contain the person he was seeking.

The sun and Francis's stomach were indicating lunchtime when the Englishman, looking a trifle overdressed in pale buff tropical suit and cravat, parted the tattered bead curtains of a smoke-filled bar and began to edge his way into the crowded room. Every available space was occupied by small card tables surrounded by seafarers of all possible colours and creeds, most of whom were apparently steeped in concentration. Polite enquiries as to the whereabouts of Captain McCoy elicited no response until the barman jerked a thumb: "Over there sir, the big fella in the white shirt with the sleeves rolled up – that's McCoy."

Heading in the direction indicated and excusing himself for disturbing the intent card-players, Francis reached his objective and, bending down to be heard, cleared his throat.

"I apologise for interrupting your leisure activities, Captain McCoy, but my name's Berry, Francis Berry, and I was hoping that we could discuss undertaking a little trade together."

Laconically, the captain scraped his chair back a little and, swiftly appraising the Englishman from top to toe, replied, "OK, but I gotta finish my hand first. The boys know I have a reputation for never starting a deal I don't finish and I don't want to lose that standing for anyone. No offence sir; be with you in six or seven minutes."

Francis acquiesced and regaining the bar, perched on one of the high stools and ordered a Scotch with water. He ran his finger under his cravat to loosen it a little as the humidity of the smoky atmosphere increased his craving for refreshment. When the whisky came he almost choked, spat it out quickly and reached for his handkerchief. The barman stifled a chortle with, "Sorry, sir, but it's all we can get and it ain't what an Englishman like you'll be used to."

Before Francis could breathe sufficiently to reply a hand clapped him on the shoulder and there was McCoy. "Right, Mr Berry, what little trade do you think we might share?"

Dabbing at his gleaming forehead, Francis regained his composure and made his offer: "The finest of Scotch whisky, Captain McCoy. I want to sell you the very best whisky there is."

The tanned features of the seaman reflected scepticism as he mouthed, "Oh sure, that's what they all say and then we just get the muck you're holding in your hand. I can tell you right now, Mr Berry, I've lost a lot of respect for you British. You might own these Bahama Islands and half the world, but your liquor men have forgotten how to offer me a good Scotch whisky. I've built up my reputation as I told you just now and I don't intend risking that."

He paused, perusing the Englishman's face and awaiting some reaction.

"Now you tell me why I should take any more notice of you than of the others I've met, and there's nothing personal in that?"

No reply came, but smiling confidently, Francis produced a small hipflask and signalling to the barman for a glass, poured the flask's contents into it and offered it to the passive McCoy. There was a moment's pause as the burly sailor swilled the drink round his mouth and gulped it down.

"Fine whisky, fine Scotch, excellent," he murmured, appreciation flickering across his clean-shaven face. Then the wariness returned.

"But if I buy any from you, how would I know that this quality would be delivered? Every damn drop that's been sent me in barrels has been tampered with. Either watered down or cheap liquor added. I don't know you, Mr Berry, and fine gentleman though you may appear to be, why should I trust you?"

Francis was momentarily taken aback. "Captain McCoy, you insult me!"

Then, recalling the captain's experience and understandable hesitation, he continued: "My family firm are no less than official purveyors of Scotch whisky to King George the Fifth of England. We too have a reputation at risk."

This seemed to make more impression on McCoy. He paused and reflected.

"Point taken, Mr Berry. Maybe we can talk turkey but I gotta think straight first. Let's stroll outside and take some fresh air."

Only too glad to be free of the oppressive atmosphere of the bar, Francis followed McCoy to the quay side. Both men were tall but distinctively different in every other respect as they strolled along in the bright heat. Occasionally stopping to identify some particular boat which was making its owners a lucrative living from rum-running, McCoy spoke in general terms of the dangers and problems inherent in his lifestyle. Suddenly he came to a halt, a broad grin creasing his face: "I've got it. I may just have the right idea. You see Berry, until this new law, most whiskies, whether Scotch, Irish, American or whatever, have been a dark colour. Now if you could come up with a whisky that's completely different in style we might be able to do a lot of business. Yes, give me an instantly recognisable style, Berry, and we can talk. Perhaps a pale special whisky – lighter in flavour, so when

Captain William "the Real" McCoy

you take your slug it goes down real smooth. Or if we wanted to sell it at the top of the market, a sipping whisky that'll be just fine on the rocks."

Francis stood still momentarily, considering the various possibilities, then shaking hands with the captain, accepted the challenge and arranged to keep in touch. As they headed back along the quay side, McCoy confided that he would be away for a couple of months in St Pierre. "Hah, the US Coastguard can't touch us there and so a few of us are organising a new base on one of the islands."

"St Pierre – is that another island in the Caribbean?"

"Hell, no!" laughed McCoy. "St Pierre et Miquelon, to give it its full title, is one of those funny little misfits from the past. It's the one tiny piece of France that's survived in North America, off the coast of Nova Scotia, and they've never heard of a customs officer. The French are hoarding Cognac there and we are going to use St Pierre as a base for our rum."

From there McCoy was already smuggling several whiskies, including Haig and Johnny Walker. Most of the Haig operation was organised by a daring young lady called Gertrude Lithy, while Johnny Walker was initially exported through the channels of a merchant called C.P. Chartier. He "acquired" it from Johnny Walker's Montreal agent, the St George Import and Export Company and later through a business called United Traders.

On 18 April 1922 the French government had craftily removed regulations that forbade the importation of non-French alcoholic drinks into St Pierre and Miquelon. This freed the St Pierre ship-brokers Folquet Frères to commence handling Cutty Sark and other drinks from both Great Britain and the Caribbean. Local legend recalls that one of the Folquet brothers was actually negotiating with Captain William McCoy in a bar in Halifax, Nova Scotia, on that eventful day, awaiting a telephone call bearing the news of the dramatic legal change.

Francis returned to London, brimming with the new idea and an equal amount of enthusiasm. He headed for Scotland to approach many of the best-known blenders, enquiring after the possibilities of producing a new, lighter style of blended Scotch. His purposes and his market Francis kept strictly confidential. Eventually he found his man and what he required in James Stannard.

"It'll take me the best part of a year, Mr Berry, but it can be done."

As Stannard explained, to provide satisfactory samples was one thing, but to ensure ongoing stocks was another. The Highlands and islands would have to be scoured for top-quality but lightly flavoured malts.

"As for the colour, that's really quite simple, Mr Berry. Everyone else adds caramel to provide a consistent colour. So we'll just leave it out."

He made the task sound remarkably easy, which was not the case, but he was a man who enjoyed a challenge and was attracted to this particular demand.

The family firm in London were naturally apprised by Francis of the course he was taking. The next step, he informed them, was to choose or devise a suitable, instantly recognisable label. An idea was to present itself sooner that he imagined.

A month or two slipped away until one morning, as he was glancing through the pages of the *Times* and sipping his coffee, Francis's attention was drawn to a major article reporting the restoration of the old tea clipper, the *Cutty Sark*. The ship, it was stated, was to be on permanent public display at Greenwich. The idea of linking the name of a fast-running ship with the speedy smuggling activities of Captain McCoy appealed to Francis. Smiling to himself, he put down his coffee cup and began to read the article in earnest.

"We certainly would welcome any publicity we can get and would have no objection to your use of the name," Commander Brittain announced to a delighted Francis Berry, on a cool, windy Greenwich day. "Now perhaps you'd be interested to know why she's called the *Cutty Sark*. Follow me and I'll show you the figurehead."

Rounding the front of the magnificent clipper, the commander pointed to the half-naked lady,

Stern view of the Cutty Sark

one arm outstretched, and luridly painted in the usual seafarers' manner. Francis was well-acquainted with such figureheads but not with the old Scots language, and had no idea that the ship's name, *Cutty Sark*, was a direct reference to the figurehead. He certainly had not entertained the idea of a lady with a bare torso on the label of his Scotch whisky.

He was recalled to himself by the commander's voice: "I hope it doesn't shock you. She was quite a character, even if she never really existed. I'm sure you are familiar with the name and poetry of Robbie Burns, Scotland's greatest poet. Well she's a figure from one of his best-known works 'Tam O' Shanter'."

Francis, as a well-read man, naturally knew the name of Robert Burns, the national poet of Scotland. Every year on 25 January, the day on which Burns was born, Scotsmen and women all over the world gathered together for a ritual celebration. His poems and songs were, and still are, recited and sung amid a great deal of revelry and consumption of whisky. Robert Burns is almost a national hero and his name is loved and revered by all Scotland.

Despite his present-day standing, Robert Burns was from very humble origins. He was born on 25 January 1759 in a clay cottage $2\frac{1}{2}$ miles south of Ayr, in the village of Alloway. His father progressed from being a gardener to the status of a tenant farmer, but making a living was an arduous task and the clay soils of Ayrshire were less than generous. Robert, however, was the eldest son and his father,

William, believed passionately in education and religion. Therefore Robert and his younger brother Gilbert were given a formal education in English language and literature, although they spoke broad Ayrshire Scots at home. In 1775, William Burnes sent his eldest son to a noted school in Kirkoswald, where he learned "Mensuration, Surveying and Dialling". It seems that at the age of sixteen he also learned while away from home a little about dancing, drinking and falling in love.

Robert became something of a rebel, dressing outrageously and behaving outlandishly, in much the same way as some youngsters today. After his father's death, Robert began to write more and more poetry, satires and love songs. His first book of poetry was a success and he was accepted into Edinburgh's literary circles. They saw him as some sort of educated ploughboy. "Tam o' Shanter" is probably his best-known narrative poem, semi-humorous and colourful.

Without further ado, Commander Brittain related the story of Tam and the witch Nanny. It seems young Tam had been riding home one night after a few drams with the lads, when he heard singing from a nearby churchyard, and there in the moonlight were three dancing female figures, naked save for their short shifts, garments known in Old Scots as *cutty sarks*. The drink he had consumed and the spectacle before him inflamed his desires and leaning forward he beckoned to one of the witches, Nanny, and grinning lecherously hailed her: "Hey, Cutty Sark!" His lustful levity soon cooled when the witch spun round on him with eyes full of lascivious malice. She lunged at him, intent on his seduction,

The Cutty Sark's *prow and figurehead*

Cutty Sark whisky awaiting smuggling from Nassau in the Bahamas, circa 1930

arms outstretched and nails clawing. In terror, Tam spurred his horse away over a nearby bridge, for it was well-known that running water was a barrier to supernatural evil. Nanny failed to catch Tam, but she caught the tail of his horse as it galloped away, and it came out in her hand. Hence the figurehead of the tea clipper has her hand outstretched, but by curious custom she only holds a horse's tail when arriving or leaving port.

The strange legend remained in Francis Berry's mind; by now he was extremely enthusiastic about the whole scheme. He would have the tea clipper represented on his Scotch-whisky label, but what about the background colour?

"Yellow!" he proposed to the artist, James McBey.

"Yellow! Yellow? I know you said you wanted something noticeable on a bar, Mr Berry, but yellow? What about something a trifle more orangey?"

But Francis was adamant and Bill McCoy delighted when he saw the final product a few weeks later in the balmy atmosphere of Nassau.

"Marvellous, Berry, damned marvellous! Pale, pale whisky and a bright, bright label. The stuff's great on the rocks and sure as hell everyone's gonna remember it with a name and label like that. In fact," he roared, "everyone'll be bewitched by it!"

He winked at the chuckling Francis and taking him by the hand said, "I'll start with 5 000 cases and that'll increase to 50 000 in a year and it's cash up front in dollars or sterling whichever you prefer. I'll soon convince the longboatmen that the whisky is genuine. They've never had anything but the finest of rum from me and now I can tell them that this is whisky from the same man as supplies the King of England.

"Better still," he said, his face brightening at a sudden recollection, "I can just say that as my ancestors came from Scotland, I can guarantee them that it's the very same as my great-great-grandfather used to drink.

"In fact," he said, clapping the amused Francis on the back, "I'll tell them it's the real McCoy!"

CULTIVATION RESTORED
Pewsey Vale, Australia

When the Yalumba Company entered a partnership with Geoff Parsons in 1961 to cultivate a vineyard in the eastern Barossa Ranges of South Australia, the parties agreed to replant on land belonging to Geoff, even though it meant starting from scratch. This was because the land already had a successful record as a vineyard. The land, with its cool climate, and located at an altitude of around 1 500 feet, had been the site of Joseph Gilbert's 1847 Pewsey Vale vineyard, which he had named after his birthplace, Pewsey Vale, in Wiltshire, England.

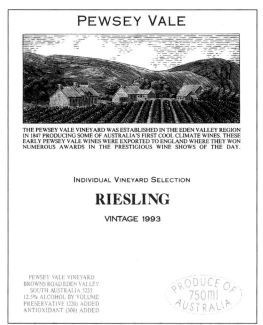

Gilbert was a wealthy gentleman farmer who lived at Puckshipton in the Vale of Pewsey and had been educated at renowned Marlborough College. He was fluent in French and apparently "well informed on aspects of viticulture and winemaking". Viticulture had continued at his South Australian vineyard until shortly before World War I.

Gilbert had succeeded with grape varieties then listed as "Verdelho, Gouais, Riesling, Shiraz and Carbonet". With the strong links that then existed between the medical world and the winemakers, Gilbert took great delight when the *London Medical Times* described his 1864 Pewsey Vale Claret as: "A fine, mature wine, grapey and potent, fit to rank with Hermitage." It was, however, the Pewsey Vale Hock made from Riesling which was most widely admired in his home state. Subsequently it was no surprise when the reborn Pewsey Vale released its Rhine Riesling in 1966, and in 1969 stunned its competitors by winning seven gold medals with it.

THE DETERMINED GERMAN
Wolf Blass, Australia

Two characteristics set the Australian wine industry apart from that of other nations. The first is a preoccupation with wine shows and the thousands of medals to be won. The second is the extraordinary number of wine personalities, deceased and still active, who it is claimed are responsible for transforming the Australian wine industry from its former, antiquated ways into its current era of worldwide recognition. As someone who has interviewed a fair number of Australian wine experts in London, I have always been overwhelmed by the welter of names put forward in this category, amongst whom only one is broadly known by consumers internationally.

In no way am I trying to undermine the importance of the contributions of Leo Buring, Len Evans, Colin Preece, Maurice O'Shea, Bill Redman and Max Schubert, some of whom I have discussed in other chapters, but the only person of this calibre whose name is widely known to consumers in the major international markets is Wolf Blass.

That recognition has been earned not so much by the man as a wine personality, but by his name being easily identifiable on wine labels in wide distribution. In particular the Wolf Blass Yellow Label Cabernet Sauvignon, with its striking Eagle-hawk logo, has become familiar to international consumers, whereas in his adopted homeland, Wolf Blass has become well-known as a pocket dynamo who always leads his troops from the front. There can be no doubt that as an early new-generation representative of Australian wines, Wolf Blass wines, in many countries, have played their part in projecting an excellent image for Australia.

In Australia, Wolf Blass has made his presence felt as a very public wine figure with numerous media appearances. In fact within minutes of meeting star Australian television host Ray Martin, I was told "how proud" Australia was of Wolf Blass.

In contrast, in some overseas markets he has visited, Wolf has not had the same reception. There is the true story of an occasion a few years ago, when Wolf Blass wines was changing distribution agencies in the United States. A meeting occurred between two executives from the companies concerned. The outgoing party was giving a word of advice to the incoming executive: "The wines are absolutely super. You'll have no trouble with them at all but whatever you do, don't let the producer into the market – he'll drive you crazy!"

Presumably those who have worked with Wolf Blass have known him best as a wine man and I have talked to a good number of them with extremely consistent results. All reported that at times he could be outrageous and extremely frustrating, and occasionally even embarrassing, but each one, without exception, has admitted in one way or another that they could not but like and admire him.

Nevertheless, the story of Wolf Blass, the young East German who emigrated to Australia in search of his dream to produce great red wine, is one that demonstrates how an outsider can sometimes observe a country's potential better than those who may be too deeply involved in the existing state of affairs.

To begin we have to travel to the Rhine Valley just twelve years after World War II. On 15 October 1957 an award to a young East German wine student at the prestigious wine college at Geisenheim was the trigger for one of the most energetic of international wine careers. Wolfgang Blass, just six weeks past his twenty-third birthday, had become the youngest recipient ever of the *Kellermeister-Prüfungzeugnis*, or Cellarmaster's Diploma.

Nowadays, amid the current generation of winemakers, there are literally dozens of experienced

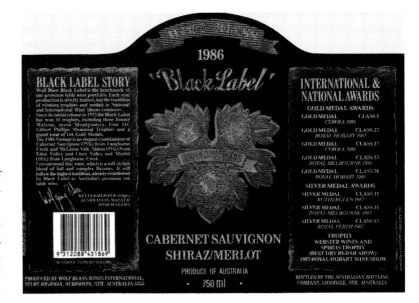

WOLF BLASS

BILYARA
ABORIGINAL WORD MEANING 'EAGLEHAWK'

CELLARS
ESTABLISHED 1966

WINES

1990
SHIRAZ

CABERNET
SAUVIGNON

'Yellow Label'

750ML PRODUCE OF AUSTRALIA

professionals who spend much of their time travelling from country to country making special wines or acting as consultants, but in the late 1950s the practice was virtually nonexistent. Yet within weeks of gaining his diploma Wolf Blass had taken his first, if relatively brief, journey to gain international experience, as he took advantage of an opportunity for a short exchange visit to the Champagne region of France.

A first appointment, as the maker of still table wines at the sparkling-wine house of Blumenthal, Linz, aided by his Champagne experience, attracted him to the production of sparkling wine for a while and the knowledge gained at Linz and in the Champagne region was soon to enable him to travel to the far side of the world.

While sparkling wines created an initial interest for the young *kellermeister*, and he later enjoyed making many examples of traditional German white wines, he realised early in his career that if he stayed in Germany he would never be able to make outstanding red wines because of the country's cool northern climate. I believe this was the dominant factor in his desire to travel, which eventually took him to the sunny weather of South Australia.

In the meantime he made England his next target as he strove to acquire a wide range of skills. After a short spell with an English-based German wine company as a wine chemist, he went to work in the cellars of Avery's of Bristol, in a city that has a wine-shipping tradition of probably more than 1 000

years. Avery's was founded in the late 18th century and had developed an excellent reputation for its bottlings of classic Bordeaux and Burgundies. Ronald Avery, head of the company when Wolf Blass joined it, was a legendary figure in the United Kingdom wine trade and was regarded an exceptional taster. He put Wolf Blass to work as a blender, a task in which he quickly displayed a rare talent and gleaned considerable knowledge.

The story is told that at Avery's, Wolf had his first experience of tasting Australian red wines. A range of them had been offered for the company's consideration and Wolf was so appalled by their quality that he vowed to go to Australia to show people how to make good red wine. This bold assertion revived his desire to become a red-wine maker, which had been frustrated by German weather conditions. This happened during a period when he was entertaining the idea of a career move, probably overseas, and Australia, with its Germanic traditions, fast became his preference. There was, however, an obstacle to this idea. In 1961 the volume of red table wine being produced in Australia was rather small and the opportunities for a young European blending expert were roughly nil. Therefore, when an opening in a quite different field, making sparkling wines, presented itself, he applied speedily and was ecstatic when the Barossa cooperative known as Kaiser Stuhl confirmed his appointment.

More than a century after the first Germans had settled in the Barossa Valley, a new-generation winemaker arrived and in his own way he too was a pioneer, for he was to introduce the latest European wine science and blending knowledge to an area that needed such a challenge. To be polite, the bulk of Australian red wine at the time was not exactly exciting and the annual national consumption of all table wines was only 2 litres per head. In 1964, when his three-year contract at Kaiser Stuhl expired, Wolf Blass purchased a Volkswagen Beetle and took to the road as Australia's only freelance winemaker, becoming a professional advocate of modern wine technology. He insisted that producers had to invest in new equipment, such as stainless-steel fermentation tanks with temperature controls, and that judicious investment should be made in good-quality new oak barrels. He encouraged owners to plant increased acreage of the best noble grape varieties, and this often meant Cabernet Sauvignon. Additionally he demonstrated the finest blending skills and showed large merchants how they could improve their blends by more carefully selecting their wine purchases.

In 1966, aged thirty-two, he acquired a small building at Bilyara Road in Tanunda and that first move as a winery owner indicated the direction he was going to take. Unlike many major companies who at that time were searching for more vineyard land, his then very limited capital meant he had to restrict himself to buying, blending, bottling and selling wines. For a few years he lived on a pittance as he reinvested his profits in the best modern winemaking equipment and his personal choice of oak casks. The word "Bilyara" offered him a small stroke of luck which he seized gratefully. He had seen positive use of wine logos in Europe and wished to select one that would easily identify his wines. *Bilyara* is the aboriginal word for eaglehawk, and the eagle is the German national symbol. So he adopted the *Bilyara* as his logo and placed it prominently at the top of his labels.

Wolf believed that the first of the two Australian idiosyncracies mentioned, the wine-show circuit, would offer him the quickest possible route to success. The Australians, as can be seen from their sporting prowess, love winners. So any wine label that can list a host of medals, and even the occasional top prize of a trophy, is likely to find ready custom. He knew that normally the competition regulations were very strictly followed, with the anonymity of the samples being guaranteed. If he could get his peers, indeed his more senior competitors, to publicly acknowledge the outstanding quality of his wines, he believed he would make speedy progress. It was a philosophy that by 1991, when he celebrated his thirtieth year in Australia, had reaped him a rich reward of more than 3 000 awards, including around 150 trophies and 760 gold medals.

He introduced a new style of red-wine making involving better use of fruit, providing much softer wines than were generally known, with supple character and a long finish. While some were concentrating on regional wines or blends from within a state, he was perfectly happy to send for samples from throughout Australia in the search for the components needed in a blend, which would then be sold as being from Australia or south-eastern Australia. At the same time, he was far from happy with the quality of the wine labels being used in the industry and so began to display a totally new fashion of brightly portrayed, boldly printed labels which wrapped around two-thirds of the bottle, giving him side panels on which he could publicise his numerous medal successes and provide some background details on the making of the wine. He was introducing a new generation of Australian wine consumers to the subject of wine education; they appreciated it and bought his wines in increasing quantity.

One success, more than any other, brought Wolf Blass to the forefront of red-wine making in Australia, although it should be remembered that the Wolf Blass label has produced many excellent white wines as well. In 1974, 1975 and 1976 he won the Jimmy Watson Trophy at the Melbourne Wine Show. When in 1974 he won it for the first time, with a 1973 blend of Cabernet Sauvignon and Shiraz from Langhorne Creek and the Eden Valley, few wine consumers knew of the trophy, which was officially presented to the winner of Class 14, for the best one-year-old red. Later, when he had become the first and only producer to win it in three consecutive years, most Australian wine lovers were aware of the name Jimmy Watson and the trophy had become the most sought after in Australia.

Some of his fellow competitors dismissed his first win as a chance result, but it was difficult to overlook his achievement when the second success occurred. The third wine proved that his wine-making skills could not be disputed. After all, many of the judges were leading figures among his keenest competitors. Instead of regarding him as an upstart, they were forced to acknowledge him as one of the all-time great figures of their industry. For the German who had known that he could never make a fine red wine in his own country, it was a superlative achievement which justified his determination to find a country where he could make such wine. His experiences in Europe and Australia, plus his natural talent and self-belief, had combined to produce great red wine; the anonymity of the judging had proved that. Throughout his many successes he has never forgotten the Geisenheim course that taught him so many skills, as is evident from some thirty years of labels which are all signed "Wolfgang Blass, Kellermeister (Diploma)", which was awarded to its youngest recipient ever.

In 1992, he sold his controlling interest in the Wolf Blass company to the Mildara Company, who formed Mildara Blass Ltd, and Wolf Blass, at fifty-eight years of age, retired to Adelaide with his famous Rolls Royce. But surely no-one can imagine that the man with such energy and drive can ever retire, for the world of Australian wine without him would be a lesser place.

AN EXPORT PROBLEM
Charles Heidsieck, France

The Champagne region has had more than its fair share of colourful personalities, but one who must rank head and shoulders above the others is Charles-Camille Heidsieck. Stories about his exploits are legion, but one in particular reveals his devotion to Champagne sales far beyond the call of duty.

In 1862, during the American Civil War, Charles urgently wanted to visit his strongest market, New

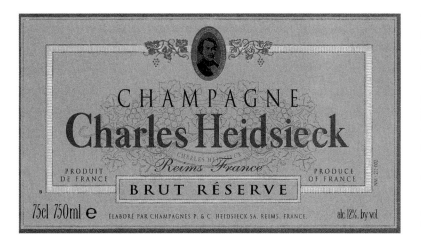

CHAMPAGNE
Charles Heidsieck
Reims France
PRODUIT
DE FRANCE
PRODUCE
OF FRANCE
BRUT RÉSERVE
75cl 750ml e   ÉLABORÉ PAR CHAMPAGNES P. & C. HEIDSIECK SA. REIMS. FRANCE.   alc. 12% by vol.

Orleans, where his house was selling an astounding 360 000 bottles per year to a population of around half a million. Substantial monies were due for collection and there was no way of obtaining them unless he travelled there in person.

Over a period of a couple of months he made numerous unsuccessful attempts to cross the battle-lines, invariably being turned back by incredulous soldiers who could not begin to understand that Champagne should be worth risking one's life. But as a man who refused to accept no for an answer, Charles persisted with his attempts, adopting a new ploy each time. Eventually he reached the Alabama port of Mobile, where the only means by which he could get a passage was to sign on as a barman on a New Orleans-bound ship. When asked by the local French Consul in Mobile to deliver the diplomatic bag to his counterpart in New Orleans, Charles willingly obliged, quite unaware that the contents contained an offer of support from the

French to the Confederate forces. Charles was arrested by the Yankees, who naturally had insisted on examining the bag and subsequently discovered the incriminating document.

For his pains the unfortunate Charles Heidsieck spent four months imprisoned in a squalid fort in the Mississippi Delta. Only after that time was the French government able to negotiate his release.

THE FRENCH CONNECTION
Seppelt, Australia

The 1991-92 International Wine Challenge awarded Seppelt Salinger the title of Sparkling Wine of the Year, which was the first time that the company's sparkling wine had received recognition outside Australia. Previous medals and awards had only been gained on home territory, but the Seppelt victory now meant that wine buffs would be giving serious attention to the company's involvement in sparkling wine and in particular to its origins in that trade. Seppelt's history is in many ways typical of rural development in Victoria in general throughout the second half of the 19th century.

The Seppelt interest in sparkling wine started as late as 1918, when the company purchased the famed Great Western Cellars. French brothers-in-law Jean Trouette and Emile Blampied first planted vines at Great Western after acquiring land on the edge of Great Western village in 1863. Their neighbours were impressed with the health of their crop. One in particular, Joseph Best, a thirty-five-year-old Englishman from Richmond, Surrey, observed the Frenchmen with much interest. In 1865, he bought nearby land and planted his own vine cuttings, calling his property Great Western Vineyards. Best, who came from a family of builders, hired teams of local goldminers to hew out $1\frac{1}{2}$ miles of underground cellars, known as drives, which he intended using for ageing his wines. Best is believed to have produced still wines only.

By 1887, the year of his death, Best had developed an extensive estate of over 500 acres, including 55 acres of vines. Some 60 000 gallons of wine, still ageing, were left. The entire property was purchased

Charles Camille Heidsieck, 1853

GREAT WESTERN
BRUT
Australian Sparkling Wine
BOTTLE FERMENTED
10.5% VOL   75CL
PRODUCED & BOTTLED BY B. SEPPELT & SONS LIMITED GREAT WESTERN VICTORIA. AUSTRALIA 3377

for £12 000 by Hans Irvine, a Ballarat entrepreneur, who in 1890 engaged the services of Charles Pierlot, a native of the French Champagne region, where he had been employed by Pommery et Greno in Reims. Together Irvine and Pierlot made a formidable duo and the businessman gave substantial financial support to the Frenchman's plans. The pair travelled to and from France on several occasions, to purchase equipment and vine cuttings and to win the odd medal in Paris.

The visits to France sometimes extended to England, where Australian wines were enjoying a healthy market and Irvine wanted to organise some shipments. These proved so successful that in 1905 Great Western opened what could be termed a public warehouse. Situated in Dowgate Hill, near Cannon Street Station in the City of London, it allowed consumers the novel experience of purchasing direct from the producer.

Salinger was the maiden name of Charles Pierlot's wife, Ellena. Over a period exceeding thirty years she provided grapes from her privately owned Salinger Vineyard to Great Western, under both the Irvine and Seppelt regimes. Even today the Seppelt company purchases Salinger Vineyard grapes and uses them as a key component in the distinguished blend that carries that name.

NOT DOLLARS BUT STERLING
Sterling Vineyards, USA

Sterling Vineyards, from California's world famous Napa Valley, is today recognised across the entire globe as a winery of undisputed international class. Sterling first met with the acclaim of French wine experts when not just one, but two of its wines were selected in 1979 by the Paris Ritz to be the first American wines ever to grace the tables of that celebrated establishment. It was considered an occasion of such importance, and such an unprecedented break with tradition, that Madame Charles Ritz herself announced to a gathering of specially invited leading gourmets and wine writers that the Sterling Reserve Cabernet Sauvignon 1973 and Sterling Chardonnay 1977 had been selected for the Ritz cellars.

Sterling was rewarded with yet another success in the same year, when its Sauvignon Blanc won first prize in Paris at the 1979 Gault Millau Wine Olympics, defeating many of France's most distinguished white wines and scores of other competitors from all over the world.

In 1977, Sterling achieved yet another first when it became the only US winery ever to be paid a visit by a member of the British Royal Family – His Royal Highness the Prince Charles. Since that visit it remains the only Californian wine in the prince's personal cellar, with the Sterling Reserve in an aptly sized imperial being the royal choice, an imperial being nine times the volume of a standard bottle.

A clue to its affinity with the future British monarch can be found in its name, for although Sterling Vineyards is claimed as the jewel in the crown of the Seagram Classics Wine Company, it was only acquired as recently as 1983. Sterling Vineyards was founded by a young Englishman called Peter Newton and some of his colleagues. Peter, who was educated at the ancient Charterhouse School in London and the historic Baliol College, Oxford, had no immediate dreams of making wine. After university his first employment was as a journalist writing for the London-based *Financial Times,* or "Pink-un" as it is often termed in Britain. Early success in his articles on the sterling currency brought him the prestigious "Lex" column. Later, in 1954, Peter Newton took a holiday trip to California, where he fell in love with San Francisco and with a lady there. He stayed and married, and began to look for a suitable journalistic post. While there were a few minor positions available to him, none of them really appealed and so he began to look for career prospects in an altogether different direction.

In downtown San Francisco today, at 225 Kearny Street, there is a pizza parlour, but in 1954, on the second floor, a major enterprise made a humble start. With just one secretary, two rooms and an imposing trading title, Sterling International, Peter began dealing in minor imports and exports in the sterling currency. In a very short space of time, it emerged that he had even greater practical acumen for financial commerce than had been evident in his brief but successful career in financial theory in British journalism. Suffice it to say that he prospered on an extremely substantial scale, acquiring major investments on both sides of the Atlantic.

As does anyone who settles in California, he enjoyed the privileges of the exciting culture and lifestyles that make the state vibrate. One growing attraction, which he greatly enjoyed, was the fascinating subject of wine and this was to lead him into making a little fun investment.

Peter Newton later recalled: "By 1964 it was no longer necessary to work 7 days a week, because things were going pretty well, so we decided to look for another interest which could be a bit of a hobby as well." "We" referred to himself and his partner, a former RAF fighter pilot, Michael Stone, and one or two others who had become involved in his scheme. "We heard that someone had 50 acres of vineyards to sell near Calistoga at a place called Bear Flats and decided to purchase them, and then over the next year we added another 50 acres and over 5 years we built up an estate of 250 acres with the intention of confining ourselves to growing grapes in order to sell them to wineries. But I suppose you could say we got the bug and finished up producing the wine as well. So we had to give it a name and called it Sterling Vineyards for obvious reasons."

Peter and his partners subsequently set out to implement one of the most positive and successful promotional programs ever seen in California. As they continued to extend their holdings, they made the decision to become pioneers in the field of conducting wine tours for visitors. They began to formulate plans for the construction of a remarkable winery that would be ideal for attracting consumers on a large scale and would also provide substantial publicity for Sterling Vineyards. Several incidental factors were influential in the construction of the winery as it stands today. One of the partners, returning from a holiday on an Ionian island, related to the others his visit to a beautiful white castle and showed them some sketches he had made of it. Their decision was instantaneous and they instructed an architect to prepare plans to build their castle winery on top of a hill, which they had acquired from the Hurd family, owners of the neighbouring Freemark Abbey Candle Factory. Later, on one of his occasional forays to England, Peter had the brainwave of buying some ancient church bells, dating from 1700, which had originally pealed from the belfry of St Dunstans-in-the-East, near the Tower of London, until the church was destroyed during a bombing raid in 1941. The bells were carefully packed and shipped to Sterling Vineyards, where they were rehung and began a new life, ringing out their call across the northern end of the Napa Valley.

One problem arose with the plans to attract visitors to the winery. Because the brilliantly white castle-like construction covered almost all of the hill, there was no room for adequate parking facilities. This seemed to be a critical situation but the infant company overcame it in an ingenious manner. Their answer was to install a tramway, somewhat like a ski lift, which could run from a lower area of ground, where car-parking space

could be allocated in the very midst of the main vineyard. The Hall Ski Lift Company was engaged to erect the 2 900-foot cable, with twelve gondolas, which were capable of transporting 320 people up to the winery every hour. The inspiration proved to be just what Sterling Vineyards needed, as the installation of the tramway attracted a great deal of media publicity, and in no time at all people were forming a line to take the tram to the castle winery on the hill, where they could not only enjoy some delightful wines but take in the breathtaking views of Mount St Helena in one direction and the entire Napa Valley in the other.

During this period, great strides had also been made in the vineyards themselves. Under the control of the head winemaker, R.W. Forman, Sterling wines had bounded up the quality ladder, with many publications acknowledging their improving standards. Together with the publicity they were gaining for their imposing building, constantly increasing streams of visitors were making their way to Sterling Vineyards, and the winery's reputation expanded enormously.

In the late 1970s, as the world economy flagged, even major financial companies experienced liquidity problems, and so it was with great reluctance that Peter Newton sold Sterling Vineyards to Coca-Cola, which was planning to diversify into wine. The venture was not a happy one for the giant Atlanta-based corporation, which soon found to its cost that the world of wine bore little resemblance to that of soft drinks. The result was that Coca-Cola sold Sterling Vineyards to the Seagram Classics Wine Company, which has attracted much deserved praise for its effort in developing the winery and its outstanding reputation. It is worth noting at this point that even in the late 1970s, Californian wines were not, in general, given serious consideration in the great cities of the eastern seaboard. But Sterling struck in a way that was to change that attitude not just in the wine world but also in many journalists and their readers.

The *New York Times* of 14 June 1978 told the whole story. "Wine World Stunned! What Were the Wines? What Were the Stunning Results?" read the banner headlines. In the article that followed, that beautifully written newspaper reported a major tasting which had produced astonishing results. The article continued:

The Sterling Vineyards 1974, estate bottled Napa Valley Cabernet Sauvignon completely overwhelmed France's most eminent Bordeaux, Chateau Lafite-Rothschild from the very same vintage. Amazingly the Lafite sells for $16.50 a bottle, the Sterling Cabernet for only $7.99! The overall votes were 158 for the Sterling, seventy-nine for the Lafite. Equally as incredible, Sterling Vineyards 1974 estate-bottled Napa Valley 100% Merlot was favoured overall by almost two to one over the great Bordeaux Pomerol, Chateau Petrus 1974. The current retail price in New York for Chateau Petrus 1974 is $18.50, for the Sterling Vineyards Merlot 1974 only $7.50!

Under the Seagram Classics ownership, and the influence of President Tom Ferrel and winemaker Bill Dyer, Sterling has moved to new heights, winning further awards and gaining widespread international praise. Steadily, its new owners have continued to purchase further prime vineyards scattered around the Napa Valley, with one at Winery Lake proving an outstanding acquisition, offering some of the most delicious single-vineyard Chardonnay and Pinot Noir in North America.

Few problems appear to face this pre-eminent winery, which remains one of the most memorable visits any wine enthusiast can make, with one exception; its wines are so much in demand that inevitably some rationing has followed. Everyone, though, should allow themselves to be tempted to try the Sterling Merlot when it has about five years maturity, for this delectably soft, smooth red wine, which is a great favourite of mine, owes its very existence to Peter Newton, the man who gave the winery its name. Peter was the first person to plant Merlot in the Napa Valley this century, and the success of Sterling Vineyards Merlot has persuaded many others to experiment and find similar acclaim. When you drink it, or any other Sterling wine, reflect upon the origin of its name and how the holiday of an English financial journalist resulted in the founding of one of America's and the world's greatest wineries.

THE THRIFTY ITALIAN
Canepa, Chile

After several years of scraping and saving, in 1914 a fifteen-year-old Italian farm worker from Liguria

managed to find sufficient money to purchase a one-way ticket from Genoa to South America. His initial destination was Valparaiso, Chile, which he reached after an uncomfortable couple of months on board ship. From Valparaiso he travelled a further 150 miles south across land to the Curico Valley, where he obtained work in the vineyards.

There, for sixteen years Jose Canepa denied himself most of the pleasures of life as he continued his thrifty existence, always saving as much as possible. His efforts were sufficient for him, at age thirty, to leave his employment and purchase 450 hectares of undeveloped land in the Sagrada Familia area. He called his estate Peteroa, which means roaring volcano, because of the unusual rumbling noises that came from underground. He then hired a small team of men to clear the land and plant many of the noble vines he had known in his youth in Italy. Ten years later he exported his first wines, and today Vina Canepa is shipped to more than thirty countries, where its Sauvignon Blanc, Chardonnay and Cabernet Sauvignon offer excellent value.

3.   PRESIDENTS, ROYALS AND THE FAMOUS

This chapter should be preceded by the argument that persons of rank and wealth or fame and distinction do not automatically have any more concept of the quality, character and style of a drink than the average consumer, unless they have been fortunate enough to be informed and guided by first-class advice.

From the following information the reader may draw his own conclusions. All I will say is that in some instances the evidence has been gleaned personally by the author, while in others it has been supplied by close or regular contacts of the celebrity concerned.

QUEEN ELIZABETH II
Chateau Talbot, France

When dining privately the Queen has been known to be a fan of the Bordeaux fourth growth Chateau Talbot, from St Julien. Her choice may seem rather surprising in view of the fact that Talbot is named after the last British leader to lose a war against the French, when he was defeated in the Battle of Castillon. Prior to that, Great Britain owned the whole Bordeaux region.

BOB HOSKINS
Sancerre, France

Bob Hoskins, the pocket dynamo who literally burst onto the screen in *Who Framed Roger Rabbit?* and acquitted himself with pride in *Mona Lisa* and *Long Good Friday*, just to name a few examples, is an individual who takes particular care of his physique. This entails drinking dry white wine and has led, in Bob's case, to a fondness for Sauvignon Blanc. His regular preferences are for estate-bottle wines from Sancerre in France's Loire Valley.

PRESIDENT BILL CLINTON
Champagne Perrier-Jouët, France

Bill Clinton's tastebuds seem to be changing with his rise in status. When in Little Rock, Arkansas, he was a regular consumer of the Gallo-owned Carlo Rossi Paisano, which is an extremely cheap alternative to Chianti. He purchased this wine in gallon screw-cap jugs and often drank it as an accompaniment to his favourite pizza.

When Clinton was elected President, a dramatic and understandable change occurred, ostensibly to suit the need for celebration, and the flower-bottled Perrier-Jouët Champagne succeeded as the Clinton tipple.

JOHN MAJOR
Carrington, Australia

Being a man of relatively moderate means, John Major has had to cut his cloth accordingly and this presumably precludes regular consumption of Champagne in private, although he does get spoiled on a number of public occasions.

Despite that, Mr Major does have an appreciation of bubbly and when watching cricket, a favourite leisure pursuit, he has been overheard requesting Carrington, the popular Australian sparkling wine.

RONALD REAGAN
Chateau Montelana, USA

As Governor of California, Ronald Reagan did much to support the Californian wine industry. When he was elected to the White House his loyalty remained unchanged and it is possible to meet a host of Californian producers who can truthfully state that their wine was served at the White House during the Reagan administration.

The evidence of his personal choice comes from the Waldorf Astoria in New York. Whenever in residence there he would order a bottle of Chateau Montelena Napa Valley Chardonnay. When the source of this information was asked for verification the reply was: "I deliver it personally and only Nancy is in the apartment at the same time and the bottle is always empty in the morning and I'm sure she doesn't drink it all!"

TOM CRUISE
Chateau Haut Brion, France

Tom Cruise, star of *Rain Man*, *Top Gun* and *Far and Away*, has a penchant for mature first-growth Bordeaux. His premier love is believed to be the supreme Chateau Haut Brion; early in 1994 he was reputedly drinking the highly acclaimed 1961 vintage. As one who played an Irishman in *Far and Away* he will surely have been told the old unproven tale that the chateau was originally founded by a man called O'Brien.

RICHARD NIXON
Schramsberg, USA

The late Richard Nixon attracted considerable attention to the high-priced Napa sparkling wine Schramsberg, when he took a case as a present on his memorable first visit to the Chinese leaders, which may be why he still retains such respect in that country.

BARONESS THATCHER
J & B, Scotland

Mrs Thatcher, when prime minister, was on record as saying that she drank J & B Rare Scotch Whisky and amusingly referred to taking a glass on Tuesdays and Thursdays, after her notorious Prime Minister's Question Time sessions when (metaphorically speaking) she ate her victims alive.

PRINCE CHARLES
Sandeman and Domecq Sherries, Sterling Reserve Wine and Royal Welsh Whisky; England, Spain, USA and Wales

The writer has been present on two occasions when the prince has chosen sherry. On the first occasion he chose the medium-dry Sandeman Character Sherry and on the second Domecq La Ina Fino Sherry. Among other treasures in his private cellar, Prince Charles has a jeroboam of Sterling Reserve from Napa Valley and the only known surviving bottles of Royal Welsh Whisky, produced during the last century. All evidence implies that His Royal Highness does not consume the copious volumes some of his ancestors were reputed to imbibe.

MIKHAIL GORBACHEV
Champagne Louis Roederer, France

In 1985, André Rouzaud, a retired director of Champagne Louis Roederer, told me of a surprise visit he had received one Sunday morning in 1976. It was when he was residing in the Roederer mansion, adjacent to the cellars. He described a phone call from the concierge next door, who said that an important Russian delegation had arrived unexpectedly and asked if they could visit the cellars. "Please can you speak to them?" the concierge requested. As André did not have any commitments that morning, he put on his jacket and went to greet them. The leader of the group, he remarked, was "a dark-suited Agricultural Deputy called Gorbachev who wanted to learn about the Champagne of the Tsars!"

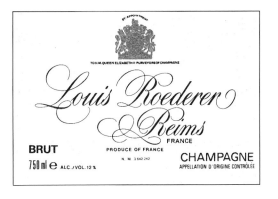

GUISEPPE VERDI
Chianti and Campari, Italy

The great operatic composer is mentioned elsewhere in this book as a patron of the original Campari bar in Milan. Verdi also had a love of Chianti, which he usually ordered from Ruffino.

KEN HOM
Chassagne-Montrachet, France

Many wine merchants recommend the charming dry white wines of Alsace, especially the spicy Gewürztraminer variety, to accompany Chinese cuisine. But leading oriental chef Ken Hom has other ideas when at home. He has a partiality for white Chassagne-Montrachet, which may well match with either European or Eastern dishes.

CLIFF RICHARD
Hardy's, Australia

The English pop singer, whose success has spanned five decades, is famed for his Christianity and temperate living, but apparently Cliff once displayed more than a passing interest in Australian wine, which he discovered on a trip down-under. While staying in Adelaide, he went on a visit to Hardy's wine cellars in McLaren Vale, where he showed a serious interest in the background and production of the various wines and a predilection for some of Hardy's sparkling wines.

NAPOLEON BONAPARTE
Madeira, Chambertin and Courvoisier;
Madeira and France

The ambitious French emperor had a fine and catholic palate. He was known to love the classic Red Burgundies of Le Chambertin, at a time when they were somewhat more moderately priced. Additionally, he enjoyed sherry and Madeira. There is a tragic story of HMS *Northumberland* anchoring off the island of Madeira on its way to Saint Helena with the diminutive Corsican on board. The British ship called there in August 1815, when Napoleon, who was still being treated in many ways as general, asked if he could purchase a pipe of Madeira to take to his exile. The 1792 vintage was selected and the cask stowed on board ship. Sadly for Napoleon he was never to partake of a single drop of the fortified wine due to instructions from his doctor on account of a stomach disorder.

The author sipping an 1883 Blandy's Bual Madeira with Richard Blandy at Reid's Hotel, Funchal, Madeira, 100 years after the vintage

Perhaps ironically, the pipe was later purchased by Blandy's, one of the best-known Madeira producers, and used as a base for a 1792 Solera. Courvoisier's claim can be justified elsewhere in this book.

ANDREW RIDGLEY
Puligney-Montrachet, France

Andrew Ridgley, who hit the heights in the 1980s in the pop group Wham, is a gentleman of some substance who loves to share fine White Burgundy with his friends. Though in London his favourite Puligny-Montrachet is readily available, supplied by leading Burgundy houses, he prefers to scour the capital's leading fine-wine retailers seeking estate-bottled examples, which are in much shorter supply. Late in 1993 his preference was for the 1989 vintage.

KATE BUSH
Champagne H. Billiot, France

Kate Bush, that sonorous siren who also electrified audiences during the 1980s, enjoys a glass or two of Champagne, often a popular drink with those who prefer something light and refreshing on the vocal cords. Her prime selection shows that either she has carried out her own research or has received some specialist advice, because her favourite is the little-known but especially agreeable house of H. Billiot.

DOCTOR SAMUEL JOHNSON
Port

Reports of that eminent man of letters and serious gourmand consuming one and a half bottles of port with his dinner at night are not quite what they might appear at first sight. In 1755, when his dictionary was published, port in London was a completely unfortified wine and it was to be another thirty-six years before George Sandeman shipped the first real vintage port. Dr Johnson's wine was a middleweight red, similar to the Alto Duoro of today, and the bottles were imperial pints somewhat smaller than the current size. Notwithstanding that explanation, he could be described as a portly gentleman who preferred to wake at a comfortable hour.

JANIS JOPLIN
Tequila, Mexico

When Janis Joplin, the American female vocalist with the resonant voice, visited London in 1970, an advance message to her London publicist gave instructions for her then favourite Tennessee sour mash, Jack Daniel's, to be made available. Today it is readily found in most London bars, but in 1970 her London agent searched the capital in vain and made innumerable fruitless enquiries before he finally traced a lone bottle, which he rapidly seized and placed in the star's dressing-room. To his dismay, upon her arrival he learned that her tastes had changed; her current favourite was Mexican tequila and she had brought her own supply.

THE FAB FOUR
Southern Comfort, USA

When the Beatles rocketed onto the scene they were young men who until that moment had survived upon relatively modest incomes and had not experienced the Champagne-and-caviar junkets of celebrity life. They enjoyed one drink regularly, which was popular with them all, and was called a Beat Special. It was simply Southern Comfort served long with Seven-Up and ice.

SIR ROBERT MENZIES
Yalumba Claret, Australia

Few leading politicians can have commanded more respect, both internationally and in the domestic arena, than the late Sir Robert Menzies. He served

Australia for a total of nineteen years as prime minister, between 1939 and 1966, and secured a stability that a significant proportion of the public would like to see restored. Uncharacteristically for a politician, he was prepared to climb down off the fence on numerous issues, including (to the delight of the Smith family of Yalumba fame) wine.

In 1965, then still prime minister, he was the principal guest at the Stock Exchange Club Dinner at Adelaide's celebrated South Australia Hotel. As the meal was drawing to a close he pronounced the 1961 Yalumba Galway Vintage Reserve Claret "the finest Australian red he had tasted". This declaration resulted in the appropriate section of Coonawarra Vineyard being renamed the Menzies Block, and it yields the finest grapes for the delightful Cabernet that now carries the great man's name.

CRYSTAL GAYLE
Champagne Louis Roederer, France

A 1990 appearance on a "Crook and Chase" television talk show in Nashville, Tennessee, found me sharing a glass in the green room with singer Crystal Gayle. She had been promoting her local speciality glass store, called Crystals, and expressed

Yalumba Winery at Angaston in the Barossa Valley, South Australia

a lively interest in Champagne. Naturally I wished to determine which was her favourite. "Oh, it has to be Cristal for me," she responded, identifying the Louis Roederer prestige cuvée.

She looked more than a little surprised when I explained that Cristal, the so-called Champagne of the Tsars, was not originally created by the Louis Roederer house but had been produced by Théophile Roederer, which in spite of its name was a small and unrelated concern. Later the Théophile Roederer house had been acquired by a descendant of Louis Roederer and the blend Cristal had been transferred to the larger house's name.

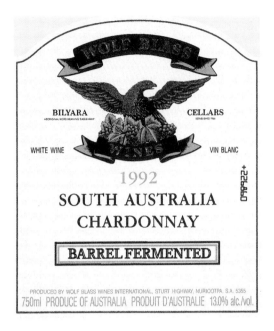

RONNIE CORBETT
Chateau Léoville Barton, France

That funny little man of English comedy, Ronnie Corbett, who retains his youth while the rest of us fade and wrinkle, is another man for Red Bordeaux, or as the British have traditionally called it, Claret. At the time of writing he was just beginning to drink his 1982 Chateau Léoville Barton, the second-growth Saint-Julien, a wise choice, as for me it was one of the few Bordeaux Grand Cru Classé wines from that wonderful vintage that had yet risen from its slumbers in 1993.

SARAH FERGUSON
Macon, France

There is a confidential tale of the lively Duchess of York and her love of wine that even this writer will not tell. On the other hand, her appreciation of French White Burgundy is known to a few. For some years, as Her Royal Highness, she partook of Meursault, but since her change in family fortune Macon-Villages has been proving a most agreeable replacement.

PAUL KEATING
Wolf Blass, Australia

The controversial Australian prime minister has endured rough press from the tabloids but that does not cast any shadow of doubt on his patriotism. In wine terms he is known to insist upon drinking Australian wines at all times and is especially fond of Chardonnay. He is reported to have two mid-priced favourites, Roxborough and Wolf Blass. He had a specific preference for the 1987 vintage of the latter, while it was available.

MICHAEL CAINE
Penfolds, Australia

Film star Michael Caine is also well-known in London as a partner in two restaurants, Langan's Brasserie and The Canteen at Chelsea Harbour. At the latter it is not unusual for friends who are shown behind the scenes to find him enjoying his favourite Australian oak-aged Cabernet Sauvignon, which is Penfold's Bin 707.

THE DUKE OF WELLINGTON
Garvey's San Patricio, Spain

The title of this story refers not to the illustrious conqueror of Napoleon at Waterloo, but to his successor, the current duke. He is, by all accounts, a gentleman with an outstanding palate, who has a penchant for the driest fino sherries. Obviously he is not a man to be swayed by self-importance, as although he is aware of the excellent fino called the Duke of Wellington and sold by Bodegas Internacionales, his preference comes from elsewhere. The duke orders from their friendly rival, the House of Garvey, their elegant fino San Patricio.

4.   PERSONAL TALES

THE BOUVET TREASURE
Bouvet-Ladubay, France

In the course of everyday life, one encounters people who prefer to avoid the decision-making. In other words, they prefer to sit on the fence. In this story there can be no fence-sitting for the readers, as they must serve on the jury and decide the truth for themselves.

In 1982, Patrice Monmousseau, the president of Bouvet-Ladubay, a small but popular house known for its sparkling Saumur Brut, was kind enough to grant me an afternoon's unrestricted access to their quaint old archive room in their cellar offices, situated in the riverside village of Saint Hilaire Saint Florent. There, in the most fertile part of France's majestic Loire Valley, he invited me, as is the local custom, to make myself at home. Patrice made it quite clear that I was free to search through their old records and lamented that he was always too preoccupied to apply himself to the task. He would, he intimated, be most interested if I found anything curious.

With that he departed and I began my exploration of one of the most unusual rooms I had ever seen. It must have measured a little less than 20 feet by 30, and the walls were completely lined with small wooden drawers. Turning around slowly, I made

a rough mental calculation that there must have been at least 4 000 of them, the vast majority of which were numbered. Numerous boxes and small cupboards – and pile upon pile of papers – lay on the floor in disarray. At random, which is as good a way as any to start under such circumstances, I tugged at one of the wooden drawers, which slid open quietly to reveal several hundred labels for the 1914 vintage, all in pristine condition. A second drawer yielded more old labels and a third a collection of cork brands, which would have been used for marking the individual vintage or name of a wine. Suddenly, and quite by chance, as is so often the case when rummaging through a dusty room, something caught the corner of my eye. It was a plain wooden cupboard, not particularly distinctive or ancient in appearance, but it gave the impression of being recently in use. Something, maybe instinct, prompted me to examine its contents. I pulled open the door and began to sift through the objects inside. Fairly quickly my hand lighted upon a small bundle of papers, which I withdrew for inspection. It revealed a letter in longhand, with some further sheets attached, which were in an older script.

The letter was from a Madame Douet. Parts of it were difficult to translate but I could feel the first tremors of excitement as I began to understand the writer's gist. She had sent the letter to Bouvet-Ladubay wondering if they would be interested to see the writings of her late uncle, who had worked for the house during a particularly fortuitous time in the last century. The realisation dawned that if the pages in front of me were accurate then I would be able to settle a ninety-year-old legend that had in the past divided the local inhabitants. Furthermore I would be able to provide the correct version of the dramatic rise to success enjoyed by Bouvet-Ladubay in the late 19th century. Like an excited boy who has just caught a lively fish, I clutched the

B*ouvet-Ladubay caves, 1898;
Saint Hilaire Saint Florent,
France*

by quarrying the soft white tuffeau limestone out of the hillside, and had lived and worshipped there for seven centuries before being forced to flee at the time of the French Revolution in 1789. When they departed in great haste, they were reputed to have left all their treasure hidden somewhere in the immediate vicinity. Her husband, Etienne Bouvet, had acquired the very cellars that once belonged to the monks and which looked like a complicated maze of chalky tunnels. She, it has often been suggested, had schemes for searching for what was believed to be a vast hoard of jewels.

Later, in the 1880s, the house of Bouvet-Ladubay appeared to experience a golden era. A costly and spacious new family home was constructed and no expense was spared on improving the company offices. Holidays were spent in the fashionable resorts of Europe and some of the Bouvet sons were even sent to be educated in England.

Rumours began to circulate that the family had discovered the treasure of Saint Hilaire Saint Florent, rumours which then escalated rapidly until gold fever hit the village and the nearby town of Saumur. Soon trouble broke out as hundreds of people disputed each other's right to dig day and night in their search for that elusive wealth. In *La Petite Loire* of Sunday, 6 March 1892, a journalist called Manoury reported at length on a public investigation into the upheaval: "According to some they had dug out gold coins, then ten gold crosses weighing several kilos and even gold statues of St Hilaire and St Florent." The main problem lay in the fact that entire families were being ruined as, seized by fanaticism, they devoted all their means to hunting for the hidden treasure. Worse still, dubious characters, parasitic by nature, were making petty fortunes by acting as clairvoyants, advising the desperate where they should dig and leading them into further despair. Witnesses even suggested that the treasure had been smuggled to England, disguised as cases of wine, and that the Dover customs had been bribed not to ask any questions.

Yet during this frantic period the Bouvet-Ladubay lips remained sealed while, it was alleged, their prosperity increased.

Madame Douet explained to me that her great-uncle Victor Lines had been a cellarman at Bouvet, where he spent much of his time bottling their wine. (She remembered him very well. He had been about eighty-three when he died just a year or so before the war.) For many years he had lived in fairly basic workmen's quarters on the premises which Bouvet provided, but then quite unexpectedly he had been given a substantial house in the village square and promoted to the position of chief foreman. Everyone had remarked that for

papers and asked to see Patrice Monmousseau again. Ah yes, he recalled receiving the package some eleven years ago, but alas had always been too busy to give it any serious attention. Nevertheless I was welcome to take it and investigate matters.

Madame Douet had given an address that was simply the name of a house in the nearby town of Doué-la-Fontaine, best known to the French as *la Cité des Roses*. Whether she was still residing there I would soon learn. Finding out was not too onerous and a few hours' sleuthing brought me to her door. She occupied a small apartment in the outskirts of Doué-la-Fontaine, in quiet and contented retirement, and it was quite apparent that she was delighted to have a foreign visitor. We sat down and I unfurled the curling papers and asked if she could identify them. "*Mais oui,* Monsieur. It was me. I wrote that letter to *la Maison Bouvet.* I thought it might interest them." Then she began to reveal the enthralling background. She thought that as it was eleven years since she had written, all had been forgotten and the secret lost forever.

She informed me that there had been many rumours concerning Bouvet, and its early history had become part of local folklore. In fact, at a later date, I was able to verify much of her explanation from other archival research.

The sparkling-wine house had been founded by a small winemaker called Etienne Bouvet in 1851 and during the early years his business had progressed quietly. Then he had fallen for the attractions of a notorious local woman known as La Dubay. This colourful character had charmed her way into his life and become the small company's bookkeeper. After some time they married and she bore him several sons.

Madame Bouvet appeared to be intrigued by the history and legends surrounding the Benedictine monks after whom their village was remembered. The monks had built their abbey in the 11th century the duration of his fifty-year employment and for the remainder of his life he wore a permanent smile.

Victor Lines was, however, more than just a contented face. He took great delight in writing for his own pleasure and it is in this manner that his secret has come to light. In his humble French he wrote in rhyme an account of the discovery of the treasure. "I was there," he wrote, "when they found their pot of gold." They actually unearthed eight large yellow barrels. The first was full of rubies and topaz, the second contained an exquisitely made cross of St Florent with a mitre which shone like a basilica. The third was filled with emeralds and in the fourth they found the crown of St Agnes. The fifth revealed diamonds whose brilliance threw dark shadows and the sixth was overflowing with precious pearls. The seventh was an enormous barrel and appeared to be nailed to the ground, and resisted all their efforts to remove it for some time because it was more than 2 metres tall and full of solid gold, weighing more than 10 000 kilograms. The eighth cask was also a huge barrel and the contents were promised to Victor Lines. Alas, it was empty!

It was that empty barrel which caused Victor to feel a little resentful, and he admitted as much in his writings. He planned to reveal the Bouvet secret after his death and probably did not foresee that it would take almost a hundred years.

Shortly after Lines's death in 1939, in the course of cleaning out Victor's house in St Hilaire St Florent, Madame Elisabeth Douet, his great-niece, found several boxes full of old papers. She kept these until 1971, when she moved from a larger to a smaller house in Doué-la-Fontaine. Just in case they should reveal anything of importance, she sifted through the papers and to her great surprise came across an old sheet covered on both sides with verse describing how Victor was present when the treasure was discovered by the Bouvet family. In the same year, 1971, Madame Douet forwarded the paper to Bouvet-Ladubay, but as it was written in old rural French, much of it in slang, and the legibility was poor, it was put to one side in the old cupboard in the archive room.

And so, as there was no response, Madame Douet had thought that all had been forgotten and the secret would remain buried forever. But now I had appeared and she would be only too happy to answer my questions. Recalling her Great-Uncle Victor, she remembered how she would sit on his lap as a child and he would repeat the story to her: "They were all there, the Bouvet family, and also a few trusted workers including myself. We found the eight barrels but one was empty. It was astonishing; there were so many jewels, rubies, emeralds, topaz, diamonds and gold, so much gold with many great crosses and *pendules*." She assured me this was exactly what she had heard from his lips.

"Do you really believe it Madame? Could it possibly be true?"

"It is a lovely story, Monsieur, and my uncle Victor loved to tell stories and he did always have a smile on his face, but you must ask Bouvet-Ladubay if they can confirm it."

So I did. I asked Patrice Monmousseau. He paused and weighed his words carefully before responding, "I believe it is true but I cannot prove it, for no-one could identify the jewels today. Certainly the family became very rich in a short time, as has been described. I suppose in the past I have always said this was because they worked so hard with their wine, but now that you have found out the secret of Victor Lines, really I will have to think about admitting the truth, that the treasure was found in these cellars. Unfortunately it has long since gone, as the sons of the family gambled it away on the casino tables at Monte Carlo. I suppose, though, it is rather lovely to think that really every time anyone opens a bottle of Bouvet-Ladubay they will be drinking a little bit of treasure, so all is not lost."

I smiled my approval and walked through to the archive room. What else would I find? I looked around and a glint of light attracted my attention. Something was lying on the floor; it looked like a small gold coin. I leaned over to pick it up only to discover it was not gold but just a 20-centime piece.

Suddenly my ears pricked up. I thought I heard laughter. No-one was there yet I could still hear the laugh. A momentary shiver ran down my spine as the laugh came again. Turning in the direction from which it seemed to come I noticed an old picture on the wall; it was a photograph of Monsieur Lines, which had faded and become almost golden with age. It was strange; he appeared to have a smile on his face.

A FOOLISH QUESTION
Chateau Cheval Blanc, France

In 1981, while still a very inexperienced journalist, I visited Chateau Cheval Blanc, the famed Saint-Émilion Grand Cru Classé, which truly is one of the first great growths and one of the world's greatest red wines. There I interviewed Jacques Hebrard, the *régisseur*, or general manager, who is also part-owner of the property.

My task was to record an interview for my BBC Radio Wales series "A Case of Wine". It was in fact the very first occasion on which I had been allowed out alone with any recording equipment on such a mission.

Almost overawed by the surroundings and Monsieur Hebrard's imposing presence, I concluded my interview with a rather naive query. I call it naive because since then I have been asked the same question on numerous occasions.

"What," I enquired, "is the oldest wine you have ever tasted?"

Monsieur Hebrard looked down upon me imperiously as if he were going to reprimand an inexperienced cellar trainee for some foolish comment, but then a slight glint appeared in his eye and I knew he was going to let me off lightly.

"It was a few summers ago," he intoned in his rich Bordelaise accent. "I was on vacation with my old friend, Jacques Cousteau, near la Corse, when Jacques, he said to me, 'Come with me. I have something to show you. I have, if you like, a little private Roman wreck which I have not told people about yet and in it are some sealed amphorae of wine. I think we should pay a little visit.' So Jacques Cousteau and I set off in his boat and headed for the Roman wreck. A short while later we were diving into the sea and quickly found the old ship from which Jacques chose one amphora, which we hauled back to the surface. With a struggle we placed it on the deck and than Jacques told me to get some glasses while he found a hammer and chisel. To my amazement he broke the amphora open and filled the glasses with wine and we drank a little drop of Roman wine. You know it was rosé in colour and it was still wine. Minutes later it was gone; the air simply oxidised it."

"How old do you think the wine really was?" I asked even more innocently.

"I do not know," came the authoritative reply. "The vintage was not on the bottle!"

Henri-Louis Pernod

HARDLY ORDINAIRE
Pernod, France

In 1789, a year in which French royalists were fleeing for their lives, some 20 000 of them made their way towards the Valais, an area of Switzerland where French is still the popular language. Among their number was an elderly scientist of some standing, known as Dr Ordinaire. In his place of exile, called Couvet, he bought a comfortable house and settled down with his housekeeper to an enforced early retirement. However he was not content to be idle, and to keep his brain active he set himself the goal of creating a unique drink.

To this end he limited himself to the herbs, spices and plants which were available in the locality. Two key ingredients in his recipe were *vermud*, or wormwood bark (Latin *Artemisia absinthium*), and the roots of the large Star Anis plant, from which

aniseed is obtained, the latter growing profusely in Valais. His unusual and superbly made aperitif was in regular demand from fellow French exiles when they called at his home and was probably simply referred to as Dr Ordinaire's drink, or his *absinthe*, a French form of the Latin word.

A few years later the distinguished doctor died and in his will left his housekeeper both his secret recipe and a small legacy, enough to purchase a café from which she could sell the drink. The good lady was faithful to the doctor's wishes and began trading from a small café-bar, where she offered Dr Ordinaire's creation. Business continued quietly for some while until the arrival of two French gentlemen, who upon tasting the aperitif declared a serious interest in its production. This resulted in the sale of the little business together with the recipe. The older of the two gentlemen, a Major Henri Dubois, was the father-in-law of the other, Henri-Louis Pernod, and they were of a mind to produce the drink on a large scale. They soon attracted many followers, chiefly among the French émigrés but also from the local Swiss residents.

Some years later, when royalty was back in favour in France, they decided to produce the drink (now known as Pernod Absinthe) in their homeland, but found that the Star Anis plant was only to be found in the Jura region. There, in Doubs, near Pontarlier, they started a second cellar, but they maintained their Swiss operation in case any shortage of the natural ingredients should arise.

As the 19th century progressed, the bars and nightclubs of Paris proliferated and in their convivial atmosphere Pernod Absinthe became a regular

feature. In later years Toulouse-Lautrec captured the essence of the drink for posterity in his acclaimed work *The Absinthe Drinkers*. For some reason Pernod has always been a favourite of artists and writers. Guy de Maupassant, Edgar Allan Poe, Alfred de Musset, Verlaine and Baudelaire all referred to absinthe in their works, while André Malraux, Jules Romains, Louis Aragon, Albert Camus and several others mentioned Pernod by name. Charles Maire painted the bottle in a famous still life, and Pablo Picasso's 1912 work *The Glass and the Bottle* clearly shows Pernod, albeit in cubist form.

Catastrophe struck when a number of absinthe drinkers, known for their overindulgence, became ill with serious mental health problems. A government enquiry ensued, from which evidence emerged that the wormwood bark was poisonous to the human system. Use of the bark was banned immediately, but extensive testing revealed that the leaves and roots were completely harmless and would provide similar flavouring. It seems, however, that certain wholesalers were reluctant to destroy their stocks and discreetly arranged for their import into the friendly Louisiana port of New Orleans, where sales of the drink were still permissible. Current visitors to that city will be familiar with Jean Lafitte's Absinthe Bar, where the banned drink has not been available for some time.

Wild rumours have suggested that between 20 000 and 30 000 cases of Pernod Absinthe were shipped there at that time, and later, when the drink was also banned in the USA, it once again followed a hidden route and was stored for some years in a secret warehouse very close to the banks of the Mississippi. It emerged during Prohibition, when its owners found an ideal opportunity to smuggle it upriver and sell it to various anonymous buyers in Arkansas and Tennessee.

Even today, anyone who cares to sample the delicious fare at the Original Grisanti's Restaurant

Pernod bottle as seen by Picasso

or at the fine retail wine and spirit store known as Buster's in Memphis, will be able to see the legacy of those days. Displayed in glass cabinets are bottles of Pernod Absinthe, their authenticity clearly verified by the name of the second place of production on the labels, the town of Doubs in the Jura region.

At the time of the fateful discovery of the harmful effects of absinthe, the Pernod company behaved in a most honourable and positive manner. They straightaway adapted Dr Ordinaire's recipe to use just the leaves and roots, and went to great lengths to ensure that their new drink, Pernod Anis, was not just good but ideal for the system. Subsequently it developed into a symbol to many of the French way of life. To this author, as a young visitor to that picturesque country in the late 1950s, the sight of persons of all ages relaxing in café-bars sipping that mysterious milky fluid was one that epitomised Frenchness.

Many years later, when I was to have the privilege of interviewing Daniel Hemard, the *president-directeur-général* of the Pernod company, he related another unusual story concerning the drink. He explained that when the successors of Henri-Louis Pernod had decided that they wanted to move their business back to France, they encountered an unexpected hitch. They were challenged by another drink producer of the same name – Pernod. He was no relative of theirs but he was making an aperitif with totally different characteristics in Avignon, in the south of France. Legal proceedings to sue them were set in motion by the southern Pernod, but fortunately the lawyer involved in the case was astute enough to realise that here was the potential for a mutually beneficial business deal. He persuaded the two Pernod companies to join forces and form a new company, in which he would invest.

It was not long before the sales of the Swiss-founded Pernod were outstripping those of the southern aperitif and a decision was taken to continue with only the former. From that point the Pernod company went from strength to strength. The lawyer became the head of the organisation and everyone concerned prospered. His name was Hemard and he was the grandfather of Daniel Hemard. "And that Mr Jones," the Pernod chief explained, "was how I came to be sitting here!"

A HUMBLE LITTLE WINE
Chateau Raymond-Lafon, France

In 1850, Monsieur Raymond Lafon, a former mayor of Bordeaux, purchased for himself a small estate in the Sauternes region, where life would be a little more peaceful than on the Chartrons, the famous quay-side of Bordeaux. Here he built a charming and comfortable three-storey house, and also some cellars, beside the narrow road that runs just north of the home of the world's most illustrious sweet white wine, Chateau d'Yquem. Following the fashion of the day the mayor named his new home Chateau Raymond-Lafon after himself.

When the 1855 classification was made, the vines of Chateau Raymond-Lafon were far too young and the wines too light to merit consideration but still Monsieur Lafon persevered and made good, if unexciting wines. The chateau remained in the family for a generation after Lafon's death and in this century changed hands twice without any noteworthy occurrences. That was until 1972, when it was purchased in "fairly run-down condition" by Pierre and Francine Meslier. It was to be one of the shrewdest and soundest purchases ever made in the Bordeaux region.

For nine years Pierre Meslier had been the manager at Chateau d'Yquem, where viticulture and vinification are practised as both art and science, so much so that the legend had developed that a single vine produces just one glass of d'Yquem. However in this case the legend is fact. The Meslier family, which is among the most charming in the region, realised that much taxing work lay ahead of it at Chateau Raymond-Lafon, but believed that with time, dedication and painstaking discipline it could produce world-class wine and even perhaps rival d'Yquem. The Mesliers still quite emphatically maintain that there is only one d'Yquem, but when you meet one of the family you gain the impression that they have secretly dedicated themselves to matching and even challenging the finest.

In England, always a keen market for the finest Sauternes, the improving qualities of the succeeding Raymond-Lafon vintages were generally overlooked. Very few experts and wine writers appeared to be aware of the rise of the almost forgotten chateau and, by and large, omitted to highlight it in their publications. By contrast, less inhibited wine journalists in the United States, always seeking enterprising selections, began to discover the emerging star. Gradually, occasional whispers came to the ears of consumers and nowadays the demand for this truly great Sauternes has risen to such a degree that many now consider it second only to Chateau d'Yquem.

It has been a remarkable rise for Raymond-Lafon. Certainly it cannot be classed as a restoration or a rebirth because the potential had always been there. It is, rather, a demonstration of the ability of a person to recognise that untapped potential and, by implementing strict discipline and working with assiduous care and attention, realise it. Working on a vineyard that was only $3\frac{1}{2}$ hectares in 1972, with vines averaging twenty-five years of age, the Mesliers have purchased neighbouring plots of considerable potential and now possess 20 hectares with vines averaging forty years of age. It is an ongoing process of reinvestment. As at d'Yquem, the Mesliers produce just one glass of wine per vine, treat their vines and wines in a meticulous manner, and pick as many as ten or eleven times in the finest vintages, often leaving the last grapes until December. Thirty-five pickers harvest the grapes by hand and the quantity is never more than three barrels in a single day.

As yet, we do not know what results the most mature Chateau Raymond-Lafon will achieve, as it will take decades for them to glide to perfection. The chateau still does not have a sufficient track record to throw light on the eventual results but it is significant that at last d'Yquem has a true rival. If the old mayor could see the state of affairs today he would surely wish that he had employed equally rigorous measures and that he had purchased the property twenty years earlier, for surely it would then have been classified at the highest level. In the meantime it remains a peaceful little chateau on a narrow road, where a warm and friendly family makes a humble little wine.

MORE THAN MEETS THE EYE!
Hastings English Wine and Castell Coch;
UK including Wales

For most international travellers and particularly for wine lovers, English wine, as a term, is something of an enigma. To be quite accurate one should talk of English and Welsh wine and certainly, if one is a devoted follower of the grape, never use the epithet "British". British wine is a term used to describe a commercial product that is generally held to be a trifle inferior and not a libation worthy of pouring for an honoured guest. It is often the product of the reactivation of partly fermented grape must, imported from dubious sources in Mediterranean or North African territory. The must is shipped in giant tanks to commercial harbours in Britain, where it undergoes the final stages in its manufacture.

Having dealt with that easily mistaken substance, we should examine the history of English and Welsh wine, which has always been one of constant struggle against the elements of a cold, damp and inhospitable climate and terrain.

The Romans apparently planted the first vineyards in an England with a slightly warmer climate than today, though historians find their cultivation a difficult matter to prove. Adhering to their usual practice, the Romans planted vineyards wherever they settled, and in my opinion the evidence that they planted them in England is borne out by archeological photography of Roman sites, which appears to reveal former terraced vineyards. Also, in Wrotham in Kent, a vine was discovered in the 1960s which was given the name of the Wrotham Pinot, but it has since been traced to an original Roman variety. On the other hand, it appears that the Romans were unable to provide sufficient volume of wine in Britannia, as there is clear evidence of its importation from other parts of their vast empire.

With the withdrawal of the occupying Romans the production of wine in the British Isles dwindled, although it would not be unreasonable to assume that the Church owned some vineyards in their early abbeys and monasteries, as was the pattern in France. Indeed the first true English historian, the Venerable Bede, himself a monk, referred in 730 to "vines in places" in Britain.

The Normans took quite an interest in wine and it is not surprising that le Roi Guillaume, better known as King William the Conqueror, chose one specific spot on the Sussex coast for his 1066 invasion. Despite millions of school textbooks referring to the encounter in which the brave English King Harold was killed by an arrow in the eye at the Battle of Hastings, the actual confrontation occurred at Pevensey Bay, at a location subsequently known as Battle. Indeed, the position may well have been selected carefully with the anticipation of victory celebration, for as Lombardi later recorded: "There was at about that time a great store of wine at Battle." A "store" indicated a depot for wines which were shipped from the French mainland for distribution in that region of England.

Castell Coch, Tongwynlais, Wales, circa 1900

A 19th-century label for a Castell Coch wine

History suggests that as the Normans brought their civilisation to England and Wales they also encouraged the spread of the vine. The monasteries were at the forefront of this wave of new plantings, as they required wine for three purposes: first, for sacramental needs; second, as an aid to digestion; and third, so that any surplus might be sold to augment their living. It was an approach that has since been repeated throughout the New World. It is notable that the first written records of a Norman vineyard are found in the works of the mid-12th century monk, Geraldis Cambrensis, who wrote of a vineyard at his father's castle at Manorbier, in West Wales.

Some 250 years later, the great Welsh revolutionary leader Owain Glyndwr, a staunch European both in politics and gastronomy, furnished his rather splendid table, at his border castle of Sycarth, with wine from the adjoining vineyards.

Down the centuries the interest in vines was generally maintained only by the owners of a few large estates and by the monasteries. With the dissolution of the latter under Henry VIII in 1536, the monastic vineyards lapsed into ruin. Gradually the cultivation of vines faded away, even among the wealthiest classes, one exception being noted in a brief record of the Duke of Norfolk having planted a new vineyard at Arundel in 1763.

Just over a century later the 3rd Marquis of Bute

attempted to initiate a modern vineyard revival in Britain in a somewhat unorthodox manner. Once again the chosen site was in Wales. The marquis owned extensive property, almost on a Vanderbilt scale, around the future Welsh capital city of Cardiff, which from the latter part of the last century through to the 1930s was the busiest coal-exporting port in the world, and from which the Scottish landowner derived most of his wealth, either directly or indirectly.

The marquis had discovered on his land near Tongwynlais an 11th-century ruined tower known as Castell Coch, or the Red Castle. It stood some 6 miles north of his imposing Norman residence, Cardiff Castle, and he planned to restore the tower as a hunting lodge, using the notable skills of the architect John Burges. The marquis issued instructions that the tower and its surroundings be developed in the style of a Rhineland *Schloß*. Fortunately Castell Coch had a panoramic view directly over the River Taff, and the marquis dreamed of having a thriving vineyard on the slopes below the castle leading down to the river which had helped to earn him so much of his fortune.

In his youth the marquis had completed the Grand Tour of Europe and truly appreciated the beauty of the Rhine vineyard regions. In his enthusiasm he began telling his friends and associates of his new project before he had done any research. In 1875 he sent his handsome young garden manager, Andrew Pettigrew, to France, with instructions to learn everything that was necessary about growing vines and making wine. The landowner could hardly contain his excitement and soon his ambitious scheme was a topic of gossip and amusement in the London clubs which he frequented. *Punch*, the satirical publication, poured scorn upon his efforts, stating: "If the wine is ever made, it will take four to drink it, two to hold the victim down and one to pour it down his throat!" In viticultural terms the marquis was undeniably naive. The French trip he organised for Andrew Pettigrew gave his manager little chance of producing the desired results. With various letters of introduction in his possession, and no doubt feeling apprehensive, the inexperienced man set off for the Champagne region, where he passed one day at Jacquesson. He later reported them as being the largest of all Champagne producers, when they were nothing other than a good small house. Some weeks later he travelled to Bordeaux, where his itinerary again allowed little time for serious study, even when visiting some of the most elite chateaux. He spent one day at Chateau Latour, the next at the neighbouring Chateau Lafitte and a third at Chateau Margaux. In between that time, he enjoyed several weeks in the vineyards of Paris, which in fairness were rather more extensive than today, when they are virtually nonexistent, but where his attention seemed slightly disproportionate. In the light of the knowledge that Andrew Pettigrew was an attractive, strongly built, well-groomed young man, perhaps Paris offered one or two temptations more worthy of his attention, for clearly he did not give much thought to careful selection of the vines he took back to Castell Coch.

It was evident that the site was near the northernmost limits for successful vine cultivation, which implied the need for white grapes. Yet he planted two-thirds of the new vineyard with the red Gamay variety, famous nowadays for the wines of the Beaujolais region. The remaining third he planted with the unfashionable white Mille Blanche variety. The choice of red wine grapes verged on the ludicrous and they seldom ripened beyond a stage sufficient for anything other than to feed the birds and satisfy the curiosity of the local youngsters, who clambered over the fence to taste the tempting fruit and found them so bitter they did not repeat the exercise. In fairness to the marquis and Mr Pettigrew, they did have one bumper harvest in 1893, when 12 000 bottles were produced, but much scrutiny of papers in Cardiff has failed to bring to light any recorded compliments.

Without proving his case, the marquis went on to plant two further vineyards in the same county, Glamorgan; one at Cowbridge, which, owing to its damp and exposed situation, never yielded a single grape; and another near Sully, which was soon grubbed out to make room for an orchard. By the outbreak of World War I, wine production at Castell Coch has ceased and in 1920 the site was returned to pasture. The Castell Coch planting had indeed proved to be a folly.

It was not until the 1960s that the latest revival of viticulture in England and Wales began and it has progressed at such a steady rate that today there are said to be more than 400 active vineyards. The best conditions for them may prove to be in Sussex and Kent, where the white chalk is virtually the same as in the Champagne region of France. Also, climatic conditions in Sussex and Kent are more favourable for grape growing.

Ironically, Hastings, which is identified with the arrival of William the Conqueror more than 900 years ago, is now one of the labels of the Carr Taylor vineyards's white wines.

THIRSTY SOLDIERS
Chateau Musar, Lebanon

"Andrew! Andrew!" an excited voice called out across the floor of Marks and Spencer's Oxford Street store in London's West End.

"How wonderful to see you," and an old friend of some eleven years standing strode swiftly towards me. "Goodness me, it is so long!"

It was one of those moments of great delight, an emotion I certainly felt at that moment. I had, in fact, only met the man once before, but it had been one of those occasions when two people discover a true sympathy for each other's interests. That first meeting had taken place at the World Wine Fair at Bristol in 1981. There I had found Serge Hochar, a young lion of a man, alive with ambition and ready to conquer the world. His delightful Chateau Musar had received some formidable reviews and was the focus of some hectic attention. Journalists and experts alike were astounded to learn Lebanon could provide a wine of such style and character.

I had arranged to record an interview with Serge at the BBC studios in Tyndalls Park Road, Bristol, where fortunately I am still a regular guest. It seemed that we breathed the same vinous air, drank the same vinous blood and shared the same basic enthusiasm for the subject that is our life. He was there as a prosperous wine producer and I as an impecunious wine journalist, but neither role mattered for we believed in our mutual subject and the delight it can bring to those who share its delicacies.

Now, in 1992, we met again at the launch of Marks and Spencer's Winemakers of the World Range. We had corresponded on a couple of matters in the years in between and I had written one or two minor articles about his wine, but now he had a new story to tell me, because his Chateau Musar had been through a situation unparalleled by any other well-known winery.

Located in Lebanon's infamous Bekaa Valley, Chateau Musar had been surrounded by the ravages

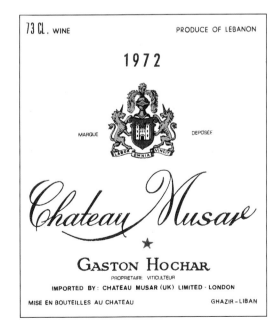

and horrors of war, had lost two entire vintages and had often found its access routes completely blocked. In fact, fighting had even strafed the vineyards but Serge was undismayed. Peace had been restored and here he was as lively as ever, full of passion for his wine and zest for living. Many celebrated names were at the launch of the new wine range that day, but one name was uppermost in my mind when I returned home that night and it set me searching for old notes on the Chateau Musar story.

I had put my notes in a safe place, certain in the knowledge that some day I would find them of great interest. When I opened the file I realised just how much I had forgotten in the time which had elapsed since our first meeting more than ten years ago.

Shortly before the 1981 World Wine Fair, I had been working on the BBC Radio Wales series "A Case of Wine", with my producer Gareth Rowlands and a tasting team that included the veteran broadcaster Wynford Vaughan-Thomas, best remembered as a war correspondent, in particular for his historic live report from an RAF bomber during action over the Rhine. Some may remember him as one of the most knowledgeable fine-wine tasters of his generation.

Others involved in the series included hard-nosed newsman Vincent Kane and genial former master *sommelier* (wine waiter) of Le Gavroche restaurant, John Jackson. We had taken over the entertainment centre at the BBC Wales headquarters in Llandaff for a weekend of tastings, during which we intended assessing forty-eight bottles of wine to cover twelve programs.

I was aware that Wynford was a member of the distinguished Saintsbury Club, a Chevalier du Tastevin and a member of various other elite wine organisations, but suspected that his experience was largely confined to traditional classic French wines and port, rather than the New World varieties. I was determined to present at least a couple of wines that were unknown to him and to that end I persuaded Gareth that New World meant anywhere outside Western Europe and promised to spring a surprise. I scoured the Loire and found a wine that I hoped would be too obscure for Wynford but my plan was to founder and he put me in my place with his gentle charm.

On the Saturday morning, we tasted four Loire wines priced at no more than £3, including a little-known and rarely seen dry white called Reuilly.

"Ho, ho, Andrew, now you're not going to fool me with this delightful little wine. There are only about ten or eleven producers of note. The wine can be white from the Sauvignon Blanc, rosé from the Pinot Gris or red from the Pinot Noir, but very little is seen of the latter."

I was taken aback and enquired, "However did you know all that Wynford?"

"Ah, perhaps you would be surprised to know that in 1964 I was intronised into their *confrérie*. I remember it well; the ceremony was held at the Mairie …" and he was off on one of the thousands of colourful reminiscences that he seemed able to conjure up in an instant. The experience left me with added respect for his knowledge and similarly increased determination to score the next day.

If I remember correctly it was a fine sunny morning when we assembled on the Sunday. "Good morning, Wynford. I think I've brought something to sort you out at last," I overconfidently predicted.

"We'll see about that; you'll have to try me," came his half-chuckled reply.

I proceeded to identify to the panel each wine to be tasted and when I reached number three I was sure the wine would stump him. "And this," I proudly announced, "is the one to put Wynford in his place – Chateau Musar from the Lebanon, from the 1972 vintage."

A wicked grin broke out across his face and I knew I had lost before he uttered a word.

"Chateau Musar, Andrew. Well, if you had intended picking one of those wonderful wines from the Lebanon you should have picked one where I haven't stayed. It was in 1933 that I spent a fortnight with Gaston Hochar there. Now Chateau Musar, that is a remarkable story." And he began to relate his experience and unveiled the colourful tale of how and why this extraordinary vineyard came to be planted.

This conversation took place just a matter of weeks before the 1981 World Wine Fair and my first meeting with Serge Hochar, son of Gaston, who built the original chateau. Serge, who was running the chateau with his brother, Roald, listened intently as I repeated the story Wynford had told us. Since then Serge has tried to verify the tale, which, after such a long lapse in time, is not always easy, but he did confirm to me that he was convinced the gist of the story was correct.

Wynford was working in Lebanon as a correspondent at a time when the French were governing the country under a mandate from the former League of Nations. Even at the age of twenty-four he claimed to have an unusually fine palate that had been spoilt on Lafite, Latour, Le Chambertin, Chateau d'Yquem and similar vinous giants. One day in Beirut, after drinking the most atrociously rough plonk, he complained to a French officer with whom he was dining that he was desperate for a glass of really good French wine. The officer admitted that he could not agree more with him and it was an opinion shared by the entire French

Army in Lebanon, but, he insisted, they had done something about it. The soldiers had complained so much that their officers had become seriously concerned lest morale should suffer, and accordingly the matter was reported to Paris, directly to the minister responsible. The minister, an enlightened man, who recognised that wine was a daily essential to digestion, took immediate action. An advertisement was placed in a Bordeaux newspaper, offering financial assistance by way of a grant to a suitable wine grower who was prepared to set up vineyards of the highest quality in Lebanon. What was more, the successful applicant would be guaranteed his choice of the finest positions for his vineyard and whatever help was required in importing the necessary noble varieties from France.

It was a most appealing offer, especially if one was attracted to Lebanon, where the climate was said to be virtual perfection. One Bordelaise, whose family had been deeply involved in the wine trade for many generations, had a Lebanese friend who visited Bordeaux from time to time in connection with his financial business. When the Lebanese man next arrived he told the Bordelaise about the advertisement; the traveller was Gaston Hochar. The year was 1930 and Gaston was feeling rather bored with his profession; suddenly, in this strange manner, a wonderful opportunity stood in front of him. But first he would have to convince the authorities that it was not necessary to import a French grower and that he would be completely capable of such an undertaking.

Gaston was very friendly with Ronald Barton, who lived at the famous Chateau Langoa in St Julien, and from him Gaston received much sound advice. On the strength of this and other support, he returned to Lebanon to seek out the ideal site and prepare his application. In the little village of Ghazir, 16 miles north of Beirut, he found an ideal building with fine cellars. It was a castle that had been built in the 18th century for domestic purposes. At the beginning of the 19th century it had been owned by Prince Beshire Chebab, then Prince of Lebanon. Later the Chebab family sold it to an uncle of Gaston's, who now wished to dispose of it. Gaston realised immediately that it would suit his threefold purpose: as a home, as wine cellars, and as a base for his future wine business. The only problem was that the surrounding land was not suitable for the cultivation of vines. To overcome this he scoured the country for many miles around until he found land that he believed would offer great potential, in the Bekaa Valley, to the east of Ghazir. There, later in that same year, after concluding all the arrangements, he planted his first batch of French noble vines at around 3 000 feet. These were providing grapes for their first wine

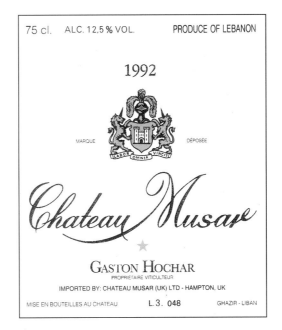

when Wynford Vaughan Thomas visited the property in 1933, with a letter of introduction in his hand from the senior French Army officer responsible for the negotiations.

The officer had explained that at that time, France had some 40 000 soldiers in Lebanon, whom he said comprised a rather thirsty bunch.

" First of all we tried to ship regular consignments from Marseilles but it didn't work at all well. The stability of the wine was often disturbed with the changes in temperature and atmosphere. The problem is that it is not possible to have proper cellars on board," he said. "What one must not forget is that an army literally travels on its stomach and without a good supply of wine the morale of our troops was not of the standard we expect of the French Army. What could we have done if there was a serious outbreak of trouble? We would have been a laughing stock. Something had to be done and done urgently. So when this man Hochar asked us for Cabernet Sauvignon, Syrah and Cinsault vines in quantity as well as some other varieties, we agreed.

"Then he planted them in the area known as the Bekaa Valley and we told our legionnaires what we were doing and everyone waited in earnest."

"When I stayed at Chateau Musar," Wynford explained, "it was still early days and most of the vineyard consisted of young vines, but Gaston did have a few old vines in one small *parcelle* he had acquired. They were just sufficient for him to produce one cuvée of wine and call it Chateau Musar. As you can imagine he was particularly proud of it, and the wine wasn't at all bad."

Even in 1981 the peace of the Bekaa was disturbed by occasional bursts of gunfire or the intrusion of SAM ground-to-air missiles, or even the heavy pounding of artillery as the PLO and Israelis scrapped either with each other or with one of the many warring factions that disputed the territory.

Since then the Musar vines have grown in stature and produced some remarkably fine wines, during more than a decade of strife that has seen two entire vintages lost. Now peace has been restored to Lebanon and there is a new feeling of hope in that ancient land, not just for the Hochar family, but also for the Bedouin who arrive at every vintage to pick the grapes (that is, for the women to work and the men to watch, as is the custom).

Chateau Musar has also become one of the great curios of the wine world, a wine that in its finest vintages can match the best that Bordeaux can offer, and as such one that can bring even the most pompous wine snob down to earth..

About a year after I first met Serge I received a call from a great wine buff, who it would be fair to describe as a country gentleman who is a stockbroker in his spare time. He had telephoned and asked to see me.

"I've got a visitor somebody coming to dinner next week," he said. "He's a director of a large company of wine shippers, he really does like to pontificate about wine and yet he hardly knows a thing. He had the nerve to ring me yesterday and ask what we would be eating. 'Right, old boy,' he said. 'I'll bring along a drop of the Mouton Roths-child '67 already decanted; you needn't worry, it will outclass anything you have in your cellar.' Now I like the old codger but he is the most ridiculous wine snob, so I'd like to teach him a lesson and that's why I've called to see what you can suggest."

I thought for a moment, hesitated for a few seconds and then nominated "Chateau Musar of the same vintage".

"Chateau Musar! What the dickens is that?" he enquired.

"It's from the Lebanon," I responded.

"From the Lebanon! You must be joking! I can imagine what sort of plonk they produce there."

" No," I said firmly. "You're wrong. Look, just trust me. It'll cost a third of the price of his Mouton and will definitely do the job. Just make sure you decant it the night before and take the top off the decanter to allow further breathing about four hours before the meal. Then when you offer your challenge his eyes will pop out."

At about 10 o'clock on the morning of the following Thursday, the stockbroker telephoned again, his voice full of elation. "Absolute bloody miracle old boy. We drank both the wines with the meat and the cheese courses and when we had finished the Major-General said, 'OK, what are you trying to pull on me? I'm supposed to be the expert. All right, what's yours? Lafite or Latour? Whichever it is, I have to admit that it outclassed my Mouton.' When I revealed that it was from the Lebanon he went purple, virtually foaming at the mouth. I actually did wonder if his eyes would pop out! The only trouble is I don't think he'll ever invite me back to dinner at his place."

Today the wine magazines of the world argue over how great Chateau Musar is. Some experts compare it with Red Bordeaux, others with Rhone, some even with Burgundy.

"It is none of these,". says Serge Hochar. "It is Lebanese and more important than that it is Chateau Musar."

Not only has it fooled wine snobs and the most experienced masters of wine, but it has been an object lesson to every wine lover on earth not to be prejudiced against the wines of any one country when one knows little or nothing about that land. The beautifully balanced, full, red wines from Chateau Musar combine finesse and maturity, and are full of fruit and flavour and an almost indefinable spiciness that hints of great camel trains that once snaked eastwards from the Bekaa on distant routes to the east.

The wine comes from vineyards and cellars where the Hochar family write the rules, where the French and Bedouin languages waft across the vines and the aging process occurs in a fine old castle which gave the wine its name. Yet if it had not been for the thirst of the French legionnaires the property would still be a decaying Moorish fort, bereft of its prince, and that Bekaa land would remain as the cornfields and orchards they once were. So may everyone who tastes this Levantine juice remember and toast the memory of the old French minister and Gaston Hochar, the Lebanese insurance man he supported, the pioneer who planted one of the finest vineyards on earth in one of the least likely settings.

As for Serge, the son who has placed Chateau Musar on the international wine map, I can only pray that it will not be another eleven years until we meet again, for we have much to share, not only a mutual love and enthusiasm for wine but a delight in the magical surprises that it can spring upon even those with extensive experience. And I, of course, will always recall that his fine chateau failed to confound the knowledge of another Welsh broad-caster and wine buff.

MY FRIEND NICOLE
Champagne N.G. Martin, France

Many lovers of true Champagne, from the chalky white vineyards of the Marne, may be surprised to learn that there are just over 5 000 producers who make and bottle their own wine. Among these the meticulous operation of N.G. Martin, in the hillside village of Champillon, must be one of the tiniest. It is also one of the most acclaimed from that village, since its petite owner was featured in the television program "Ladies and Champagne", seen in many countries during the mid-1980s. Nicole Genièvre Martin is the fifth generation of a small family of growers who can trace their ancestry back to the end of the Napoleonic Wars. From her 1½-hectare vineyard Nicole looks westwards from Champillon to Hautvillers and the Abbey of Dom Perignon, one of the most rustic vineyard vistas you could ask to see, especially in autumn. It is the very same plot that her ancestors cultivated but it was not until 1976 that she joined the growing band of small vineyard owners who bottle their own Champagne. Prior to that she sold her grapes to Pol Roger in Épernay. Her cellar is in the basement of her comfortable bungalow, where she produces a maximum of 12 000 bottles per year.

Nicole was apprenticed to fellow Champillon *récoltant-manipulant*, Bertrand Devavry, and also

My friend Nicole

gained experience in California, working for his small Monterey operation there. In addition she has followed a special CIVC course in viticulture in Épernay. She is married to her vines, which through her talents provide a charming Champagne that delights those who taste it. She is everything in her organisation: viticulturist, winemaker, sales director, transporter, secretary and accountant. She sells, she says, "to my friends and the friends of my friends". I count it a privilege to be among the former.

NORMAN, THE MEMORY MAN
The Ritz-Carlton, USA

Norman, the head bartender at the Jockey Club in New York's luxurious Ritz-Carlton Hotel, has the most capacious memory that one is ever likely to encounter in the world of wine and drink. A couple of years ago I met a member of the Ritz-Carlton staff who mentioned Norman's unusual gift and said that if he was given your name when you ordered a drink, whether it was a glass of Franciscan Chardonnay or a vodka martini, if you returned six or even twelve months later and reminded him of your name he was capable of recalling your choice of drink.

Taking the first possible opportunity to act upon this information, I turned towards Central Park South and the homely surroundings of the Jockey Club. There, behind the bar, was Norman, a lean figure moving swiftly along the bar, acknowledging regular visitors, proffering the occasional witticism and then bursting into torrents of conversation.

As soon as he had finished serving at one end of the bar he headed straight towards me. "Sir, welcome to the Jockey Club. What can I get you?"

"Orange juice on ice," was my reply, simply because I had already enjoyed my fill of wine earlier in the evening.

Six months later I happened to arrive in New York with my road manager, Dave Hollyman, having just flown in from Cleveland on a flight that had been delayed, a situation which usually leaves the need to unwind. Dave suggested a late-night drink in the Jockey Club and so we made our way directly there.

Without moving from the centre of the bar, Norman spotted me coming. "Good evening, sir. You are the Flying Wine Guy and you tried to catch me out last time by ordering orange juice on ice. Here it is, but no ice please. It ruins the best freshly squeezed orange juice you can get in New York."

THE OLD LADY OF CHAUME
Chateau de la Guimonière, France

Quarts de Chaume must be one of the most puzzling appellations ever to claim my attention. Set in the heart of the ancient kingdom of Anjou, which is found in the middle of France's great Loire Valley, Quarts de Chaume is a much disputed name among local growers. Each grower will swear that his family have always owned a small *"parcelle dans les Quarts"* and they alone know the truth concerning its origins. Needless to say, upon enquiry, his neighbour will take great pleasure in warmly contradicting and disproving him. As you can imagine, identifying truth from fiction among such a proliferation of claims is an onerous task.

Chateau de la Guimonière, in the Rochefort area of France

Some say that in medieval times the feudal landlord of Rochefort-sur-Loire owned all the vineyards around the hamlet of Chaume and, as was often the practice, vineyard sites were allocated to winegrowers in return for a quarter of the vintage. Others say this explanation is only partially correct. According to their version of the story the landlord provided homes, wagons, buildings, tools, manure, vines, and in fact all the village's requirements in return for three-quarters of the crop; hence the plural form of the word *quarts*. One local expert confided the following tale to me. It appears that when the authorities were organising the appellation contrôlée status for the vineyards in this region, to put an end to the confusion, they invited all those who wished to prove their claims to "Quarts de Chaume" to attend a meeting. To their chagrin, only twenty-two owners of *parcelles* arrived and in their anger at the casual way in which their office was being treated, the authorities granted the rights of the official appellation to the twenty-two growers who had condescended to present themselves and to no-one else.

To my mind the most intriguing footnote to the Quarts de Chaume controversy arose when I had occasion to visit the nearby tiny appellation of Bonnezeaux, which vehemently disputes the claims of Quarts de Chaume to be the finest sweet white wine from the hills bordering the meandering river Layon. One established vigneron of some repute told me that while there were some extremely energetic wine producers in the Quarts de Chaume, who had done their best to create a legend, they did not have the best wine. There was no doubt in his mind that their vineyards were not even as good as his. And surely I did not need him to tell me that the finest vineyards were those on the upper slopes, which benefited from the best exposure to the sun. Now, if I wanted to visit the finest around Quarts de Chaume, then I would have to go up the hill until I reached the higher slopes. There, the appellation was not even Quarts de Chaume but Coteaux du Layon-Chaume. In his opinion the landlord was a fool who knew nothing about wine; he simply chose the wrong land. If I just followed his instructions and took the road from Rochefort in a southerly direction, then drove to the very top of the hill, I would find wines which were far better than I was seeking here.

Following his advice I returned to Rochefort and took the road to the top of the hill. There I was confronted by the sight of the somewhat dilapidated but still imposing great old chateau called Guimonière. After ten minutes of fruitless searching, in my experience a common feature on such occasions, a window creaked open and an old lady peered out, wary and suspicious.

"What can I do for you Monsieur? My son, who makes the wine is away in Paris for the Concours, but if you think I can be of any help I'll come down."

I indicated that I would be obliged if she would be prepared to join me and added quickly that I was interested in only a few bottles, having learnt that the quickest way to frighten any *propriétaire* was to mention large, possibly commercial quantities.

Waiting for her in the yard, I rubbed my hands as my breath steamed in the chilly morning air. Carefully negotiating the frontal staircase, and well-wrapped against the cold, the old lady guided me into a small but attractive tasting room. As is the custom among the hospitable folk of Anjou, her first move was to offer me a glass of the most recent vintage. Her interest grew when I asked her opinion of all the vintages since the war. Quickly turning the question back on me she retorted, "Which do you prefer, Monsieur?"

"Of the vintages I've been fortunate enough to taste to date, probably the 1955 or the 1959."

"I detect that Monsieur knows a little about our region," she good-humouredly acknowledged, and with that crossed the room to some old square wooden boxes and searched carefully among some dusty half bottles. "I think, Monsieur, we had better prove you right."

And so it came about that on a bitter March morning, this charming old lady and I tasted, gossiped over and finally devoured the rich golden delicacy. My friend from the Bonnezeaux was correct – the wine was finer than any from lower down the slope.

As the morning progressed and we relaxed together, I was prompted to ask her which was the oldest vintage of Chateau de la Guimonière she had ever drunk. She thought it must have been from the last century, as she was born and brought up here and she remembered that her father, whenever there was cause for celebration, would always open some old bottles and the wine had a deep, dark, golden colour. Even as a child she had thought it rather entrancing.

"You know," she added suddenly, "I could sit here for hours talking to you and opening other old vintages. It's always a pleasure when two people share the same feelings about wine."

It was a tempting idea but I had to politely decline her offer as it was time for me to leave, and I suggested we had better leave some bottles in the cellar for future generations. Only one question remained unanswered, and I simply had to ask her what she considered the finest vintage she had ever drunk.

"Oh, that's not difficult," she responded swiftly, and proceeded to relate one of the most touching tales I have ever heard.

"During the last war the family were given just twenty-four hours' notice to flee our home and head south from the advancing *Bosch*. The message was received by my husband over the telephone and gathering everyone into the house he ordered us to pack straight away, essential items only, clothes, food and valuables.

"'What about the wine?' we blurted out.

"'There's only room for one case,' he said, 'so you must decide which vintage.'

"We just looked at one another and declared unanimously, 'The 1921.' It was the finest vintage I had ever drunk. Two years after leaving home my son was born and to celebrate we opened a bottle. When he was baptised we opened another. Later my daughter was born and another two were drunk. With the restoration of peace we returned home and another was devoured. Years later, when my son married, we drank one, and also when my first grandchild was born. And so on, Monsieur, until today, when only one bottle is left."

"When will you drink that one, Madame?" I enquired.

"Never, Monsieur!"

"Never, Madame?"

"No, Monsieur, it will be buried with me when I die, because it is deserving of a higher place."

It was with a reflective but cheered heart that I said goodbye to the little old lady of Chaume,

whose name I later discovered was Madame Doucet. Her lovely wine and personal story were quite unforgettable. As I turned my car around and headed for the open countryside, the squabbles down below paled into insignificance beside the best wine and finest tale.

PROFESSOR HERMANN BAUCH
Winzerhaus, Austria

The simplicity of the watercolours painted by Professor Hermann Bauch is captivating, and he loves his Weinviertel region, just outside Vienna, with all his heart. His entire being breathes the spirit of the land in which he has spent his life.

Professor Hermann Bauch in his beloved Weinviertel Museum

Visitors to his living museum at Kronberg are usually conducted around its contrasting exhibits by the talented and enthusiastic professor, who is so emphatic in his explanations that his reasoning often transcends language. He is, he says, a man of simple tastes, a man of bread and wine, who looks to nature for his inspiration, a statement that is borne out by so many of the items on display.

Hermann Bauch is local historian and guardian of his beloved Weinviertel, and is so passionately fond of the arts, crafts and traditions of the region that he has developed his museum with the intention of preserving past character and skills for current and future generations to observe and appreciate.

His selection as the artist to provide a watercolour for the Winzerhaus label was an honour that

was naturally granted to Professor Bauch. His response was typical; he painted a brief series of simple watercolours that illustrated a *Winzerhaus*, or little wine store, just as one might find tucked into a Weinviertel hillside.

SOMETHING OF A RUSH
Inniskillin, Canada

In June 1984, a brief stop in London, Ontario, resulted in a fleeting visit to the Inniskillin Winery in its scenic setting near the Niagara River, just north of Canada's border with the United States. It took place during a never-to-be-repeated period of experiment in which I attempted to meet a demanding schedule of extensive travel across North America by rail. So much frustration followed complications and delays that the net result was my avowal that all future travel of any extent would be undertaken by road and air.

For some months I had been presenting a weekly spot on LBC Radio in London, England, which proved a helpful link with CFPL, the main talk-radio station in London, Ontario, where the subject of wine was creating increasing interest. My host, Jim Weir, urged me to spare the time to visit the Inniskillin Winery and before I could open my mouth to reply, he had picked up the phone and called Donald Ziraldo, one of the two partners there. Donald said he would be delighted for me to pay a rush visit, which is exactly what it proved to be. My radio host kindly drove me to a local car-rental company, where I hired a mid-size vehicle, having received assurances that I would have enough time to drive to the winery, spend at least one and a half hours there and return to London to take the night express for Toronto.

It turned into one of those journeys familiar to all those experienced with demanding schedules, where one realises the necessity of timing the outward journey carefully in order to calculate how much time one can actually spare upon arrival at one's destination. Initially there were no major problems, but gradually the volume of traffic, coupled with a chain of roadworks, slowed my progress, until by the time I was 10 miles from Inniskillin I was beginning to feel agitated – especially when a careful calculation told me that if the return journey matched the outward trip, then I would only have thirty minutes to view the winery and talk to the partners. Another delay reduced the permissible time to a farcical twenty minutes. It was not the manner in which I would wish to treat anyone, let alone someone who had offered to make me welcome at such short notice.

Upon arrival I rushed up the steps and desperately asked the other partner, Karl Kaiser, if he could direct me to Donald Ziraldo and hastily made an apologetic explanation, which I repeated to Donald some minutes later. To add to my embarrassment, I mortally wounded the feelings of Karl Kaiser by innocently accusing him of being German, when he is in fact a proud Austrian. With both partners bemusedly watching a harassed and perspiring journalist struggling to compose himself, I produced a microphone and Marantz recorder and began to record a radio item for the other London some 4 500 miles away.

Somehow the patient pair tolerated my eccentric haste and provided a first-take interview, when a second attempt would have seen me sleeping in Ontario rather than Montreal. Karl, having recovered from what must have been a more than occasional Teutonic error, explained that their Niagara latitude is the same as northern Spain, while Donald added that despite their southerly aspect, Canada's legendary winters meant every chance of producing some interesting Icewine, which he would dearly like me to taste. Indeed, Donald and Karl must have thought my behaviour bizarre, as I insisted I must leave in five minutes. With that Donald grabbed my arm and tugged me around a five-minute winery visit, placed a bottle of Chardonnay under one of my arms and some literature under the other, led me to the car and helped me into it. The last I remember was an Austrian accent yelling, "You must come back!" as I waved a rapid farewell and departed in a cloud of dust. I dreaded to think what the two partners thought of me as they went back up the stairs. I am quite certain they thought they would probably never hear of me again.

In the meantime, I raced back to London, praying that I would not attract the attention of any stray policeman, ever-vigilant for offenders of the traffic speed regulations, and repeatedly glanced down at the odometer, making mental calculations of how much time remained to catch the night express. It is enough to record that I was thankful that the international railway code of

being later than advertised was observed as meticulously in Canada as it is in Britain. The return of the rental car remains a blur, in which I donated a brand new pair of glasses to the lost-property fund. So too does the final sinking into my railway seat, an exhausted action endorsed by words of heavenly thanks.

For some years Inniskillin was far from my mind until David Pinchard, a wise old friend of many years' standing and a director of Avery's of Bristol, told me that they had introduced some exciting New World agencies, including a Canadian wine from near Niagara. A little later a sample bottle of red Inniskillin hybrid Marechal Foch arrived and I remember wondering to myself if its name indicated that like many North American hybrids it would have a slightly unpleasant, foxy nose. The possibility was quickly dismissed, as I rated it by far the best example I had tasted of that little-seen variety. A few months later a retailer supplied me with a gold-medal-winning half bottle of Inniskillin 1989 Icewine, which proved to be filled with mouth-watering Canadian nectar, fit for sipping and discussing among the most serious tasters. It completely substantiated Donald Ziraldo's suggestion and reawakened my curiosity about the winery.

I had no early plans to travel there and would only do so when a full eight hours were at my disposal. This time I would indulge in a little history by correspondence and other research.

It appeared that when the foundations of the first winery building were started in 1975, they broke the earth on a plot that had been rented to the Royal Inniskillin Fusiliers when the Irish regiment had been stationed in the area during the Canadian War of 1812. When the conflict was over and the regiment returned home, the land was allocated to an officer of another, unknown regiment, Colonel Cooper, who named it Inniskillin Farm.

In the nine years since my rushed visit the calibre of patronage of the Canadian winery has improved. Prince Henrick of Denmark has stayed to lunch, Boris Yeltsin has devoured the 1988 Chardonnay (one cannot imagine him sipping it), and he made short work of the Pinot Noir Reserve, while the sweet-toothed Princess Diana has been delighted by the Icewine. As for myself, I hope one day, after giving proper and respectful notice, to return to the site of my only Canadian winery visit, request permission to use the overnight hospitality suite and taste their entire range to discover exactly what I have missed.

5.   HUMBLE BEGINNINGS

DISHWASHER MAKES GOOD
James Herrick, France

Among the emerging generation of winemakers is a scattering of enthusiastic and skilled individuals who have gained their experience in various countries around the globe. One such character, who has recently caused much blood-letting in southern France, is an English-born producer of confused heritage called James Herrick.

Drawing upon knowledge he has gleaned in the Champagne region of France, and in Australia and California, this extrovert traveller has finally put down his viticultural roots at Domaine de la Motte, just outside Narbonne, in the Vin de Pays d'Oc, which is often claimed to be the first region to be planted with vines when the Romans came to Gaul. Here, chauvinistic Midi farmers gawped as he grubbed out some little-known varieties and replanted three separate vineyards with Chardonnay, a grape that is often assumed to be the sole possession of the Burgundy area in France. With well-known Australian wine names Mark Swann and Robert Hesketh as financial partners, James Herrick has been able to turn the local wine world upside down. The result is a wine that seems to marry the power of Australian sunshine with the

elegance of French Chablis, which means that James Herrick Chardonnay is achieving healthy sales in several countries, even if consumers have to look at the bottle twice before deciding on the nationality of the wine.

To date, James Herrick's most significant qualification for his role is the character of the wine he makes, for he is a man of no pretensions, as is evident when he reveals his background.

"I was born in a London hospital, the son of a New Zealand sailor and an Irish mother. We lived for a while in East Anglia in England before we began travelling. As far as my education was concerned, upon leaving school at eighteen I travelled to Bavaria, where in the quaint hamlet of Iznell, I began my first job as a dishwasher. I then dreamed of higher ideas and went to Sussex University and studied philosophy but I never finished that and returned to Iznell to continue my career as a dishwasher and it wasn't because of a woman, whatever anyone might think!"

Sometime later James took a journey away from the hopfields of Bavaria and tasted some wine

James Herrick, the one-time dishwasher who made good

Mike Hogue by the Hogue Doll's House, cellar for the first vintage

which enticed him to a trial career in France. Being a determined young man of positive outlook he aimed at the top, or so he thought, and applied to Moët et Chandon, who hired him as a *stagiaire* (trainee) for three months. He translates *stagiaire* as cellar rat.

"I had to do every dirty job imaginable," he recalls. "But I suppose I learned a bit."

Convinced of his oenological talent, James decided upon emigration to Australia, a land where he hoped people would treat him more gently, and there he became a friend and colleague of Mark Swann and gained a great deal of viticultural and oenological experience in South Australia.

Somewhat later his itchy feet saw him crossing the Pacific to California, where he became involved in the sale and marketing of Mark Swann wines in North America. Now he swears that he has settled down and is married with three small children, who are all learning French while speaking English at home. His loves, apart from his family, are skiing, sailing, reading and wine. He is beginning to sound a little normal, which must be quite pleasing for a Bavarian-trained dishwasher who can justifiably claim that he has "made good".

DOLL'S HOUSE WINE
The Hogue Cellars, USA

The founding of the Hogue Cellars must be unique in the annals of wine history. This fast-emerging star, from the semidesert conditions of Washington state, describes its beginnings as basic, a term which could be considered euphemistic. Yet those early days illustrate many of the fundamental principals of wine production.

This book is not intended as an appraisal or critique of wines but I feel compelled to admit that in my opinion the Hogue Cellars, in less than a

generation, has provided the United States with its most attractive value in Merlot and a Reserve Merlot that is stunning, as well as some most appealing Johannisberg Riesling, Chardonnay, Fumé Blanc and Chenin Blanc and the little-known provision of small quantities of one of the continent's most acceptable *méthode champenoise* wines. Having prefaced my comments with such tributes, I must add that I find their attempt at Gewurztraminer an exercise which requires a return to the drawing board.

The origins of their meteoric success lie in some most unlikely circumstances, for Michael Hogue admits quite frankly that the Hogue family drank cheap Portuguese wine and had no real idea about the subject at all when they first embarked on their venture. Their inspiration was a friend from Chicago, a lawyer, the late Mark Schwarzman, who first intimated in 1969 that they should plant some vines on their family farm at Prosser, in the Yakima Valley, as it was his belief that ideal growing conditions existed there. Persuading the family took a decade but in 1979 Michael Hogue turned over his father's favourite cattle pasture to the cultivation of vines, thus establishing a vineyard that had already received years of natural fertilisation.

Wayne Hogue was rather disgruntled and complained at the loss of his good pasture. He later recanted these opinions in public, however, when speaking in his official capacity as mayor of Prosser, a responsibility held for some thirty years. Evidently he had a suspicion that good results would be achieved at an early stage and he was ultimately completely convinced when wine journalists began to compliment the rising name from the Pacific North-West.

The Hogue family first arrived in the Yakima Valley from Montana in the early 1920s and settled as fruit and vegetable farmers, who over the years became prolific producers of hops, asparagus and the most delicious bell peppers, as well as a wide variety of fruit. Mayor Hogue probably knew only too well that if those grew in such profusion and good health that there had to be a good chance that some grape varieties would fare equally as well.

In common with neighbouring farmers and growers, the Hogue family became involved in one of the great examples of natural engineering. They irrigated the desert-like conditions of the Yakima Valley with the melted snows of the towering 14 000-foot Mount Rainer, which divided them from Seattle and Tacoma and their picturesque valleys, with their freshwater lakes and saltwater inlets. They studied how other grape growers used narrow-pipe irrigation and like good farmers adopted the same practice in their new Schwarzman vineyard.

In 1981 the first Johannisberg Riesling grapes were ready to be pressed, a situation which threw the entire Hogue family into a state of consternation as they had no suitable building for the purpose. Michael, ever anxious to keep a close watch on his new venture, decided that he wanted to make the wine at home at all costs. Having already taken over his father's favourite cow pasture, he commandeered his daughter's dolls' house, which stood in their garden, and within the wooden walls of that favoured playroom the Hogue Cellars' first wine was produced – all 110 gallons of it!

"We didn't really know what we were doing. We just produced it for fun," Michael told me on two later visits in 1991 and 1993. Incredibly, within a decade of that "Dolls' House Wine", the Hogue Cellars had become a blue-labelled success, sweeping the American mainland from coast to coast. Within a few years of their first vintage, Gary Hogue, Michael's eldest brother, returned to the family fold after twenty years in the furniture business in Seattle. Gary, with his commercial skills, provided the perfect balance to his brother's farming experience and their combined efforts have resulted in their wines becoming great favourites in cities from Boston to Miami and San Diego to Chicago, a colossal achievement and one which happened so rapidly. However, success has not swollen them with pride, for the brothers and their father, Mayor Hogue, happily relate the story of the 1981 vintage, that very first production, their Doll's House Wine.

THE DREAM CHATEAU OF CHESTNUT MOUNTAIN
Chestnut Mountain Winery, USA

Drivers who regularly travel eastwards on the US I-85 freeway from Atlanta towards Anderson, South Carolina, may perhaps remember noticing the sign for exit 48 that announces Chestnut Mountain and Winder. Yet few will have taken a slight diversion from that exit in search of James Laikam's dream chateau at the Chestnut Mountain winery.

The dream chateau of Chestnut Winery, Braselton, Georgia

The ambitious winery, founded in 1988, is already attracting growing interest in its pleasing range of *vinifera* wines, the Cabernet Sauvignon being rated as the star by many consumers. The numbers of persons who visit the winery are rising but those who search for the elegant chateau, as depicted on the label, may feel bewildered, for in January 1994 it would still take "about two to three years to finish" according to a winery official, and that statement may be optimistic. One could see that most of the metal superstructure was complete but the roof had not been laid and the interior was at a very early stage.

It is a dream that most serious wine lovers can readily comprehend, a dream of a man and his team, who live their wine lives with enthusiasm and hope, and have a vision of bringing to Georgia a classic wine chateau that will match the delightful wines they are already beginning to make. If Chestnut Mountain can sell enough of its wine then the dream will come about and the artist's impression will convert to reality.

The image displayed on the label evolved when one visitor arrived in the spring of 1990. David Bauer called at Chestnut Mountain, suggested that some label improvements might be in order, and mentioned that he was "an artist". When James Laikam expanded to him about his dream of building a chateau there, the artist prompted the winery president to describe his vision, which he reproduced on the label which the winery now uses.

So if you are able to cruise along the I-85 and take exit 48 in the near future, please do, and help the building work. If you cannot manage it for a few years, do not worry, for with a little good fortune the Dream Chateau of Chestnut Mountain may by then have materialised.

DROPPINGS OR DROP-OUT?
The Peel Estate, Australia

The Chenin Blanc must rate as one of the most misunderstood grape varieties. It seems to be able to create a different image in no matter what country it is grown and made.

In France's Loire Valley it produces a whole gamut of styles, providing the long-lasting and classic dry whites of La-Roche-Aux-Moines, La Coulée de Serrant and Savennières, and also the dry, medium-dry, and occasionally sweet and *moelleux* whites of Vouvray. In Anjou and the Coteaux du Layon it gives long-ageing dessert delicacies bearing names such as Moulin Touchais and Bonnezaux.

In California it is generally perceived as a moderately priced, moderately acceptable semi-dry white, although there are occasional superior examples, but they are the exception rather than the rule.

In Western Australia the Chenin Blanc truly comes into its own and develops into one of the most mouth-filling and surprising dry whites that you would ever expect to find in that continent of young bottled-sunshine whites. In fact the variety's success at Baldivis, some 50 kilometres south of Perth, at the Peel Estate, is truly marvellous. There it is vinified by a man called Will Nairn, who will make an admission which is truly shocking in wine circles. He will readily own that when he turned on the power switch of his new wine press, in March 1980, to crush his first vintage, he had never even seen one working before. He was, so it would seem, greener than his grapes. Yet just nine years later, Will Nairn was to make a Peel Estate Chenin Blanc that was so full of vitality and zest and so out of character for the grape variety with which we

are acquainted, that in blind tastings, examinations and quizzes across the world, tasters could easily be caught out.

It might not be unreasonable to say that those Californian wineries that still have extensive plantings of Chenin Blanc, which only supplies them with moderately priced wine, might do well to invest in return tickets to Western Australia to glean a few magic tips from the talented man who describes himself as "a drop-out". For the Peel Estate, small though it may be, is commanding and deserving a full premium price for its Chenin miracle. Somehow the untrained has given the wine world something new and exciting.

Perhaps the answer lies in a quote from an interview which Will Nairn gave to Mike Zekulich for his book *Wine and Wineries of the West*:

> It has only taken fifteen years to break even, so we are not in it for the money. It is a lifestyle that becomes an obsession. You get a tremendous amount of satisfaction in making a good wine, creating something people really enjoy.

On the other hand, I have a theory of my own which may just have some substance. The Peel Estate is a vineyard literally cut out of the bush, where the main vineyard pests are parrots, which

WESTERN AUSTRALIAN WINE

PEEL ESTATE

Chenin Blanc
WOOD MATURED 1991

PRODUCED BY
PEEL ESTATE
FLETCHER RD
BALDIVIS WA
13.5% VOL 750 ML

PRODUCE OF AUSTRALIA

devour the fruit from the vines and leave their acrid droppings on the soil. Is it possible that the parrots' contribution provides a unique fertiliser, unknown in Chenin Blanc vineyards elsewhere in the world? Or is it simply that Will Nairn, the drop-out, has the magic touch?

Whatever the truth of the matter, few will argue that Will Nairn's Chenin Blanc is in a class of its own. Why, then, has he not named his wine after himself? Why Peel Estate? The answer lies in the colonial history of the region. In the early days of Western Australia the size of the land grant that one might obtain was directly related to the size of one's labour force and, of course, to one's status and influence. It was on this understanding that Thomas Peel arrived in the colony in 1834 with a large army of skilled and unskilled workers. He also brought his own fleet of carriages and even a selection of pianos for a little light entertainment. As for status and influence, his family undeniably had both, for he was the nephew of Sir Robert Peel, the British prime minister and founder of the public police service. It is therefore not surprising that Thomas Peel was granted an initial land allocation of 1 million acres, although this was later reduced to a quarter of that after vociferous complaints from other settlers. Despite such a head start, Thomas Peel did not prosper, as he had little or no idea of how to deal with the virgin territory and its inhospitable sandy soil. In fact he made so little progress in transforming the wilderness into productive property that most of his land was reclaimed. Today's Peel Estate lies on part of the last piece of land that remained in his ownership. Will Nairn, with permission, now uses the Peel family name and crest on his wine, which he has succeeded in producing from the barren wilderness that defied the attentions of Thomas Peel.

FOGGY WINE
Monteagle, USA

The very name Monteagle conjures up a picture of life at altitude, which is particularly fitting for the title of a Tennessee winery that produces a delicious Sauvignon Blanc amidst an unorthodox list of noble varietals, hybrids and fruit wines.

My November 1993 visit took place during a rainstorm that gave way to a dense, muddy grey fog in a matter of minutes. The conditions altered so rapidly that I could scarcely see far enough ahead to pick my way from the car park to the winery. When I did reach my goal I was assured that these sudden and dramatic weather changes were part of normal proceedings. After all, the winery was perched at an altitude of 2 100 feet on the Cumberland Plateau of Tennessee's Monteagle Mountain.

My curiosity that the Marlow family should have chosen to plant vines at such an altitude was soon satisfied. They explained that when they chose the position in 1986 they had entertained no doubts that it would suffice, because around 1870 a colony of Swiss immigrants had settled nearby and enjoyed noteworthy viticultural success.

Names like Sewannee White and Assembly Blush might lead some serious wine lovers to question the true intent at Monteagle, but one slurp of the Sauvignon Blanc should put any doubts to rest, and with young Merlot and Cabernet vines being grown, an interesting future lies ahead.

In any event, if you do leave exit 134 on the I-24 between Nashville and Chatanooga to search for the winery, do not go when it is raining, because the weather can swiftly turn to fog and you may not be able to locate that Sauvignon Blanc.

W*ill Nairn of Peel Estate*

GASPARE'S LITTLE CAFÉ
Campari, Italy

If any drink in this world has the right to call itself unique then it must be Campari, the bittersweet aperitif from Milan. It is made from a recipe so carefully guarded that its ingredients are assembled personally by the president of the company with a small team of dedicated workers, each of whom is party to only a few of the ingredients on that secret list. The security surrounding the herbs and spices store is so strict that any employee found in breach of it is instantly dismissed.

That recipe is considered by the Davide Campari Milano company to be priceless, and yet it may never have come into being but for a string of events in the personal life of its creator and the coincidence that he happened, at one particular moment in history, to own small premises in the Coperto dei Figini, right in front of Milan's magnificent *duomo,* or Cathedral.

It is a story with more than its fair share of tragedy and yet is full of colour and character. To begin to understand its depth of human experience one has to imagine oneself in the heart of the Italian countryside, about 60 miles north-west of Milan, during the first half of the 19th century. In that context Gaspare Campari was born on 11 April 1828, at 57 Contrada Novara, a rickety courtyard building in the small farming town of Casselnuovo, in Lombardy. He was the youngest of ten children from a farming family which owned a small plot of land and enjoyed a reasonably secure, if basic, standard of living. His father was aware of the need to find suitable employment for his children, as their land could not support all ten. With this in mind he arranged an apprenticeship for Gaspare, and so, on one emotional day in 1842, the fourteen-year-old youth was taken by horse-drawn coach to the great city of Turin, the capital of what was then the kingdom of Sardinia and Savoy. There he became an apprentice *licoriste* in the imposing Bass bar which stood in the shadow of the great Basilica di Superga.

The mainland area of the ancient kingdom of Sardinia and Savoy was, and still is, regarded as the birthplace of aperitifs and vermouths, and it was normal practice for every reputable bar and restaurant to have its own house drink. The creation of these involved jealously guarded recipes of which the *maître licoristes,* or master drinks-makers, kept only one or two written copies. The first would be used for practical purposes and the second hidden in a place of security, such as a bank or other deposit, a precaution which continues to this day.

These recipes involved the fortification of drinks with young brandies and other spirits, and the addition of infusions and macerations of numerous herbs, spices and barks. Many of the recipes were wine-based but a good number had no wine content at all. From this tradition a small commercial production began, based in Turin, with eminent names such as Martini & Rossi, Cinzano, and Carpano, with its Punt E Mes remaining prominent to this day.

It was in this environment that Gaspare Campari learned his trade and matured. Upon completion of his apprenticeship it was time for the newly registered *maître licoriste* to seek a position of his own in a similar establishment. In a short space of time he succeeded in his quest when an opportunity arose at the elegant Cambio restaurant in the Piazza Carignano, just a few steps away from Turin's famous old Teatro Carignano.

In the Cambio, Gaspare felt as if he were in paradise. The 18th-century interior design, with its finely decorated panels, tall mirrors and glittering chandeliers, attracted the cream of Turin society, and Gaspare found himself serving both the king, Vittorio Emmanuel, and his redoubtable prime minister, Cavour.

The word *cambio* literally means exchange, and while no doubt financial dealings proliferated in the café-restaurant, it was not so much a local centre for business as a place of social exchange. Here the aristocracy and talent of the day met for lunch and dinner or quite simply for refreshment. The gentry of Turin had, at that time, the practice of arranging to meet friends and acquaintances in a fashionable bar for an evening aperitif. This would often be the house speciality, and after a couple of glasses it was customary to take a stroll, to permit the digestive juices to settle, for a comfortable distance to a restaurant of their choosing. For many the Cambio served both purposes. To the present day this elegant café-restaurant, founded in 1757, plays the same role alongside its theatrical neighbour and enchants its customers not just with its time-honoured gastronomy but with its unique decor, which has remained virtually unchanged since its establishment. The only difference now is that while there is still a knowledgeable and skilful head bartender, he could scarcely be termed a *maître licoriste*.

Life blossomed for Gaspare, and his happiness was crowned by his marriage to a young woman called Maddalena Alman, who bore him two healthy children. Then, with awful swiftness, tragedy fell with the sudden deaths of his wife and both children in what is believed to have been an outbreak of cholera. Devastated, he felt quite unable to continue his existence in Turin, the capital city which had brought him such joy for fourteen years, and so he turned his steps homeward. But apparently the experience of urban life directed him not to his native village but to the neighbouring town of Novara.

From 1856 to 1862 he was the proprietor of a small bar and cake shop in the Corsa di Porta Torino, in the centre of Novara. His fortunes here were mixed. He found fresh happiness in a second marriage to an auburn-haired young lady from Milan, Letizia Galli, but financial disaster struck when his business failed, the most likely reason being the sheer amount of competition prevailing in the day. Records show that many businesses producing cakes and biscuits flourished at the time, offering pleasing delicacies but with a limited demand.

With just 60 lire remaining the distressed couple were forced to call upon the aid of Letizia's parents in Milan, with whom they lived temporarily while Gaspare sought a position as a waiter.

Letizia's father, Ignazio Galli, was a man of some substance, the owner of a commodious house on the prosperous Contrada delle Stelle, where a number of relatives were welcomed, and he appears to have considered two extra no problem. Ignazio had, it seems, a liking and respect for Gaspare, whom he knew to be hardworking by nature. Without much ado he provided a loan to help the couple acquire another small café in the Coperto dei Figini, a location which was to prove their catalyst to fortune and fame.

In 1860, while still trading in Novara, Gaspare and Letizia had married at the church of Santa Maria della Passione in Milan. When, at a later date, they moved to that city, they made the impressive *duomo* their place of worship.

In the space of a few years their new geographical locations were to prove of the greatest consequence.

Their arrival in Milan has to be viewed against the backdrop of the momentous political changes taking place at that time, for this was the era of the unification of Italy. Gaspare, who had once served Vittorio Emmanuel and Cavour when they were the leaders of Sardinia and Savoy, now saw the two outstanding statesmen take control of the newly emerging nation. They persuaded and bargained their way through numerous treaties and agreements with the heads of a colourful assortment of small countries, dukedoms and tiny republics, which at this stage did not include Rome. Such negotiations created a considerable amount of competition for influence in the infant country. The situation was highlighted in the matter of selection of the capital city, a title claimed by both Turin and Milan. Turin was the home city of the king, while Milan was the growing centre where he enjoyed spending a considerable proportion of his time.

What follows comes from a compilation of written records and verbal accounts and, while some items cannot be verified, much of it seems to make a great deal of sense and, to date, nothing has come to light to contradict it.

The City Council of Milan consisted of a far-sighted group of men who were ambitious for the future of their expanding city, which then had approximately a mere 250 000 inhabitants. They knew that their new king, Vittorio Emmanuel II, liked to attend mass on Sunday mornings in the *duomo* and then take a stroll past the untidy scramble of buildings that was the Coperto dei Figini, and through various side streets towards the historic La Scala Opera House, where he would partake of lunch and a little entertainment. Bearing in mind that Milan is set in the foothills of the Alps, this meant that in the summer the king could stroll in glorious sunshine but in the winter he was likely to become rather dishevelled when exposed to rain, sleet or snow. The city leaders reasoned to themselves that if they wanted Milan to become the capital of Italy, they needed to attract their king to spend the majority of his time there and so some careful planning was needed.

Also, there was the pressing problem of the tens of thousands of country folk pouring into Milan on the newly constructed railway system in search of prosperity. In view of this the Milan Council wasted little time in drafting ambitious programs for the transformation of the city centre and the provision of housing in the suburbs, in the belief that they would be providing both employment and homes. They did not foresee that the economy would rapidly become overstretched, both in the public and private sectors, and the realisation suddenly dawned that it would be necessary to attract capital investment from outside Milan and even perhaps from abroad.

For many years the edifice they viewed as their

Demolition work on the Coperto dei Figini

The entrance of the Galleria of Vittoria Emmanuel, circa 1900

greatest architectural asset, the magnificent *duomo*, with its numerous spires, had been all but obscured among the sprawling back streets, and now they had at least some excuse to take positive action. They envisaged demolishing the clutter of narrow roads and passageways in front of the *duomo*, and those between it and La Scala, to make space for the construction of the finest arcade in the world, to be called the Galleria of Vittorio Emmanuel. It would be graced with elegant shops and cafés on the ground floor and majestic apartments above. That same Galleria was destined, in years to come, to give its name to shopping arcades around the globe.

A widely publicised competition was announced for the design of the Galleria, and after scrupulous examination the much vaunted prize was awarded to Guiseppe Menghoni of Bologna. Menghoni was regarded as a genius in his generation and justified the accolade with the completion of this, his most ambitious project, which has been called "the finest iron and glass covered arcade of the 19th century". Ironically, the Galleria which brought him such acclaim would also cost him his life.

After the selection of Menghoni's design, further debate ensued regarding the choice of firm to be responsible for the Galleria's construction. The contract was finally awarded to a British firm especially created for the task, the City of Milan Improvements Company Limited. Among its trustees were such noble names as the earls of Warwick and Sommers and its board of directors boasted in its lists the likes of the Right Honourable Stuart Wortley and Sir James Lacaita.

On 7 March 1865 the new King of Italy laid the official foundation stone amid a general feeling of elation and optimism. The City Council of Milan had stated that their great scheme would be completed and officially opened in 1867. However the prevailing mood proved to be somewhat short-lived as, for reasons too diverse to be enumerated, the municipal exchequer ran desperately short of funds. Various efforts were made to raise additional capital in England and Italy but to no avail, and it was beginning to look as if matters were destined to come to an early standstill when the idea of a giant lottery was sanctioned. This was run continuously over a period of ten years and eventually accumulated the necessary profit.

The citizens of Milan could be pardoned if at times they suspected the existence of a jinx on the Galleria. Apart from financial problems, there were a number of other delays and the promised opening date of 1867 loomed ever nearer. Milan Council intended, it seems, like all good politicians, to at least be seen to have achieved their target – if only in part. Thus it was that on 15 September 1867, in a somewhat muted ceremony, they officially opened the main arcade, despite the fact that much other work remained. It then took the decade of lottery revenue to fund the completion of the contract. The two-year target had been wildly optimistic, as it embraced not just the construction of the Galleria but also the arrangements to move all the existing occupants of the various streets designated for demolition. One of the occupants, in the Coperto dei Figini, chanced to be Gaspare Campari, and when he was approached regarding the demolition of his property his true business acumen was revealed. Gaspare had served the king as *maître licoriste* in the Cambio in Turin and attended the same masses in the *duomo*. He was also aware that the Galleria was to be dedicated to Vittorio Emmanuel II and was extremely reluctant to be removed from the scene of such excitement. Gaspare negotiated the most beneficial transaction for himself, insisting on being provided with new premises at the very entrance of the Galleria, just 30 metres from the steps of the *duomo*. His king was certain to stroll past the Café Campari Sunday after Sunday and perhaps one day Gaspare would have the privilege of serving him again.

On 16 September 1867, the day following the official opening, Gaspare, Letizia and their three children moved into their new home and opened the Campari Café-Patisserie, as it was termed. There, in a spacious basement cellar, Gaspare developed his own small private laboratory and during the latter part of 1867 and the first part of 1868 he toiled ceaselessly to create a unique aperitif, with the intention of serving it to the customers in his café-bar.

Ten years later, towards the end of 1877, work on the Galleria was at last completed and only the architect's final inspection remained before the second official opening ceremony could proceed, which on this occasion was to be graced by the king. Sadly the jinx was to strike again – not once, but twice. As the forty-eight-year-old architect, Guiseppe Menghoni, was examining the Triumphal Archway he slipped and fell to his death. Great consternation was caused by such an ill-omened tragedy, but nevertheless, in the light of so many previous delays, the council announced that there would be no change in the official opening date of 24 February 1878. Everyone involved in any way with the Galleria, and indeed the entire infant nation, were shocked yet again when on 9 January 1878, just six weeks prior to the opening day, Vittorio Emmanuel died. It remains a bizarre circumstance that despite the enormity of the king's loss the ceremony was still held on that February day – but with flags at half-mast.

Nonetheless life in the Galleria had been far from melancholy during those ten and a half years between opening ceremonies. A Galleria society had developed embracing many of the most talented academics, artists and professionals of the region, and they in turn greeted their prosperous friends and relatives from across Europe. The Galleria became Milan's most fashionable meeting place, where sartorially dressed widows could sip their cappuccinos and the handsome young gentry and dandies of the day could enjoy their aperitifs. It became a custom for socialites to gather in the Galleria in the evenings and, after a glass or two of bitters, stroll quietly through the arcade into the outside world in search of a restaurant.

For many the focus of that Galleria meeting was the Café Campari and a significant attraction was Signor Campari's bittersweet *aperitivo*. Indeed, this patronage of the Café Campari was pivotal in the Galleria's continuing success throughout the next half century. Verdi and Puccini were regular in their attendance, Mascini came from time to time and it was a favourite haunt of Ernest Hemingway. Even the Prince of Wales, the future Edward VII, patronised the café and it came to be a recognised meeting-place for the aristocracy of Europe on the Grand Tour.

Gaspare and Letizia could hardly credit the upturn in their fortune. Apart from their financial setbacks, poor Letizia had lost two children at birth, which was a double tragedy for Gaspare after the death of his first wife and two daughters. But now everything had changed. The man who had expected to wait on others found himself employing more and more waiters. His "bitters" was fast becoming the most popular *aperitivo* in Milan, and elegant customers with refined manners and full wallets and purses were crowding his premises day after day. The Campari family was making a small fortune.

Despite the financial struggle Milan had endured, it was about to enjoy a golden period of prosperity. In March 1877 it became one of the first cities to lay on public electricity and later that year introduced a telephone service. Davide, Gaspare's son, was always extremely proud that for nearly half a century his official number was Milano 19. Later, in 1883, Milan became the very first city in Europe to employ electric street lighting, when 3 300 lamps were fitted in the centre of the city. It developed into a metropolis for visitors to explore on foot and the Galleria benefited directly from Milan's growing reputation.

Gaspare's second son, Davide, was to become the driving force behind the company, and literally took the drink Campari from the café-bar in the Galleria to the world. Davide Giovanni Maria Gaspare Pietro Campari was born in their Galleria apartment on 14 November 1867, just two months after the official opening of the arcade and at the very time when his father was developing his historic recipe. It is to Davide that credit must be attributed for the worldwide reputation of the drink named after his family. While Gaspare and his wife Letizia had worked energetically and had attracted considerable and consistent custom to their business, it remained purely an individual and very successful enterprise in a unique and majestic setting. It was only when Davide became involved that matters really began to develop on any scale. He soon demonstrated a native instinct for commerce and a natural talent for leadership.

This business acumen first manifested itself during his early teens, when Davide was assisting the rest of the family in the café and was astute enough to recognise that other café owners were sending their staff to purchase what was then advertised as Fernet G. Campari. On his suggestion, other premises could only be permitted to sell his father's

The Café Campari

recipe if they displayed a small sign stating that they served "Authentic Campari". It was his first step in marketing and heralded the embarkation of Campari as a unique drink on its way to widespread success.

On 14 December 1882, just fifteen years after the opening of the Galleria, Gaspare Campari, who had become a greatly respected figure in Milan, died prematurely at the age of fifty-four. The celebrated Milanese newspaper *Corriere della Sera* reported that he had:

> … come to Milan with 60 lire and the idea of working as a waiter and afterwards got to occupy the big corner shop at the Galleria entrance where now every day an astounding quantity of spirits are drunk and where nearly a dozen waiters are busy from 8 am till midnight in attending to the customers.

At the time of his father's death, Davide was just fifteen and had several years' experience working with Gaspare upon the production of his various liqueurs and aperitifs, and also in the café–bar with his mother. Davide did have an older brother, also called Gaspare, but he had chosen to pursue an academic career, and so with Letizia and his brother Guido operating the café, Davide concentrated on the preparation of the drinks, at all times scrupulously adhering to his father's secret recipe. This work involved regular journeys to the market to buy the herbs, spices, wood barks and dried peels; the creation of the macerations and infusions; the careful compounding of the concentrates, and the final blending of these with water, syrup, young brandies and other spirits.

Davide Campari

In 1900, Davide, then thirty-three, and Guido opened their first commercial Campari production headquarters in a fairly nondescript building a few blocks away. The same year they invested some of the fruits of their labour in a country villa with a large plot of land at Sesto San Giovanni, a small village on the outskirts of Milan. This purchase was to prove fortuitous, as the Campari business was now growing rapidly and the aperitif had become popular in a number of European countries and was already being imported into the United States, where it was a great favourite with the immigrant Italian population. The brothers immediately realised that their production building in central Milan would not be able to provide the capacity they required and had a new purpose-built Campari headquarters constructed on the land alongside the Villa Campari, which remains the centre of Campari activity to this day.

Davide was an enthusiastic patron of the arts and helped to fund the cost of one of the magnificent sculpted doors of the *duomo* by Gianino Castiglioni, the same artist who in 1939, three years after the death of Davide, was commissioned by the Campari

family to sculpt an inspiring tableau of the Last Supper above the Campari tomb in Milan's Cimitero Monumentale.

Davide also regularly patronised La Scala and other opera houses, and it was his interest in opera that was to lead to his becoming entangled in a remarkable relationship that spanned three countries and some thirty-four years. Today the only remaining evidence of that love affair is the portrait of a beautiful lady in blue that decorates some Campari promotional ashtrays from earlier in the century and which are still in the company's possession. The portrait is of a young opera singer, Natalina Cavalieri, better known as Lina. Having been born on a Christmas Day, Lina was one of those characters who believed every day should be a party and, irresistibly attracted to her magnetic personality, Davide fell hopelessly in love with her.

Lina arrived in Milan in 1902 to perform at the Lirico Theatre. She was then just twenty-eight years old and Davide was seven years her elder. It was the beginning of an enduring relationship that Davide never wanted to abandon, and when in the following year Lina was appearing at Dal Verme in Milan and she announced to him that she was leaving to perform in Nice and savour the good life of the Côte d'Azur, Davide was dismayed. With little hesitation the wealthy and extremely eligible bachelor followed her, probably advising his family and colleagues that it was a business trip, for he certainly transformed it into one by establishing the company's first overseas warehouse, in Nice. It

House audience". From that point onwards Lina became known as "the kissing primadonna". During that same trip she shocked Manhattan society by an absurdly hasty marriage to multimillionaire, Robert W. Chanler. It lasted a mere seven days and after another divorce a more stable marriage, to Italian tenor Lucien Muratore, followed.

It seems that at times Lina lived and loved as if there was no tomorrow, and during her travels she appears to have acquired some curious assets. Quite how she gained title to a prime piece of commercial land in the Parisian suburb of Nanterre remains a mystery, but it is recorded that when her fortunes were at a temporary low, in 1932, when she was again single, the land was purchased from her by the Davide Campari Company for a substantial sum. It was used as the site for their new offices and remains today the Campari Company's French headquarters.

At the time the company purchased the land in Nanterre, Davide was sixty-four and married to his next-door neighbour in Milan, Quintilia Poggeschi. He had wed her in 1917, when he was forty-nine and she fifty-nine. But clearly the Cavalieri spark had never been completely extinguished, for after Quintilia's death in 1934, at the age of seventy-six, and Davide's death in 1936, when he was sixty-nine, a further marriage came to light. This union was only unveiled when Lina, then sixty-nine, died in February 1944 in Florence, when it came under bombardment. The documents that recorded her death referred to an apparently secret marriage late in life to one Giovanni Campari, and Giovanni was Davide's second name.

A PAIR OF PANTS
Cousino Macul, Chile

Vincente Perez Rosales, the eminent Chilean historian of the last century, recounts a story of gratitude from his own experience, which strikes a chord in all human hearts. Rosales recalls that in his younger days, as manager of a substantial farm, on one particular morning he sighted a pair of bedraggled youths approaching. The senior of the two was on horseback, while his partner tugged the lead rope of two cows and an ox. In Rosales' own words, they looked "frayed and tattered". The youth on horseback indicated that they wished to sell the cows and ox for the meagre price of 23 pesos. Realising that the young men must be desperate, Rosales was moved to generosity. His first act was to feed them a good lunch. Then, noticing that the senior and more lively of the two was wearing a pair of trousers that were literally falling to pieces, he told them that they had a deal

was a decision he later regretted, as he closed the warehouse twelve years later and transferred his French distribution to Paris.

The length of time Lina remained in the south of France is not known but undoubtedly the romance blossomed there for some while. Afterwards her travels took the opera singer to tsarist Russia and St Petersburg, where the hot-blooded Lina embarked upon a fresh affair. From the attentions of a wealthy drinks producer she moved up the social scale to minor royalty when she journeyed to Moscow and, for the first time in her life, succumbed to an official wedding ceremony where she exchanged vows with Prince Sasa Bariatinskij. Settling down to married life, even in Russian aristocratic circles, did not suit Lina's temperament for long. From the age of thirteen she had been singing in public and she was accustomed to the exciting and stimulating lifestyle of the international world of opera. A divorce followed, and shortly afterwards Lina found herself on the opposite side of the world, in New York, and achieving notoriety for two quite distinct reasons.

It was the 1906-07 season at the old Metropolitan Opera House at the junction of Broadway and 39th Street, and Lina Cavalieri was cast in the role of Fedora, singing opposite the Great Caruso himself. The part required that she and Caruso embrace, which she did with such passion and gusto, refusing to release him, that she brought the entire audience to its feet. The next day the *New York Evening World* wrote: "Cavalieri and Caruso in fervent embrace arouse a Metropolitan Opera

but he would accept no protests. His price for the cattle was 28 pesos and he would throw in a well-worn but good pair of his own trousers.

Thirty years later, when Rosales held the post of Governor of Concepción, he received a surprise visit from the most prosperous and best-known entrepreneur of the region. To Rosales' astonishment the entrepreneur threw his arms around him and informed the speechless governor that he had been the recipient of the trousers and his generosity so many years ago and now he had returned to repay the debt. The entrepreneur's name was Don Matias Cousino and in the intervening years he had risen from an impoverished livestock dealer to become a shipping, mining and farming magnate, and among his farming interests was one of his greatest loves, namely wine.

At the age of forty-six, in 1856, Don Matias Cousino had acquired one of the oldest vineyards in the Americas, when he had purchased the Macul Estate. It had originally been planted in 1554 by the Spanish conquistador Pedro de Valdivia, when he had been granted land in the south-east of the Santiago region and settled what was called the Jufré Hacienda. Within his land grant, Valdivia selected the right-hand side of the Maipo Valley as the most suitable site for a vineyard and called it Macul. The word "Macul" is taken from the ancient Quecha language and was the name of an Inca village which had previously stood on the spot. Here the Spanish pioneers planted their European vine cuttings, not unlike the Spanish Mission variety initially used in California.

Coincidentally, Don Matias Cousino made part of his fortune during the Californian gold rush. When he heard of the multitudes streaming to the US West Coast, dreaming of untold wealth and prosperity, he remembered lessons from those who had scoured the American continents in earlier years in search of El Dorado. He decided not

CABERNET-SAUVIGNON

to seek gold but to obtain his share of wealth by supplying the prospectors with goods and necessities. At that time, he already owned a number of ships and so he used them to transport cargoes of coal, wheat, flour and vegetables, all of which gave him double profits, once as their producer and again as transporter. His ships returned with timber such as oak, redwood and pine, and also with exotic plants, which he sold to wealthy ranch owners of his homeland.

It is no small coincidence that in 1856, when he purchased what he renamed the Cousino Macul Estate, the vineyards of California were in their infancy. The Santa Clara Valley and Santa Cruz mountains were showing some hopeful activity, but it would be a year before Buena Vista in Sonoma opened its doors, and the vineyard sod would not be cleared in the Napa Valley for another five years. News of California's vinous awakening must have reached Don Matias and it may well have played a part, albeit a minor one, in inspiring him to take a more serious interest in wine production.

By 1850, Don Matias headed an extremely wealthy family and was already travelling the world both for business and pleasure. From such experience he decided to send his son, Don Luis, to study at university in Paris when he was just fifteen years of age. The young Cousino proved talented, and completed his studies without any reported problems, the main effect of his education being the commencement of the family's love affair with France. In 1860, just four years after his vineyard purchase, Don Matias Cousino, being acquainted with numerous fine Bordeaux wines, travelled to that vineyard region to study the working practices of various wine producers there and to purchase vine cuttings to ship to Chile. In Pauillac and Margaux he acquired Cabernet Sauvignon cuttings and then took the short journey to Martillac in the Graves region to buy Sauvignon and Semillon plants. Later he imported some Pinot Noir vines from Burgundy and even some Riesling from the Rheingau. A French architect was hired to design an ideal winery and cellars for the future needs of the estate. But tragically, Don Matias never saw the completed project, as the contract began in 1870, three years before his death in 1873, and it was not completed until 1878.

Without realising the enormity of his action, Don Matias had, to a degree, created a mirror image of a great Bordeaux chateau of pre-phylloxera days, because the cuttings he had shipped from France were selected before phylloxera became a serious threat. As for his new winery, he had considered all eventualities, even down to temperature control. In 1878 it was arguably the most complete and comprehensive purpose-built winery in the continent of South America. Five years later, his widow, Dona Isadora Cousino, hired Godefroy Durand, a leading Bordeaux winemaker, and so completed their plan. The Cousino Macul winery became an example and role model for other Chileans and entitles the family to claim that as long ago as the last century they actually began the modernisation of Chilean wine production, which has brought so many delicious and favourably priced wines to the tables of wine lovers today.

PERFECT CHOICE
Caymus Special Selection, USA

When Henk Schuitemaker, the dynamic young food and beverage director at the Angas Barn in Raleigh, North Carolina, wanted to send me a liquid present, he made what was in my eyes the perfect choice. With the Angas Barn having one of the most impressive wine lists in the United States, the choice open to him was daunting, but he

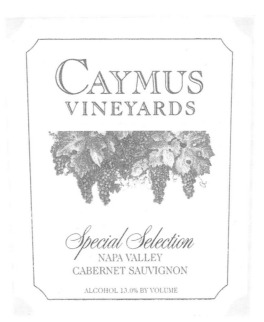

thought carefully and decided upon an outstanding bottle of American wine. It was one that would benefit from many years of cellar ageing and of course recall the memory of the gift and the giver when finally enjoyed.

His decision was Caymus Vineyards Special Selection Napa Valley Cabernet Sauvignon, from the superb 1987 vintage, a red wine that should peak at about fifteen to twenty years of age. With the Napa Valley having a relatively short history of futures or laying-down wines, Henk recognised the exceptional merits of a wine which many rank among the Napa superstars, if not as the current champion.

Yet Caymus Vineyards only embarked on its official career in 1972 and developed in a manner that confounded many experts who scoff at the humble efforts of home winemakers, which is exactly what Caymus founder Charlie Wagner was at that time. As a veteran Rutherford farmer, Charlie grew some grapes, among other crops, sold them to several well-known wineries and retained a small quantity to crush for the family's own consumption. Like many amateurs, Charlie became quite enthusiastic about his efforts and in 1972 decided to relinquish his amateur status for that of part-time professional, when he made 230 cases of Cabernet. The following crush of 1973 saw his full-time professional status arrive as he produced a stunning red wine that excited the length and breadth of the valley. In two years he had risen from home winemaker to one who was attributed with greatness by his peers, an achievement that was more than mildly pleasing to a man who was then in his sixties.

Today, in tandem with his talented son Chuck, Wagner has increased his overall production to

Charlie (left) and Chuck Wagner, Caymus Vineyards

around 27 000 cases a year, of which only 1 000 are Special Selection and the old Rutherford farm makes a tiny bit more profit than when it sold its grapes to others and old Charlie hovered over his home-made wine in a farmyard outhouse.

A PILE OF SHELLS
Limeburner's Bay Vineyard, New Zealand

The name of the New Zealand wine Limeburner's Bay Vineyards has an intriguing and involved history; it embraces both pure chance and dogged determination, as well as being a dire warning against the perils of overindulgence. It is based on the story of one hardy character, Rice Owen Clark, whose life underwent so many sea changes that he must have wondered what the next day would bring.

Clark was born into a prosperous upper-class English family in Great Marlow, Buckinghamshire,

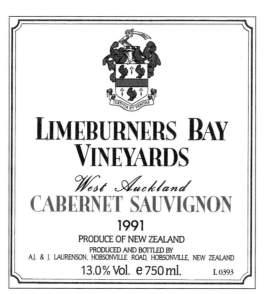

LIMEBURNERS BAY VINEYARDS
West Auckland
CABERNET SAUVIGNON
1991
PRODUCE OF NEW ZEALAND
PRODUCED AND BOTTLED BY
AJ. & J. LAURENSON, HOBSONVILLE ROAD, HOBSONVILLE, NEW ZEALAND
13.0% Vol. e 750 ml.   L 0393

Limeburners Bay, West Auckland, New Zealand, circa 1900

early in the 19th century. His father must have considered him a gifted student, for he sent him in his teens to study in France and upon his return, three years later, he easily found work in the world of commerce in London. There, in the sample room of a prominent wine merchant, Clark was able to put his fluent French to good effect. But he was a restless character and soon felt prompted to seek his fortune elsewhere than in the world of wine, and so he transferred his attentions to the city and particularly to Lloyds of London, the giant shipping and insurance centre.

As a young man in his early twenties, Clark was able to enjoy the exciting world of trade by day and the good life of the bustling city by night. London at that time was, according to many historians, a capital infested with every kind of debauchery and decadence. Prostitution of young men and women was rife, and for many of the paid participants it was their only means of survival. Worse still, the "good life" was largely encouraged by the extravagant behaviour of certain elements among royalty, the aristocracy and the upper classes, who also had the excessive wealth to indulge their whims. The leaders of Great Britain were publicly smiling and revelling in the vastness of the British Empire while masses of their own people suffered lives of appalling squalor and degradation. It was a world of stark contrasts and one which the young Rice Owen Clark was on the verge of experiencing.

There is no evidence that R.O. Clark, as he was later known, was a regular participant in this dawn-to-dusk society, but it is likely that he had more than a passing acquaintance with it. One specific incident in which he was involved precipitated his downfall. No doubt what came about began as horseplay, and as a jest originating in the overflow of high spirits natural in young men, but the outcome was the sole reason for Clark's sudden emigration to New Zealand.

As a young bachelor of twenty-four, Clark was apparently held in good esteem. However, one night he accompanied a group of young gentlemen revellers to a place of dubious repute. There he became helplessly intoxicated and his fellows placed him in the company of a young male transvestite, with whom they made their drunken friend transact a form of marriage ceremony. It was an elaborate hoax, but when Clark awoke in the morning he was appalled by his folly. To escape the misalliance with this "woman", he determined to flee and his comrades, albeit with great difficulty, maintained their silence, while he made all haste to the nearby London docks to buy the first available passage to the far side of the world.

Four and a half months later his lifestyle underwent a dramatic change when he discovered that the

New Zealand of the 1840s had little use for his French, his limited wine knowledge or his mercantile insurance skills. To feed himself he was forced to turn to manual labour and apply his physical strength to making roads at half a crown per day. The employment was short-lived and was followed by a succession of jobs of equal brevity before he was appointed teacher at a small Wesleyan school in Wellington. The upturn in his fortunes was to be temporary, for in one of the 1848 New Zealand earthquakes the adjoining church collapsed across the school building, destroying it.

Over the years Clark had become deeply religious and was now married with a one-year-old daughter, and so the small family moved to Auckland, where they remained for some while until, in 1854, they trekked a further 10 miles or so north-west to claim some land. Initially Clark was the first and only European settler in the area, but that situation did not continue for long. New Zealand's governor had asked for the assistance of some British Royal Navy surveyors to map out territories for land grants. One of these surveyors, called Warner, was instructed to prepare plans for the area surrounding West Auckland. In the course of his duties Warner was utterly confounded when he reached one particular bay, for he found there an unexpected English settler, standing on the beach, burning mounds of shells and then slaking the embers with sea water to produce lime for the acidic soil he had cleared, where cultivation was proving a serious problem.

The land that R.O. Clark had settled was low and in need of drainage, and to this end he began digging out the clay which surrounded the edges of the bay. He would mould the clay around tree trunks to form pipes, which he would then fire. Despite that ingenuity, his efforts at a market garden never quite prospered to his satisfaction and so he concentrated instead on selling clay pipes and tiles to new settlers as they arrived. He set up Clark's Brick and Pipeworks at the very edge of the water and by so doing attracted competition, until by 1870 there were four rival companies trading there. However, by the end of the century his company had outgrown and absorbed the others and went on to become the international giant Ceramco, owner for some while at a later date of the celebrated Royal Grafton company in Stoke-on-Trent, England.

It is sufficient perhaps to report that after all his trials and tribulations, Clark died an extremely wealthy man, one of his numerous activities preserved in the name of a highly rated New Zealand wine. His attempts to produce lime from a fire of seashells led the naval surveyor Warner to name the cove Limeburner's Bay. Today Alan and

Jetta Laurenson's vineyard is planted on the upper part of the original Limeburner's Bay Estate and their mouth-watering results suggest that they do not have too many problems with the soil.

As for R.O. Clark and his marital status, some time after his arrival in New Zealand he received a letter from one of his brothers referring to that drunken night in London. He assured him that there had been no valid marriage and that the "lady" had been a young man in disguise.

PINEAU NOT PINOT
Pineau des Charentes, France

Holiday-makers driving through the gentle chalky hills of the Charentes region of western France are accustomed to the proliferation of small signs that advertise En Vente Pineau. These announce that a small farmer is offering his own production of a sweetish, grapey, delicious aperitif, called Pineau des Charentes, for sale. This can officially be either Blanc or Rosé. With the latter lies a clue, for the Rosé is not in fact Rosé but Rouge, a contradiction which has never been adequately explained to me by any Pineau personality. The situation has left me wondering if these charming and hospitable folk are perhaps a little confused about other items of a viticultural nature.

The Menuet property – a typical Pineau estate

My research into Pineau began in the early 1970s, when with two long-standing friends, Derek Grindell and Bernard Rees, I was involved in buying a holiday home in the Charentes. Many a morning break was taken at the antiquated Café de Commerce in the hamlet of Thairé d'Aunis, where we would delight to see the patron open the door of his large refrigerated cupboard and pour us a glass or two of the local nectar. Our regular visits to the ancient province of Aunis aroused my interest in its history, particularly its viticulture, a subject that was becoming increasingly attractive to me. In the course of my research I chanced upon a grape variety which originated there, called the Pineau d'Aunis, and which had been popular throughout the Charentes in the 15th and 16th centuries. The information was to lie dormant in my memory for many years to come.

Then a visit to record some radio items took me a little further south in the Charentes region to cover the topic of Pineau and just as I was listening to a colourful explanation of the drink's background, the information came flooding back. On this occasion I was in Les Trois Pigeons, a greatly favoured gourmet restaurant on the outskirts of the rather sombre town of Cognac, listening to the story of the aperitif's origin while devouring Moules au Pineau, followed by a mouth-watering dessert accompanied by a couple of glasses of Vieux Pineau. An unidentified senior official of the local Pineau Comité was relating how it had all come about quite by chance 400 years ago. A farmer in the vicinity had erroneously poured some fresh grape must into a barrel which contained a small amount of Cognac. A few days elapsed and he returned to check the fermentation and was surprised to see no activity. Curious to know what had happened he tasted the liquid and found it quite superb. He realised at once the mistake he had made and decided to leave his new drink to age for a couple of years before retasting it and sharing his discovery.

"And that," the official explained, "is quite simply how Pineau des Charentes was born."

Later, another Pineau des Charentes official told me that the reason for its name was that the farmer was actually a Monsieur Pineau.

"Oh yes!" I exclaimed. "Monsieur Grape Variety."

"Well," came her reply, "you have to understand that it is local legend and we are talking about 1590."

6. VIRTUE AND CHARACTER

CLOS STE HUNE
F.E. Trimbach, France

Many leading wine journalists regard Clos Ste Hune as the finest of all Alsace wines, and some even consider it among the world's greatest dry white wines. Its maximum production of 8 000 bottles per annum comes from a tiny plot in the ancient village of Hunawihr, within sight of the parish church of Sainte Hune, who was the inspiration behind the development of the vineyard. Sainte Hune was a young woman who lived in the 8th century and who dedicated herself to serving the sick and poor of the neighbourhood. She was reputed to have healed many parishioners of their maladies by using the local wine as a medicine.

ALSACE
APPELLATION ALSACE CONTROLÉE

Clos Ste Hune

RIESLING 1982
WHITE ALSACE WINE   750 ml

F. E. TRIMBACH PROPRIETAIRE-VITICULTEUR A RIBEAUVILLE & HUNAWIHR (HAUT-RHIN)
PRODUCT OF FRANCE   ESTATE BOTTLED   BOTTLED IN FRANCE

Imported by: SEAGRAM CHATEAU and ESTATE WINES COMPANY
ALCOHOL BY VOLUME 12%   NEW YORK N.Y.

COLOURFUL KRUG
Champagne Krug, France

Krug is without doubt the classic Champagne, and the Krug family is also a classic, with many figures of considerable individuality and talent in its history. Of these one of the most notable was the late Madame Joseph Krug II, whose husband was imprisoned in 1915 during World War I. In his absence she not only took charge of the firm's

cellars but, during the siege of Reims, organised a pharmacy from them to help supply the local hospital. She reasoned that the medicines and drugs could not be destroyed 100 feet below the surface of the ground, whereas in a building above they could be obliterated in one flash. Despite being gassed twice the brave lady persisted in her heroic endeavours.

Later, during the course of World War II, Madame Krug became involved in the smuggling of Allied airmen out of France, hopefully on their way to freedom. She was twice imprisoned and suffered greatly, but even after the war she continued helping with repatriation work.

Madame Krug was said to have been responsible for the only time Krug produced, in 1915, a single vintage Champagne tinged with pink. The problem was that the Battle of Champagne took place during September of that year. This and other effects of the Great War created numerous problems, with roads that were inaccessible, transport that was commandeered and fuel that was only supplied for priority use. Apart from these issues, all able-bodied men had been enlisted, along with many women, who were assisting in the field services. The end result was that experienced pickers were in short supply.

Madame Krug assessed the difficulties confronting her. She knew that instead of the house's normal practice of purchasing the finest Chardonnay grapes from a range of villages spread across the Côte des Blancs, it was almost certain that they would be restricted to using the two black varieties only. Pinot Noir and Pinot Meunier were regularly supplied by villages on the Montagne de Reims. Fortunately she was able to obtain a limited quantity of Chardonnay from the village of Villers-Marmery, on the eastern side of the Montagne, and concluded that they should produce a good wine.

Consequently she made the 1915 vintage in a unique style which may have been due to her efforts to compensate for the lack of Chardonnay. She decided to allow the skins to be pressed a little longer than usual and the colour gave that particular Krug vintage a true *oeil-de-perdrix* (eye of the partridge; see page 200) hint, as well as providing a Champagne that was judged to be full of body and flavour.

CURES AND CLAIMS
Bernkasteler Doktor, Anjou and St Pelligrino;
Germany, France and Italy

Wine is the Best Medicine is a delightful little book, written by Dr Maury, a French physician who established a sound reputation for himself in both Paris and London after World War II. In his book he extols the medicinal virtues of good French wines, as he takes his readers on a geographical tour of those vineyards which he endorses as beneficial to the health. Personally I have no need of such convincing since witnessing, at the early age of fifteen, the healing properties of wine. The experience I refer to occurred at a swimming pool in the French Atlantic resort of la Baule, where I was one of a group of French and Welsh exchange pupils who were enjoying a midday frolic in the warm sun. All of a sudden, during the course of some typical adolescent horseplay, one of our Welsh group, Brian Tanner, my room-mate, slipped and fell incurring a nasty graze on his right leg; he was also a little shaken. Immediately, a cool glass of muscadet was produced as a cure and Brian's only hesitation was in deciding whether to rub it on or drink it. In his innocence he did both and in an instant was completely restored.

The medicinal properties of wine have been recognised at least since Roman times, when Julius Caesar, in 50 BC, advised his legions to drink it as a protection against cholera and typhus. Some sources go as far as to suggest that he imposed a compulsory ration of $1\frac{1}{2}$ litres per day. A hundred years later, St Paul also advised Timothy to "take a little wine for the sake of thy stomach".

Later, in 14th-century Germany, wine's medicinal reputation received a further substantial boost from the claims of the Docktor vineyard in the quaint old Mosel Valley town of Bernkastel. For many years the local population had believed the wine had health-giving properties and when the news reached them that their much loved leader, Archbishop Bohemund II, Elector of Trier, was on his deathbed, they sent a cask of the wine to his Landshut Castle, with the request that the fading ruler should partake of it. The effect was startling and after a deep sleep, Bohemund was restored to strength amid much public rejoicing.

The account of this apparent cure quickly became widespread throughout the Holy Roman Empire and the demand for the wine of the Bernkasteler Docktorberg, increased dramatically, along with its price. The name has since been modified to Bernkasteler Doktor and the wine is acknowledged as one of Germany's greatest, and indeed one of the finest Riesling wines in the world.

Early in the 20th century the medicinal benefits of the Bernkasteler Doktor were put to the test by a member of the British royal family. When the late King Edward VII learned of the healing properties claimed for the wine, this portly gentleman, suffering, so it is reputed, from years of dissipation, decided to take a regular dose in an attempt to rid himself of gout.

He consulted with the London office of the Koblenz wine merchants, Deinhard & Co., who had in 1899 acquired a one-third share in the prestigious company, and subsequently the king travelled to Germany to visit the Mosel and hopefully benefit from regular dosage, rather in the manner of partaking the waters in a spa town, as was the current vogue.

Whether the gout-ridden king was cured by the Doktor is not recorded, but the accounts of the company of Deinhard & Co. show that from that day to this they have supplied the royal household with various German wines, and the Bernkasteler Doktor is frequently on the list.

Again in the 14th century, in the neighbouring Rheinhessen, the unfortunately named town of Worms gave us Liebfraumilch, a wine of a humble level which has nonetheless introduced millions, including the author, to the wine-drinking habit.

At that time, Worms was a centre for the training of young guildsmen, where they spent six months as part of their apprenticeships. To protect these young innocents from the ways of the world, they were normally given board and lodging in local monastic hostels. As an accompaniment to their evening meal they were generally given milk to ensure that they remained clear-headed for evening devotions. But the hostel of the Liebfrauenkirche, or the Church of Our Lady, an attractive building which remains standing to this day, was an exception. Here the youths quenched their thirst with a fresh, fragrant wine from the vineyards surrounding the church. In the mornings they would boast to the other apprentices how they had been enjoying the Milk of Our Lady, or Liebfraumilch.

In one of my favourite stamping grounds in France, the Touraine vineyards of the Loire Valley (not that they have stamped on any grapes there for about a century), I once met a most interesting winegrower, who sported an iron leg. He owned a small property, with an equally small underground cellar, a common feature in the vicinity, and it was located alongside the quiet road that leads from Vouvray to Montlouis. When I met him he must have been in his eighties, but despite his artificial limb and the treacherous steps that led to his little cave, he experienced no difficulty in showing me the way to his cobweb-covered tasting room, which in reality was the end of the cellar where the least activity took place.

He was the only man I have ever encountered who produced a dry Rosé wine from 100 per cent Cot grapes, a seldom-seen ancient variety which is still approved under the appellation contrôlée regulations. As we tasted this unusual drink, he seemed to relax and appeared pleased that a foreign wine enthusiast should have knocked on his lonely door. Noting this I took the liberty of asking him if it were especially difficult to maintain a vineyard with his disability. He glanced up at me with a twinkle in his eye and assured me that it was not too much bother. He was of course rather elderly now, but it was his advanced years rather than his iron leg which slowed him down. He had lost his own leg in the trenches during World War I, but his replacement had not given him any trouble since, because once a week he cleaned it using his own dry white wine.

His tale did not deter me from savouring the delicious wines of the region, which can range from driest to sweetest, and although it is many years since I conversed with that octogenarian, I still have not been able to think of some way in which to take advantage of that unique beneficial property which he confided in me that day.

Forty or so miles west of Montlouis are the ancient vineyards of Anjou, so named after the medieval kingdom that once dominated this area. Its Rosé wine was, for many years, an inexpensive favourite in the United Kingdom but lately it has somewhat lost its sway. Its semi-dry, fruity flavour is for most consumers inoffensive, and for some positively delectable. In Dr Maury's opinion it was an important prescription for lack of appetite and one that I have put to the test both in the Anjou

region and at home in Britain. After the fifth or sixth course, I always begin to doubt the great medic's credibility, for try as I might, no matter how high a dose of Rosé d'Anjou I take, I cannot persuade myself to eat another morsel. Clearly, his proposition, to date, remains unconfirmed.

In January 1983 I was invited by the leading Beaujolais producer Marc Pasquier-Desvignes to accompany him to the village of Pommiers to serve on the Grand Jury, whose task it was to select the outstanding wine of the previous vintage. The Grand Jury comprised just five people: Marc, an elegantly dressed country gentleman of some refinement, as the chairman; a Monsieur Ribut as the representative of the growers, who was also at the time president of the UIVB, the official organisation responsible for the promotion and good health of all Beaujolais wines; another man, who represented the artisans, and who had his own bottling and filtering machinery which travelled from farm to farm providing its service; and finally myself, as a representative of the press, and a tubby, purple-faced man, whose status puzzled me – that is, until we set to work.

While four of us sniffed, swirled and spat samples from the unlabelled bottles before us, it came to my attention that the last of the above-mentioned individuals was the only one to swallow every single drop of the competitors' wine that was poured into his silver tastevin. As he drank, he would mutter remarks either to himself or to the rest of us, his barely audible claims usually being to the effect that he could recognise Jacques' wine, or Albert's, or Jean's, because of its style or body. The more I observed the more curious I became until, after we had tasted some forty or so wines and were taking a short respite, I plucked up the courage to ask him just what his role was.

"*Monsieur, je suis le consommateur!* (I am the consumer!) and who knows more about Beaujolais in Pommiers than me? In thirty years I have drunk

The Bernkasteler Doktor vineyard can be seen between the walls behind the church

over 25 000 bottles from this commune alone!"

As he finished his sentence he began to leave the platform, just as I wanted to pursue my enquiries.

"S'il vous plait, Monsieur, please Monsieur, wait a moment. I would like to ask you some more questions."

"Certainly," came the reply, "but you'll have to follow me."

"But where are you going?"

"Across the road to a bar. I'm dying for a good glass of Beaujolais," he shouted. "And there's nothing better than Beaujolais for your health."

One of the most wasted efforts to provide a medicinal cure using wine was inflicted upon my late grandmother, Cicely Cory, who, I admit to my sorrow, could appreciate two or three gins and tonic before lunch or sixty Craven A a day, but could not comprehend why the gourmets of this world poured adulation upon the name of Champagne.

In her forties she suffered a succession of chest and lung diseases which left her rather debilitated and her general practitioner felt the need to recommend a good tonic. The doctor, John Sewart, was either a contemporary thinker of Dr Maury, or had chanced to read of the French physician's remedies, as he prescribed one half bottle of Champagne per day. The tragedy was that my grandmother simply detested the King of Wines, and was horrified at her physician's insistence that she should improve her health in this manner. Worse still, it was at a time when many would have loved such a prescription but would not have been able to afford it. In order to follow her doctor's instructions, my grandmother forced herself to submit to agonies of displeasure.

Sad to say, my mother was, in those days, a teetotaller and cannot recall which brand of Champagne was prescribed.

Incidentally, Dr Maury writes that Champagne is rich in potassium but somewhat deflates any chauvinism in that region by admitting, with surprising candour, that Asti Spumante from Italy, at about one-third of the price, has exactly the same property.

Probably more has been written about the medicinal virtues of bottled water than of wine, although it has to be said in all fairness that few of the reputable companies today make exaggerated claims for their waters. Not so in the 1960s, as I discovered on a trip to Sardinia. There I came across an ashtray that promoted one of Italy's sparkling waters, a brand which is still one of my favourites – San Pellegrino. I was so amused by what was written on the ashtray that I requested, and was granted, permission to keep it as a souvenir. As this chapter is being written, nearly a quarter of

a century later, that souvenir is alongside me, but, I hasten to add, never has it been used for its original purpose.

The ashtray is rectangular with wavy edges and is blue with a white border. Near the centre, presumably to catch the eye, there is a red star and beneath it, in four languages – Italian, French, Spanish and English – are printed its startling claims. It reads (and I quote the English):

Unrivalled for curing the:-
URIC DIATHESIS: gout, gravel, stones of the bladder, kidney and liver:
CATARRH of the stomach, bowels and bladder:
CONGESTION and SWELLING of the LIVER from diseases of the stomach intestines, infectious fevers, malaria and alcoholism:
The DISEASES of the KIDNEYS and ALBUMINURIA in uric acid diathesis:
The gouly MANIFESTATIONS OF THE SKIN:
Excellent, cooling, aperient, hygienic drink.

One water with all these properties. If only Dr Maury could have read the list; I wonder what he would have said.

DOCTORS OF WINE
Lindeman, Penfold, Pendarves Estate; Australia:
David Bruce, California

Two supremely gifted men, both born in 1811, a mere 40 miles apart in southern England, went on to be contemporary trainee surgeons in London's St Bartholomew's Hospital. Later both emigrated to Australia and pursued identical yet quite separate paths as "Doctors of Wine".

Upon arrival in Australia, both were employed as general practitioners and recommended wine for its medicinal benefits. Today these illustrious men are remembered on two of the most familiar and respected labels of our generation. Their names were Henry John Lindeman and Christopher Rawson Penfold. It is not claimed that they were the first Doctors of Wine, but the contribution they made to the reputation of wine and its positive properties, and their influence on the story of Australian wine, is incontrovertible.

For several thousand years, history has recorded the use of wine for medicinal purposes, but it is well nigh impossible to identify the first occasion on which it was put to such use. In Old Testament times it was given occasionally for its recuperative value, but it would be an exaggeration to maintain that doctors actually prescribed it.

Yet during the lifetime of Our Lord, a charitable band of women existed in Jerusalem who would mix drugs with wine to ease the pain of those suffering from serious illnesses. Some experts have

pointed to these women as the possible source of the bitter wine offered to Our Saviour when he was hanging on the Cross of Calvary.

Early European history refers to the Greek physician Hippocrates, born on the island of Cos around 460 BC, as recommending wine as a medicine. Even so, that does not justify any claim to his being the first Doctor of Wine. In truth, the first was probably public commonsense.

The earliest Doctor of Wine who is known to have planted vines to produce wine for its health benefits is possibly Jan Van Riebeeck, the naval surgeon and explorer who was also leader of the first Dutch party to settle South Africa's Cape in 1652. Van Riebeeck already had a reputation for recommending wine as protection against scurvy and planted the first vines on South African soil in that year, with that very purpose in mind.

To return to Lindeman and Penfold, both were born into middle-class English families during the first year of the Regency period, during which George IV assumed the royal responsibilities of the demented George III. The doctors lived in times of great change and they played their own parts in the development of a transforming world.

Of the two, Dr Lindeman was the first to emigrate, disembarking at Sydney on 18 August 1840, following a brief stop at Melbourne. The most comprehensive details of Lindeman's life, for which many readers, including myself, are most grateful, are found in Dr Philip Norrie's exhaustive book *Lindeman, Australia's Classic Winemaker.* Dr Norrie, the subject of a later section of this chapter, explains fully that the Lindeman family were

living in Hythe, Hampshire, in 1811, but that Henry Lindeman's mother returned to her home town of Egham in Surrey, not far from the site of what is now Heathrow Airport, for her confinement. She gave birth on 21 September 1811 and, presumably after a suitable rest, returned to Hythe to continue her daily life. The name Lindeman is believed to have originated from the Rhine a century earlier and is still commonly found there as well as in the eastern United States. Henry's father was a prosperous general practitioner, and the family were devout Anglicans. Indeed, Dr Henry Lindeman remained an energetic Christian all his life.

Nothing is known about his schooling but the Lindeman family's diligent record-keeping informs us that he was apprenticed to his father, a common practice in those days. The arrangement was in no way casual and the father and son signed indentures which stated that the fourteen-year-old Henry John was apprenticed to become a "Surgeon Apothecary and Man Midwife" after five years. Anyone of legal background might question how such an agreement between a minor and his father could be enforceable, but such a question would not even have been considered in that day and age.

When his apprenticeship was completed, Henry Lindeman succeeded in gaining a place at the highly esteemed medical school of St Bartholomew's, near the ancient Smithfield Market in the City of London. In the autumn of 1830 he embarked upon his course as a student surgeon in what remains one of the oldest continuous hospitals in the world, and which stands on its original AD 1123 site. Lindeman shared his classes there with Christopher Penfold, although there is no evidence of a close friendship. In 1834, Lindeman enrolled as a member of the Royal College of Surgeons and afterwards apparently practised as a surgeon until his emigration six years later. Unfortunately, in spite of efforts to trace any records of this period, none have come to light. However it is believed that at some stage in the mid-1830s Dr Lindeman toured some of the vineyard regions of Germany and France.

Dr Henry Lindeman

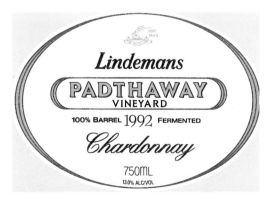

In February 1840, aged twenty-eight, Lindeman married Eliza Bramhall, who was only eighteen, and six weeks later, on 24 March, they set sail for Australia on board the 494-ton barquentine *Theresa*. Lindeman was listed in the ship's papers as its surgeon. After berthing in Melbourne, the *Theresa* eventually arrived in Sydney on 18 August. The young couple had spent twenty-one weeks on board, as the ship's voyage had been extended by a stop at Plymouth to collect additional emigrant passengers and by the ship's first docking at Melbourne.

After a short stay in Sydney, Dr and Mrs Lindeman progressed inland to the Hunter Valley in New South Wales, to Gresford on the Paterson River. There Dr Lindeman opened a general medical practice from his home, where his daughter Harriet was born on 1 October 1841. Her name had been carefully chosen so that she would have the same initials as her father.

In January of the following year Dr Lindeman bought some 800 acres of a property called Cawarra, or "running water" in Aboriginal language. In all probability he acquired it for an extremely low price, as it was the subject of a failed land grant. In 1843 a slab cottage was constructed and Dr Lindeman planted his first vines. The meticulous Dr Norrie writes that: "He selected the rich alluvial flats on the north-western side of the Paterson River to plant Riesling, Verdelho and Shiraz grapevines". This would suggest that neither Alsace nor the Rhine or the Mosel were included in his European vineyard tour, as in those regions the Riesling is usually planted in poorer soil. Nevertheless, over a period of time the vineyard was extended to around 40 acres and in 1847 Dr Lindeman applied for a government permit for the immigration of a German vinedresser and a cooper. Three years later, in 1850, he joined the Hunter River Vineyards Association, of which he was president from 1863 to 1870.

In the meantime, Dr Lindeman's practice and his prescription of wine for good health increased, as did his family. Eliza produced ten children over a period of twenty-two years, their Cawarra house being extended as necessary. Furthermore, the Lindemans provided a home for the doctor's younger brother, Arthur, who came to them after an earlier interval in Jamaica. Arthur was a scholarly man who devoted himself to the children's upbringing, which suited Henry, as it enabled him to develop his growing reputation as a promoter of the health benefits of wine. Aware of the abuse of spirits that was prevalent in Australia, he publicly campaigned for wine to be the national beverage and wrote various published articles on the subject. One of these, addressed to the editors of the *Medical Gazette*, was entitled "Pure Wine as a Therapeutic Agent and Why I Believe it Should Become our National Beverage". Amusingly, when published, the article bore the initials of the signatory's name as W.T. instead of H.J. It seems Dr Lindeman suffered from that all too common doctor's disease of illegible handwriting.

To prescribe wine was one thing, but for his patients to find wine of satisfactory quality was another, for most of the local vines were extremely young and many of the winemakers inexperienced. To achieve his ends Dr Lindeman divided his attention between the two professions. Soon his wines became better known than his medical practice and they attracted noteworthy sales in Newcastle and Sydney. At the age of forty-seven, in 1858, the doctor had good cause to be a proud man, when he exported his first consignment of Cawarra Claret to London. In 1870 he became the first wine producer to transfer his headquarters to Sydney, where he opened the Exchange Cellars in Pitt Street, three of his sons helping him to organise his booming business.

Dr Lindeman had a reputation as a very good employer who took a serious interest in his staff. Indeed, after a July 1993 television appearance I made on the "Midday Show, with Ray Martin", on Australia's national Channel 7, I received a letter from a viewer which emphasised this very point. Patricia Tarhy of Sylvania wrote that her direct ancestor on her mother's side was an Irishman called Laraghy, who in 1864 was hired by Dr Lindeman to be a vinedresser at his Cawarra property. Dr Lindeman quickly grew to appreciate the interest in vines shown by Laraghy's eldest son, Ambrose,

Lindeman export bottle, 1889. The term Australian Hock shows that it was aimed at the international markets

and encouraged him to learn all he could about viticulture. This education was sufficiently beneficial that a generation later Ambrose Laraghy travelled 300 miles north with his family to Tamworth, where he founded the Darook Vineyard, which was later sold to the Wyndham Estate.

Dr Lindeman's contemporary, Dr Christopher Penfold, was born in 1811 at Steyning, Sussex, just inland from England's chalky southern coastline. His father was Rector of Steyning for forty years, and to their credit the modern Penfold family in Australia have maintained their relationships with his beloved church in the quiet town. After his success at St Barts, as St Bartholomew's Hospital is familiarly known, a longer space of time than in Dr Lindeman's case elapsed before he emigrated. In 1845 he married Mary Holt from Edmonton, Middlesex, and moved to Brighton, fairly near his elderly parents. There he ran a general practice for some years, his decision in all likelihood being influenced by the age and infirmity of his parents. Following the death of his father in 1840 and of his mother in 1843, he began to make careful plans for the long journey to his new homeland. Free from family responsibility, the Penfolds headed for Europe, possibly the south of France, where they visited wineries and made a brief study of the subjects of viticulture and oenology, and purchased vine cuttings to take with them.

Seven years after the Barossa Valley wine pioneer Johann Gramp had sailed from Deal in Kent, Dr Christopher Penfold, Mrs Mary Penfold and their maid, Ellen Timbrell, boarded the *Taglioni*. Under the command of Captain Black, the vessel slipped its mooring on 10 February 1844 during a ferocious storm and eventually arrived 127 days later, on Tuesday, 18 June, at Largs Bay near Port Adelaide. For some unknown reason, various Penfold records give conflicting dates for their arrival, with 8 August being most popular. However, there is irrefutable evidence of the date 18 June in a report in the *South Australian Register* of Wednesday, 19 June, which identifies the captain and several prominent passengers, among them "Mr and Mrs Penfold and Miss Timbrell the maid".

With little ado, it seems, the party of three set off for Magill, in the foothills of the Mount Lofty ranges. Magill was then some 7 miles from the centre of Adelaide; now it is a suburb. Only three days before his departure, Penfold had paid a deposit of £100 to the Colonial Land and Emigration Commission as a down payment for 500 acres of land, worth £1 200. Two hundred acres of the land were sown with crops and the property was described in the *South Australian Register* as a "truly valuable estate".

Some accounts state that he built a wooden bungalow immediately, which he replaced in the following year with the stone-slab Grange Cottage, which has since become a national landmark. The spacious single-storey building had whitewashed elevations and a low verandah, and the interior walls were lined with red cedar. A corridor led to the doctor's surgery and an anteroom, and to the left were the domestic quarters. When I visited Grange Cottage in July 1993 it was still preserved in something approaching its original condition. It is a priceless treasure in the worldwide story of wine and we must hope that when it is restored its renovators will faithfully retain its authentic appearance.

Alongside the house, Dr Penfold planted his initial 12-acre "Home Vineyard" using the French vine cuttings he had brought with him and possibly some others he had obtained locally. The likely date for the establishment of the vineyard is 1844. A little later he introduced the sherry variety, Palomino, and also Frontignan and Muscat, with

D*r Christopher Rawson Penfold, who founded Penfolds in 1844 when he planted vines on his property at Magill on the outskirts of Adelaide, capital of the infant colony of South Australia*

G*range Cottage, a stone dwelling built by Dr Christopher and Mrs Mary Penfold in 1845 on their property Magill*

VINTAGE 1990

EST. 1844

Penfolds

KALIMNA
BIN 28

Penfolds Kalimna Vineyard, in the Barossa Valley, is considered to be one of the premium red wine vineyards of Australia. Shiraz from Kalimna is blended this vintage with Shiraz from the Barossa Valley, Langhorne Creek McLaren Vale and Padthaway to produce a soft, elegant, yet powerful wine that will continue to improve with further bottle age.

PENFOLDS WINES PTY. LTD. TANUNDA ROAD • NURIOOTPA • S.A. • 5355 • 13.5% ALC/VOL
750mL • WINE MADE IN AUSTRALIA

the intention of producing fortified wines. These vines were purchased locally.

Two minor unsolved mysteries remain associated with Dr Penfold. The first concerns the source of his French vine cuttings. There is the suggestion that he may have spent his time in Bordeaux, but there does not appear to be any evidence of this. Records state that the majority of his vine cuttings were Grenache, a variety that has never been used in the Bordeaux region, but which has thrived in the southern Rhône and throughout the Midi and parts of south-west France. The second mystery surrounds his relationship with Louis Pasteur, the celebrated chemist. The late Max Schubert, formerly Penfold's legendary winemaker, stated that in his understanding:

> Christopher Rawson Penfold went to France to see Louis Pasteur about bringing vines to Australia. They became friends and Pasteur taught him a lot about fermentation and provided him with the first cuttings of Hermitage wines to be brought to Magill.

This sounds possible but cannot be proven. However, there is some degree of corroboration from Gérard Jaboulet of the leading Rhône wine producers Paul Jaboulet Aîné. Gérard Jaboulet said that he had learned that the first Syrah (Shiraz) vines to be used in the Grange Hermitage wine were old stocks that had originated in the actual Hermitage vineyards near their cellars. Penfold is unlikely to have been aware of Pasteur's existence at the time of his emigration, as the French genius would then have been only twenty-one years of age and had not come to fame. Whatever the truth, there is no doubt that Dr Penfold employed the strictest rules of hygiene in his winemaking and was always fastidious about ageing his wines sufficiently in small oak casks before selling them. Indeed much of his winemaking conduct was modelled on Pasteur's recommendations.

Dr Penfold died a little prematurely aged fifty-nine, leaving a reputation which in many ways had

developed in parallel with Dr Henry Lindeman's. He served his community both as a medical practitioner and as a spokesman for wine, prescribing it for good health. Both aspects of his career flourished, albeit on a smaller scale than Dr Lindeman. He was indeed fortunate in his wife, Mary, who some have called, perhaps overgenerously, the first of the lady winemakers. Mary was certainly a great support, for after her husband's demise, she took up the reins of the wine business, first on her own and later with her son-in-law. Her assistance during the doctor's lifetime meant that he could travel to his patients for miles around, and the fact that he was held in great respect is corroborated by the flags in Magill being flown at half-mast on the day of his funeral and all the local stores being closed. It was "a fitting recognition of the esteem in which the deceased was held", the *Register* reported. Dr Penfold was buried in the cemetery at St George's Church in St Bernard Road, Magill, a church of which he was a founding member.

It is entirely appropriate that today's best-known Doctor of Wine is the biographer of both Lindeman and Penfold, Philip Norrie. A man of prodigious energy, Dr Norrie is a busy general practitioner in northern Sydney, a prolific author and, with his wife Belinda, co-owner of the beautiful Pendarves Estate, with its successful vineyard in the lower Hunter Valley.

Dr Norrie's career appears partially preordained, for his ancestor on Australian soil was his great-great-grandfather, Alexander Norrie, from Aberdeen in Scotland. Alexander Norrie settled in Gresford, where he owned Commodore Farm and

Belinda and Philip Norrie

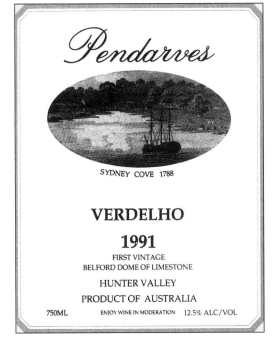

Pendarves Estate and Tasting Rooms

in his spare time, conforming to the Protestant work ethic, he ran the Gresford General Store. One of his customers was none other than Dr Henry Lindeman, who settled in Gresford four years after Norrie.

Dr Philip Norrie has already made his mark in the history of Australian wine. His book *The Vineyards of Sydney* is an integral part of Australian national history. In it he recounts the trials and tribulations of the early settlers, and through his painstaking research he paints a memorable picture of that developing scene. His works on Lindeman, Penfold and Leo Buring, another Australian wine pioneer, and his publication in 1986 of *Medicinal Wine*, have made him a major influence in the history of wine, an influence that no sane writer or journalist can afford to overlook.

Medicinal Wine helped confirm a large part of Dr Norrie's philosophy. In his accounts he presents no less than 150 Australian wine doctors, including individuals such as the jolly Dr Max Lake of Lake's Folly, and Dr Lance Allen of Tamburlaine, who, like Dr Norrie, extol the virtues of wine. He has further underlined his beliefs in his founding role as President of the Australian Medical Friends of Wine Society, an organisation which battles against some of the more extreme measures advocated by the anti-alcohol lobby.

The 30-acre vineyard of his Pendarves Estate is planted both with popular and less widely seen varieties, such as Verdelho and Chambourcin, the latter being a French hybrid which Dr Norrie believes has tremendous potential. The property is situated on the Belford Dome, a limestone outcrop north-west of Pokolbin, which contrasts sharply with the volcanic soil found in most parts of the region. The Pendarves Estate label was designed by Belinda Norrie and features a picture of Sydney Cove in 1788, when Australia's first vineyard was founded on the cove's south-east coast.

Phil Norrie, as he is known to his friends, sent me some information on 10 January 1994, and found time to include a five-page handwritten letter. It apologised for his late response due to the Sydney bushfires, and it exemplified the unselfishness of his character, dwelling more on the problems of his patients than on himself. His words recorded the alarming situation from his viewpoint as the local doctor at Elanora Heights:

> We have been preparing our house in case it came under threat (fortunately the wind changed from the westerlies to a southerly yesterday, otherwise it would have been very interesting). Also we have had extensive blackouts due to the fires burning down power poles and sub-stations but now we are back to normal. Approximately ten of my patients have lost their homes. The area behind the surgery looks like a war zone or as one patient puts it – the day after the bomb without the radiation!

He went on to relate much more, including an explanation of the Pendarves name. This comes from Belinda Norrie's great-grandfather, who came from Cornwall, and who arrived in Sydney in the 1870s. He called both his properties, at Woollahra and Bowral, Pendarves, which he chose because of fond childhood memories of a family of that name near Camborne in Cornwall.

Dr Philip Norrie is one of the major wine figures of our day, and yet until this is read in other countries, few outside Australia will realise the significance of his contribution, which it is hoped will evolve on an international basis. James Halliday, a leading Australian wine writer, gives a vivid description of him as "the perpetual motion general practitioner and founder of the Australian Medical Friends of Wine". He praises Dr Norrie as a born communicator and marketer, as well as a wine historian and author of note, before suggesting that the 1991 Chardonnay and Verdelho at Pendarves Estate are bound to flourish. I will go a step further by recalling that nearly 150 years elapsed before an author like Dr Norrie published biographies of doctors Lindeman and Penfold, while this account of Dr Norrie is being written while he is still alive and only in his forties.

Leaving the Antipodes, a flight of roughly thirteen hours eastwards across the Pacific will take one to the vineyards of California, where the link between wine and good health is a much-debated issue. There in the Santa Cruz Mountains, some 70 miles south of San Francisco, one finds another Doctor of Wine, Dr David Bruce. His spectacular mountainside estate, on Bear Creek Road at 2 200 feet, commands a breathtaking view as well as producing a wine which many non-Napa residents rate as the state's finest and most consistent example of Pinot Noir.

In the terms of the Santa Cruz Mountains, Dr Bruce is a veteran. The purchase of his land in 1961 and the opening of the David Bruce Winery in 1964 placed him in the vanguard of the new "sixties" generation, both of Santa Cruz and Californian winemakers. Vines had been planted in the area as early as 1853 by Lyman J. Burrell and by the mid-1880s the vineyards were thriving. They continued to progress until Prohibition dealt them an untimely blow.

Since his student days at Stanford Medical School, Dr Bruce had always enjoyed wine as a serious hobby, but when he purchased the Santa Cruz site he was forced to include wine in his plans for his future career. At first he continued as a general practitioner in the Santa Cruz valley, but this soon became a part-time occupation and eventually he

made the brave decision to concentrate full-time on wine.

David Bruce may well have found the perfect microclimate for Pinot Noir, a grape variety which is proving a stumbling block for many of California's winemakers. But he has established a style and consistency with that grape that is probably not matched elsewhere in the state. Many wine writers feel that he has not been successful with other varieties, but the proof may yet lie in the extensive following that his wines have attracted.

Dr Bruce loves to recall his fortuitous introduction to wine. He was raised in a teetotal family in postwar California and progressed along a promising academic path that took him to one of the West Coast's most respected medical schools. No doubt encouraged by others there, he felt prompted to taste and judge an outstanding wine for himself. As a serious student he felt he should read a wine book and then select a wine of great repute to try for himself. For his initiation he chose Domaine de la Romanée-Conti, one of the world's greatest red wines.

"That evening I had the wine and I was just about as close to ecstasy as I could imagine anyone being," he recalls, though reports of his attendance at lectures the following morning being equally ecstatic are not recorded. "That's when I decided that I was going to have a vineyard and plant Pinot Noir and while I was going about it I was going to make the greatest Pinot Noir ever made." This was a boldly enthusiastic claim for one so young. However, he did rise to his aspirations, even if the attempt has taken some thirty years of endeavour. As he states, "This was my decision at that point in time and I have been working at that ever since."

Dr David Bruce is a campaigner against the current misguided anti-alcohol lobby in the USA. His letter of 24 March 1993 to President and Mrs Clinton emphasised many of his arguments for the benefit of regular wine consumption. Among wine's advantages, he listed the following in his leaflet "Ten Little Known Medical Facts about Wine that You Should Know":

1. Non-drinkers have approximately the same level of cardiovascular death as heavy alcoholics.
2. Wine is significant in the treatment of both anorexia and obesity, the wine should by dry.
3. Moderate drinkers are, on average, of higher intelligence than either non-drinkers or heavy drinkers.
4. Liver disease is decreasing during a period of increasing wine consumption and decreasing spirit consumption.

They are the words of a doctor who is prepared to get off the fence. One must hope that he will not

Estate Bottled   1990

David Bruce

Santa Cruz Mountains
Pinot Noir

PRODUCED AND BOTTLED BY DAVID BRUCE WINERY
21439 BEAR CREEK RD., LOS GATOS, CA 95030 • (800) 397-9972
ALCOHOL 13% BY VOLUME • CONTAINS SULFITES • 750 ML

only continue to increase his campaigning but also proceed with the supply of the best medicine possible.

Of course, there are and have been more Doctors of Wine than are mentioned in this chapter. Let us hope that in the future there will be others who will be as great an influence as doctors Lindeman, Penfold, Norrie and Bruce.

THE MODEL EMPLOYER
Jameson Irish Whiskey, Ireland

In 1780, when John Jameson was preparing to open his Dublin distillery, he surprised his competitors by offering potential employees remuneration at one and a half times the accepted rate. This policy, together with three conditions of employment, aimed at hiring the best possible labour force.

Jameson had been born in Scotland in the expanding stone city of Glasgow, and like many other Catholics had fled south at an early age, following the defeat of the Stuart forces of Bonnie Prince Charlie. He made his way to Dublin, then still part of Great Britain, where he knew many of his compatriots had settled.

Bearing in mind his background, it would have been understandable if one of his conditions of employment had been adherence to the Catholic faith. But this was not the case; his stipulations were far more practical and even in today's ever-changing world might be viewed as sound guidelines. His first insistence was that all employees must be nonsmokers, the second that they should be married with at least two children, and the third condition was that their habits should be temperate. In return, John Jameson provided a hospital clinic within the distillery grounds, housing and some educational welfare and support.

In New York City there is an unproven tale among whiskey drinkers that a pub called O'Lunneys in West 44th Street can claim a unique St Patrick's Day record. The claim is that a greater volume of Jameson is consumed on the premises on 17 March than any other drink, on any other single day, in any other pub in the world. Presumably the reason for the feat being unattested is that nobody can remember the occasion afterwards.

SCHUBERT'S VINOUS SYMPHONY
Penfolds Grange Hermitage, Australia

For music lovers the name Schubert evokes magical images of symphony and song, of intricate compositions that in their notational form resemble hieroglyphics to some, but when performed sound sweet to many. It is therefore fitting to form an analogy between the musical genius of Franz Schubert and the vinous talent of his albeit distant namesake, the late Max Schubert, whom the English wine magazine *Decanter* in 1988 described as the "Father of Australian Red Wine".

I am in no way qualified to express an opinion on the work of the composer, as my musical talent is nonexistent. But I do claim the right to eulogise on the talent and tenacity of the blacksmith's son from Nuriootpa, in the heart of Australia's Barossa Valley. In the early 1950s, Max Schubert proved himself a man of steel in his efforts to produce Australia's finest red wine. He was mocked by fellow professionals and publicly insulted, but he pressed on doggedly and eventually received the acclamation he deserved.

Max Schubert's personal involvement in wine began in 1931, as a messenger boy with the Penfold Winery in Nuriootpa. Even then Penfolds were regarded as one of the giants of the Australian wine

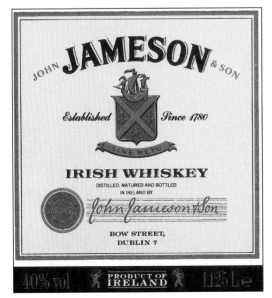

Max Schubert at the Penfold homestead, Grange Cottage

world, but that world was quite different from the one we know today. At that time, to the majority of Australians, wine meant fortified wine. Max showed sufficient interest in the subject to be promoted to the role of assistant to the Penfold chemist at Nuriootpa, who was responsible for ports, sherries and muscats. It soon became evident to one of the directors, Leslie Penfold Hyland, that Max had an exceptional curiosity for wine, and arrangements were made to transfer him to the Penfold cellars at Magill. There he was taken under the wing of the old English winemaker Alf Veysey, who had been working in the cellars since he was first employed in the 1880s by Mary Penfold, widow of the company founder, Dr Christopher Penfold. Max attended night school to study chemistry and its application to winemaking.

Within three years he was appointed a member of the winemaking team and six years later he was made assistant winemaker. At the age of thirty-three, in 1948, he was given the title of Penfold's chief winemaker. In 1949, Max was sent to Europe for several months to observe the vintage and study winemaking in Bordeaux. On that expedition, Max Schubert formed his ambition of making a world-class Australian red wine that would age well for up to twenty years.

He has always acknowledged the influence of Christian Cruse of the famous Bordeaux *négociant* house Cruse. The Frenchman took a liking to Max and went to considerable lengths to teach him everything possible in a relatively short space of time. Later Max reported:

Christian Cruse invited me to his home where he showed me magnificent old French wines, some 60–70 years old but which still had life in them. I have never forgotten those wines and I don't think I have ever tasted anything like them again in my career.

Max also visited chateaux Margaux, Lafite, Rausan-Segla, Beychevelle, Léoville-Poyferre and Pontet-Canet in the Médoc; Haut-Brion in the Graves; Chateau d'Yquem in Sauternes; Cheval Blanc and Ausone in Saint-Emilion; and L'Enclos and La Croix de Gay in Pomerol. Of these, he found most help at Rausan-Segla. There he made careful note of the use of small oak casks for ageing the new wine, a discipline that was not generally practised in Australia at that time.

Max embarked upon research into oak ageing and toyed with various ideas. He concluded that French oak from Allier, Nevers and Limousin would, in general, be better for elegant wines, and American oak would be more suitable for wines which were full-bodied. In late 1993, Max recalled that period. "When I decided to make red wine

that would last for twenty years I immediately thought of using new oak hogsheads for fermentation rather than large French neutral casks." He went on to explain, "No experimentation was performed outside my own head. Grange Hermitage was designed in my mind before I returned to Adelaide." He stressed that French oak had never been used in the making of Grange Hermitage, a fact which makes the label for the 1966 vintage all the more puzzling. It states quite simply that the wine was matured in "small French oak casks", and the label printed below even bears Max's autograph, which must make it quite a collector's item. But there is no skulduggery to report. The label shown came from a poster produced to celebrate twenty-five years of Grange Hermitage and poor Max had to sign countless hundreds. Apparently an oversight in the proofreading meant that the world "French" was used erroneously instead of "American".

Grange Hermitage label with the incorrect French connection – "small French oak casks" should have read "small American oak casks"

Chateau Rausan Segla, source of inspiration for Max Schubert

Upon his return from France in 1949, at Magill, in the suburbs of Adelaide, Max pondered whether it would be possible to use Cabernet Sauvignon. At the time the variety was in short supply in South Australia and so he decided on Shiraz. Knowing the reputation for ageing of the red wines of Hermitage and Côte Rôtie in the Northern Rhône, Max was confident of the grape's potential. He selected some fruit from the Grange vineyard and some from a privately owned one at Morphettvale, to the south of Adelaide, and named the wine Grange, after the Penfold homestead, Grange Cottage, which still stands today. An experimental vintage was made in 1951 but it was not released. Max had developed complicated innovations in the fermentation process, which encouraged a remarkable depth of colour. The wine was aged for eighteen months in five American oak hogsheads before spending a further period in bottle. In the meantime, the 1952 vintage had taken place and it too began its ageing process. In 1953, Max experimented with Cabernet Sauvignon, but problems maintaining a suitable supply of fruit persuaded him to return to Shiraz.

By 1957 some of the Penfold directors were becoming rather anxious about the amount of capital invested in Grange Hermitage, which, in their sight, was "lying idle in their underground cellars at Magill". Consequently the managing director of the day ordered a tasting of each of the six vintages from 1951 to 1956. Wine authorities, connections and friends, as well as most of Penfold's senior management, were invited to attend. Max was horrified by the response. No-one liked, let alone understood the wine, with the exception of one family member, Jeffry Penfold Hyland, who was then the company's assistant general manager for the state of South Australia. With Jeffry's active support, Max and his team began giving samples of Grange Hermitage to clubs and societies whose members were either serious wine professionals or knowledgeable amateurs.

Max has commented:

It was the worst time in my life. It may be illuminating to record some of the assessments made by experts and critics, both in public and in my presence, during the darkest hours of Grange Hermitage. Some of the remarks were downright rude and pained me no end.

These included: "A concoction of wild fruits and sundry berries with crushed ants predominating"; and, from a respected wine figure, "Schubert, I congratulate you; a very good, dry port, which no-one in their right mind will buy, let alone drink." Also there was the individual who asked Max to give him a couple of dozen bottles. He was not

going to pay for them, as he did not think the wine was worth anything.

The death knell tolled a few weeks before the 1957 vintage, when written instructions were issued by the board of directors to cease the production of Grange Hermitage. But Max was not a quitter, and with Jeffry Penfold Hyland accidentally looking in the wrong direction, the Grange Hermitage operation continued under a veil of secrecy. Without an official budget, production was reduced and there were no new oak barrels. In July 1993, one Penfold veteran described to me how the forbidden vintages were hidden in the Champagne cellars, in Cellar 20. Max played his cards close to his chest and only a few key members of the Magill team had any notion that he was deliberately disobeying orders. He realised that he would have to bide his time, and time alone would see the wine achieving greatness. He hoped that as the years passed, the occasional compliment might be forthcoming and that is exactly what happened. Experts began to take note of the evolution of Grange Hermitage, and rumours reached the board of directors that they may have made a monumental error. The trickle of comments grew into a steady stream, and shortly before the 1960 vintage, after three years of clandestine production, Max was permitted to resume the Grange Hermitage program.

A little later came the revoking of another Penfold company practice. For many years they had eschewed Australian wine shows and competitions, a field many would uphold as the lifeblood of the industry. With forecasts of a change in market conditions, from fortified to table wines, the directors felt the time was right to enter the fray again, and Grange Hermitage 1955 was chosen as the entry in the Open Claret Class at the 1962 Sydney Show. That 1955 vintage won a gold medal, and during the following few years gathered a total of fifty gold medals in shows across the country. Only one cloud remained on the horizon for Grange Hermitage and it came from those quarters where previously it had been ridiculed and now the wine was an object of envy as it rose to fame. The same senior Penfold figure told me that in the following three years, the vintages of 1956, 1957 and 1958 were entered in a major show but they failed to win any medals because an anonymous saboteur smeared Joy Patou and Old Spice onto the glasses. I have no corroboration of this but if it is untrue then it is a remarkably elaborate invention.

Max Schubert led his team through twenty-five successive vintages before his retirement in 1975. He developed for Grange an international reputation as yet unrivalled by any other Australian wine, and he also gained international recognition for his own work. The leading British wine writer and broadcaster Hugh Johnson has described Grange Hermitage as "the one true first-growth of the southern hemisphere", and the former editor of *Decanter*, the colourful Tony Lord, called Max "the Grand Old Man of the Australian wine industry, its maestro and the creator of Australia's greatest wine." In addition to those compliments, Max has been awarded the Order of Australia by the country's government for his services to wine.

When I interviewed Max for LBC Radio in London in March 1988, it was minutes after he had been honoured with *Decanter* magazine's Man of the Year award, and many of the illustrious vintages of Grange Hermitage were available for tasting. As I listened to Max speaking about them and how their reputation had developed, it became apparent that the *Decanter* panel had made only one error. The award should not have been restricted to Man of the Year but expanded to Man of the Decade, for surely Max deserved such acknowledgement. He had written the music and conducted the orchestra which produced the wine that had gained such plaudits. If only his distant namesake could have seen him, he would surely have had to acknowledge that Grange Hermitage had become a great vinous symphony.

A SPIRITED LADY

Metaxa, Greece

In 1888, Spyros Metaxa built his first distillery and then proceeded to confound his opponents by not actually producing a brandy, as they had all anticipated, but what could technically be described as a flavoured spirit.

He was aware that at the time there was a preponderance of second-rate Greek brandy being sold, and believed he could provide a superior result with a little planning. Taking brandy as his base he added muscat wine to it. He also purchased an assortment of herbs and spices from the Aegean Islands, and made some infusions with them, which he added to his blend. By so doing he developed a softer, more elegant drink, which soon found popular favour.

Suddenly tragedy struck, with the premature death of Spyros Metaxa. The whole company was crestfallen by the unexpected news, particularly with the knowledge that there was no son to take control, and in Greek society at that time the male role was predominant, to state the case mildly. Imagine the shock when some days later Spyros's widow, Despina Metaxa, assembled the staff and announced that she would be taking charge personally. Thus she became the first Greek lady to head a major Greek company and her successors seem to think well enough of her proficiency to tell visitors of her achievements with notable pride.

THE TRUTHFUL DISTILLER

Asbach Uralt, Germany

The title is not meant to suggest that the majority of distillers are untruthful, despite the fact that the odd one or two have been known to spin the occasional yarn. Hugo Asbach, the Rheingau distiller who founded his business in 1892, was a man who built his reputation on honesty and integrity. Born the son of a carpenter in the busy city of Cologne, he dreamed of a more enterprising life and, for reasons unknown, at an early age developed an ambition to be a brandy producer.

At twenty-four years of age, having saved his money scrupulously, he began trading in the prominent wine town of Rudesheim, with just two small stills and three employees. His aspiration was to make a brandy as fine as Cognac, which he admired as one of the world's greatest spirits.

Hugo travelled to and from Cognac learning more about the methods employed there and no doubt undertaking a little trading at the same time. By 1905 he was thriving so well that he took on Albert Sturm, the major local wine merchant, as partner. With this new financial backing, Hugo Asbach went straight ahead and purchased two small Cognac houses, Jean-Baptiste Lainé and Pinaudaine and Co., which he merged and renamed Asbach & Co., Cognac, and proceeded to trade in both Rudesheim and Cognac.

Hugo knew that for Cognac to be so called it should always be distilled and aged in the official area and even though he shipped young eaux-de-vie and brandies back to Rudesheim, his Rudesheim production was always labelled Brandwein, and only his Cognac production was labelled Cognac. He persisted with this practice despite the disagreement of all his German rivals who identified their brandies as Cognac.

When in 1919 the Treaty of Versailles resulted in the confiscation of such German assets in France and forbade the use of the term Cognac on any German label, the honest Hugo Asbach was the only German distiller who did not need to visit his printer. Today the only visible memento of his Cognac house is the lion symbol used on the Asbach bottle, a logo which he adopted from his Cognac company.

Visitors to Asbach in Rudesheim, if they are observant, will notice a pot still that is quite unique, for it stands on four brass feet, each of which is moulded in the form of a different animal. These four animals, so Hugo Asbach maintained, represented the four basic characteristics necessary to produce the finest brandy. A fox's paw represents the alertness needed by a distiller; a raven the

The *four-footed pot still at Asbach Distillery*

vigilance; a wild boar the strength; and an owl the wisdom. These are all, no doubt, qualities which the truthful and highly successful Hugo Asbach possessed.

7. OTHER ROYAL CONNECTIONS

BONNIE PRINCE CHARLIE'S SECRET RECIPE
Drambuie, Scotland

Bonnie Prince Charlie, the Young Pretender

In 1745, Prince Charles Edward Stuart landed on Scottish soil with a mere handful of supporters in an abortive attempt to regain the British throne for

his exiled family. He was only twenty-four years of age, yet already he had earned a reputation for generously rewarding outstanding loyalty and service. He continued to bestow gifts throughout the Jacobite rebellion, and the practice led eventually to his name being proudly displayed on the label of one of the world's most prestigious liqueurs.

Better known as either Bonnie Prince Charlie or the Young Pretender, Prince Charles was a courageous and idealistic young man whose overriding vow was to win back Britain for the Catholic Stuarts from the Protestant House of Hanover. Sadly, his one great foray, which began in July 1745 and ended with his departure from Scottish soil to France in September 1746, was in many ways ill-conceived and lacked careful military preparation. On reflection it was probably one of the more bizarre attempts to overthrow a European monarchy that has been recorded.

His father, James Francis Edward Stuart, known as the Old Pretender, was the only surviving son of James II of England and Scotland. In exile, he claimed the title of James III but his only official recognition came from the Pope. He did, however, have many Jacobite supporters, who made several attempts to restore the Stuart throne, after which Prince Charles Edward assumed the mantle of responsibility. In that cause he found some sympathy from Louis XV of France, who in 1745 was already embroiled in war with England. Clearly it must have suited the French king to encourage some military distraction to the north, which could well draw forces away from England's southern coastline.

On 25 July, Bonnie Prince Charlie set foot in the west of Scotland at Moidart, at first attracting little support. Gradually, however, his purpose began to gain somewhat wider attention, and on 19 August he was able to raise the Stuart standard at Glenfinnan. There he declared his father James VIII of Scotland

and James III of England, and himself regent, as he took command of some 1 200 men who had arrived in ever-growing throngs to serve in the Jacobite cause. Among them was one John Mackinnon, son of the Laird of Strathaird on the Isle of Skye. Mackinnon was appointed a captain and remained loyal and determined in the service of his prince throughout the uprising and even after the terrible loss at Culloden Moor, near Inverness, on 16 April 1746.

Months later, in July, Mackinnon and his father, the old Laird of Strathaird, also John Mackinnon, were able to provide such assistance to the Young Pretender that he gave them, as a thanksgiving present, the ancient recipe for an old elixir which had apparently been a secret possession of the Stuart family for many generations.

After a couple of early successes, probably gained more by the element of surprise than military prowess, the Jacobite army had headed south into England, taking Carlisle without any real opposition, and marching deep into the Midlands as far as Derby. There the young prince listened to the advice of his senior officers, who realised that their force of around 2 000 men was in danger of being outnumbered, and retreated to Scotland, enjoying a further couple of small victories before being completely routed at Culloden by a Hanoverian army headed by the Duke of Cumberland.

Then began the famous trek across the Highlands and Islands, in which the Young Pretender was chased from pillar to post by the victors and their supporters. Yet despite a reward of 30 000 gold sovereigns being offered for his capture, a sum worth just over $4 million today, throughout the arduous five-month journey not a single attempt to betray him was made. Instead, Prince Charlie was hidden, fed and protected by small groups of Highlanders and Islanders, who remained utterly loyal to him until his eventual departure for France in September 1746. During that period he was passed on from one little band to another as he ran the gauntlet of the British Army and Navy. His very survival depended on always being with men who were totally trustworthy and who knew the lie of the local land.

Those who know a little of the Scottish climate, and in particular the changing weather of the west coast and the western isles, will appreciate that in five months the fleeing prince must have endured many soakings and much discomfort. He could only be thankful that his journey was between April and September and not in colder times. In addition to that problem, there was the simple necessity of nourishment. Many a day he went without, and for the prince, a reputed gourmet, some of his experiences must have been a little disturbing, such as the island habit of bleeding the black cattle. To sustain themselves during food shortages, the villagers would bleed one of their black cattle, then add salt to the blood and boil it. Left to cool, it set into solid, cold, gelatinous chunks. There were, on the other hand, days at the occasional solitary inn that provided some recompense for the young man, who not only enjoyed his food but a glass or two of the finest malt whisky.

On 29 June, in the company of Flora Macdonald and five other islanders, he had arrived on the beautiful and mountainous Isle of Skye disguised as an Irish woman servant using the name Betty Burke, in what is probably the best-known tale of his flight and which is immortalised in the "Skye Boat Song". Immediately the boatmen who had rowed the party from South Uist returned home they were arrested. They confessed to their captors, with apparent readiness, that their prince was dressed as a woman, because they were quite certain that he would have quickly changed back into men's clothing. The net was closing in rapidly and so other supporters whisked Prince Charlie away to the nearby island of Raasay. But after just one night in a small hut it was deemed safer to return to Skye.

On 4 July the fugitive prince and his party arrived at the home of Captain John Mackinnon at Elgol, on the lonely southern coast of Skye, only to find his officer away from home. This time the prince was playing the part of a male servant called Lewie Caw. His protector on the journey to and from Raasay had been Captain Malcolm of the Macleod clan, who knew the Mackinnons well. Eventually Captain Mackinnon returned, and the two men and their prince arranged a fresh plan. Later, upon the arrival of the Old Laird Mackinnon, Captain Malcolm withdrew, and from 4 to 10 July, when the prince was in continual danger, his wellbeing was safeguarded by the Mackinnons. In fact it is fair to say that their subsequent action, shared in part by four Skye boatmen whose names remain unknown, saved the life and liberty of their prince.

The Jacobite army on Culloden Moor

The revised plan was that they would row from Strathaird Point across the Sound of Sleat to Mallaig on the mainland. This they did, and then the Mackinnons remained with Prince Charlie for four days, through rough and perilous conditions, until they could link up with other trusted supporters at Morar. They knew that once Bonnie Prince Charlie was on the mainland he had a far greater chance of survival, and eventually, in September, he was able to make good his escape on a French ship.

It was abundantly clear to the prince that without the action of Captain John Mackinnon and his father he would have been lost. Since he had no material items on his person with which he could reward them, it is reported that he passed on an ancient recipe for an elixir that had been a Stuart possession for very many years. It is a remarkable and indisputable fact that today Drambuie is still produced using the same basic recipe, and that the Drambuie Liqueur Company is wholly owned by the Mackinnon family, who have certainly been well-rewarded. There is no doubt that those courageous Mackinnon ancestors were quite correct in their fear for Bonnie Prince Charlie's life, for the news of the dramatic escape by boat was immediately reported and both of them were arrested within twenty-four hours of leaving their prince at Morar.

Both the Mackinnons were incarcerated in some of the notorious floating prisons that were being used in England at the time, where they suffered considerable hardship and deprivation before being released under a general amnesty a year later. The

Mackinnon family then kept the secret recipe to themselves until 1904, when Malcolm Mackinnon decided to blend it and sell it from a retail store he owned in Edinburgh. In the first year, he sold just ten cases, but within a few years the liqueur was held in such esteem that its reputation spread with surprising speed and it could be found all over Scotland. Then, during the 1914-18 World War, Scottish soldiers took it with them to the trenches in northern France, where they shared it with their allies from other countries, including those from Canada and the United States, where of course it found great favour with those of Scottish ancestry, many of whom would have had forebears who fell at Culloden. After World War I, it was taken back across the Atlantic by such soldiers as a souvenir, and thus started a demand for its importation. In America, sales were soon buoyant, but were brought to an abrupt halt by the introduction of Prohibition.

Strangely it was a similar wartime situation during World War II, which brought about a repetition of the circumstances which had first brought Drambuie to the attention of the United States, and once more there was a call for its return to the retail shelves. Nowadays the drink made from the secret recipe of Bonnie Prince Charlie is widely acclaimed as one of the world's great liqueurs. It can be seen in more than 100 different countries, and is still the jealously guarded possession of the Mackinnon family.

The recipe itself is one of, if not the most, carefully guarded such secrets, with security at the Drambuie headquarters at Kirkliston, just outside Edinburgh, being of an extremely strict standard. The formula is under the sole control of Mrs Mary Mackinnon, the widow of the late Mr Norman Mackinnon, who was a direct descendant of Captain John Mackinnon and the Old Laird of Skye. On one morning every month, Mrs Mackinnon uses the little herbs and spices room in the very heart of the Drambuie headquarters to make up the essences of the ingredients, which she blends together to make the tincture which gives Drambuie its unique taste. Only at this point does she hand over the tincture to the head blender, who mixes it with its remarkable malt-whisky base. This sees as many as thirty single-malt Scotch whiskies used in the final blend, in addition to other blended whisky, a sugar syrup and pure Scottish water. In the head blender's laboratory it is possible to identify the samples of the single malts involved, with such celebrated names as the Glenlivet, Highland Park, the Glenfiddich, Glenmorangie and the Macallan prominent. It is a reflection of the true quality and character of Drambuie that this is the case. In France, for example, it is not difficult to find liqueur and other drink recipes that in the past were always made

Mrs Mackinnon's secret essences

Aging of malt whiskies for the Drambuie blend

using Cognac, but where less expensive commercial grape alcohol has been substituted. Not so at Drambuie, where the whiskies are always the finest.

As to the history, origin and form of the recipe, one can only surmise, for the Mackinnon family will not discuss the secret of the essences with anyone. One wonders whether originally, when Bonnie Prince Charlie gave them the information, he was not passing on instructions for an elixir of long life made by using herbs and spices, and involving the maceration of such ingredients in a base spirit, in the manner of similar elixirs which were at that time still being produced in many monasteries in France, a country where he and his ancestors had spent much time. If so, no doubt a brandy base would have been used and he simply would have suggested to the Mackinnons that they substitute whisky.

Then there is the matter of the Lairds of Strathaird and their descendants, and why they did not produce Drambuie commercially for more than 158 years after receiving the recipe. Putting aside the suggestions of some that the Scots can be a trifle over-careful with their possessions, there may be a very simple explanation which can be gleaned by studying the history of another outstanding liqueur – Chartreuse.

That recipe was said to be a gift from royalty to the Carthusians in 1605. It then laid untouched in a Carthusian monastery near Paris for a further 132 years, probably because no-one could understand it. Then, by chance, the document was taken to the Carthusian headquarters at La Grande Chartreuse, where it took a master pharmacist, Brother Jerome Maubec, another twenty-seven years to comprehend and produce the blend. Perhaps a similar situation existed for the Mackinnons, for there is little chance that the prince had on his person any kind of document. It was probably a case of a royal fugitive saying thank you, and passing on the information that he could recall. He only had to make the odd mistake and one can understand why such a time lapse occurred.

These days, of course, there is a printed copy of the recipe locked in a bank vault, which one day will be passed on to one of Mrs Mary Mackinnon's

descendants. In the meantime, Bonnie Prince Charlie's recipe remains very much her personal secret.

CROWN VILLAGE
Krondorf, Australia

The award winning Krondorf Show Reserve Chardonnay is a much requested wine that, with its delicious fruit and firm body, might well be deemed fit for a king's table.

In its Barossa Valley village of Krondorf, the wine always receives royal attention, as the town's name means "Crown Village" and was given to it by a breakaway group of Prussian Lutherans in 1847. Ironically, most of these Prussians came from the regions of Brandenburg, Posen and Silesia, within the boundaries of modern-day Poland. Yet when the two world wars broke out, the community in the Barossa Valley village and similar settlements were the target for much anti-German feeling. In fact, in 1918 the peace-loving citizens of Krondorf were greatly distressed when their government changed the village's name to Kaldukee. Their persistence in seeking a repeal of that imposition was rewarded fifty-seven years later, in 1975, when the name Krondorf was restored.

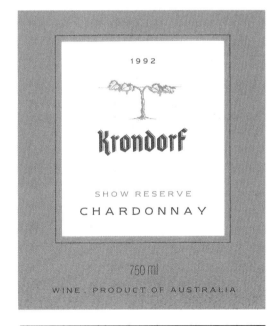

THE ELEVEN-YEAR VISIT
Justerini & Brooks; Italy and England

The overseas visitor to central London who takes a stroll up the gentle slope of St James's Street is sometimes surprised at the sight of a prestigious wine shop on the left-hand side. It is a small but elegant premises which is adorned by the Royal Warrant as a retail wine merchant to Her Majesty the Queen, and is one of only three such

retailers to be awarded this distinction. The reason for the surprise is that the warrant-holder's name will be familiar to many visitors, not in connection with wine, but as the name of one of the most popular and successful blended Scotch-whisky brands, namely J & B. The shop, which is popularly known among the wine trade and by its regular clientele as Justerini's, is an excellent source of fine and mature wines, as well as the home of a number of outstanding whiskies.

Yet anyone who has seen the J & B Rare or Select labels has actually had the outline of the Justerini history in front of them on one of the most informative labels of all. The warrant to the Queen is displayed at the top, and below it are listed the eight other British royal warrants that the company has held in succession since the first was granted in 1760.

To trace the foundation of the house requires a return to the year 1749 and to the location of Bologna, where a young Italian, Giacomo Justerini, was employed as an assistant to his uncle, the owner of a distillery. Giacomo would have been considered an eligible match for any young lady in his strata of society, and possibly for one from a level slightly above his station. There seemed every opportunity for him, in time, to succeed his uncle and become a man of wealth and substance. He was an intelligent young man with drive and enthusiasm, who had studied the distillation and blending of many drinks; and he was a talented individual, well-respected in the community, with a bright and stable future ahead of him.

Giacomo's downfall was a beautiful young theatrical singer, Margherita Bellino, who dreamed of becoming an opera star and who longed for a life of romance and travel. Giacomo fell in love with this tantalising young singer, and was swept off his feet by her heady and thrilling talk of adventure. For a while, life must have seemed bliss, until one day Margherita informed Giacomo of her plans to go to London to appear in the Italian Opera House. Being completely enamoured, he instantly responded that he would give notice to his uncle and follow her to the English capital.

In London, harsh reality dawned upon Giacomo and his ardour cooled in the light of the truth that Margherita did not have any role in the Italian Opera. In fact she could not even get a part in the chorus. Despite the prospect of no employment, Margherita still moved in popular fast society, where she had her own group of friends and acquaintances.

Giacomo soon realised that he would need to work to subsidise such an expensive lifestyle. He had brought a fair amount of money with him from Bologna, but it was inadequate to meet his designs to open his own Foreign Cordial Warehouse. He found suitable premises in the Haymarket at the junction with Pall Mall, at an address suitably advertised as "Two doors below the Opera House". To produce his drinks he needed equipment, so while he was making all the arrangements to commence trading he also made enquiries to find a financial partner. Through Margherita's theatrical circles, Giacomo was introduced to a young country gentleman called George Johnson, who invested capital in the enterprise and took charge of the administration, while Justerini controlled the production.

The word "warehouse" that they employed was not strictly accurate, but it must have been a most interesting premises to visit. Below street level was a quite substantial cellar, where Justerini toiled among his copper still and row of infusion pots. Above were the shop, office, tasting room and storage. There he made a diverse assortment of concoctions that soon had the gentry and aristocracy knocking at his door. One recipe for ratafia included black cherries, cinnamon, gin and sugar. Another for Aqua Mirabilis required cinnamon, galega, cloves, cucumis, mace, nutmeg and cardamines, to which the juices of celandine, spearmint and balm were added, as well as fourteen other ingredients. He also produced what were described by George Johnson as "strong waters", which included Cordial Poppy Water, Walnut Water, Rose Water and the curiously named Penny-Royal Water.

At the other end of Pall Mall stood St James's Palace, an important royal residence of the day, where the young Prince George was regularly installed. In an era in which it was reasonably safe for a member of a royal family to stroll along such a fine avenue, it may well be that Penny-Royal Water was manufactured especially for the prince's needs. There is no doubt that Justerini's became a favourite supplier of the prince's early on, for when he ascended the throne in 1760, among the very first royal warrants he sanctioned was one for the growing company of Justerini & Johnson. The foundation date for the business, 1749, is definitely accurate, and the 1760 warrant date is incontrovertible. Whether Justerini's produced or sold any whisky of any kind during this period is uncertain, although highly likely. At the same time, it should be remembered blended whisky was still a century away and that the whisky produced in Ireland, Scotland and Wales was basically the same as single malt today. The first indisputable evidence of Justerini & Johnson selling whisky is in a 1779 advertisement in the *Morning Post*, which offered "Usquebaugh", using the old Gaelic word for the spirit.

The light-yellow J & B Rare label came into use at the start of the 20th century, and was one of two principal styles of blended whisky offered through mail order. Justerini & Brooks noticed that the overwhelming majority of customers ordered it because it was so much lighter and more elegant than the brands of many of its competitors. In this manner it became the brand upon which the company concentrated, with the other early blend, known as Club, being dropped.

It was not until 1993 that J & B reintroduced a further blend, the much darker, fuller Select. On the labels of both one can inspect the names of each royal warrant. They read:

By Appointment to Their Late Majesties
King George III
King George IV
King William IV
Queen Victoria
King Edward VII
King George V
King George VI
And to His Late Royal Highness
The Prince of Wales (1921-1936)

At the foot, as if almost an afterthought, and in much lighter print, is:

And to HRH Prince Bernhard of the Netherlands.

The Brooks name was introduced in the 19th century, when the entire business was purchased by a wealthy Londoner called Alfred Brooks. He was a great lover of Bordeaux and Burgundy, and expanded the company's wine trade considerably, one noteworthy customer being Charles Dickens.

As for Giacomo Justerini, his participation in those early days lasted only eleven years. Once the Royal Warrant had been granted by George III, he sold his share at a handsome profit and returned to Bologna, perhaps for the same reason that he left it.

*R*ecords of transactions between *Justerini & Brooks* and *Charles Dickens*

A NAGGING WIFE
Corton Charlemagne, France

This is a cautionary tale for all those millionaire couples who have invested in showpiece winery empires in the New World. If you specialise in red wine grapes and their success becomes a temptation to overindulge, then husbands in particular beware, or you might have to change your priority to white.

If you visit the Côte de Beaune village of Aloxe-Corton, with its wasplike roofs and spiralled church, you will learn the origin of the name Corton-Charlemagne. At Bonneau de Martray, the cellar-master will point at the vineyard slope and raise a broad smile, for he is pleased with a royal decision made near the end of the 8th century to plant white grapes there. However, if you make your way to the other side of that sweep of vineyards and converse with a producer of red Corton wines, he will shake his head disparagingly as he recalls the decision to grub out the finest red vines and replace them with white.

The difference in local opinion stems from Emperor Charlemagne's decision to replace the red vines in the vineyards he owned in Corton with white. It was not a matter of taste or opinion but a ploy to avert the attention of his nagging wife. The empress, so local tradition insists, nagged Charlemagne for his overgenerous tasting sessions.

For some while these had escaped her notice, but with his advancing years the hairs of his beard turned white and she could see the droplets of Red Corton which stained it. Reflecting that life would indeed be empty if an emperor could not indulge in a glass or two, the cunning Charlemagne instructed his men to tear out his red vines and replace them with white. The empress, whose eyesight was also probably failing with age, never saw a droplet on his beard again.

THE PRESIDENT, THE QUEEN AND LARRY GLICK
Reichsgraf Von Keselstatt, Germany

The scenes of East Germans chipping at the Berlin Wall and even holding parties on top of it amid the great popular revolution of 1989 drew billions around the world to their television screens, transfixed with amazement, to witness the historic events. The sudden appearance of those scenes one October evening left viewers incredulous, wondering whether the old axiom "seeing is believing" could really be true.

At noon on the following day, I happened to be a guest on WHDH Radio in Boston on the last daytime performance of Bostonian radio legend Larry Glick. Frankly, the show turned into a party for Larry, who had developed his reputation over very many years as the amusing voice of the New England night-waves. After a couple of years' daytime experiences as a talk-show host, he had decided to return to his nocturnal habitat. As Larry's eyes lighted on my usual assortment of bottles, each with a story behind it, he noticed one with a German label, picked it up, referred to the dancing on the Berlin Wall, and asked me to forget the wines just for a minute and give, "as a journalist and experienced traveller", my opinion on the amazing pictures everyone had seen.

By pure chance Larry had selected a bottle which had a particular connection with that exciting event. It was from the highly acclaimed Mosel estate of Reichsgraf Von Kesselstatt, and was a Piesporter Goldtröpfchen Riesling Kabinett 1988.

The vineyards at Piesport, in Germany's Mosel Valley

I explained two things to Larry and his listeners; in the first place, I was a wine man not a news journalist, but I did know parts of Germany quite well and I did have an opinion, which was that while it was all extremely exciting, everyone should apply a little caution and insist on German government statements that they had no further territorial claims on Poland or Czechoslovakia.

Second, I explained, his choice of wine was a remarkable coincidence, because we were, after all, in Boston, birthplace of John F. Kennedy, who, as President of the United States, on 26 June 1963 had stood at the Berlin Wall and associated himself with that divided city, and particularly with those who were not free, when he gave his unforgettable "*Ich bin ein Berliner*" speech.

I went on to relate how some time earlier I had been fascinated to find out what Kennedy drank with lunch that day, and that Larry was now holding the bottle – well, not the actual one, but its counterpart twenty-seven years on. The president had been the guest of the popular Berlin mayor Willy Brandt, whose staff had served a 1961 Piesporter Riesling from Reichsfgraf Von Kesselstatt.

Some might even suggest that this celebrated estate has some special claim to be served at the most important state occasions, and perhaps I can prove that with further illustrations.

On 2 June 1953, at the coronation of Her Majesty Queen Elizabeth II of the United Kingdom, once again a Reichsgraf Von Kesselstatt Piesporter Goldtröpfchen Riesling was chosen. It was also served to the Queen and the Duke of Edinburgh on a state visit to Germany some ten years later. But it was in April 1986, on the occasion of President Mitterand of France visiting Chancellor Kohl in the ancient city of Trier, in the Mosel Valley, that appeared to receive the fullest official approval. For the German Chancellor treated the French president, a man whom he would certainly wish to impress in gastronomic terms, to lunch in the Reichsgraf Von Kesselstatt restaurant, which is part of the delightful baroque Palais Kesselstatt, home of the wine estate. Naturally a Reichsgraf Von Kesselstatt wine was served for lunch but this time it was not a Piesporter but another Riesling, from the unique Josephshöfer vineyard at Graach, which is owned solely by the Trier-based winery. The vineyard records can, in fact, be traced back to Bishop, and later Saint, Magnerice in AD 596, making it the oldest continuous vineyard in my experience.

There are several other illustrations of the wines of Reichsgraf Von Kesselstatt being chosen for such significant occasions. One reason is probably that these elegant wines from the Mosel valley are among the lightest and most delicate to be found

CONTAINS SULFITES PRODUCED OF GERMANY

ERZEUGERABFÜLLUNG A.P. NR. 3 561077-08-87 QUALITÄTSWEIN MIT PRÄDIKAT

750 ml e

alc. 7,0% by vol

MOSEL · SAAR · RUWER

1986 PIESPORTER GOLDTRÖPFCHEN

RIESLING KABINETT

ESTATE BOTTLED

REICHSGRAF von KESSELSTATT

TRIER · DEUTSCHLAND

anywhere. Often the Kabinett style will only have 7.5 per cent alcohol by volume, compared with many Chardonnays, for instance, at 13 per cent. It therefore makes good sense to choose such a wine for lunch when there is still much business to attend to in the day.

Another reason for selecting these wines can be recognised from the estate's name. The word "von" in Germany, like "de" in France, suggests that one is a member of the old aristocratic order. The Von Kesselstatt family have been listed among the most prominent Trier citizens since the 14th century, and from 1761 until 1794, Johann Hugo Casimir Reichsgraf Von Kesselstatt was a member of the royal court of the Holy Roman Empire. In 1776, as the American colonies won their independence, Emperor Josef II honoured him by making him a *Reichsgraf. Reich* meant royal kingdom and *Graf* was a level above baron, indeed a most royal position. Therefore it is perfectly understandable that the wines of Reichsgraf Von Kesselstatt should be chosen for the most memorable events, whether for President John F. Kennedy, Queen Elizabeth II or Larry Glick.

THE ROYAL BREWER
Kaltenberg, Bavaria

Kaltenberg is the only beer included in this book and deserves to be on the basis of its unrivalled history and because its principal is the most accommodating and friendly man.

The title may mislead readers to assume that this is an account of a brewer who holds some particularly impressive royal warrant, an honour which is not uncommon. However such is not the case. In contrast, this is a tale of a prince who has become one of the most dynamic and colourful brewers of his generation and who makes beer for his subjects. In the land which possesses more breweries than any other, he is not just a prince among brewers, but the direct descendant of King Wilhelm IV of Bayern (Bavaria), who in 1516 imposed the famous purity law known as the *Reinheitsgebot*, which must

be strictly adhered to in Bavaria to this day, and which demands that the only ingredients used for brewing are barley, yeast, hops and water.

The brewer concerned is Prinz Luitpold Von Bayern, the grandson of King Ludwig III, the last King of Bavaria, who relinquished the throne in 1918, terminating 738 years of family rule which began when Otto von Wittelsbach was made Duke of Bavaria by Emperor Friedrich Barbarossa in AD 1180. Prinz Luitpold is also a descendant of King Ludwig II, the Dream King, sometimes referred to as Mad King Ludwig because of his legacy of extravagant fairytale castles scattered throughout the mountains of Bavaria.

Prinz Luitpold is the head of the Kaltenberg brewery in the village of the same name. The brewery is one of 1 094 registered in Bavaria; between them the breweries produce more than 6 000 brands of beer, which constitutes 25 per cent of the world's supply. The *prinz* literally lives in the brewery, since it is located in his home, the Castle of Kaltenberg, which has a history that can be traced back to 1179.

The low point of Prinz Luitpold's career came in the 1970s, when Kaltenberg was barred from participation in Munich's world-famous Oktoberfest on the grounds that the brewery fell outside the city's geographical boundary. His response was calm but positive. If he was not welcome in Munich then he would organise his own event and hold it not in October but in July, during the fine

K*altenberg, the brewery castle*

weather. It was a bold decision but it has reaped abundant rewards.

With his lively talent for promotion, the *prinz* seized the opportunity to revive the exciting medieval sports of jousting and combat at a castle where they had not been practised for six centuries. From that embryonic idea in 1979, a major Bavarian tournament and market has blossomed, an event which draws tens of thousands of visitors to the province from all over the world. The *Kaltenberger Rittertunier,* or Tournament of Knights, has grown into the largest spectacle of its type in Europe. The event, which boasts 2 000 participants, presents four days of dramatic and vigorous action, which climaxes in the final jousting tournament between the German Knight and the villainous *Schwarze Ritter,* or Black Knight. Each year, quite by chance, the Black Knight is defeated and reaps his just rewards to the cheers and boos of the capacity 13 000 audience.

The Kaltenberger Rittertunier, or Tournament of Knights, the largest spectacle of its type in Europe

Since Prinz Luitpold is of noble lineage, he naturally believes in fairness and therefore gives strict instructions that the minimum of blood should be spilled. This ensures that each knight is capable of quenching his thirst after his exertions and remains fit for the duration of the *Rittertunier.* The *prinz* is also eager to encourage the knights to mingle with the throng, which makes its way patiently through the market that borders the gently sloping approach to the portals of the castle. Here visitors find a fascinating display of medieval Bavarian life, with a wide selection of stalls demonstrating ancient crafts and trades. Most important, of course, are the places of refreshment, and one is designed with the merrier and more adventurous tourist in mind. It is a mixed bathhouse, open to public view, where slightly inebriated young men and women, sipping Kaltenberg or the tasty Prinzregent Luitpold wheat beer, soak themselves in a hot tub constructed out of a large wooden beer vat. As they soothe their aching limbs they are serenaded by a medieval musician.

The showman *prinz* is not just a successful promoter but also a serious brewer. His regular and often unscheduled inspections of his castle brewery highlight his insistence on scrupulous cleanliness. However, punishment for any infringement of the *prinz*'s high standards of hygiene poses a problem, as his staff already work in the dungeons. That apart, what comes across most strongly in conversation with him is his philosophy regarding beer. "Beer is a food," he insists. "You should not think of it as alcohol. In Bavaria beer is a way of life." Only when asked his opinion of beers and lagers from other countries does his voice take on a sharper edge: "Chemicals, that is the problem, chemicals. Under our Bavarian law, created by my ancestor, we are not allowed to use chemicals in our beer and neither do we want to."

When Prinz Luitpold negotiated a major licensing arrangement for the British brewer Whitbread to brew Kaltenberg in England, he surprised the giant company's directors with two unexpected conditions. Apart from the water, he insisted that the ingredients used should be supplied from Bavaria and also that Whitbread should contract a head brewer approved by him. Whitbread, duly impressed by the *prinz*'s determination that every drop of Kaltenberg brewed in England should be completely authentic, agreed to his conditions. Subsequently, they sent a young brewer, David Jacques, to Prinz Luitpold in Kaltenberg for training there. The ultra-professional royal brewer decided that was not quite sufficient, and afterwards sent David to the University of Weihenstephan, where he obtained his doctorate in "brewing".

A ROYAL FAMILY OF WINEMAKERS
McWilliams, Australia

When it comes to claiming to be the Royal Family of Winemakers, the title could justifiably, in the past, have been awarded to the Fetzer family from California's Redwood Valley. Until 1992 the

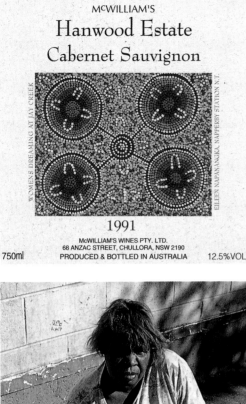

Semillon with considerable softness and charm, while Philip is a more masculine red Hermitage or Shiraz.

To some, the McWilliam's name is better known for its support of Aboriginal art. An excellent example is seen on their Hanwood Estate Cabernet Sauvignon, which features *Women's Dreaming at Jay Creek*, by Eileen Napanangka, who specialises in using natural dyes.

Don McWilliam, the executive chairman of the independent, family-owned wine company, which was founded in 1877, adds support to their bid for the title of a royal family by explaining that there are thirteen McWilliam men in the business, sufficient for a Rugby League team.

*E*ileen Napanangka, Aboriginal artist of the Hanwood Estate label

ROYAL WINE
Sandeman Character Sherry, UK

It was a damp Sunday afternoon in the spring of 1987 when my wife Branwen and I had the privilege of being among the guests of David Sandeman, the Chairman of the House of Sandeman, at Smith's Lawn, Windsor, possibly the best-known polo field in the world. There we had the good fortune to be welcome in the royal box for the Sandeman Character Sherry Trophy. As a matter of courtesy I had asked official permission in advance to bring my camera and, a little to my surprise, approval was granted. Since then I have experienced another royal event and can sympathise even more with the royal family, who cannot move outside the confines of their palaces and homes without hearing the continual sound of clicking shutters. It is such a problem that perhaps they might undertake to offer an international award for the first camera manufacturer to produce totally silent shutters. As it turned out, that permission enabled me, a mediocre amateur photo-

winery had no less than nine directly related members of the family working under their mother's leadership. Success and expansion brought its rewards and also its price, for in the second generation the Fetzer family opted to sell control of their excellent business to the Brown Forman company.

So ironically it is to Australia, where Prime Minister Paul Keating is apparently preparing for a republican breakaway, that one must go to find today's truly Royal Family of Winemakers, which is quite a distinguished title for a family descended from a Scots-Irish sheep farmer. McWilliams produce two decidedly royal wines from their Hunter Valley vineyards. Elizabeth is a classic dry white grapher, to capture two unique moments, one of which is shown below, as I kept firing away.

Prince Charles had been participating in the polo while Fergie, otherwise known as the Duchess of York, had agreed to award the prizes. Accompanying her was her husband, Prince Andrew, the Duke of York, and the ever-popular Princess Diana. Everything went smoothly, apart from the ceaseless drizzle; Prince Charles's team won by a couple of lucky goals, and then Fergie walked onto the

Prince Harry falls for Sandeman

centre of the field to distribute the prizes, with Prince Andrew and Princess Diana in support. One's respect for Fergie grew when she saved the day for the throng of press photographers, who were uncomfortably penned in about 200 yards away, by refusing an umbrella so that everyone could take their pictures of the presentations.

It was on the return journey to the pavilion that the two amusing incidents occurred. Little Prince Harry did not seem to appreciate his mother, Princess Diana, carrying him while his elder brother, Prince William, was allowed to walk. Harry wriggled and squirmed, distracting Princess Diana, who accidentally stumbled on a boundary rail, causing her to slip and drop the young prince onto the wet grass. It was all over in a few seconds, but I kept snapping and for once was in luck.

Next it was the lively Prince William's turn to make a contribution. He had seen his father, Prince Charles, leaving the field carrying a couple of prizes and a bottle of Sandeman Character Sherry in a carton. Suddenly he jumped in front of Prince Charles saying, "I want the sherry. I want the

sherry," and he simply grabbed it, turned his back and walked away, with Prince Charles left shouting, "You can't drink that! You'll go blind!" I was later assured that the prince's remark was no reflection on the Sandeman Sherry, but on the danger of a seven-year-old drinking a fortified wine. A security man was requested to assist, and very quickly the young prince lost his prize.

ALMOST ROYAL
Chateau Ducla, France

The connection between Chevy Chase, the Bordeaux property Chateau Ducla, and an almost royal Scottish family might sound like a bit of a brain teaser. It is, though, quite real. The explanation, however, has to be provided in reverse order.

The almost royal family is the clan Douglas, which ruled much of south-west Scotland from around the end of the 12th century. Chateau Ducla derives its name from a member of that clan who acquired land in the Entre-deux-Mers region in the 14th century. In all probability he was either the direct descendant of a 13th-century Douglas crusader knight, or of a clan mercenary who had decided to invest his newly won fortune in a peaceful occupation. Indeed the name Douglas was of sufficiently ferocious reputation to be immortalised in the "Ballad of Chevy Chase", which has little to do with a talented film star or a suburb of Washington, DC.

8.　AMERICANA

AMERICA'S MOST VISITED WINERY
Biltmore, USA

In the rustic fall of 1989, as the leaf people flocked to the Great Smoky Mountains near Asheville, North Carolina, my colleague Dave Hollyman and I were paying our first visit to that small but enchanting city. My task was to present a lecture tasting on selected European wines and my audience was composed of guests who were customers of the Weinhaus in Patton Avenue, a traditional retail wine store with a burgeoning number of enthusiastic supporters.

It was a Friday evening and the weekend lay ahead in an area of unparalleled natural beauty. Our host, Davy Mallet, a local wine distributor, who is recognised throughout the state by his personalised car registration "LAFITE", enquired how we intended spending our time.

"In this delightful climate, we would really like to play a game of tennis," I suggested.

With that, David Mallet Sr, Davy's father and owner of the Weinhaus, chipped in with the

Biltmore House, a French Renaissance-style chateau, and home of America's most visited winery

bilt between 1889 and 1895, and which attracts more than 500 000 guests a year. Perhaps it was a little surprising that George, who had his imposing residence designed in the style of a Loire chateau, should have overlooked including a winery in his original plans, as was so often the practice in France. This lamentable situation has been suitably rectified by the current owner, George Vanderbilt's grandson William A.V. Cecil, and it has raised North Carolina to number ten in the batting order for wine production among American states.

It must not be overlooked, however, that the Biltmore Estate Vineyard is not the first on the property. In pre-Civil War days, vines were successfully grown on the site, although little is known about them. These may well have succumbed to phylloxera at a later date. Also, Mrs George Vanderbilt is reported by some local inhabitants to have planted a small vineyard using indigenous grape varieties "somewhere on the south side of the estate", but there is no written record of any wine having been produced, and it may well have been limited to dessert grapes.

Whatever the truth, the present Biltmore Estate Vineyard can certainly claim to be the first vineyard operation of any size on the site, and it is indisputably America's most visited winery.

recommendation that Davy should book a court at the Biltmore Club, where they were members.

"And while you're at it, take them to the Biltmore Estate Winery," he added, indicating a bottle displayed on the main counter.

The following afternoon, with Eberhard Heide, a friend and employee of the Mallet family, we played doubles in the impressive surroundings of the Biltmore Club – for a small challenge of a bottle or two. Davy was a keen but not particularly skilled player, while Eberhard offered plenty of cunning spin, which was fortunately matched by the inaccuracy of an out of practice opponent; the sum total of all this was two pedestrian Welshmen plodding to a three-set win in a match that has since become almost an annual trophy for us. The outcome was fortuitous, not merely with regard to the way we played, but because the rules of that select club preclude visitors from buying drinks.

"We may not have time to visit the winery but you must try the Chardonnay," Davy suggested. He then told us a little about the Biltmore Estate Winery, which had opened just four years previously. He explained that a French winemaker had been hired and an ambitious project undertaken. A little further research revealed that a significant sum had been invested in the conversion of an old dairy farm into a state-of-the-art winery. Since then, progress has been swift for the Biltmore Estate, with a stream of medals and awards for its wines, which are fermented from many of the most successful noble varieties.

Indeed, few would realise that the Biltmore Estate, with its 78 acres of vineyards, is already America's most visited winery. It stands in the 8 000 acres of grounds which belong to America's largest private mansion, the 255-room Biltmore House, which was constructed by George Vander-

COINCIDENCES AND CONNECTIONS
Trimbach, France

As Hubert Trimbach rose to accept the *Wine Spectator* Special Award for 1986, the distant hum and throb of busy New York City receded under a wave of applause. The hot June sky formed a bright backdrop to the heads of the guests as their eyes followed Hubert's path towards the rostrum. Behind his smile of genuine gratification at such an accolade, Hubert was forced to pause momentarily to reassure himself that this was not a dream. Yes, he was in that famous Park Avenue restaurant, the Four Seasons, and yes, his family's ancient Alsace house of F.E. Trimbach was being honoured in front of winemakers from numerous countries – names known and respected throughout the world.

It was in some ways difficult to grasp, to realise, the importance of the occasion. Yet, on reflection, was it really beyond imagination? After all, could the family business not claim to be older than most, and could its dry white wines not compare, in terms of breeding and elegance, with the best the world had to offer? New York City itself could testify to that, since many of its leading gourmet restaurants had discovered just how well the Trimbach Alsace wines complemented the finest *haute cuisine*. And New York, great metropolis though it may be, had more than one connection with the Trimbach family and their small home town of Ribeauvillé, in France's beautiful Alsace region.

The name Ribeauvillé may not come readily to every New Yorker's mind but it has a special significance to the city, and indeed to all Americans. Legend claims that Helen of Troy was so beautiful that her face launched a thousand ships, but little Ribeauvillé can boast the face that welcomed millions. For that face, the familiar face of New York's Statue of Liberty, was modelled on an ordinary but beloved lady of Ribeauvillé. Most Americans will know that the statue was a gift to the United States from France, but few realise that when in 1875 the French sculptor Auguste Bartholdi began designing the statue, he decided to model it on the kindest and gentlest face he had ever encountered, that of his mother, Charlotte, who was born Charlotte Beysser in Ribeauvillé in 1801. This was a touching tribute from a son to his mother. Being a loving and honourable son, Auguste Bartholdi represented his mother at half the age she was in 1875.

My interest in the face of the Statue of Liberty came about some eight years ago, during a period in which I was making regular annual visits to Alsace to taste the Trimbach wines of the previous vintage. On one of those trips, in 1989, I undertook a little research. My first stop was in the Vieux Quartier of the ancient town of Colmar, to a small but most edifying museum dedicated to the art and sculpture of Auguste Bartholdi. The staff there were most helpful and confirmed that Auguste had indeed modelled the face of the Statue of Liberty on the face of his mother. Furthermore, her husband, the sculptor's father, had been the mayor of the nearby vineyard town of Ribeauvillé, in the foothills of the Vosges Mountains, for many years.

It took just twenty minutes to reach that quaint old town, which I already knew so well, and the Trimbach cellars on the Route de Bergheim. Hubert Trimbach had agreed to spend a couple of days working with me in an effort to trace the birthplace and origin of the Statue of Liberty's face.

It was known to some local citizens that she was supposed to have come from Ribeauvillé and my intention was to try to uncover some irrefutable evidence. Quite frankly, in retrospect I realised that the people we had called upon were generally old friends of Hubert, and in many cases their eyes lit up when they saw him again. Some had heard vague rumours of the Statue of Liberty connection; others knew nothing. We visited a variety of private homes, small inns and businesses, and it was delightful to see how the vast majority were timbered properties centuries old, kept in immaculate condition. Gradually the information we gleaned began to take on some consistency, particularly when we visited, quite separately, two local historians. These elderly sages were much more serious and specific; one provided us with an address, and the other with Charlotte Bartholdi's maiden name, Beysser. It was suggested that we visit the *mairie* (town hall) and peruse the municipal birth register.

It was on the second day of our search, at about 4.30 p.m., that we eventually gained access to the necessary records. I had been fortunate to obtain the year of her birth, 1801, from the museum at Colmar. Many such records in France had been destroyed during the French Revolution of 1789, so many searches start with the year 1790. We were in luck and found the entry for the birth of Charlotte Beysser in 1801. On the strength of our promising start, we felt we merited a little self-indulgence, and so retired for the day with a glass of bone-dry Trimbach Riesling.

Charlotte Bartholdi, whose face graces the Statue of Liberty in New York

The next morning brought both disappointment and pleasure, for we soon learnt that the house in which Charlotte had been born had long since been demolished to make way for a hospital. But a stroke of luck led us to a dentist's comfortable old house, set back from the road behind an arched entrance, where Charlotte was said to have been raised from the age of eight until she left home to marry a Monsieur Bartholdi, who later became the town's mayor. The fruit of their marriage was a son, baptised Frédéric-Auguste, but who preferred to be identified simply as Auguste. An amusing incident occurred when a little while later we were filming outside the house. The dentist and his wife returned from a shopping expedition and earnestly implored us not to reveal their address, as they were anxious to avoid an influx of American visitors.

One curious piece of information which we stumbled across in the process of our investigations was that the Bartholdi family was of German extraction. There their name had been Barthold, but when they crossed the Rhine to live in France, for some unknown reason they chose to add the "i" to the end of their name, perhaps assuming that this would make it sound more French.

Coincidentally, the Trimbach family also had another New York connection, this time concerning their foundation year, 1626. Hubert knew that 1626 was the earliest year in which any record of sales of Trimbach wines could be found. Therefore, on the basis of this evidence, it was claimed to be the year the House of Trimbach was established. By chance, 1626 was also the year Peter Minuit and his Dutch settlers purchased the island of Manhattan from some Iroquois Indians in exchange for trinkets and bundles of cloth – "Bangles, baubles and beads worth just $24" – a real estate contract that might be regarded as the first Manhattan scam, since the Iroquois concerned were merely a hunting party which had strayed from its own territory. Interestingly, two bottles of my favourite Trimbach Pinot Gris cost the same today as the Island of Manhattan did in 1926.

New Amsterdam was in those days in a similar position to the town of Riquewihr, where the Trimbach family commenced trading in 1626, and the neighbouring towns of Hunawihr and Ribeauvillé, where they have lived since; for all found themselves at that time in a political situation which would be most unorthodox today. None of these townships formed part of any individual country. In 1626, the portion of Alsace where the Trimbachs lived came under the terrifying control of the *Seigneurs,* or Lords, of Ribeaupierre, who occupied lofty castles perched on the hillsides above the towns, from which they could easily gratify their needs. It was not until 1670 that the

region came under the domination of the mighty Austro-Hungarian Empire, before, in 1681, Louis XIV succeeded in absorbing it into the first acknowledged boundaries of modern France. Across the Atlantic, New York, as New Amsterdam was eventually renamed, did not become part of the new country of the United States of America until 1776.

In the 17th century, both in Alsace and northeastern America, or Vinland as the Vikings named it, the vine grew wild, but only in Alsace was it cultivated with skill and care on any scale. The region's first noble vines were planted by the occupying Romans in the 2nd century AD, and the art of winemaking was practised and furthered during the hundreds of years that followed. By 1626 it was, at least in good vintages, a region from which the most attractive "Ossey" wines could be shipped to the Low Countries, as the Netherlands were then known, and to England. In the wine world today, the term Alsace brings to mind elegant dry white wines, but in the 17th century the majority of Alsace wines would have been red.

Such was the state of affairs when Jean Trimbach first reached the quaint town of Riquewihr in, or possibly before, 1626. His was a short journey from the nearby hilltop town of Sainte-Marie-aux-Mines, where he had spent a few years after quitting his native Switzerland. At that time, Saint-Marie-Aux-Mines was the most prosperous silver-mining town in Europe, with more than 20 000 miners toiling night and day to tear the valuable ore from the rock. Why Jean changed his plans and did not settle here permanently remains a mystery, but it seems that one day he gathered together his few possessions and travelled over the mountain top to the busy little town of Riquewihr, where he acquired premises and began trading in wine. What we know of Jean's earliest origins is that he hailed from a small Swiss town named Trimbach near Basel. Upon arrival in Alsace he took the name of his home town to identify himself and thus became known as Jean Trimbach.

From the moment of their settling in Riquewihr the Trimbach family gained the respect of their neighbours and Jean was acknowledged as a winemaker of certain merit. He must also have been something of a minor politician, since his son Jean-Jacques and his grandson Jean both became mayors of the town and brought honour to the family name.

In later years, sometime around 1840, Jean-Frédéric Trimbach moved his family and their business to the nearby peaceful hamlet of Hunawihr, where he was astute enough or fortunate enough to purchase what many regard today as one of the finest vineyards in the world for dry white wine. Clos Saint Hune, as it is nowadays called, is found in great restaurants in many countries, and is the only Alsace wine offered on important state occasions at the Élysée Palace in Paris. Just how it came to gain its special place in the Élysée's wine cellars is a homely shopping story.

It seems that one day in 1955 the late Madame de Gaulle was making one of her regular expeditions to the celebrated Parisian gourmet shop Fauchon. She asked for a suggestion for something different in dry white wine to serve the general and was sold Clos Saint Hune. The general was so delighted with her purchase that he gave instructions for it to be placed *tout de suite* on the palace's list.

At the time when Jean Trimbach and his family arrived at Riquewihr in 1626, the land was ruled by those awesome and powerful Siegneurs of Ribeaupierre. Theirs was a rule exacted by force and fear and they lived according to their whims. High among their priorities were feasting, drinking and wenching, and for many years their reign went unchallenged.

Legend has it that two of these counts, who were brothers, were extremely boastful of their prowess with the bow. They occupied separate towers some 300 yards apart and practised an unusual eccentricity. On alternate mornings at dawn one brother would wake the other by firing an arrow into the wooden shutter of his brother's bed-chamber. Apparently, one morning after a night of excessive indulgence, the brother whose turn it was to fire the arrow overslept. Upon waking, he recalled that he had not performed his duty and hastened to open his shutters and fit his arrow to his bow. Simultaneously, in the opposite tower across the hillside, the other brother wakened and, realising that he had not had his alarm call, opened his shutters, only to be instantly struck dead by an arrow in the head.

Clearly life was brutal and severe under the Counts of Ribeaupierre, and it did not change for the better when they were succeeded in 1670 by the Austro-Hungarian Empire. In 1681, however,

an era of relative peace and prosperity ensued when Alsace was absorbed into France. But in 1870 came the Franco-Prussian War, and from then until 1918, a period of forty-eight years, the people of Alsace were denied even the right to speak their own language, as their land was annexed to the newly formed country of Germany.

The armistice of 1918 saw the return of Alsace to France, and it remained under French control until its occupation in 1940, when once more it was annexed by Germany. Towards the end of World War II, in 1944, it was liberated by the Allies and once more returned to France. This, for Alsace, was the beginning of a new period of prosperity; life has bloomed as its wine and gastronomy have attracted international fame. It has also brought unusual reflections for Hubert Trimbach's nona-genarian mother and her contemporaries, for she, who is indisputably proud of the French flag, has witnessed her official country of residence change on four occasions during her lifetime.

Many believe that the vineyards and wine villages of Alsace make it the most beautiful wine region in the world. Ribeauvillé is perhaps the most typically French of these villages, and the wines of its leading producer, F.E. Trimbach, would be a credit to any country, and in fact grace some of the world's greatest tables. But most importantly, Ribeauvillé's most famous face is possibly the most recognisable face in the world.

THE FRENCHTOWN SCHOOL
L'École No. 41, USA

The L'École No. 41 label from Washington State brings increasing compliments for its Semillon and Merlot wines, and has an intriguing history behind its name.

The Frenchtown School, L'École No. 41

It refers to the winery's name and building in the great metropolis of Lowden, population forty, in the south-west sector of the state, not far from the Oregon border and about a five-hour drive from my favourite city, Seattle. There, close by the banks of the Walla Walla river, stands an unusual if not unique winery. The building was constructed in 1915, when Lowden was still known as French-town and had a slightly larger population, and it was officially registered as School District No. 41.

In 1983, when the local government authority abandoned it, retired banker Baker Ferguson and his wife Jean claimed the school house and set about converting it into a winery. The Fergusons have subsequently passed control to their daughter, Megan Clubb, and her husband, Martin, and the seat of infant learning has been transformed into a hive of vinous activity.

The French translation of the name came about during a period early in the last century, when the Hudson Bay Company had a base at Walla Walla, and several French Canadian communities developed in the vicinity, including Frenchtown. Local oral tradition claims that some of those French-Canadians planted vines and produced wine, thus being the first true wine pioneers in the future state.

When it became necessary to name the winery in 1983, Baker Ferguson had two intriguing ideas. The first was to translate the name of the school into French and use it for the wine label, L'École No. 41, and the second was to run a competition among the local population to find the appropriate artwork for the label design. All the elementary-school children of Lowden were challenged to submit entries. Refuting any hints of nepotism, Ferguson awarded the honour to his eight-year-old nephew, Ryan Campbell.

GEORGE WASHINGTON'S WINE
Barton et Guestier; France and USA

It is with good reason that Americans celebrate the year 1776 with some vigour and enthusiasm, as it is the year in which freedom from colonial rule was achieved. It was an objective, historians explain, that could not have been attained without the active support of such heroic French figures as Paul Revere and the Marquis de Lafayette.

On the other hand, those same historians seem to have overlooked one other French name that played a significant role in turning the tide against the redcoats, that of Daniel Guestier, of the cele-brated Bordeaux wine shippers Barton et Guestier. And his action, many in Bordeaux claim, had more that a trifling effect on the outcome of the uprising.

Daniel Guestier was a sailor and merchant who ran away to sea when he was only fourteen. In the following six years he made his fortune, to become the equivalent of a modern multimillionaire trader, as he sailed to and from the developing ports of South America, providing for every possible com-mercial need. Naturally enough, since his home port was Bordeaux, one of his regular cargoes was wine, a commodity which attracted considerable custom. This trade eventually took him north of the Caribbean as he began visiting the American colonies, and in due course he developed a base in Baltimore Harbour, where he opened a depot for his increasingly popular Bordeaux wines.

For twelve months or so his Baltimore business expanded steadily, and soon his name was being praised by the landed gentry in their fine homes scattered around Chesapeake Bay. His trading contacts brought him word of the growing disputes between the colonists and the government of the British king, George III. However, little did he realise at the time how much the accumulating furore was going to involve him in its headlong course and simultaneously ensure him a memorable place in its history.

As initial threats led to full-scale war, France made the momentous decision to cast her lot on the side of the rebellious colonists. The French government was apparently confident of the eventual outcome of the war, and naturally wanted to protect her extensive settlements in Louisiana and Canada. The result was both military and commercial support. All kinds of armaments and supplies were transported across the Atlantic to the home forces, and where Daniel Guestier and his colleagues were involved, there was always sufficient room for the odd dozen or so *barriques* of wine. The consequences were more than the British could tolerate, and the King's Navy was ordered to form a blockade of the French ports along the entire

BEAUJOLAIS-VILLAGES

APPELLATION BEAUJOLAIS-VILLAGES CONTRÔLÉE
BOTTLED BY BARTON & GUESTIER
NÉGOCIANTS – ÉLEVEURS À BLANQUEFORT
750 ML
RED BURGUNDY WINE • ALC 12 % BY VOLUME

length of the Atlantic coast. With Britain already having a garrison in Gibraltar, which secured the entrance to the Mediterranean Sea, the French supplies came to an abrupt halt and merchant ships from Calais in the north to Bayonne in the south remained tied to their moorings.

Daniel Guestier, then twenty-one years of age, was not to be frustrated. He commissioned the building of two specially armoured balahows, one of which we know was called *Le Grand Nancy*. These ships were constructed in the sheltered bay known as Le Bassin d'Arcachon, some 40 miles south of the city of Bordeaux. From the small port of Arcachon, perhaps better-known for its oysters, Daniel set sail in an attempt to revive trade with his Baltimore outpost. He had chosen his route well. Using the cover of pitch-black night and his knowledge of the treacherous currents outside the little port, he managed time and again to slip silently through the British blockade without ever being spotted.

Imagine the excitement on the first and subsequent occasions when *Le Grand Nancy* was sighted sailing up Chesapeake Bay into Baltimore, proudly flying the French flag, with the promise of its much-desired cargo. Particularly for the gentlemen officers of George Washington's army, it meant the opportunity to return to their pattern of civilised dining. They had become so habituated to enjoying fine French wines with their meals that the unexpected arrival of Daniel Guestier with his prized cargo must have boosted morale to a large degree.

Exactly how much influence this had on the performance of Washington's men must remain a matter for conjecture. A reasonable estimate may be made from the following authenticated matter. As the newly independent United States began to reorganise its everyday life, shipments of Daniel Guestier's wine became increasingly popular until today it is the mostly widely seen French label in the USA. In 200 years, it has survived temperance movements, Prohibition, the Civil War, two world

wars, and the slumps of the 1920s and 1930s. It almost seems as if Uncle Sam is remembering to say thank you for Daniel Guestier's efforts.

On the other hand, the wine trade in Great Britain reflects just the opposite. Historically its business has always been conducted by the aristocracy, who supplied the fathers, brothers, sons, uncles and nephews who made up the ranks of the redcoats. They never forgot that Barton et Guestier had broken through the British naval blockade to help the rebellious colonials, and so, it seems, have declined since then to trade with the eminent Bordeaux house. Surprisingly, the British gentry were, and still are, perfectly happy to purchase from either of the great chateaux owned by the Barton family, namely Chateau Leoville Barton and Chateau Langoa Barton. But then neither of these chateaux remain under the auspices of the company Barton et Guestier, and it is that name Guestier which is rejected.

Some of my readers may think I am exaggerating, but is has not taken much research to reveal the lack of availability of Barton et Guestier wines in Britain today, with just one exception, the chain of more than 100 fine wine shops called Oddbins. That fact in itself is significant, because Oddbins is a relatively recent purchase of the North American wine and drinks giant Seagrams, and prior to their purchase of the chain in the mid-1980s, Oddbins also declined to stock Barton et Guestier wines. Of course, no-one will admit the real reason for America's first-choice French wine being taboo to the wine trade in Britain. Evidently it can have no reflection on its quality, which, after all, was good enough for George Washington and is welcome on my table at any time.

GOD KNEW FIRST
Llano Estacado, USA

A host of wines from around the globe can claim the privilege of having been selected to grace a multitude of magnificent state occasions, but few can have been so honoured as the delicious Llano Estacado Texas Chardonnay. It alone can fairly claim to have had some influence on one vital occasion that was to bring about the demise of the dreaded Iron Curtain.

The location was the presidential weekend retreat of Camp David in Maryland and the date, Saturday morning, 2 June 1990, on the last weekend of talks which did indeed help to change the world. A number of minor obstacles still confronted George Bush and Mikhail Gorbachev. However much they wanted to reach a settlement, they always seemed to encounter some small barrier which prevented a final solution. "Surely," they must

Cotton and vines share Llano Estacado soil near Lubbock, Texas

believe that conditions which attract wild vines should also be sympathetic to the cultivated varieties.

It was while browsing in a Houston wine store one afternoon that I first came across a bottle of Llano Estacado Sauvignon Blanc and, being of Welsh extraction, pronounced its first name with the strange double "ll" sound peculiar to the Welsh language. It is a sound which always poses a problem to English visitors, and may be known to many in the name of one of our most famous Welsh rugby clubs – Llanelli. But on this occasion it was my pronunciation which was astray and I was quickly put right by the helpful Houston shop assistant, who gave me the briefest possible lesson in Spanish. "Yarneau Estercardough" is how I interpreted the name, and so far no-one has corrected me.

I reasoned to myself that if a Texas winery could produce such a fresh, attractive Sauvignon Blanc with a good balance of fruit and acidity, then obviously much could be achieved there. And so that weekend, in a San Antonio hotel room, my road manager, Dave Hollyman, and I drank the bottle as a little digestive assistance to a takeaway shrimp feast. It was everything I dared hope and more. The proof as ever was in the tasting. In my mind, Texas was indeed a serious wine state and now the time was ripe to learn a little more.

Then quite fortuitously, the very next day, my extremely basic knowledge of Texas wine was increased considerably when Lee Foulkes, then wine manager at Don's and Ben's Liquor Barn, on West Avenue in San Antonio, poured three further samples for me in their tasting room. They included a Slaughter Leftwich Chardonnay 1989, which was most impressive, a Fall Creek Emerald Riesling which, while not suited to my taste buds, was well made and excellent value at less than $7, and a Fall Creek Cabernet Sauvignon 1989, which was most agreeable. Lee enthused about the future of Texas wines and spoke of Llano Estacado and Pheasant Ridge as the emerging stars. A few days later in Arlington, a suburb of Dallas, at a store called Big Daddy's, the wine consultant Joe Callahan was also full of praise for the rise of Texas wine and once more the name Llano Estacado was prominent.

And so, when some months later I flew from London to Houston, then on to Dallas and finally to Lubbock, I at least knew that I was on the trail of a superb Sauvignon Blanc which came from a winery with a growing reputation. Some had warned me that they had never even seen a Welshman in Lubbock, but I was sure that at least photographic images of Tom Jones, Richard Burton, Sir Anthony Hopkins and the like would have reached them. After all, Lubbock had been well-known to many of my generation as the birthplace of the very

have agonised, "we are not going to fail now when we are so near?" Yet certain problems still persisted.

At this point a presidential aide suggested a break in the proceedings for a light lunch to be shared with Barbara Bush and Raisa Gorbachev. The menu was a simple dish of crabmeat salad, and the wine was Llano Estacado Texas Chardonnay 1987. Its delicate aroma and mouth-filling flavour may, one might have thought, have possessed some magic power to charm its presidential consumers, for it is a matter of fact that after lunch the few remaining stumbling blocks seemed to dissolve in a new light of understanding.

George Bush, proud to be a Texan, had simply provided his illustrious guests with an example of an outstanding Texas Chardonnay and one of the prime such selections in the entire United States.

"Texas!" some might say derisively. "You can't really be serious!" But the doubter makes the mistake, for anyone who has tasted that rich Llano Chardonnay will know that George Bush, on that weekend, was not a fool but a wise man. So how can it be, many will ask, that Texas can boast a winery that has won so many awards as Llano Estacado, and also several other wineries that deservedly bring pride to the Lone Star State? The answer is, simply, God knew first! For it is an indisputable fact that there are more species of wild vines growing in Texas than anywhere else on earth.

To put the matter into perspective, let us consider that there are said to be some twenty-six species of grapes, which provide in excess of 2 000 grape varieties. The giant state of Texas is the natural home of fourteen of these species, with many thriving in the High Plains region near Lubbock. So if the wild vine chose Texas as its favourite land it is because it found ideal conditions there for it to thrive and multiply. Hence it is reasonable to talented Buddy Holly, whose electrifying performance at the Gaumont Theatre in Cardiff had enthralled me just weeks before his tragic death at the tender age of twenty-one. Also there was Texas Tech, as the state university in Lubbock is known. Its reputation preceded it, both in sporting and academic terms, but I had not realised that it was going to play such a vital role in this story.

Many years of visiting wineries around the world have taught me a number of lessons about the impressions made upon guests, the majority of which are gained upon one's initial reception. Sometimes there is an air of simple welcome. By stark contrast, on other occasions one may be greeted by a cool, if not even arrogant, indifference. Naturally many shades of distinction lie between these two polar opposites. At some wineries one is struck by the air of grandeur, and at others – a minority I might add – one gains the impression of having arrived in some antiseptic world of space-age technology where the individuals are merely androids programmed by their masters from a distant planet. The worst experience of all, as many will know, is to be kept waiting for an inordinately excessive period of time with no explanation. It is so often true that, as with a glass of wine, one's first impression lingers through to the finish.

Upon my arrival at Lubbock Airport, Mary-Louise Fuchs, a vice-president of Llano Estacado Winery, met me in a giant leather-seated Lincoln Town car and drove me to the comfortable Lubbock Plaza Hotel, ensuring everything was to my satisfaction before leaving, even though it was 11 p.m. Later I found out that she was a part-owner of Royal Coach Towne Car Service and had decided to parade their best car to ensure I was comfortable.

The following morning I was enthralled by Walter Haimann, the dynamic winery president, as he enthused about their exciting future and his projections of early progress. He introduced me to then Head Winemaker Don Brady and his assistant, Grant Douglas, who together must have made one of the most talented winemaking teams I have met in the United States. The message again was one of enthusiasm and ambition tempered by discipline.

Shortly, Don Brady was driving me across some tortuous terrain as we went on a wild-vine hunt. In the process it became clear to me that God really must have known that here were both the ideal microclimate and terrain for the vine, and so Mother Nature had sown her vines in abundance in the limestone soil, where, especially at an altitude of 3 200 feet, they could flourish.

By this stage my interest in two names that Don had mentioned – T.V. Munson and Bob Reed – was beginning to grow. The former was a 19th-century figure to whom the entire world of wine

should be indebted, and the latter a humble but charming Texas professor who at that stage, probably had a wider experience of viticulture in the state than anyone else.

Thomas Volnay Munson, better-known as T.V. Munson, was one of the first intellectuals in the United States to become involved in the profession of viticulture. In 1876, at Denison, Texas, which lies about 40 miles north of Dallas, he initiated extensive experimentation with wild vines and hybrid varieties. Sarah Jane English, in *The Wines of Texas*, relates how T.V. Munson went to the length of "saving the seeds, carefully separating and labelling each one". He was the first to classify the vines of Texas, and many others from different states, as well as breeding considerable numbers of new grape varieties. His most important contribution to viticulture was his pioneering work that saved many of the greatest French vineyards from phylloxera. For this he was awarded the Legion of Honour and showered with many other medals and awards by leading French viticultural and agricultural societies. Munson's simple but brilliant plan was to graft French noble vines onto phylloxera-resistant American rootstock, and then send the examples to leading French growers and authorities. In the utter doom and gloom of the latter part of the 19th century, when many French growers feared complete vineyard devastation, T.V. Munson provided not just a ray of hope but a giant sunbeam.

Bob Reed, a lean outdoor type in his late fifties, took some tracking down but he proved to be a fascinating man who turned viticulture, normally a tedious topic, into one full of curious interest. He was quite frank with me: "I really know nothing about wine. I'm not a wine drinker to any real degree. I'm a grape grower."

Bob recalled his pioneering role in the story of the Llano Estacado Winery. In 1962 he was Professor of Horticulture at Texas Tech University, Lubbock. As the university expanded westward, the next victim destined for the bulldozers was an old peach orchard and so Professor Reed decided to take a last look in case there were any plants which might yield useful cuttings. It was at this point that six vines claimed his attention and, rather than see them destroyed, he removed them and replanted them in his garden. Of these six vines, one was used to create an arbour as a sun shield over his patio. This was a black grape variety which even to this day he has been unable to identify, except to determine that it is a European-American hybrid. In 1966 his old friend and neighbour, another Texas Tech professor called Clinton McPherson, approached him with the suggestion that they should make a little wine from the grapes. The result was quite pleasing and so when 1967 produced a bumper crop of some 240 pounds, they were able to make good progress. The succeeding 1960s vintages provided increasing encouraging results, convincing them that winemaking in the area could become a serious proposition.

In 1970 they purchased a parcel of about 15 acres of land, which included a well, and from this plot selected 3 acres, on which they planted more than 200 different varieties of vines, all of which were either of the native North American *labrusca* species or were hybrids.

"At that time," Bob Reed said, "we didn't even contemplate growing any *Vitis vinifera* varieties, as we had been convinced by Californian publicity claiming that it was impossible to grow *vinifera* east of the Rockies, a misleading piece of propaganda that too many New York State growers, along with many others, continue to believe."

In 1972, as Bob explained, the temptation to experiment with *vinifera* proved too strong and they purchased some fifteen plants from a Californian nursery, out of which Chenin Blanc proved to be the most successful. Spurred on to further ambition, they introduced, in the following year, White Riesling, Sauvignon Blanc, Gamay, Pinot Noir, Gewürztraminer and Cabernet Sauvignon. The Pinot Noir, true to its temperamental nature, as elsewhere posed many a problem and still does, while all the other varieties settled comfortably into their new home. Later that year, Bob and Clinton held a field day for visitors, which resulted in a group of farmers forming an association named the Sandy Lane Grape Growers. Among them, the members planted 20 to 30 acres, but for the most part success was erratic, with one notable exception. George Martin's vines, on his 8 acres at White Face, thrived and later, in 1976, he provided the association with their first commercial quantity of grapes for crushing.

That same year, the two professors, one banker and three lawyers invested $3 000 each, published a prospectus, raised $275 000 and broke ground for the construction of the Llano Estacado Winery. The name was taken from the actual geographical region, which was so called after the Coronado expeditions of the early 1540s. Coronado had led his men north from Mexico in search of his personal El Dorado. Legend recalls that native Americans he had enslaved told him of seven great cities of gold to the north, and so he had struck deep into the unknown in search of glittering wealth. When the expedition reached the High Plains, apparently they entered some areas of tall grass, and so Coronado instructed his men to fell timber and make wooden stakes, taller than a man, to be placed in the ground every few hundred

yards. In this manner he ensured that his force would not lose their way. These grassy areas were referred to as the *Llano Estacado*, or quite simply "the staked plains", and so the region retains the name to this day.

It is perfectly feasible that Coronado may have carried vine cuttings with him, as this was normal practice among early Spanish settlers. Certainly we know that in 1659 two Franciscan fathers, Garcia Zuniga and Juan de Salazar, planted vines of the Spanish Mission variety at their Mission Senora de Guadalupe at El Paso, in what appears to be the earliest recorded bountiful cultivation of grapes for wine on the land of today's United States. There were several earlier plantings in Virginia, but none of these really proved successful and all were abandoned. The Franciscans used the wines primarily for sacramental purposes and also to aid digestion, much more than a century before Father Junipera Serra introduced the same vines to California for identical purposes.

During the following centuries, the planting of vineyards and the production of wine proliferated in the El Paso area, and Sarah Jane English relates the curious tale of Lieutenant Zebulun M. Pike, a US officer caught trespassing by the Mexicans early in 1806. She writes that he was taken to Chihuahua via El Paso, becoming:

> ... the first Anglo to travel through the pass. In March 1806, he recorded the event in his diary and wrote of "numerous vineyards from which were produced the finest wine ever drank."

It is difficult to imagine that his captors allowed him to indulge in a wine-tasting tour, so while the record of his eye remains indisputable, that of his palate may be a trifle doubtful. Today the longest continuous Texas winery is Val Verde, near the

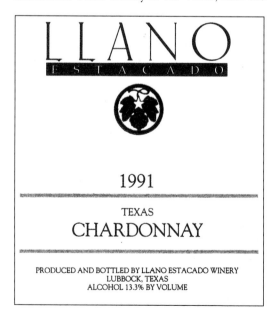

LLANO
ESTACADO

1991

TEXAS
CHARDONNAY

PRODUCED AND BOTTLED BY LLANO ESTACADO WINERY
LUBBOCK, TEXAS
ALCOHOL 13.3% BY VOLUME

Rio Grande in the south-west of the state, founded in 1883.

To obtain the very best from agriculture, most farmers will readily admit that teamwork between God and man is needed, and understanding this leads us to another unique and almost accidental factor in this story. Many of the Llano Estacado vineyards are planted in blocks amid what are claimed to be the world's largest cotton fields. These comprise not the cotton bushes of the Mississippi, but upland cotton, slender individual stems that provide for the almost insatiable international appetite for denim. The planting has become so extensive that hundreds of square miles have succumbed to cotton and its cultivation has even effected a change in the climate. In July, when the lush new green growth appears, it provides such an efficient sun barrier for the soil that the average daily temperature in the vineyards drops by more than 10°F per day. Late in June, near Lubbock, temperatures may often be in the low 90s. Yet two weeks later, as the grapes are ripening, this first growth on the cotton plants results in the temperature remaining in the upper 70s or lower 80s. Despite this, Llano Estacado has the earliest regular picking date that I have experienced anywhere in the Northern Hemisphere – 31 July.

A little later, with the autumnal blooming of the cotton, the effect becomes even more remarkable, as the white of the cotton bolls appears like snow to those flying over the region, and just as the Arabs of the desert wear white clothes to reflect the heat of the sun away from them, so the cotton can then cause a drop in temperature of 15°F or more. It also provides cool nights that can be particularly helpful with late-harvest wines.

The pioneering Stephen Austin, who was responsible for so much of the early settlement in Texas, wrote: "Nature seems to have intended Texas for a vineyard to supply America with wines." Leon Adams, one of the most respected of American wine writers is more specific. "There is no question the High Plains is a viticultural miracle. No-one realised this area could produce world-class wines. It is an amazing story." To this the present writer can only add one question. If the wines of Llano Estacado are so outstanding that already they have been used for President Gorbachev, Queen Elizabeth II of Great Britain on three occasions, the American Ambassador in Paris, and at a host of other memorable events; and if they have won gold medals from London to San Francisco, while the majority of their vines still average only ten years of age; and if they have received plaudits from the *Wine Spectator*, the *Los Angeles Times* and the *San Francisco Examiner*, then what will the vines of Llano Estacado achieve when they are fully mature?

HOME FROM HOME
Beringer, USA

Few of the countless thousands who drive along the picturesque Napa Valley through St Helena can fail to notice the impressive Rhine House in the grounds of the Beringer winery. The seventeen-room building overlooks the valley as it has done for a century. Designed by San Francisco German architect Albert A. Scroepfer, the Rhine House was completed in 1884 at a cost to Fritz Beringer of $28 000, and was designed in the style of their original Beringer family home in Mainz-am-Rhein, Germany.

It is a solidly constructed house, made of brick, local limestone and redwood, and cost nearly twice

Frederick Fritz Beringer, 1840-1901

Jacob L. Beringer, 1845-1915

The historic Rhine House in the grounds of the Beringer winery

Napa Valley

ESTABLISHED 1876

Beringer.

1990

ZINFANDEL

NAPA VALLEY

the style to which he had become accustomed as they move from room to room, noticing in particular the unique display of stained-glass windows. Some of these are painted, and others are jewelled and said to have been purchased as part of his private collection of Art Nouveau, of which he was most fond.

The Beringer brothers left the Napa Valley with one of its most prestigious wineries, one which is enjoying resurgent popularity for its superb range of premium, estate and reserve wines under the ownership of the Swiss group Nestlé. Fritz also left future generations his distinctive home, and would have been proud to see others enjoy the little piece of Rhineland he had built in California.

INCORRECT FOUNDER
Inglenook, USA

As a Briton involved with wine, I am always surprised that a major Californian winery, owned by the British Grand Metropolitan Group, should repeatedly make the error of claiming the wrong person as its founder – even the nationality is wrong.

Inglenook, near Rutherford, is the culprit, and while I am a keen admirer of its pleasing Cask Reserve Cabernet Sauvignon, I do not like to see that rare British Napa heritage denied.

For many years, Inglenook have claimed the 19th-century Finnish sea-captain and vineyardist Gustave Niebaum, as the person responsible for their origin and have given their foundation date as 1879. The likelihood is that someone within the company some years ago decided that Niebaum would lend more credibility to the winery's tradition than its actual founder.

The captain was an eminently respected father-figure of Napa wine and, following his 1879 purchase of Inglenook, brought new disciplines and standards to the valley which were a fine example to all. In addition, his name is connected with a number of surrounding wineries and vineyards. All of this is praiseworthy, but not a reason for overlooking our proud Briton.

To be accurate, the Inglenook founder was a Scot called William Watson, who acquired the property in 1872 and planted a 70-acre vineyard upon it – rather too large, one might think, to be overlooked. As Watson travelled northwards, along the road from the growing city of Napa, he saw the occasional new vineyard site being cleared from the forest. These vineyards were easily accessible from the road, but William Watson was intent on finding a more secluded position. For this purpose he continued his journey north, reaching Rutherford, where he was attracted by a peaceful location,

as much as the $15 000 Fritz and his brother Jacob had paid only nine years earlier for 215 acres of land at St Helena, which included 23 acres of vines and a modest farmhouse. At the time, Jacob was working nearby as a cellarmaster for Charles Krug, and he was fully aware of the valley's potential for wine production. He persuaded his maltster brother Fritz to finance him in a new vineyard venture. Seven years of occasional visits to the peaceful surroundings of Napa were sufficient to entice Fritz to build his dream house on their land. Later he sold his east-coast assets and moved to St Helena to join his brother and become an active partner in the vineyard enterprise.

Sadly, Fritz enjoyed only seventeen years in his Napa Valley home, for he died at the relatively early age of sixty-one. Today visitors can experience

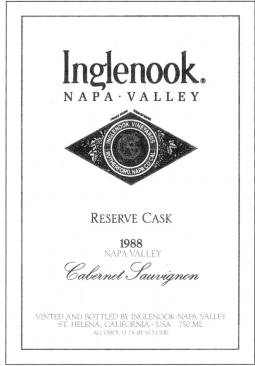

sheltered by the valley's western slopes. He considered the situation ideal for his plan to develop a health and holiday resort, a proposition for which he needed a suitable name. He selected some land there, built a house upon it, and quickly began planting vines. He called his property Inglenook, as it was the Scottish word for a cosy corner and he thought it would appeal to potential guests. Unfortunately, the limited travel of that era found Watson's Inglenook resort failing to attract sufficient customers and his dream gradually faded away during the seven years of his ownership. In contrast, his vines matured sufficiently to attract that interest of Captain Niebaum, who was able to purchase an established vineyard in peak production.

LILLIE'S COUNTRY ESTATE
Guenoc Winery, USA

The Guenoc Valley in Lake County, California, just north of the Napa Valley, is the home of

Guenoc, a winery that has two attractive red meritage wines, or Bordeaux-style blends. Released under the names Guenoc and Langtry, they both identify the legendary actress Lillie Langtry, owner of the estate in the Guenoc Valley between 1888 and 1906.

Some historical accounts have given a rather unbalanced view of Lillie Langtry by placing too much emphasis in her role as one of the mistresses of Prince Edward the Prince of Wales, the debauched son of Queen Victoria, and later King Edward VII of Great Britain. It should be remembered that Langtry was "the most popular actress of her day" in London, and her successes included important Shakespearean plays such as *Macbeth* and *As You Like It*, and Goldsmith's *She Stoops to Conquer*.

Lillie, who was born on the Channel Island of Jersey in 1852, was the daughter of a clergyman. She travelled extensively in South Africa and the USA, and selected her west-coast estate when she was thirty-six. There she built a fine home, which has been tastefully restored by the current owners, and where, according to local tradition, she also grew vines and made wine.

WHACKY WINEMAKERS
Adler Fells, USA

For a couple of generations it was very much the fashion in California to employ a winemaker who was a graduate of the Wine School at the University of California, Davis. It therefore raised quite a

Vineyards beside the Langtry house as they were from 1888 to 1906, when Lillie Langtry was the proprietor and vintner at Guenoc

dler Fels Winery stands high in the Mayacamas Mountains that separate the prestigious Sonoma and Napa Valleys. Turrets, towers and flourishes are the forefront of a commanding view down the Sonoma Valley and beyond to California's dramatic coast line. Founded in 1979, owner-winemakers David and Ayn Coleman built their mountaintop winery to produce highly awarded wines that have been acclaimed internationally. Production is limited as the wines are a product of small premium vineyards selected for their intense varietal character allowing the wines "to be made in the vineyards . . . not in the laboratory."

PRODUCED AND BOTTLED AT THE ADLER FELS ESTATE
SONOMA VALLEY, SANTA ROSA, CA, U.S.A.
BONDED WINERY 5024 • ALCOHOL 12.5% BY VOLUME

1991 SONOMA COUNTY
GEWÜRZTRAMINER

few eyebrows among wine-industry professionals when eccentric wine-label designer David Coleman and his wife Ayn decided to build a substantial mountain-top winery in the Sonoma Valley. There they intended to make their own wines from grapes purchased from other growers.

The couple named their European-style mock-Tudor castle Adler Fells, from the German for Eagle Rock, after a craggy granite outcrop adjacent to their property in the Mayacamas Mountains. On this site, in 1980, they constructed their home and winery, complete with towers, turrets and flags, and the most amazing golf hole in the state. Designed to keep the crazy couple in swinging mood, it offers a par of fifty as they and their occasional visitors and golfing victims aim successive golf balls into a perilous ravine hundreds of feet beneath.

These days, as David points out the floor of the Sonoma Valley nearly 1 500 feet below, he philosophises about "his grudge against Champagne", which he once described as "an unnatural combination of unripe fruit, dead yeast cells, sugar and water", before offering a taste of their Melange ê Deux sparkling wine, made from 50 per cent Gewürztraminer and 50 per cent Riesling in their own inimitable style. Then, in a moment of seriousness, Ayn will suggest their Sauvignon Blanc, which has been highly praised by such eminent journals as the British magazine *Decanter*, the *Los*

The mock-Tudor castle Adler Fells, perched high in the Maya-camas Mountains in California

Angeles Times and *Bon Appetit*, and has also won a host of medals.

At this point, David is likely to hold your attention while he delivers a lecture on the technical details of his personally designed top fermenter, which follows the procedures of a jet-fighter quick-release door. Or if you are extremely privileged, he will confide in you his nearly complete plans for a new ageing system, which will make barrels obsolete and alter the pattern of wine production worldwide.

As time passes, the realisation dawns that Ayn is really quite down-to-earth, as she admits that for reasons politic she has retained her maiden name for everyday use, as "she often finds it advantageous to be Ms Ryan rather than Mrs Coleman". As Ms Ryan she can often smooth the ruffled feathers of clients who have been riled by the outspoken David.

Of course it may well be that Adler Fells means Eagle's Bluff, and that David is really calling the bluff of the entire Californian wine establishment.

WHAT ELSE IS THERE TO SAY?
Robert Mondavi, USA

So much has been written by so many about Robert Mondavi that there is little I can add. He is undeniably one the most redoubtable figures in the history of wine in the New World, and has been a major influence on the modern development of Californian wine. His fellow producers obviously appreciate the magnitude of his contribution to the promotion of Californian wine, both throughout the USA and worldwide. He has justly received a flood of prestigious honours from a wide variety of organisations and countries. He is included in this book because, I believe, he is an outstanding example of the American dream.

Robert Mondavi was born in Minnesota just before the outbreak of World War I. He was the son of an Italian immigrant father, Cesare Mondavi, who for some years struggled to earn his living as a miner before he had accumulated sufficient funds to begin trading as a grocer and eventually a grape dealer. Cesare's wife, Rosa, was, according to all accounts, a family matriarch who practised what she preached, based on her ten years' experience in Minnesota running a miners' hostel. Here she cooked, cleaned and scrubbed for some fifteen men, whom she treated as her own kin. During this period, the English wine writer Cyril Ray recalls, she never enjoyed more than six hours' sleep a night.

When Prohibition arrived, the price of grapes suitable for home winemaking quadrupled, and the Mondavi family packed their bags and travelled

1989

NAPA VALLEY

CABERNET SAUVIGNON

RESERVE

ROBERT MONDAVI WINERY

to Lodi, in California's Central Valley. Twenty years later, in 1943, Cesare Mondavi had acquired enough capital to purchase the Napa Valley's oldest surviving winery, Charles Krug, at St Helena, for what was then the substantial sum of $75 000. Initially Cesare took control, but later Robert and his younger brother Peter assumed responsibility, with their mother acting as president.

So much has been said about the acrimonious dispute that followed, which culminated in a major court action, that it is probably best to gloss over that era, merely reflecting that there are usually two sides to every story. What is indisputable is that the total split between the two brothers instigated the birth in 1964 of the Robert Mondavi wine business, with the construction of the first major new winery in the Napa Valley since the Volstead Act. Especially noteworthy is that, at the time, Robert Mondavi was already fifty-one years old, and it has been during the succeeding thirty years that he, more than any other person, has placed the name of the Napa Valley among those of the top wine regions of the world, something he achieved by producing an outstanding range of wines and by demonstrating his natural skill as a promoter.

WHERE THOMAS JEFFERSON FAILED
Prince Michel Vineyards, USA

In 1983, when Prince Michel Vineyards owner Jean Leducq instructed his staff to graft noble vines from France onto American rootstock, it was as if history were repeating itself, for grafting of this nature had saved the vineyards of his native France from phylloxera a century earlier. The striking difference for Jean Leducq was that he undertook the task in the light of modern wine science, in contrast with the basic knowledge available to earlier generations. Aided by his substantial personal wealth, he was able to integrate traditional French winemaking disciplines with modern American oenological and viticultural practices.

Jean Leducq was attracted to his Virginian challenge after his company's acquisition of a Culpeper, Virginia, business. He found himself suitably impressed by the new breed of Virginian wines that he had tasted, and vowed to join the small but growing band of vineyard owners who were succeeding in the state where Thomas Jefferson had failed in his attempts to produce wines of the quality and character he had found in France.

Jean hired the services of the respected Joachim Hollerith, who supervised the planting of 110 acres of *vinifera* vineyards, the most extensive to date in Virginia, and then began the uphill fight for the recognition that is so difficult to obtain outside one's home region.

The choice of the name Prince Michel recalls a

number of men of European heritage who bore that name and who were renowned for their sympathy with the subjects of wine and gastronomy. Perhaps the most notable among them was Prince Michel of Byzantium, later Emperor Michel III, who actively promoted the cultivation of vineyards and the enjoyment of wine throughout his empire. To many, the same Prince Michel is best-known for his conversion of the Slav peoples of his empire to Christianity.

9. HOPEFUL INFANT: OREGON, STATE OF THE FUTURE

The wine industry in the scenic state of Oregon, USA, has such a short history that it would need some careful creative writing to describe its heritage, but I am so irresistibly drawn to the state and its delicious new crop of wines that some small tribute is mandatory. Sporting some 6 000 acres and seventy producers, Oregon wine production is hardly a large-scale business, but it is supplying noble wines of class and style that can only go on to achieve recognition and praise.

My annual broadcasting visits to Oregon have allowed plenty of scope for tasting, and I have gleaned much information from friends like Brian Pearson and Greg Lemma of the Lemma Wine Company. Also, I have scoured the surface of Oregon wines, searching for the occasional tale worthy of merit.

HAWK-EYED VINTNER
Eyrie Vineyards

The family of hawks that peer down from the tall pines onto David Lett's Willamette Valley winery do not pose any threat. On the contrary, their presence probably deters vermin and, best of all, inspired the name of the vineyard. Without doubt,

other Oregon wine producers have been watching the amusing Mr Lett like hawks ever since his Pinot Noir won such acclaim for his winery (and the state's viticultural reputation) at the 1980 Gault-Millau Wine Olympics in Paris. The performance was repeated in the Drouhin tasting later that year, and Monsieur Robert Drouhin, one of the most esteemed Burgundy producers, was astute enough to recognise what Oregon had to offer. He proceeded to invest his own funds in a new venture, Domaine Drouhin, in the nearby Dundee Hills.

WINE FOR THE COUCH
Cooper Mountain Vineyards

First-time visitors to Cooper Mountain Vineyards usually find it a haven of peace in which they can relax in the presence of owner Robert Gross. On other occasions the atmosphere is a little livelier at the picturesque setting, which might suggest that the winery has something of a split personality.

None of this is surprising, as Robert Gross is one of the few oenological psychiatrists in existence, who in his spare time treats his patients in Portland, hopefully with his outstanding Chardonnay, as it could cure a few problems.

CHOOSING THE RIGHT NAME
Argyle Brut

The owners of the Oregon winery that can justifiably claim one of the finest sparkling wines in America apparently could not agree for some time on a suitable name. Brian Croser, an Australian sparkling-wine expert, and Robert Chadderton, an American wine shipper, decided to amalgamate their names to form the "appealing" title of Crochad. During that time, according to specialist wine writers Ronald and Glenda Holden, Croser and Chadderton were not too enthusiastic about journalistic enquiries. The Holdens reported in *Northwest Wine Country* that in July 1988 the winery wrote to them in the following terms: "Please do not include Crochad in your publication. Crochad has no wine available, no label and no name."

Perhaps a little rethinking was inevitable, for in 1990, when the new sparkling wine was released, the Scottish name Argyle had emerged, no doubt inspired by their Dundee location. It had to be an improvement on the idea of consumers in a wine store or restaurant requesting that "beautiful bubbly Crochad Brut".

PROBABLY THE FIRST
The Laurel Ridge Winery

The oldest vineyard site in Oregon is probably the Laurel Ridge Winery at Forest Grove. Unfortunately, specific details of its history are not readily available, but there is sufficient evidence to confirm that in the late 19th century a vineyard existed at that location, owned by a German immigrant,

Frank Reuter. He boldly and correctly prophesied that the Willamette Valley could become "the Rhineland of America", a statement borne out by its current abundance of fruit, including grapes.

Prohibition brought the demise of Reuter's Hill Winery, as it was then called. The Laurel Ridge Winery is the third attempt to revive the German's viticultural dream, the Charles Coury Winery and a relaunched Reuter's Hill Winery both having met with failure.

HOW OLD IS OLD?
Hillcrest Vineyard

Hillcrest is the oldest vineyard in Oregon, one wine buff told me, and I had to make some careful mental calculations as to how old that might be. I had heard that the Hudson Bay Company had, as early as the 1820s, planted a vineyard at Fort Vancouver, some thirty years before Oregon became a state. But then down in the Umpquah Valley, below the quaint and folksy city of Eugene, "old" did not really mean that old. In fact, local winery pioneer Richard Sommer had planted his first *vinifera* vines at Hillcrest Vineyard as late as 1963, and soon became a popular source for Riesling. Now with vines that are more than thirty

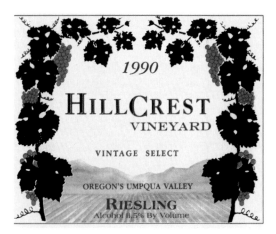

years old, the Umpquah veteran is gaining a reputation for late-harvest wines as he gently takes things in his stride. He and his successors will be able to look back and remember that he was the owner of the oldest continuous vineyard in Oregon, but we must not forget that the Canadians planted vines first, and Frank Reuter a little later.

IT'S A SMALL WORLD
Ponzi Vineyards

Not fifteen minutes from downtown Portland lie Ponzi Vineyards, where the Pinot Gris is one the finest in the New World. Frankly, the drive is one of the less scenic in a state where magnificent vineyard backdrops abound. But pay the vineyard a visit just to buy the wine and discover whether any imaginative engineering has begun, based on Dick Ponzi's lifetime experience. Trained as an aeronautical engineer, Ponzi transferred those skills

to designing rides for Disney World and Disneyland. Then, apparently, one day he took a stroll from his back garden into a neighbouring vineyard and a change in lifestyle followed, one which has resulted in increasing journalistic acclaim.

10.   CHRISTIANITY AND WINE

GEORGES DE LATOUR PRIVATE RESERVE
Beaulieu Vineyard, USA

In the American state of Ohio, one of the most respected gentleman of the wine trade is a dear friend of mine, George Hammer. He is the head of a family company which is a wholesale distributor of many fine European and American wines. The Hammer Company is also one of the most important sources of sacramental wine for hundreds of miles around, which is fitting for a company with a strong Catholic tradition. Indeed, the subject of sacramental wine has brought the Hammer family a special relationship with the outstanding Napa winery Beaulieu Vineyard.

Beaulieu is French for "a beautiful lie of land", and was the name given to the winery in 1900 by Frenchman Georges de Latour, who planned to produce a classic Cabernet Sauvignon at Rutherford, to rival the first-growth red wines of Bordeaux. Among red wines that require ageing, Beaulieu's superb Georges de Latour Private Reserve has the longest continuous record for

consecutive vintages in the Napa Valley, California, and has been marketed since 1936. Most wine journalists agree that during that time it has set a record, so far unsurpassed in the region, for such consistent quality. Much of the praise must go to the late Georges de Latour and his Russian-born winemaker André Tchelistcheff.

Yet four years before that landmark 1936 vintage, the name of Georges de Latour was well-known to the Hammer family of Cleveland. When Prohibition came into force, Beaulieu Vineyard survived by transforming its operation into one that specialised in sacramental wines, and it found in the Hammer Company a ready outlet. Soon the various members of the Hammer family were travelling the states surrounding Ohio, offering sacramental wine to local stockists and churches from this most highly regarded winery. As a result a friendship between Georges de Latour and the family grew, and when my friend George Hammer was born in 1932, his parents invited the Napa Frenchman to be his godfather, and had their son baptised Georges de Latour Hammer.

The following year, 1933, saw the repeal of Prohibition, and Beaulieu Vineyards began a gradual change back to traditional winemaking. The first release of Georges de Latour Private Reserve in 1936 was followed by nearly sixty consecutive vintages, which have won much acclaim and been distributed in Ohio through the Cleveland headquarters of the Hammer Company. Nowadays, Beaulieu no longer offers any sacramental wines, but the Hammer Company does and is one of the most successful participants in that unusual trade.

THE MOST HONOURED NAME
Vigne de L'Enfant Jésus, France

The most honoured name of any wine must be that of the Vigne de L'Enfant Jésus, a single-estate

Burgundy from the Beaune-Grèves vineyards belonging to Bouchard Père et Fils. From around the 14th century, this premier cru is believed to have been owned by the Carmelite sisters of Beaune. They would have used the wine for three purposes: for sacramental needs, for daily consumption as an aid to digestion, and to sell any surplus to help support their living. The drawing on the label is believed to be a processional figure from that era. After the 1789 French Revolution, however, the property was confiscated and sold by public auction.

The current owners, Bouchard Père et Fils, are one of the largest *domaine* owners in the Burgundy region. The original Père, or Father, Bouchard, as he is remembered, was a travelling cloth salesman from northern France, who used to make an annual journey through Burgundy and the Rhône, selling his materials as he travelled south, and then purchasing wines for his return north. He soon established a preference for fine Burgundies and began to concentrate upon their sales. In a relatively short time he found that his wine trade became more profitable than his business as a draper, and he moved to the picturesque medieval city of Beaune, where in 1731 he founded the independent family house.

THE POPE WHO KNEW BEST
Chateauneuf-du-Pape, France

The mouth-filling red wines of Chateauneuf-du-Pape are renowned for their character and vigour, qualities derived in part from the fact that their vines enjoy exposure to one of the warmest climates in France, something which raises a question concerning its selection as a vineyard site and the name of the wine.

The name Chateauneuf-du-Pape means "the new castle of the Pope", and identifies a surviving ruin which is in the heart of the vineyards of that appellation. It was built as the summer residence of Pope Clement V (born Bertrand de Got), the first of the popes domiciled in Avignon during the so-

called Babylonion Exile, which lasted from 1309 to 1377. The alleged purpose of the new castle was to provide, in summer, a peaceful and cool base for the pontiff, away from the onerous duties and the heat and humidity of the papal palace in Avignon. Yet Clement chose one of the warmest microclimates in France.

Thus the question remains: would it not have been relatively easy for Pope Clement V to have chosen a situation at a somewhat higher altitude, but still within a reasonable distance from Avignon? At that time, the papacy owned vineyards which embraced a large section of today's official Côtes du Rhône area, and which is still known as L'Enclave des Papes. If the Pope had really wanted a cooler position then he could, without difficulty, have acquired just a few miles to the east, an ideal site on the foothills of Mont Ventoux, affording panoramic views in at least three directions. Here he could have experienced a more temperate climate, where he could have relaxed and grown the healthiest of vines.

The clue to the answer, which can be deduced from substantial background evidence, is that Pope Clement V was very much a man of wine. Immediately prior to his appointment he had served as Archbishop of Bordeaux, and his entire childhood had been spent in the Bordeaux *paysage*, where he had been raised in a world of winemakers and had come to appreciate what the grape could achieve, with a little blessing from God and some physical guidance from man. It was an era in which the wine trade was formed of growers and merchants and little else. The growers were responsible for the entire production of Bordeaux wine, and the consumption of a tolerable proportion as well. The remainder was either paid to their landlords, often monastic orders, as rent or as a share of the crop, or it was sold to *négociants,* or merchants, who even at that time were shipping in casks to the British Isles and other northern European countries.

Until that stage the concept of a wine chateau had not even been considered, yet in many ways it is perfectly fair to credit Pope Clement V with

being responsible for both the first and second wine chateaux in France. In 1300, during his term in office as Archbishop of Bordeaux, Pope Clement V's brother made him a gift of a vineyard, in the hamlet of Pessac in the Graves region, as a diocesan investment. The estate later became known as Chateau Pape Clement, and it remains one of the most eminent of the Graves Grand Crus Classés to this day. The word Graves arises from the fact that the soil was full of gravel, with much of the stone lying on the surface. There the archbishop planted several hectares of wine grapes, and no doubt was highly delighted with the results. Six years later, when he was elected Pope, he had to hand over his investment to the Archbishopric of Bordeaux, under whose jurisdiction it remained until 1789, and he probably felt a little saddened to leave that task before the vines had developed to maturity.

In this manner, by the time of his appointment, Clement V had become an enthusiastic man of wine, and so when he came to consider the position of his new summer palace a few years later, he preferred to choose one where he believed the best wine could be produced. Between Avignon and Orange, on a bluff overlooking the Rhône, he selected his land. There he found not gravel, but smooth pebbles, not unlike the small Cavaillon melons, which almost completely covered the surface of the earth. After his experience at Chateau Pape Clement, he realised that these stones would absorb the heat of the sun by day and radiate it to the vines during the night, encouraging the strongest growth.

The stony terrain of Chateau-neuf-du-Pape, once an inland sea

Unfortunately, Clement V died in 1314 with the work in its infancy, and the new chateau, Chateau-neuf-du-Pape, was not finished until the reign of Pope Clement VI, some thirty years later. Some authorities believe that the vineyard there was first planted by John XXII, who held office between the two Clements, but no conclusive proof is available. Others consider that Clement V may well have appreciated that planting his vines would be a much speedier task than building his summer castle, and therefore it is likely that this work was completed first. As it is, we will probably never

know, but it does seem a justifiable assumption to credit Pope Clement V with being responsible for the two oldest wine chateaux in France, and for getting his priorities as a wine enthusiast right when choosing his holiday home.

PRAISE BE TO GOD
Nederburg, South Africa

A diary entry of Jan Van Riebeeck, the leader of the first party of Cape settlers, reads: "Today, praise be to God, wine was pressed from Cape grapes for the very first time." In 1652 he had landed in what has since been named the Cape region of South Africa, with instructions to develop a settlement for the Dutch East India Company, as a sort of halfway post for their ships as they made the great spice run to and from the Netherlands and the East Indies. He found idyllic climatic conditions, which he knew would sustain all kinds of fruits and vegetables and, being wise, he quickly took advantage of those conditions to plant some vines.

Praiseworthy reports of the earliest Cape wine led to the Dutch government taking a serious interest. Obviously the Dutch could not have vineyards in the Netherlands, owing to its geographical position in Northern Europe, but South Africa afforded them considerable potential for the production of vines within their expanding empire.

As a result, in 1679, the colony's governor, Simon Van der Stel, implemented a planned expansion of viticulture in the Cape, and even appointed inspectors to improve vineyard and winemaking disciplines. He also planted the legendary Constantia Vineyard, which was shipping its famed dessert wines to several countries by the end of that century. These wines rapidly earned a reputation for their voluptuous concentration. In the 19th century, Constantia became a favourite of Napoleon Bonaparte, the Russian tsarist court, and various British monarchs. Only a few years ago the late Earl Spencer told me that he still had some bottles of 1787 Constantia hidden away.

The best-known name in the current generation of South African wine is Nederburg, a proud company with a two-century German tradition. Nederburg produces a wide range of wines, including less-familiar names like Edelrood, Baronne and Prelude. The winery was founded in 1792 by a German immigrant, Philip Woolvart, who built its historic homestead, which is a noted example of early Cape architecture. After phylloxera ravaged the Cape vineyards in the 1880s, Nederberg faded from the scene, but in 1937 the arrival of another German immigrant, Johann Graue, saw a resurgence of activity, which later, in the 1950s and 1960s, brought an array of medals and trophies.

These successes reduced drastically with the imposition of sanctions against South Africa in the international fight against apartheid, but are now increasing again.

SAINT MARTIN
Chablis St Martin, France

His name appears on thousands of Christian churches and cathedrals scattered around the globe and will be familiar to hundreds of millions of people. Yet one must wonder how small a fraction of those will know of the historic role he played in the story of wine in Europe. When one takes into account the substance of his influence, it is hardly surprising that many vignerons recognise him, and not Saint Vincent, as the true patron saint of wine.

His life, which spanned eighty-one years from AD 316 to 397, was one of exemplary Christianity, and for centuries he was revered by millions of devout believers. Sad to relate, his prominence has faded over the last 200 years, a circumstance which in no way detracts from the importance and relevance of his contributions to the development of early European Christianity, and to the serious organisation of viticulture which has formed the basis for the growth of the wine trade as we know it today.

He was born into a family living in Sabaria, in Pannonia, part of modern-day Hungary, and a region which would have been considered an outpost of the Roman Empire. Martin's father was a serving officer in the Roman Army, and his mother raised him in a pagan home, yet despite this, Martin, as a youth, became familiar with Christianity, and it was a matter of considerable

inner turmoil to the young man whether to dismiss this religious movement or accept it. The question was not settled until many years later when the memorable incident for which he is best-known occurred in northern France.

Initially, Martin followed in his father's footsteps and enlisted in the Roman Army, quickly rising to the rank of a junior officer, a role in which he is believed to have served for some five years. He was posted to Amiens, about 100 miles north of modern Paris, where the legion was trying to contain successive waves of incursions by the ferocious Allemani tribe.

Here he first demonstrated his humanitarian principles when he shocked his fellow officers by insisting that he should not be entitled to more privileges than his servant. He pursued this ideal by sharing his tent and his meals with this servant, and also by helping him with his workload. It was about this time that the famous incident of the cloak occurred, which demonstrates most aptly his, albeit subconscious, application of Christian precepts. At the time, he was on guard duty, inspecting the legionnaires at their various postings around the city walls. As he rode his horse through the Gate of Amiens on a freezing-cold day, a half-naked beggar approached him pleading for alms. It was instantly apparent to Martin that the poor man had nothing, and so he removed his *capella,* or cloak, and, unsheathing his sword, cut the cloak in half, giving one piece to the shivering vagrant in a deed which has since been portrayed by many artists and sculptors.

That night, in his dreams, Martin had a vision of angels surrounding Christ, who was sporting the half-cloak he had given to the beggar, and who was saying to the heavenly host, "This is the cloak which Martin has given me." Upon his awakening on the following morning, Martin had no further need of inner debate; he was convinced by his dream that he must follow Christ, and so made the decision to be baptised. Shortly afterwards he applied to his senior officer to be granted release from the army on the grounds that he wished to become a monk. The immediate reaction was to accuse him of cowardice, but his response was that he was willing to march forward to meet the Allemani without armour or weapons, trusting to his Lord to protect him. Here the accounts of what happened next vary. Some authorities say that Martin was put to the test and given the opportunity to demonstrate his courage, but his senior officer was sufficiently convinced to call him back before he reached the astonished enemy, and instantly granted him his freedom. Others relate that he was thrown into prison and only released when the Romans had quelled the Allemani uprising.

From his early days in Pannonia, Martin would have been aware of wine and its importance in everyday Roman life. Indeed, it is likely that his birthplace had been the very cradle of European viticulture, as it is generally accepted that the Celts, who inhabited the region before 600 BC, owned their own vineyards, although it is not known from what source they had gained their knowledge of wine production. As a young Roman, Martin would have learned that it was considered essential to drink wine on a daily basis, as the cleanliness of water supplies could seldom be relied upon. In the Roman Army, he would have been instructed that the legionnaires should have a daily wine ration as protection against various diseases, and to this end they took vine cuttings and planted vineyards wherever they went. It was a basic discipline that Martin was to retain when he was eventually discharged from the army, and which he was to adapt for the Christian Church.

Upon his release from the army, he travelled some 200 miles south-west to join St Hilaire, or St Hilary, in Poitou. Here the two men followed lives of asceticism and self-denial in monastic cells, which were probably caves cut out of the tuffeau, or soft chalky limestone, of the region. In no time, Martin developed a wonderful reputation for serving the poor and sick of the nearby communities, aiding them with his herb lore and the use of wine in enhancing their health.

In 372 AD, following the death of the incumbent Bishop of Tours, the local Christian community and some of their priests sent word to Martin that they wished him to fill the position. He declined, explaining that this was not the sort of service to God that he wished to undertake, but it seems the populace were not going to be denied so lightly. A delegation was sent to seize Martin by force and have him consecrated as bishop. Eventually, accepting that by early Church law a bishop could be elected by popular demand, Martin submitted to this act, which he deemed God's call to the Holy See.

Martin became a living legend, with many contemporary examples recorded of his conversion of

pagans, healing of lepers, and numerous other good deeds. Contradictorily, his was apparently a short, scruffy, rather unkempt figure, certainly not an example of cleanliness being next to godliness. Yet he displayed a particularly adept and concise mind in church matters, a facet which could no doubt be attributed to his Roman upbringing and five years service as an officer. Using his talents, he began to organise parishes along the Loire Valley, appointing individual priests to take charge of them, with instructions to plant vineyards. He visited these parishes on a regular basis to ensure that they received the requisite pastoral support and guidance. It was one such visit that led to an amusing local legend, which is recalled to this day in Touraine:

Martin had set out one morning to visit a parish about a day's ride from Tours. When he eventually arrived it may have been in the dusky evening light. He tethered his donkey to some vines, which he probably assumed belonged to the parish, before calling upon the local priest. The following day, when it was time for him to proceed to his next call, he went to retrieve his donkey, only to be greeted by a local farmer, the owner of the vines, who was furious. He complained vehemently that the donkey had eaten all the greenery on his vines, and had in fact chewed the plants right back to their stocks, and that he would have no crop next year. The farmer insisted on compensation, and the humble bishop apologised for his animal's behaviour, opened his purse, and settled his account.

A year later, Martin revisited the same parish, but this time found an elated vigneron waiting for him, full of profuse welcome for the bishop and his donkey. He had, he recounted to Martin, experienced the most abundant crop he had ever known. Martin's donkey had "miraculously" discovered the benefits of pruning.

Quite how the tale came to spread no-one will ever know for certain, but there seem to be several clues which substantiate it. Wild vines had grown in profusion in the Loire Valley for centuries, but none of the local populace had any knowledge of how to cultivate them. The Romans had used pruning knives for generations, and Martin would have explained to his priests the benefits of pruning as part of crop maintenance, just as he would have emphasised the benefits of vine growing and wine production in general. The church would gain from the ownership of vineyards in three principal ways: wine was used in the communion service for sacramental purposes; it was an aid to good healthy digestion; and the church could sell any surplus wines to provide for the financial support of the parishes. It was this same philosophy which was adopted fourteen centuries later by Father Junipero

Serra and his followers as they settled their missions in California.

One other possibility about the donkey story is that it derives from an even more ancient legend with an Egyptian background. It was reported earlier this century that when the eminent archaeologist Howard Carter opened a tomb near the Nile, which he believed had been sealed for some 3 000 years, he was surprised to discover some wall paintings in excellent condition. One of these showed a donkey chewing back vines as if it were an established practice. Similar accounts have also been received from the Middle East. If the assumption is correct, then it may well have been that for thousands of years growers used animals to prune their vines in this most natural way. If it was an accepted practice, then perhaps it is more likely that Saint Martin put a stop to it and introduced the Roman pruning knife into the parish vineyards.

To even begin to appreciate the influence of St Martin one has to remember that he not only constructed the first monastery in Gaul, at Marmoutier, but founded one of the earliest of all monastic orders, which seems to have been later absorbed into the Benedictine order, and which soon spread Martin's practices across the continent. In AD 386 he was summoned to attend a heresy trial in Augusta Trevorum, or Trier as it is now known, at the great cathedral which was first built by the Emperor Constantine about sixty years earlier. While there, he so influenced the local Christian community that a monastic order of St Martin was established. This had a direct bearing on another notable connection with wine when, two centuries afterwards, the Bishop of Trier, later St Magnerice, donated to the order a large area of land near Graach, in the heart of the Middle Mosel. Upon it they constructed a monastery and a winery, where they produced one of the truly outstanding Mosel wines, called Martinshofer. After secularisation in the 18th century, the property was sold to a banker called Joseph Hain and the name was changed to Josephshofer, and still remains so. Here visitors can see the ancient chapel and, over the main doorway, the carving of St Martin cutting his *capella* in two.

Thus, for some 1 200 years, the wine of Martinshofer, or St Martin, was produced and sold in the Mosel Valley, where it underwent differing periods of either French or German name, depending on the identity of the occupying power.

It is surprising that the name is only occasionally seen on labels, with the inexpensive Californian San Martin and the French Chablis Saint-Martin, from Laroche, being two exceptions. The headquarters of the latter are in l'Obédiencerie, the oldest building in the historic town of Chablis, which dates back in part to AD 867. At that time,

L'*Obédiencerie cellars, where St Martin's bones were once hidden*

it was constructed on the foundations of the ancient Saint Loup monastery, which was founded in AD 510. In AD 867, an edict of King Charles the Bald had ceded the tiny monastery to the monks of St Martin, who had fled from Touraine with the relics of their founder, after losing their land to Norman invaders. For many years the bones of St Martin were guarded in l'Obédiencerie, before being taken to the Abbey of Vougeot, which was also to become the home of one of the world's most celebrated wines. Later the relics were returned to the tiny parish church of Candes Saint-Martin, where the often forgotten saint continues to lie in peace in the heart of the Loire vineyards to which he contributed so much.

THANKS TO A BAPTIST
Kentucky Bourbon, USA

There are few subjects upon which more nonsense has been written or aired than the fast-fading relationship between the Christian churches and temperance. Nevertheless, during the latter years of the last century and the early years of this, it is understandable that so many denominations actively supported the demise of the demon drink. Life for countless millions had become a pitiful shambles, as they gulped the roughest liquor in a cyclical attempt to forget the dismal conditions that surrounded them.

No country took more drastic measures than the USA, with its public pledge-signings held on a huge scale, and its eventual unfortunate episode of Prohibition. Therefore it will surprise some to learn that the man responsible for the creation of Kentucky Bourbon was none other than a Baptist pastor of high standing, the Reverend Elisha Craig.

Of Scots-Irish descent, the preacher divided his attentions between his calling as a minister and his part-time occupation as farmer and distiller. At that time, it was common practice for nonconformist clergy in rural areas to have their own stills and produce rye, or in Kentucky corn whiskey for three chief purposes: for use as a medicine, to restore travellers after long journeys, and as an occasional relaxing drink. The accidental discovery of a clergymen, however, was to bring a mellowness to the fiery spirit and dramatically increase its popularity in a matter of a few years.

In 1785, Elisha Craig was Baptist pastor at Great Buffalo Crossing, Kentucky, where he had apparently settled after an inland trek from Pennsylvania. There, it was reported, he kept his still and barrels in a small store. At some stage a fire broke out in the store and there followed an unseemly rush to rescue the still and barrels. Unhappily, only some of the casks were recovered and the remainder were heavily charred. When, some while later, Craig resumed distilling with some friends, he was suddenly confronted with a problem. The run, as it was sometimes called, meant that there would be more whiskey distilled than they had barrels to contain. Initially he used the barrels he had managed to recover from the fire. They were made of clean new oak, but even so, he needed further casks. So, reluctantly, he put the remaining spirit into the charred barrels.

A year or so later the first whiskey from the clean barrels was drunk, as obviously he thought that it would taste best. Some time later, when the first supplies had been exhausted, he removed the bung from one of the charred kegs and began to pour. The whiskey's darker colour was immediately apparent and its mellowness could be appreciated instantly. He had quite fortuitously benefited from using the charred oak and from ageing his whiskey longer than usual.

Being an unselfish man, Elisha wanted others to learn of his serendipitous result, and soon word of the Baptist pastor's success spread among the surrounding counties. At the time, the farmer-distillers of Kentucky were becoming increasingly conscious of the need to identify their corn whiskey in a different manner from the rye whiskey being produced in some quantity in Pennsylvania. There was no doubt much debate about the name of the new style. Indeed, it is interesting to note that it was not until some twenty years later that the Scots-Irish adopted the whiskey spelling that their ancestors had previously known in Ireland. One obstacle remained. The early Kentucky distillers would have wanted to select a name that would identify their product as being specifically from their state, and though Elisha Craig lived in Scott County, the name Scott held little appeal. Their whiskey was not Scotch but American, and more specifically it was from Kentucky. So it seems that the title of the neighbouring Bourbon County was chosen, probably because it had no previous connection with whisky, and possibly because there were more distillers operating there than in Scott County.

It is noteworthy that by 1792, Bourbon County had twenty-five flourishing distilleries, and that the per capita whiskey consumption was $2\frac{1}{2}$ gallons per annum, with much of it being partaken before breakfast in the form of juleps, from the Arabic word *julab*, for a drink mixed with rosewater.

TSUGUHARU AND RENÉ GIVE THANKS
Champagne G H Mumm, France

Visitors to the historic city of Reims, home of a considerable proportion of the Grande Marque Champagne houses, flock in their thousands not only to see and taste those famous names, but also to view two ancient and notable churches. Large numbers of tourists are drawn to both the 11th-century Basilique de Saint Remi and the 13th-century cathedral of Notre Dame, to wonder at their magnificent architecture and awe-inspiring stained-glass windows, breathtaking examples of the craftsmanship of their periods. Yet I prefer to spend the occasional half-hour in a lesser-known church in that ancient city, a church which, by contrast, was completed not hundreds of years ago, but as recently as 1966.

La Chapelle de Notre Dame des Vignes is a small, grey, stone building, which stands on a plot of land immediately adjacent to the famous Champagne house of G H Mumm. It is an unique memorial that every visitor to Reims and to G H Mumm should ask to see, for the story of its construction and decoration is a refreshing and remarkable witness in what would appear to be a largely agnostic world. The chapel was the conception of two fine and greatly respected men, who gave bounteously so that it would recall the exciting and memorable conversion to Christianity of one of them.

For many years, Tsuguharu Foujita, a Japanese by birth and a Buddhist by faith, had lived and worked as an artist in Paris. There he had gradually risen in international esteem as he became one of the few fine artists who are widely acknowledged in their own lifetime. Throughout this time, a close personal friendship developed between Foujita and a small but energetic lawyer named René Lalou, a highly regarded individual, who was destined to become the head of G H Mumm for more years than anyone could ever have imagined.

René Lalou's marriage to the grand daughter of Joseph Dubonnet, creator of the quinquina aperitif, was the catalyst that changed this diminutive figure's professional life from law to wine, a choice he apparently never regretted. In 1920 the Dubonnet family invested in a new major company formed to acquire the Champagne house of G H Mumm,

which had been confiscated, as war reparation, from its German ownership. Emile Dubonnet and his brother-in-law, René Lalou, were among the new board of directors appointed, and the former Parisian lawyer was to serve on the company's board until he died in his ninety-sixth year, in 1973. He had served as vice-chairman from 1929 to 1939, and as chairman from 1939 to 1973, with the exception of the wartime years. It was during the latter period that he persuaded Tsuguharu Foujita to paint a rose to decorate Champagne Mumm Cordon Rosé. It was the first of several Foujita works commissioned by René Lalou, yet their friendship had evolved as early as the 1920s.

The double relationship of friend and commissioned artist strengthened the bond between the two men, and there can be little doubt that the Japanese master was influenced by the Christian outlook of the Mumm chairman. It was not, it seems, the only Christian influence that affected Foujita, for it is reported that he had been puzzled for many years by the inspirational work of the great Christian artists, such as Michelangelo and Leonardo da Vinci.

It was on an auspicious day in 1959 that Foujita, with his friend, the writer Georges Prade, visited the Basilique de Saint Remi, and while there lit a candle. At that moment he had some kind of revelation, which prompted him to declare instantly his new-found Christian faith. It was an experience he later related to his wife, and she too acknowledged her conversion. Overwhelmed by the situation, Foujita made all haste to see René Lalou and tell him of the remarkable occurrence.

On 14 October 1959, Tsuguharu and his wife, Kimiyo Foujita, were baptised in the Cathedral of Notre Dame in Reims. Foujita, who took the Christian name of Leonard, was then seventy-five, and his godfather, René Lalou, was eighty-two. The whole experience had such a profound effect upon both men that they made a decision in 1964 to create some permanent memorial of their personal thanks to God. René Lalou provided the money and Leonard Foujita the majority of the skill. Their memorial was La Chapelle de Notre Dame des Vignes.

René Lalou purchased a small plot of land adjacent to the G H Mumm offices in the rue de Champ de Mars, and Foujita instructed an architect regarding the chapel's construction, and then designed the wrought ironwork and stained-glass windows. The stained-glass window designs were put into effect by a gifted Remois craftsman, Charles Marq. By mid-1966 it was time for the decoration to begin, and it is in this area that, for me, the chapel acquired its unique appeal. For three months, working twelve hours a day, Foujita decorated the building with frescoes, an art form he had never previously attempted. The work on the ceiling was particularly exhausting, as it necessitated his lying on his back for long periods at a time. He has been quoted as saying on more than one occasion that only two things enabled him to persevere: his faith, and a daily supply of Champagne from next door.

Among Christ's followers, he painted the face of his great friend and benefactor, and he also left one other personal note. On one hand he painted six fingers. Some say it was the error of an exhausted eighty-year-old man, but when you look closely at it, it seems too deliberate an action. As deliberate perhaps as the action of those two fine elderly Christian men, who, following the chapel's consecration and inauguration in October 1966, handed its keys to the city, and there the chapel stands, awaiting your visit.

WINE AND THE BIBLE
Golan Heights Winery

There is substantial archaeological and historical evidence that the vine had its origins in the Middle East and, further, that wine has been produced within the boundaries of modern Israel for more than 2 000 years. It is not the object of this chapter, however, to examine these topics. Instead the intention is to observe viticulture and winemaking and the general understanding of the subject of wine during biblical days, and also to look briefly at a prime example of wine production in Israel today.

The chapter might make interesting reading for those who try to correlate their religious beliefs with the practice of temperance; they should be

Vines in the foothills of Mount Hermon, Golan Heights

aware that my observations are made as a wine journalist and a Christian, but not by interpreting isolated biblical texts literally.

The Armenian people, who lay claim to Mount Ararat, state that Noah planted the first vineyard at Erivan, and they do at least have the support of the Book of Genesis. After the flood had receded, Genesis 9:20-21 tells us, "Noah, a man of the soil, began the planting of vineyards. He drank some of the wine, became drunk and lay naked in his tent". Whether or not that vindicates any Armenian claims that their country is the true cradle of viticulture must be a matter for conjecture. It is certainly accurate, however, to report that wine, as portrayed in the Bible, did not have too auspicious a start. On the other hand, old Noah did have something to celebrate and had to be fairly patient before he could indulge. Apart from spending just over a year in the ark, he had to wait another three years from the planting of his vines if Armenian practices were observed, or four years if he pursued the rule that rabbinical law was later to teach. So in human terms, his overindulgence is understandable.

From that point the Bible offers 161 references to wine, seventy-two to vineyards, fifty-seven to vines, and many more associated references.

Genesis 49:11 holds the first possible clue to viticultural practices: "to the vine he tethers his ass, and the colt of his ass to the red vine". It is quite feasible that this is an example of vine pruning by donkeys eating the green wood and foliage. This suggestion is not a jest, and reference should be made to the story of St Martin on page 157. In that tale, the incident involving the bishop (later St Martin) and his donkey is apocryphal, but the evidence which Howard Carter found in Egypt is incontrovertible, and is referred to in the chapter on St Martin.

To be frank, wine in the Bible does at times receive a mixed press, but the balance is redressed by the benefits claimed. A straightforward example is given in 2 Samuel 16:2, when one of wine's most popular qualities is recognised, that of its use for recuperation. When Ziba, the servant of Mephibosheth, was asked what he was doing with a vast quantity of food and wine, he replied that the wine was for "anyone who becomes exhausted in the wilderness", while in Psalm 104:15, the psalmist writes of "wine to gladden men's hearts". In Deuteronomy 7:13, the Israelites are promised that if they observe their commandments and laws, then God will bless them with "the fruit of the land", which included new wine. It is evident that God would not involve wine in such a blessing if he did not approve of its nature. Proverbs 3:10 follows a similar vein. The author begins the chapter reminding the reader, or listener, not to forget his teaching, and to "guard the commands in your heart". He continues by stating in verses 9 and 10 that if men will honour the Lord with their wealth, "as the first charge on all your earnings, then your granaries will be filled with corn and your vats bursting with new wine". Similar positive references are made in Hosea 2:8 and Joel 2:24. Yet in Deuteronomy 28:30, in the midst of dire warning to the children of Israel of the punishments that await them if they do not obey God's commandments and statutes, Moses states that one of the penalties will be vineyards that do not produce any grapes. There are also similar supporting Old Testament references indicating God's positive consideration of wine.

The Bible also cautions against the abuse of alcohol. Proverbs 23:31 is a pointed example, "Wine is an insolent fellow and strong drink makes an uproar", and two chapters later, the Book of Proverbs is critical of "those who linger late over their wine". Isaiah 5:11 seems to add fuel to the fire with: "Shame on you! You who rise early in the morning to go in pursuit of liquor and draw out the evening inflamed with wine." But in my opinion, Isaiah's comments appear slightly contradictory. After all, those who overindulge at night seldom rise early in the morning. Sufferers from morning hangovers are reluctant to partake of another glassful when they rise. Perhaps the verse would make more sense if the two sentences were viewed as referring to quite separate practices, the first to the habit still seen in the rural areas of many winegrowing countries, where agricultural labourers start the day with a glass of robust young wine consumed in great haste.

Of most interest to serious wine enthusiasts is the viticultural and oenological detail the Bible gives us, presenting us with a historical record of vineyard cultivation, winemaking methods and the understanding of the subject in those times.

To some degree one can follow the whole cycle of wine from passages scattered throughout the Bible. The Song of Solomon 7:12 is written of June or thereabouts, with the suggestion to go early to the vineyards and see if the vine has budded or the blossom appeared. The writer must have been experienced with vines, because few unversed people can easily identify the moment when the vine blossom opens, the flowers being so slight and without a corolla.

There are also accounts such as the one found in Isaiah 5, which has given us a picture of the time around 700 years before Christ. It begins: "My beloved had a vineyard high up on a fertile hillside." This shows that the inhabitants were planting on elevated sites rather than in the valley bottom or on flatter ground. "He trenched it and cleared it of stones and planted it with red vines" – the trench would have been dug to divert heavy rainfall and prevent mud slides. At the time, and until around two centuries ago, it had been the practice in many countries for growers to separate red vines from white, but often they did not identify individual varieties, a task that, if organised, would have enabled them to concentrate on those which gave the best results in local microclimates. The specific reference to red vines indicates that the vineyardists of that era were aware of different varieties, for otherwise "My beloved" would have mixed white grapes with red.

The mention of the watchtower in Isaiah 5 appears to refer to a local practice where growers were prepared for any attack by enemies and it made sense that the press should be built into the tower so that the grower and his men were in the most secure position in the vineyard whenever possible. The watchtower was placed in the middle of the vineyard for the greatest security, and this also suited the practical need to carry or cart the grapes to the press as quickly as possible after they had been picked.

As the passage continues, Isaiah complains that the vineyard keeper "looked for it to yield grapes but it yielded wild grapes". Israel had wild native vines growing in abundance in certain areas, but it was generally known that to produce drinkable wine, cultivated vines were necessary. A few lines later there are references to pruning and hoeing, which speak for themselves.

Irrigation of the vineyards was quite common, as testified by Isaiah 27:2-3: "moment by moment I water it for fear its green leaves fail".

Some wine professionals will be enlightened by 1 Chronicles 27:27, which states that during the reign of King David, around 1000 BC, he employed the ancient equivalent of both a head viticulturist and a winemaker: "Shimei of Ramah was in charge of the vinedressers, while Zabdi of Shephem had charge of the produce of the vineyards for the wine-cellars".

As to the actual pressing of the grapes, this appears in general to have been carried out by treading, and while it would have been possible to construct large wooden-framed presses operated by levers, there is no obvious evidence that these existed. Job 24:11, "they tread the winepress", is supported by Isaiah 5:2, "and then hewed out a wine press", and there are a number of similar remarks elsewhere. There is also some non-biblical evidence of lever presses being used in the Middle East at the time, but none that appears to refer to Israel.

Nehemiah complained how he saw "men in Judah treading winepresses on the sabbath", and Isaiah 63:2 asks, "who treads grapes in the vat?" This is a rhetorical question which draws attention to the clearly defined stages of wine production that existed even then. Most presses were either made of wood, from which the juice would run off into casks and pots, or possibly vats formed from hard-packed baked soil. Nearly 800 years later, when St John had his revelation on the island of Patmos, he tells us that "the wine press was trodden". The wine press was additionally used as a suitable place for threshing wheat or similar crops. Judges 6:11 writes of "Gideon threshing wheat in the winepress".

Around six centuries before Christ it is evident that the Israelites understood the concept of a wine from a particular area having a reputation – a sort of precursor of the named appellation. They clearly recognised that some regions were superior to others. Ezekiel 27:18-19 identifies "the wines of Helbon and Izalla", and Hosea 14:7 confirms the popularity of the wine of an ancient neighbouring land with "famous as the wine of Lebanon".

Continuing the quality theme, Isaiah 25:6 confirms that as long ago as 700 BC the better wines at least were subject to some kind of filtration or fining process. There were three possibilities: straining through some kind of woven cloth, fining with egg whites or fining with clay. The writer cannot be more definitive than that. The same verse also makes it abundantly clear, by repeating the term twice in successive lines, that the best wines were understood to be those which were "well-matured".

The cellaring of wine was a regular practice. In Jeremiah 40:12 the Judeans are reported to have "gathered in a considerable store of food and wine". Additionally, the use of wine vats is mentioned, although these were probably just large barrels and earthenware vessels. Jeremiah 48:33 speaks of stopping the "flow from the vats".

Often wine was made in much smaller volumes than today, and small quantities would be poured into leather wineskins straight after the fermentation was believed to have been completed – a sort of Beaujolais Nouveau of biblical days. Joshua 9:4 indicates that these skins were repaired and reused, while many will recall Jesus asking who would put new wine in old wineskins. The very question implied that everyone would know that there was a risk of disaster involved. In past times, in many countries, grapes would be pressed, and the must would begin to ferment naturally and continue to do so until the first cold weather of the season arrived, which would usually bring the activity to an end. When spring brought a rise in temperature, many wines would resume fermentation. Hence anyone who had wine in an old wineskin risked calamity, as the reviving fermentation emitted carbon dioxide and the volume expanded. Burst wineskins meant loss both of wine and containers.

One of the most enlightening quotes regarding the condition of a wine comes from Proverbs 23:31: "Do not gulp down the wine, the strong red wine when the droplets form on the side of the cup". The author of the book had sufficient knowledge to recognise the glycerine in a full-bodied wine that has some years of life ahead of it. These droplets, often called "legs" or "tears", are acknowledged as a sign of some promise in a wine, and also as an indication that it has not yet reached its peak. His sensible advice was to take care of such a wine, as he obviously was aware that it still needed time.

On the other hand, the winemakers of the day knew what to do with wine of a lesser quality. Both Psalms 75:8 and Proverbs 9:2 refer to spiced wine. The addition of herbs and spices had two distinct aims: either to improve inferior wine, or to help make the consumption of various herbal medicines more palatable. Indeed, what Dubonnet and St Raphael introduced in fortified form in the middle of the 19th century had existed more than 2 000 years earlier, though without the addition of any alcoholic spirit. In fact it is known to historians that, at the time of Christ, there was a group of charitable women at work in Jerusalem who administered a form of drugged wine, believed to have been flavoured with herbs and spices, to relieve pain and suffering. It is not unreasonable to surmise that this provides an explanation of the sour wine, or "vinegar", which St Matthew's Gospel refers to as "wine mixed with gall", that was offered to Our Lord on the Cross of Calvary. St Mark 15:23 tells us that before Christ's crucifixion he was offered "wine mixed with myrhh".

The social attitude to wine was generally a responsible one in biblical days, and it is interesting to note that while in the current generation there are many Jewish people involved both in wine production and the wine trade, they generally have a reputation for sobriety. Ecclesiastes 10:19 advises that "the table has its pleasure and wine makes for a cheerful life", but adds the philosophical comment, "and money is behind it all", a sentiment with which many readers will readily agree.

On the other hand, Proverbs 31, when it relates the sayings of Lemuel, King of Massa, gives some fairly uncompromising recommendations:

> Not for kings to drink wine, nor for princes to crave strong drink. Give strong drink to the desperate and wine to the embittered; such men will drink and forget their poverty and remember their trouble no longer.

This is definitely not an attitude many would wish to take more than 2 500 years later.

The Old Testament also provides us with an illuminating example of wine consumption from outside the Holy Land. Esther, who was selected, during the Babylonian Exile in the 6th century BC, to be the queen of the Persian King Ahasuerus, described the lavish splendour of his court and enlightened us with two specific comments. She wrote that "wine was served in golden cups of various patterns", and also noted a responsible attitude to alcohol by recording that "the King's wine flowed freely as befitted a King and the law of drinking was there should be no compulsion".

Throughout the Bible the vine plays a pivotal role. Isaiah explains that "the vineyard is the House of Israel", and six different prophets make use of the vine as a symbol of Israel as a healthy nation. In the New Testament, Our Lord, indicating the New Covenant, identifies himself as "the true vine", and finally permits wine to take its most sacred position in the Last Supper. Many theologians have commented on the relationship between the choice of bread and wine and the act of the Resurrection of Christ. Both bread and wine, when activated by an agent, yeast, rise from something which is lifeless into food and drink that nourishes, actions which are reflected in the rising of Jesus from the tomb.

Subsequently wine has a most privileged position in the Bible and in Christianity. Its role is of such influence that it surely indicates that fermented wine should always be used in the Eucharist, an argument that appears reasonable in the light of Our Lord's association with wine and the knowledge available to us of Israel's history and tradition as a winemaking country. Perhaps the consumption of wine in the communion feast should be re-examined carefully by all those who partake. Sadly the understandable evolution of the temperance movement, which began in the second half of the last century, has led some away from the essential living character of real wine. Some years ago, I remember being confronted by a teenage girl in a restaurant in Cleveland, Ohio. She insisted that her pastor had told his flock that at the Last Supper Jesus had used only unfermented wine. In response, I tried to explain that, as far as I was aware, there was not a shred of biblical or historical evidence for that claim, and that Our Lord's generation was unable to make anything resembling a low alcohol or de-alcoholised wine. They simply did not know how to prevent wild yeasts from causing the fermentation of fresh grape juice. She replied that she would take the matter up with her pastor, for he had been most emphatic about the subject, and I wished, for a brief moment, that I could be a fly on the wall at that meeting. The clergyman's statement was, to be polite, somewhat inaccurate and apparently without any justification.

In Old Testament times there were three different words for wine. ‏יין‎" was generally used to identify all types of wine. ‏תירו‎‏‎ referred both to fresh grape juice and new wine. Indeed, Hosea 4:11 warns us that ‏תירו‎‏‎ "takes away the understanding", making it quite clear that the prophet was referring to alcohol. ‏עסיס‎ was the third word, and was derived from a verb meaning "to foam or ferment", and it indicated intoxicating juice.

Those who continue to use non-alcoholic wines for sacramental purposes should remember that the churches became involved with the temperance movement because of its merit-worthy social responsibility during an era of great alcohol abuse, but not for theological reasons, although of course there have always been those who have selected limited biblical quotations to support their negative arguments, while ignoring the involvement of Our Saviour with wine in the most sacred way. Also it should be noted that in St Luke's Gospel 22:18, Our Lord, at the time of taking the cup during the Last Supper, said: "From now on, I tell you, I shall not drink wine until the kingdom of God comes." This verifies that Jesus did drink wine until that moment.

In the early 1970s, I was privileged to undertake a somewhat hair-raising journey into the Kyrenia Mountains in Cyprus, to visit the tiny chapel of the prophet Elias. The occasion was the saint's-day celebration of the birthday saint of the Greek Orthodox village *papas* (or priest) in the village of Karmi, where I was working at the time. Large numbers of villagers and friends tumbled into far too few vehicles and headed for Lapithos Spring. At the end of the metalled road, we drove for another hour, gradually ascending amid the most majestic scenery, and on through a military range, before reaching a lonely summit, where a great

feast was enjoyed by all present, but which was preceded by a thank-offering. Worshippers filed quietly into the simple white chapel to give thanks for the service of their priest, which they did by donating fresh food that could be eaten straightaway, preserved foods that could be kept, and numerous bottles of good-quality local wine, which would be retained for its eucharistic purpose during the following year. I well remember that there were quite a number of bottles of Saint Pantaleimon, a popular medium-sweet white Cyprus wine. It was the normal habit to use the staple needs of everyday life, the very bread and wine that the local people ate and drank each day, and that surely must have been what happened at the Last Supper and is the theme we should have continued.

Apart from the Last Supper, the first miracle performed by Jesus, at Cana in Galilee, relates his other important involvement with wine, and the story paints a vivid picture. St John's Gospel records how at a wedding feast, Mary, the mother of Jesus, told him the wine supply had been exhausted, and the Gospel explains his action:

> There were six stone water-jars standing near, of the kind used for Jewish rites of purification; each held from twenty to thirty gallons. Jesus said to the servants, "Fill the jars with water", and they filled them to the brim. "Now draw some off", he ordered, "and take it to the steward of the feast"; and they did so. The steward tasted the water which had by then turned into wine, not knowing its source; though the servants who had drawn the water knew. He hailed the bridegroom and said, "Everyone serves the best wines first, and waits until the guests have drunk freely before serving the poorer sort; but you have kept the best wine till now."

In the same manner as restaurant diners publicly nose and taste their wines today, so the steward had

*V*ines in winter at the Golan Heights Winery, near the Sea of Galilee

to evaluate the new supply. He immediately appreciated that the sample given to him was superior to the wine already consumed, and his comment reflects on what was the normal trend on such occasions; that is, to enjoy the finest wine first. In current times, this pattern is less frequently observed, though a contemporary comparison might be made with weddings, where the expense of providing good French Champagne for everyone is outside most budgets. Some couples, wishing to partake of the finest of all sparkling wines at their wedding celebration, order it exclusively for the top table and provide a less expensive alternative for their guests.

The New Testament, in Matthew 21:33-43, also has the famous parable of the landowner whose son is murdered by the tenants of his vineyard. In the account, the owner built a wall around the land, suggesting a relatively small estate, similar to a French *clos*, or enclosed vineyard. The participation of tenants indicates that during New Testament times the leasing of vineyards was a normal business transaction, and verse 42 refers to the method of payment being by a "share of the crop".

Finally on the subject of wine in the Bible, St Paul must be permitted his say, as wine professionals should be indebted to him for his sensible support. In 1 Timothy 5:23, he sends the unhealthy Timothy a message of good sense: "Stop drinking nothing but water; take a little wine for the sake of your digestion, for your frequent ailments." The apostle was aware of the health benefits of the moderate consumption of wine and told his assistant in straightforward terms. St Paul also wrote of those to be selected as leaders or bishops in the early church, that "he must be sober, temperate", and

"not be given to drink". That did not imply a total abstainer but a man of restraint who only consumed in moderation.

So how does wine in modern Israel compare with its ancient and historical tradition? Late in the 20th century, Israel has around 5 000 acres of vineyards in five main regions: the Golan Heights, Shomrom, Samson, the Judean Hills, and Negev. The best-known winery in modern Israel, in international terms (at least in the eyes of the gentiles), is the Golan Heights Winery, responsible for the Yarden, Gamla and Golan labels. Since its 1982 foundation, this state-of-the-art winery has won a virtual torrent of medals in major worldwide competitions. Its 675-acre vineyards rise from near the northern shoreline of the Sea of Galilee to an altitude of some 4 000 feet at the very foot of Mount Hermon, not far from its popular ski resort, making it one of the highest elevations for cultivated vines to be planted anywhere on earth.

Owned by a company controlled by four kibbutzim and four moshavim, it is responsible for about 30 per cent of all wine exported from Israel, and ships its wine to many major international markets including the United Kingdom, the United States, Australia and Japan. In contrast with biblical days, when little was known about grape varieties, today every Golan variety is clearly identified, and much of the viticulture and oenology is practised as in the New World, with similar varietal labelling being used. The vines flourish in a climate that varies from snow in winter to baking heat in summer. To counter extreme temperatures during the seven or eight-week picking season, floodlit night harvesting has been adopted, using both manual and mechanical means.

The winery's premium label is Yarden, which is the Hebrew name of the River Jordan. Gamla is the name of an ancient Hebrew city on the Golan Heights, which heroically withstood the Roman onslaught for a number of years, and Golan simply refers to that famous locality. All three are kosher wines, which basically means they have been produced under strict Jewish hygiene regulations. The most important of these are that only kosher items may be used in the winemaking process, and only religiously observant Jews may touch the product or equipment at the winery concerned. There are also some lesser regulations of a traditional nature.

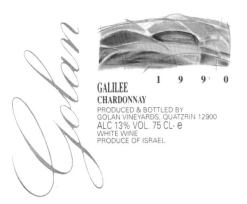

GALILEE
CHARDONNAY
PRODUCED & BOTTLED BY
GOLAN VINEYARDS, QUATZRIN 12900
ALC 13% VOL. 75 CL- ℮
WHITE WINE
PRODUCE OF ISRAEL

1 9 9 0

11.   WHAT'S IN A NAME?

BOUTARI
Greece

The leading Greek wine producer, Boutari, is a family-controlled business with an extensive array of vineyard properties. In the north, at Naoussa, their modern estate is situated on the very slopes of Mount Vermion, home of the mythical Greek god of wine, Dionysus. In the south of mainland Greece, in the Peloponnese, their full-bodied red, Nemea, comes from what were once called the pastures of Nemea, where, so it is claimed, Hercules slew a lion with his bare hands. Several other holdings are scattered across the Aegean islands, producing wines which include Kretikos, a dry white wine hailing from Crete, and Paros, a light red from the island bearing that name. The most attractive of their dry white wines comes from the

Santorini, volcanic island home of Boutari's best white wine

volcanic island of Santorini, which has no water supply other than that which descends daily from the clouds which shroud its pinnacle.

The Boutari family began producing wine in Naoussa more than a century ago, and yet the family name suggests a much longer wine tradition, for they originate from the Vlachs tribe in the mountains to the north-west of Greece, where the word *boutari* meant "I have barrels".

RAIMAT
Spain

In the Lérida region of Catalonia lies the Raimat estate, owned by the Raventos family, famed elsewhere in the Penedes region for their Codorniu Cava, which is believed to be the largest-selling of all bottle-fermented sparkling wines.

When earlier this century the family decided to search for potential vineyard sites in Lérida, they stumbled across a lone ruined castle in the midst of what was virtually a desert wilderness. While surveying the land, they unearthed the ancient keystone from the castle gateway. The stone, carved in 1627, displayed a bunch of grapes and a hand. In the Catalan language, *raim* means "grapes" and *mat* means "hand". The message was that God provides man with the gift of grapes, but it takes man to cultivate them. This discovery, along with

Marques de Monistrol, with its ancient monastery church in the background

RAIMAT

Abadia

COSTERS DEL SEGRE
Denominación de Origen

75 cl

CRIADO Y EMBOTELLADO
EN LA PROPIEDAD

Alc. 12,5% vol.

the sheer desolation of the surrounding land, inspired the Raventos family to dream of transforming the wilderness into the magnificent 3 000-acre vineyard that it is today.

In the Raimat Estate, they have planted the finest both of Spanish and French grape varieties to blend them together in delicious wines such as the full-bodied Abadia, which uses Cabernet Sauvignon and Tempranillo.

MARQUES DE MONISTROL
Spain

This highly rated Spanish Cava, from the largest such single estate in the Penedes region, is known to some for its charming little 8th-century monastery church, a surviving vestige from the era when the entire area came under monastic control. To others it is known for its mature non-vintage sparkling wine. The name of the wine has, in essence, two origins: first from the original monastery or *monasteriolo* of San Sadurni d'Anoia, and

second from the 19th-century *marqués* whose full name was Don José Maria Escriva de Romani Y Dusay, Marqués de Monistrol Y de Aguillar, who introduced the production of sparkling wine on the estate in 1882. He came to the conclusion that his name was just a little too complicated to put on the labels of his bottles, and so he simply abbreviated it to Marques de Monistrol.

NOILLY PRAT
France

The name Noilly Prat has attracted much debate and has become the subject of some ridiculous attempts at French pronunciation by many individuals keen to demonstrate their prowess as linguists. Few of these have ever been eager to emphasise the "t" in Prat, which is indeed the correct pronunciation. English Francophiles, in particular, often seem to delight in saying "Praah!"

The winery, situated in the diminutive port of Marseillan, near Montpellier, on the south coast of France, was founded in 1800 by a local winegrower called Joseph Noilly, who eleven years later ceded his small business to his son Louis. The younger man soon increased the production and sales of their white-wine aperitif which was then sold simply as "Noilly". In time he was prospering but also working increasingly hard.

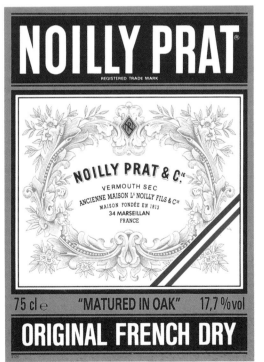

Louis had an eligible and beautiful young daughter whose name (somewhat unjustly) has been lost. She was the centre of attraction for many of the young beaux of Marseillan, but her father was wary that their intentions were directed not just at his daughter but at gaining an easy share of the family's

newly acquired wealth. To allay these fears he let it be known that if any man wished to court her he must work for the Noilly family business for several years to prove his industry and honourable intent. Apparently the young men of Marseillan preferred a more sedate lifestyle and opted out of such a trial. But just when Louis was wondering if he had pursued the right course, an eccentric young English traveller, Claudius Prat, arrived and fell in love with his daughter. Claudius accepted the terms, and in time became such an indispensable asset to the thriving winery that Louis Noilly made him a partner in the business, which was renamed Noilly Prat.

DUBONNET
France

In the 1840s, as the French armies of occupation colonised North Africa, malaria became the chief cause of fatalities, rather than any military action. Of those who recovered from the disease many were prey to recurring bouts throughout the remainder of their lives.

It was known that quinine, or *quinquina* as the French called it, was a preventative, but its taste was so bitter and unpalatable that the majority of the forces declined to consume it. In an effort to overcome the dilemma, the French government

To crown his success, Monsieur Dubonnet collected a handsome sum from the French government, who were well pleased with the results of his research and with the drink he created.

Today, Dubonnet produced at Thuir according to the classic recipe and blend, is owned by the Pernod-Ricard company, while in the USA a slightly different version is produced by another ownership which some years ago obtained the American rights.

OMAR KHAYYAM
India

The 11th-century Persian poet and mathematician, Omar Khayyám, in his beautiful *Rubáiyát*, left us some vivid illustrations of the enjoyment of wine that all wine lovers can appreciate. Three specific quatrains, translated by Edward Fitzgerald, speak volumes to the initiated:

Here with a loaf of bread beneath the bough,
A flask of wine, a book of verse – and thou
Beside me singing in the wilderness
And wilderness is Paradise enow.

And lately, by the tavern door agape,
Came stealing through the dusk and angel shape
Bearing a vessel on his shoulder; and
He bid me taste of it; and 'twas – the grape!

While the rose blows along the river brink,
With old Khayyam and ruby vintage drink:
And when the angel with his darker draught
Draws up to thee – take that, and do not shrink.

Little could Omar Khayyám have imagined that some 900 years later his inspiration would lead to a devoted wine enthusiast in another country, somewhat further south than Persia, selecting his name to honour a unique *méthode champenoise* wine.

Today, Omar Khayyam is an attractive and extremely well-made sparkling wine from the Sahyadri Mountains, near Bombay in India, some 200 miles south of the Equator. The result of a

offered a bursary to anyone who could find an acceptable way for the substance to be ingested.

One of a number of applicants for the bursary was a Parisian chemist and merchant, Joseph Dubonnet, who spent most of 1846 working in his laboratory upon his theory that *quinquina* could probably be disguised in a fortified-wine aperitif, where the bitter taste could be masked by the flavour of added herbs, spices and wood barks. In his search to perfect his theory, he scoured the famous Les Halles, the historic wholesale market in Paris where most of the world's exotic herbs and spices could be found. He also travelled the length and breadth of France, seeking the fruity red wine he needed to balance the compounded recipe he was attempting to formulate.

Eventually, in the foothills of the Pyrenees, in the Roussillon region, he found the wine which answered his requirements and, to his surprise, discovered that he could also obtain the requisite herbs and spices in the same area. A man of commerce as well as a man of science, Joseph decided it would be wise to move to the small town of Thuir to pursue his venture, and so forsook the bustling capital which had been his home for most of his life.

To the peaceful Pyrenean farming town, Joseph Dubonnet brought a touch of flair and imagination, and he soon decided to publicise his new wine aperitif by ordering the construction of what was then believed to be the largest barrel in the world, for the ageing of the drink. This aroused much publicity, which in turn led to Joseph starting what were probably some of the first visitor tours in the history of wine and drink.

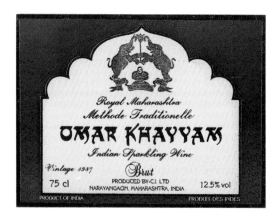

project founded by a prominent Bombay business-man, Sam Chougule, in 1981, it now sees its bottles being imported into several countries, including Great Britain, where it ranks alongside *méthode champenoise* wines from France, Spain, Australia and California.

Much of the oenological and viticultural input has come from Champagne Technologie, a sub-sidiary of Champagne Piper Heidsieck, and the head winemaker was previously employed by Moët et Chandon. The grapes are mainly Chardon-nay, but some Pinot Blanc and Ugni Blanc have also been planted. The soil is chalky limestone, and the winery manager, Praihad Parvatikar, reports that they use 100 litres of irrigation water per day for every litre of wine they produce, the water being supplied from a nearby dam.

How the Persian Omar Khayyám became Indian is still a mystery, but one can be sure that the great poet-philosopher, with his love of wine, would have approved.

KNOCKANDO
Scotland

In November 1991, together with my wife, Branwen, and our son Huw, I travelled to Scotland, where I was due to record a radio item for a syndicated American NPR show called "Living Well". As we approached the scenic Speyside region, I rechecked the road atlas to ensure that we were actually heading in the direction of the distillery.

"There it is," I advised with confidence, suggest-ing that the map was using the Old Gaelic language in its spelling of Knockandhu.

Some forty-five minutes later, having traversed a rather steep and narrow road and obeyed the map's instructions to take the first road to the left at the foot of the hill, we approached what appeared to be the village of that name. It was really nothing more than a hamlet with a small scattering of homes, and I had noticed, or not noticed, something odd. I could not find any signposts to identify it. Driving on until we were again passing through the countryside I decided that the village must have been Knockandhu, and somehow or other I must have missed the sign to the distillery. One three-point turn later and we were retracing our steps. Again there was not a sign to be seen. Then I noticed a small shop operating from a house and decided to enquire.

"Not another one!" came the surly reply. "We're fed up with people asking; that's why we had the signs taken down. You're miles away. It'll take you another forty minutes to get there. You don't want Knockandhu you want Knockando!"

Her pronouncement poured at me like a Highland torrent in full flood on a stormy day.

"And what's more" – she had not finished yet – "there's no distillery here!"

In due course, we found the small side-road that leads from the banks of the Spey to the Knockando distillery, but it soon brought us another rude shock. Directly across the road in front of us was a wooden barrier with a "Road Closed" sign painted on it. At this stage, I made the second of what was to be an embarrassing string of phone calls to Innes Shaw, who by then was a rather puzzled distillery manager, wondering if we were ever going to arrive.

"Well you see, Andrew, you'll have to head back up the main road, then take the next left until you come to a T-junction. Left goes to Lower Knock-ando and right to Upper Knockando. Don't you go right now; you turn left for Lower Knockando, but when you get near there you don't want to go there." I had to think about that statement for some while.

"Well, you turn left there," Innes continued, "and carry straight on until the end of the road and you will have arrived!"

Fortunately Innes Shaw is a soft-spoken man and, as is often the case in the Highlands, his Scottish accent was not too strong. So surely we would arrive within the ten minutes he had esti-mated. We had not foreseen one more handicap to overcome. We were in the north of Scotland, it was the middle of a November afternoon, and it was already turning to dusk at 3 p.m. How quickly would darkness fall, and would I be able to read the road signs? The first two instructions were relatively straightforward, but we did manage to miss the crucial final turning and arrived in the tiny community of Lower Knockando. By a stroke of good fortune its occupants were much friendlier and soon set us on the right path.

Darkness was beginning to descend as I knocked on the old wooden door of the distillery. It opened and a smiling face announced: "Hello Andrew, my name's Innes Shaw. I'm the distillery manager. You know, some people have quite a problem finding us, but you haven't done too badly!"

Innes Shaw, Master Distiller at the Knockando distillery

The recording proceeded and Innes showed me how the distillery was unique in its style of ageing its single-malt whisky as it endeavoured to produce the palest in colour and most elegant in flavour of the Speyside malts. A complete tour was organised for my wife and son, and we all met later in the tasting room, where not a single drop was sipped but every glass was nosed.

Soon it was time to leave for the delightful Craigellechie Hotel, but I had one last question: "What was the English for Knockando?"

"Oh, it means 'little black hills', and there are hundreds of them around here. You'll always be far better off asking your way to Knockando."

CHATEAU SAINTE MICHELLE
USA

Whenever I arrive at a previously unexplored winery, I am eager to learn the origin of its name,

Chateau Sainte Michelle

and often there is a quaint tale or a curious piece of history to explain it. A 1988 visit to the Woodinville headquarters of Chateau Sainte Michelle brought an explanation the merit of which the reader is invited to assess. When Victor Allison, the founder of the largest winery in Washington State on America's west coast, decided to proceed with its development, he is reported to have asked his daughter, Michelle, to select a name. Her reply was that one of the favourite places she had visited was the French abbey of Mont Saint-Michel. In recognition of his daughter's preference, Victor Allison altered the Saint-Michel to the feminine Michelle, and named the new winery accordingly.

FIRESTONE VINEYARD
USA

This popular Californian producer of agreeable mid-priced Cabernet and Merlot wines is headed by Brooks Firestone, a direct descendant of the Firestone tyre family and, while their sales motor along smoothly, they still maintain their interest in the metalled road. As late as 1990, Firestone Vineyards was sponsoring the early career of Nicholas Firestone in his quest for motor-racing success on the European junior circuits. As for his choice of tyres, who knows?

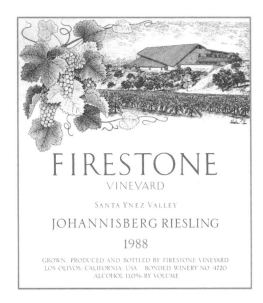

BLACK OPAL
Australia

Certain persons develop into talented winemakers, others prove themselves gifted as marketeers. Some, by force of circumstance, have to undertake both roles, while a minority become so absorbed in the world of winemaking that they need to control all aspects of the business. Most noteworthy, perhaps,

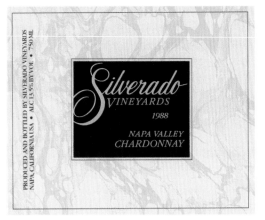

among the most skilful winemakers are those well-balanced individuals who can recognise where their dominant talent lies and concentrate on making that their specialist area, while allowing better-qualified experts to deal with other issues.

Such a man is the New South Wales wine producer Mark Rushmore, who has earned himself a deserved reputation as an outstanding winemaker and blender. He believes that he can achieve the best results year after year only by blending a variety of wines from a careful selection of the finest vineyard sites spread across several states of south-east Australia. When in the 1980s he developed an outstanding new Chardonnay, which he regarded as a jewel of a wine, he hit on the idea of calling it after Australia's most valuable gem, the black opal, a particularly apt title, as the first black opals were discovered in New South Wales, at White Cliffs, in 1875.

Having produced the wine and chosen the name, Mark asked the powerful Mildara Wine Company, now Mildara Blass Pty Ltd, to market it internationally, which they have done with notable success. In the Washington, DC, competition in November 1990, the Black Opal Chardonnay 1989 proved its right to its name when it won the gold medal and was voted top Australian Chardonnay.

SILVERADO VINEYARDS
USA

The name Silverado, which refers to the legendary Napa Valley trail that silver miners took in the mid-

19th century, is also known for the top-quality wines of Silverado Vineyards, founded in 1981 by Diane and Ron Miller. It extends from the Silverado Trail in the east of the valley, for some 110 acres towards Yountville in the west. Bearing in mind some of the crazier labels that one sometimes finds in California, Diane Miller has been restrained in avoiding the influence that her late father might have had on the design of their labels, or they might have been a real "Mickey Mouse job". Her father was, of course, Walt Disney.

FIRELANDS
USA

The name of this Lake Erie, Ohio, winery recalls the cruelty of the British redcoats towards the colonists of New England during the Revolutionary War. The Firelands was the name given to the land granted in north central Ohio to resettle those from Connecticut whose homes had been burned to the ground by British soldiers.

The actual Firelands Winery, at Sandusky, was founded a few generations later, in 1880, by Edward Mantey, when the name Firelands was still being employed with some bitterness. Even today, Firelands is retained as a local geographical title.

Firelands Winery provides wines both from *vinifera* and *labrusca* varieties, as well as some hybrids. It has a creditable Gewürztraminer, which is made along the lines of the classic dry Alsace style. The winery also has a growing reputation for its Chardonnay, Johannisberg Riesling and Cabernet Sauvignon. Among its most popular *labrusca* favourites are Concord and Catawba.

LONZ PINK CATAWBA
USA

History books relate that the late Harry S. Truman was a fairly ordinary middle-class citizen from Independence, Missouri, a very close neighbour of Kansas City. To many in his home town he appeared to be a quiet, unpretentious fellow and the last person likely to rise to great heights of power. Yet he was the man who took the ultimate decision to use the atomic bomb in the war against the Japanese, and the man who gave us two unique and memorable aphorisms: "If you can't stand the heat keep out of the kitchen", and "The buck stops here!"

Such utterances suggested hidden personality traits many had overlooked, but there was one person who could detect the underlying characteristics of Harry S. Truman, and he was Ohio vintner George Lonz, owner of the Lonz Winery on Middle Bass Island in Lake Erie.

Lonz would invite the president to visit the winery on weekends, close down the entire operation and send all the staff home. Then he and Mr Truman would sit down in a tasting room, consume generous quantities of Pink Catawba, and while away the time watching Lonz's collection of blue movies.

The Lonz Pink Catawba label of that favoured wine has its own story to tell. Depicted on it is a Lake Erie steamboat called the *Put-in-Bay*, which traversed the lake between 1911 and 1948. It carried as many as 3 500 passengers to and from Detroit, the Bass Islands and Sandusky. Somehow the enterprising Mr Lonz persuaded the boat's owners to stock a wide selection of his wines on board, and through this outlet they became familiar to a multitude of Canadians and Americans.

The *Put-in-Bay* was named after the last naval battle on Lake Erie, when an American naval officer named Oliver Hazard Perry led an unexpected attack that routed the British Navy and placed the most eastern of the Great Lakes under American control for the first time. Perry then issued the famous dispatch: "We have met the enemy and they are ours!"

STONELEIGH
New Zealand

This winery is much acclaimed for its Sauvignon Blanc, which has won accolades in a number of international markets. It is a mere infant winery in terms of age, having been established in the 1980s, but it is also the result of intelligent planning. Its founders had the foresight to search far and wide for the New Zealand location most favourable for this particular grape variety.

The stony vineyard at Stoneleigh

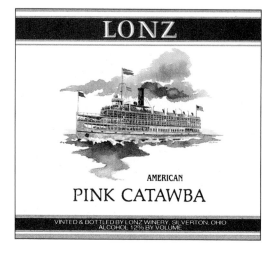

It was only when they inspected the Marlborough region of the South Island that they found a "stoneleigh", or dried-up river bed. They realised that, as in the well-known case of Chateauneuf-du-Pape, it would be advantageous to plant their vines among the stones. When the sun warms the pebbles they retain the heat and give it out again at night when the temperature falls.

ALEXANDERS
Australia

In the 1950s, Ron Haselgrove, managing director of Mildara Wines, turned his attentions to the Coonawarra region of South Australia, and there he met his most formidable foes, two spinster sisters by the name of Alexander.

Long-time local residents recall that the sisters' father had a habit of regular overindulgence, conduct which influenced his two daughters to reject the demon drink and vow it would never enter their portals again. When Mr Alexander died, the ladies inherited the vineyard, which an ancestor had settled in the 1880s. The two women, embittered by their memories, took drastic action, demolishing the winery and removing all trace of it. They also had the entire vineyard ripped out and the land put to other use.

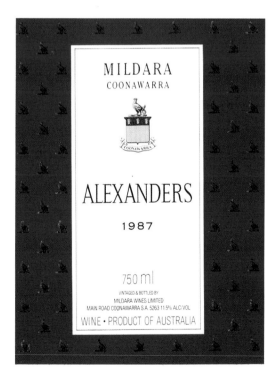

In 1955, Ron Haselgrove called upon the now elderly spinsters and asked if they would consider selling the site. But when they learned that he was the head of a wine company, they promptly ordered him to leave their land, and subsequently

ignored all his efforts to negotiate the matter by correspondence. It was not until both ladies had died that he was able to approach their beneficiaries and purchase the old vineyard block. Mildara Wines planted Cabernet Sauvignon, Cabernet Franc, Merlot and Malbec vines there to produce a Bordeaux-style blend, which has won a string of gold medals, and which has been described by an English wine publication, in terms which would have further shaken the Alexander sisters, as "positively orgasmic".

JAMIESONS RUN
Australia

The picture on the label of Jamiesons Run indicates the origin of the name. The *terra rossa* vineyard, which was the founding home of Mildara Wines in 1888, is situated on land which previously was quite simply a sheep run, the property of a settler called Jamieson. I will always recall Jamiesons Run as the red wine that I drank with my first kangaroo dish at the Chardonnay Lodge, which stands almost opposite the vineyard in Coonawarra.

CALITERRA
Chile

The country with the longest viticultural history in the Southern Hemisphere is Chile, where the first vineyards were planted in the middle of the 16th century. Three hundred years later, Chile gained much praise for the development of its red wines using Bordeaux grape varieties. However, it has only been in the final quarter of the 20th century that the South American country has achieved widespread international success with red and white wines.

In Great Britain, sales of the Caliterra label have proven something of a phenomenon, with the

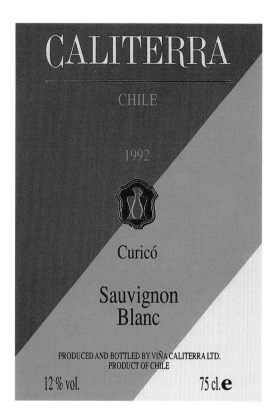

winery, only four years after its inception in 1989, becoming the top-selling Chilean wine in the market. This exciting success, according to its UK importers, B.R.L. Hardy, is linked to the name of the wine, which they assured me meant "hot earth". Later, a little detective work by Brigitte Xelot, a French member of the company's staff, proved the translation wrong. Not convinced that hot earth could produce a cool, refreshing Sauvignon Blanc, she re-examined the Spanish and found it meant "calcareous earth", or "limestone earth", which made much more sense. Apparently hot earth refers only to the sales policy.

IRON HORSE
USA

A 1985 visit took me to Sebastopol, in the Sonoma Valley, some 65 miles north of San Francisco, California. There I met Barry Sterling, who, with

wife Audrey and partner Forrest Tancer, owns the Iron Horse Vineyards, best-known for its top-quality sparkling wines. Barry pointed down the slope below the winery to a passing road and told me how a branch railway line had once run parallel to it and had provided the winery's name.

A later explanation revealed that part of the land had been occupied by what was called Ross Station, and though the building no longer survived, it was indeed an historic site. Following the USA's purchase of Alaska, groups of Russians had temporarily emigrated south to the area's warmer climate. The little railway provided them with access to neighbouring cities, so the local halt became known as Russian Station. In a typically American manner this was abbreviated to Ross, which resulted in the winery's address being Iron Horse Vineyards, Ross Way, Sebastopol.

SEAVIEW
Australia

Sounding more like a boarding house at a seaside resort than a winery, Seaview was only given its illustrative name by its owner, Bill Chaffey, a century after its foundation. That inspired moniker was chosen on the same basis as for a holiday home. The first recorded vineyard date at Seaview is 1850, when, from its elevated position in the McClaren Vale, those who had only recently taken the long journey from Europe could look back across the waters of Gulf St Vincent to the great Southern Ocean and muse over the last leg of the course they had sailed.

In international markets, Seaview is seen primarily as a maker of sparkling wines of an attractive quality. In Australia it has a different image, and my publisher rates the Cabernet Sauvignon most highly. It certainly appears to have many followers in its homeland for what eminent Australian wine writer James Halliday calls its "frequently absurdly underpriced" wines.

COMMANDARIA ST JOHN
Cyprus

Commandaria comes from the vineyards around three villages in the Troodos Mountains of Cyprus; they are Kalokhorio, Yerassa and Zoopiyi. Its original ageing process, still practised by some small producers, is one of the most ancient in the world, and is known as Cyprus Mana. It involves maturing the fortified wine in earthenware pots that are buried in the ground, though current production takes place chiefly in concrete vats. Traditionally the wine was poured from jar to jar, in a parallel of the Spanish *solera* system.

During the Crusades, Cyprus was occupied by the Knights of St John of the Hospital, later known as the Knights of Malta. They wore plain black robes with a white cross at the front, and ministered to the sick and injured who had suffered as a result of the skirmishes. They included among their medicines Commandaria, which in those days was not fortified.

VIA DELLA CHIESA
USA

Every time he drives to his Raynham, Massachusetts, winery, Italian-American Bob DiCroce has to go to church. Perhaps that is a slight exaggeration, but he does have to drive along the *via della chiesa*, or road to the church. Even a stroll through his vineyards takes him right to the church door. Bearing all this in mind, Bob came to the conclusion that there was only one name to give his winery in its pretty and secluded setting not far from the town of Taunton.

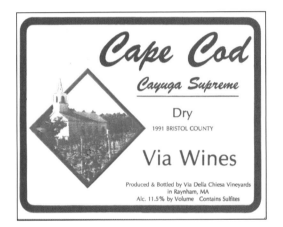

There, at the gateway to Cape Cod, the friendly winery-owner takes great pride in his title *il Padrone*, one which tells you just how much he values his Italian heritage. It was from that background that he learned how to make home-made wine, which he says was good, but nothing in comparison with the quality of wine his European staff are producing today from a variety of hybrid and *vinifera* grapes, at one of the prettiest winery locations in New England.

KRONE BOREALIS
South Africa

The highly reputed South African sparkling wine, from the south-eastern slopes of the Obliqua Mountains in the Coastal Region, is so called because "all its grapes are harvested by starlight". The name is also considered particularly apt because the behaviour of the tiny bubbles, which burst upward from the surface of the wine and then disappear quickly, is reminiscent of shooting stars.

Produced by the Krone family, whose surname means crown, the wine is made on the Twee Jonge Gezellen estate, which is South Africa's second-oldest vineyard property, founded in 1710. By coincidence, the name Krone Borealis does not just originate from the family, but from the constellation of stars known as the Corona Borealis. In Roman mythology, Bacchus, who enjoyed the occasional goblet or two, fell hopelessly in love with Ariadne. To demonstrate the depth of his passion for her he threw a golden crown, a shining wreath of jewels, high into the heavens, where it would remain forever as a testimony to his love.

The Afrikaner name Twee Jonge Gezellen has no connection with that starlit explanation, but refers to the "two young companions" who originally settled the land on which the estate is found.

P*ickers harvesting grapes for Krone Borealis in the cool of the night. From a distance the picker's headlamps look like stars twinkling in the vineyards – appropriate for a product namesd after the constellation Corona Borealis*

CASTRUM COESARIS
France

The coat of arms on the various labels of the owner and *négociant* Joseph Mellot carries a Latin inscription which may have puzzled consumers. Some may have assumed it is a motto. It is in fact a reference to the family's ancestor, César Mellot, who in 1698 was appointed wine adviser to the Sun King, Louis XIV, who used more than the odd barrel at his Palais de Versailles. *Castrum Coesaris* simply means César's castle, and refers to the Sancerre chateau from which the privileged vintner organised a family business that had been founded by Pierre-Etienne Mellot 185 years earlier, during the reign of Louis XII.

DOMAINE SAINT-DENIS
France

Domaine Saint-Denis, pronounced "Sant-Denee", is honoured with the name of France's patron saint. His name is sometimes spelt Denys, Dionis, or even Dionysius, and he is said to have been one of six bishops sent by Rome to evangelise France in the 3rd century. He was most influential in Paris, where he occupied an island in the Seine and made it the centre of his activities. Domaine Saint-Denis is one of the rising stars of the new wave of noble varietal wines from the large Vin de Pays d'Oc region in the Midi. It produces a pleasing Cabernet Sauvignon which will further increase in reputation as its young vines mature.

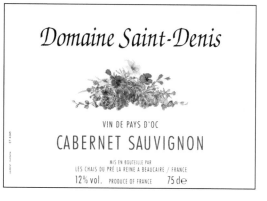

MAUREGARD
France

The names Mauregard and Yvon Mau are seen on Bordeaux bottles in many countries, but equally recognisable is their back-label logo, "the man on the penny-farthing". It relates to the early days of the company founder, Yvon Mau, who was born in 1900 and who initiated his original sales campaigns by riding his trusty iron steed from village to village in the Gironde as he sold his wines in increasing quantities. Today, Mauregard is possibly the best-known Yvon Mau label, and means "looking for Mau", which is apparently what his opposition were doing in the 1920s, and are still doing; for the first gentleman of Gironde-sur-Dropt spends less time on his bicycle, but still enjoys wine tasting in his mid-nineties. The Mauregard label is most unusual, as it represents not one chateau, but a carefully selected sequence of *petits chateaux* which separately would not be able to provide enough wine for major marketing but together offer some delicious and inexpensive Bordeaux.

DOMAINE COLLIN ROSIER
France

Being something of a romantic, I tried to translate Domaine Collin Rosier by reasoning that *colline* is a hill and *rosier* must mean rosebushes. Sadly, the name of this Vin de Pays d'Oc estate, near Limoux in the foothills of the French Pyrenees, has a much more mundane background. The property simply was founded by two men, called Collin and Rosier, with the sole intention of specialising in white wine while most of their neighbours produce red.

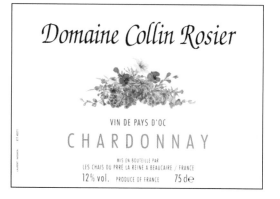

12.   VISUAL IMAGES

Many of us, at some time in our lives, harbour a secret dream that we might possess a God-given talent in a particular art or craft, so great that our fellow mortals would be obliged to acknowledge it as genius. This is a touchy subject, which brings us to the hackneyed argument of whether genius is born or made. Among the ranks of geniuses, names such as Michelangelo, Renoir, Picasso, Mark Twain, John Steinbeck, Rudolf Nureyev, and many others, come to mind. But how many who possess, or who have possessed, true genius are easily forgotten? For me, one such genius was the French belle époque artist Emile Gallé. He was a man who arrived in a turn-of-the-century Paris of faded and sombre hues, which he then transformed into the vivid colours of real life. The drab decor of nightclubs, restaurants, and the homes of the wealthy all came under the influence of his brightening touch. The sheer elegance of Gallé's work, which varied from figurines to furniture and glasswork, took nature indoors. His floral designs evoked the pure, pristine freshness of summer mornings, and he was daring in his use of the rich colours of the external world.

It was his genius, along with that of others, that introduced a new era to the French capital, an era which naturally enough came to the attention of the sales staff and directors of the great Champagne houses, who moved in the very same circles of society that consumed so much of their production.

At the very beginning of this century it was virtually impossible to visit the fashionable *arrondissements* of Paris without being aware of some new evidence of the belle époque era. Even the metro had succumbed to being decorated with floral designs, as had the brasseries, restaurants and *haute couture* salons. Paris revived and revelled in a new and exciting period of renaissance, and the French adored every moment.

This upsurge of excitement was a movement recognised and appreciated by Henri Gallice, a director of Champagne Perrier-Jouët, a middle-sized house in Epernay, which was experiencing a

The flower bottle of Champagne Perrier-Jouët

The legendary Maurice Chevalier at the Paris launch of the Perrier-Jouët flower bottle in 1969

unique problem, and which Gallice hoped the belle époque would help them solve.

The problem confronting them was that Perrier-Jouët had been achieving remarkable success in Britain, to which they were exporting 90 per cent of their production of about 1 million bottles a year. They had been fortunate enough to be granted the Royal Warrant by Queen Victoria, and also found particular favour with a senior member of the royal household called William Payne. Whenever requesting further supplies for both the Queen and His Royal Highness, the Prince of Wales, William Payne always included his own personal order. Those who enjoyed the hospitality of the royal family in Britain soon spread the word that Perrier-Jouët was being served at the Queen's table, and in no time many of the principal establishments of the day followed suit and ordered the same Champagne. It was wonderful business for Perrier-Jouët, but Henri Gallice was alarmed by this situation in a Europe that was often threatened by war. He had the foresight to realise that they had too many eggs in one basket, and it was time to capture their fair share of French trade, which hopefully would be less of a risk.

In 1902, this situation prompted Henri to approach Emile Gallé and enquire if it would be possible for him to create for Perrier-Jouët a bottle design which could be produced in some quantity and used for the ultimate luxury vintage cuvée. At his *verrerie* in Nancy, Emile Gallé carefully and skilfully crafted four magnums, all hand-painted with colourful floral designs. Henri Gallice and his colleagues must have been delighted with them, but by then a major problem had arisen. Each bottle would have to be produced manually, and while the cost might be acceptable to a few of their

wealthiest customers, it would be prohibitive to use the magnums as a regular line. Additionally the market for Champagne overall was showing a downhill trend. Disappointed, Henri wistfully gave instructions for the sample flower magnums to be stored away in the hope that at some time, in a brighter economic future, conditions would be favourable for one or more of them to be brought into use.

Time passed and for nearly thirty years the entire market continued to decline. In some countries, losses were owing to wars or skirmishes, in others they occurred owing to the rise of the temperance movement. In 1914, World War I had broken out, and it was followed by the economic slumps of the 1920s and early 1930s. Champagne sales plummeted alarmingly, not just for Perrier-Jouët, but for all the houses. Many producers in the Champagne region talked about changing their production to that of a still table wine, because so few people could any longer afford to purchase the King of Wines. The four flower magnums were considered unlikely ever to be of any use, and they remained tucked away in storage in an old straw pannier.

From the 1930s to the mid-1960s the Perrier-Jouët house quietly re-established its business, gaining an increasing reputation for the quality of its elegant wines. Despite this, there were difficulties in expanding sales; that was until the arrival of one man, a sales director, an enterprising young Belgian named Pierre Ernst, the Hercule Poirot of the Champagne trade. His was the unenviable task of increasing turnover, and subsequently production, without diminishing the reputation that the house had gained for the character and quality of its wines.

In the manner of Agatha Christie's great detective, Pierre Ernst began to search through the Perrier-Jouët cellars from top to bottom. He was convinced that there must be some facets of the past which could be of help in the future, even though he did not know exactly what it was that he was seeking. Then one day in 1964, which would have been like any other, almost by chance he stumbled upon his answer. While conversing with André Bavaret, the house's then renowned cellarmaster, Pierre's eye lighted upon an old basket in a corner of the office. It appeared to be holding some ancient magnums which he had not noticed before. The cellarmaster brought the basket across to Pierre and opened it, explaining that the contents were an idea from the past which had never been put into effect. Wiping the dust away, Pierre was taken aback by what was revealed – three exquisitely decorated magnums with floral designs in perfect condition, and one broken bottle of a rather melancholy aspect, but which still had its original pattern. "Eureka!" might be the word which summed up Pierre Ernst's feelings at that moment, as in a flash the knowledge that he had discovered something exciting dawned upon him.

It took another five years to prepare for the rebirth of the flower bottles but it was not wasted time. The belle époque had long ago vanished, and Emile Gallé and his *verrerie* no longer existed. This meant that the first challenge to be met was to ascertain whether it would be possible to produce such masterpieces on an economically viable scale. Here, once again, Pierre Ernst's Poirot reputation was to prove justified, for after months of enquiry, he came across, in a Paris suburb, a family company which still had such skills. The head of the family was a man in his sixties called Jean Bigou. When Pierre Ernst contacted him, he merely advised that the Perrier-Jouët sales director should visit their small *verrerie* and bring with him the original flower magnum that he had chosen. When Bigou saw the anemone-covered bottle he agreed that it was delightful and set to work. Apparently, in a very short time he inspected, photographed and possibly even sketched the impressive magnum. Then he simply told Pierre that it would not be a problem to copy it and that he had a procedure involving the baking of such bottles at just below the melting point of glass that would enable him to provide the most faithful reproductions. Pierre could leave, and only needed to advise the family when the first order was to commence.

Even today, little has changed in this tiny workshop, whose location remains a carefully guarded secret, discreetly hidden away down a gravel path behind a cottage garden. Here the family continue to decorate the flower bottles by hand and bake them in a small oven which is typical of a model still found in older bakehouses.

What happened next Pierre Ernst told me one day – I believe it was in 1989 – in their cellarmaster's office as we munched on the most unusual Champenois lunch of foie gras sandwiches washed down with Perrier-Jouët's delicious Blason de France cuvée. It had been both astonishing and distressing, as he began to explain. He had driven from the glassworks into the centre of Paris, to the Place de la Madeleine, to deliver the Gallé magnum for use in a special belle epoque window display in Fauchon, which many say is the finest gourmet store of all. That night, by appalling coincidence, turned out to be the first night of the infamous Paris student street riots, and a favourite store of the rich quickly became a prime target. A paving stone smashed through the window and in a split second Emile Gallé's unique work was destroyed.

The next day an emotional Pierre Ernst returned to Jean Bigou with the shattered pieces in a bag.

The craftsman sympathised, but told him that it was not a total disaster because he had completed all the necessary preparation the previous day and they could still proceed with the copies without any problems.

Then, though, there was the all important question of creating a prestigious cuvée. Fortunately this did not pose a problem, as the house's late managing director, Michel Budin, with the cellarmaster, André Bavaret, made a blending team whose skill was second to none. Michel Budin was convinced that the answer lay largely in two areas; first, that it was vital to include a higher proportion than usual of Chardonnay, using the ripest grapes from the house's outstanding vineyards at Cramant, and second, to give the Champagne five years bottle ageing in their cellars. At this juncture it is worthwhile noting that anyone purchasing Fleur de Champagne in the United States in, say, 1989 would have found only 1982, or sometimes 1983, on the retail shelves or on the wine lists of leading restaurants, a fact which confirms that Michel Budin's original instructions continue to be carried out to the benefit of the consumer. In the 1960s, when Michel Budin and André Bavaret decided on their blend, most Champagne houses preferred to have more Pinot Noir grapes in their blend, and so their decision caused a few eyebrows to raise. Although at the time some hailed Michel Budin as an innovator, he was a humble man who would make no such claim for himself, but who simply believed that he was using his skills and experience to provide the most charming of styles.

The original Gallé magnum before its destruction in student riots in Paris

The design that was selected featured white anemones, and it was destined to inspire Pierre Ernst's next, and rather more audacious move. In the 1960s he had been, for some time, a friend of Louis Vaudable, owner of the internationally acclaimed Maxim's Restaurant in the centre of Paris, a restaurant renowned for its belle époque decor. Pierre telephoned and asked Louis for an appointment, saying that he had something extremely precious to show him. The result was instantaneous, and in 1968 Louis Vaudable urged the delighted Belgian to allow Maxim's an initial twelve months exclusivity in France for the new prestige cuvée. The clientele of the great restaurant, which included the cream of Parisian society and the most demanding of overseas visitors, were charmed and fascinated, and as Pierre had secretly hoped, a steady flow of discreet requests to take the empty bottles away began to occur. It was another minor masterstroke on the road to success.

To obtain wider publicity it was decided, in 1969, to officially launch the bottles that are now known as La Belle Époque in Europe and Fleur de Champagne in the USA. Sadly, the former name was already registered as a trademark in the USA, hence the selection of the latter. But what a day (and night) to remember! It was the occasion of the seventieth birthday celebration of the visiting jazz giant Duke Ellington, who played amid the hazy, dusky atmosphere of the famous Alcazar Club, with the exquisitely decorated anemone magnum resting on top of his piano, and with his old friend Maurice Chevalier sitting nearby. Finally, as everyone sang "Happy Birthday", the two legendary entertainers and all the assembled guests sipped their glasses filled from magnums of the new flower bottles. The new belle époque, or flower era, at least in Champagne terms, had arrived.

GEORGE AND THE DON
Sandeman; Portugal and UK

In the 200-year old history of the growth of the House of Sandeman, there are two names which are impossible to ignore, those of George and "the Don". Our story begins to unfold in the year of 1790, which could be called the Year of the Georges; George Washington was serving as the first President of the United States of America, King George III was proving a particularly unin-spiring British monarch, and a young Scotsman from the city of Perth, George Sandeman, was opening the doors of what was to become one of the most renowned wine houses in the world. In due course, Sandeman was succeeded by his nephew, George Glas Sandeman, whose son, Albert

George, came in his turn to lead the company. Even today, seven generations later, there is another, youthful George Sandeman at the head of the company in Portugal. All these Georges have been prominent either in history or in the wine trade, yet despite that, there is one other George who left his mark, literally, and quite indelibly, in a way that would be instantly recognisable to many, and it is his story which is both fascinating and compelling to relate.

His tale is one to cheer the flagging spirits of anyone who is struggling to make his way in the world. Here was a man who had been frustrated by his commercial environment, and yet at the final moment displayed two small touches of genius, which have resulted in his work being seen and recognised all over the world, right up to the present day, a couple of generations after his death.

His full name was George Massiot Brown, and he was born in the golfing town of Troon, on the Ayrshire coast of Scotland, in the latter part of the 19th century. The deed for which he is chiefly remembered is his creation of the Don, arguably the best-known trademark in the history of the wine trade. That creation was his first touch of genius; his second was how he came to sell it to the House of Sandeman.

It is believed that George arrived in London shortly after World War I. He was in his late twenties, a quiet, inconspicuous bachelor, and appeared unlikely to shake the world. He probably had a number of jobs before he obtained a position with a small firm near Victoria Station, known as the Lochend Printing Co. Ltd. The business was run in the calm, quiet, Scottish tradition conducive to George's character, and he seemed to fit in quite harmoniously. There he shared a small studio with a fellow countryman, W.Y. Calder, who was the art director, and a junior artist, Ronald Brett.

It was the art department's task to supply a steady flow of creative ideas in the form of outline drawings which might hopefully turn out to be the requisite touchstone for some attractive new ad-vertising campaign. The three artists would scour the backgrounds of their existing clientele and of other potential customers in the hope of finding that magic spark which might lead to continuing success for a current customer, or to acquiring some major new account for the Lochend Printing Co. Ltd.

The early 1920s were halcyon days for George. Work had not been difficult to find and British poster artists were very much in demand. But by the later 1920s the business trends affecting him had completely altered. A new wave of poster advertising from Paris had become the current vogue – the latest fashion. The House of Sandeman, for example, had employed in 1926 a leading French poster artist, Jean d'Ylen, for an advertising campaign. Additionally, the world economy had suffered a great slump and in the same year, 1926, Britain experienced its first national strike, which meant the succeeding two years were marked by a massive loss of national confidence. In no time at all, George found his professional existence threatened. His company began to take drastic measures as the once rushing river of commerce dwindled rapidly to a small stream. Sales staff were placed on short-term contracts and the art department were probably next on the list. In the little studio, there must have been a growing feeling of desperation.

It was at this stage that the normally placid, orthodox Ayrshire man took the one step in his life that was not only dramatic, but which toed the very line of impropriety. As he witnessed the results of the French advertising vogue and felt personally under threat, he embarked upon a course of action quite alien to his nature. He decided to masquerade as a French poster artist in order to strike back and claim a share of the business that had been slipping across the English Channel. It was a ploy he could only adopt with the connivance of his colleagues, and one can imagine the timid man's trepidation as he discussed his plan with his two fellow artists.

For many years he had believed that his middle name, Massiot, was of French origin, possibly from Huguenot or even Norman days, and perhaps it would not be such a dishonest move to assume his old nationality and pretend to be not George Massiot Brown, in which the "t" was pronounced, but Monsieur G. Massiot, with the final "t" dropped and just an "o" sound ending the word. Surely, he reasoned, if people thought the Lochend Printing Co. Ltd employed a French poster artist, then they would be attracted to bring their business there. He was also perfectly convinced that their ideas were as good as those of the French and so what harm could be done?

There are two versions of the next part of the story, and it is difficult to pinpoint facts accurately. One version recalls that matters came to such a pitch that Monsieur G. Massiot lost his permanent position with Lochend, but remained in contact with them as a freelance artist, and in this capacity he went walking through the City of London with his sketchpad, searching for inspirational ideas. The story continues that one day in October 1928, while he was strolling near the Bank of England, he crossed Lombard Street and turned right, into a narrow street called St Swithin's Lane. When he reached No. 20 he found himself standing outside the House of Sandeman. Glancing up at the wrought-iron gate, his eyes were drawn to the highly polished brass plaque, which read "Sandeman, Jerez, Oporto, Lisboa etc.", and this gave him his unique moment of inspiration. Dipping his hand into his pocket he pulled out his charcoal and began to form the outline of a sketch. He simply drew a Spanish sombrero to represent the Sandeman sherries from Spain, and then a Portuguese student's cloak, a garment which had once caught his eye, to represent their port wines. Instantly he realised that he had captured something very special in what he was already enhancing as a shadowy black silhouette.

Tidying his appearance, he hastily crossed the little road, headed straight for the reception hall and asked to see the advertising manager. How he then came to explain his signature as G. Massiot is a matter of conjecture, but it does not seem to have presented an obstacle to his approach.

The advertising manager, E. Marshall Hardy, was a delightful character, who appeared to belong to the heart of the last century rather than to 1928. He was an author in his own right of two or three instructional books on fly-fishing, and was a familiar sight at weekends, in his Scottish tweeds and plus-fours, on the most active stretches of salmon and trout streams. In contrast, during the week he was one of the smartest figures in the city, impressive in bowler hat, morning suit, starched white collar,

A *bottle of Sandeman Founders Reserve Porto displaying the famous cloaked figure of the Don*

immaculate spats and brilliantly polished boots. He was a man ideally suited to his job and to the particular occasion, as he loved to write and had a great sympathy for the arts and for those he considered his fellow artists. It was to this man that George Massiot Brown, or Monsieur Massiot, was fortunate to present himself when he entered the office, and he thus found a welcoming eye.

The moment he saw the sketch, Marshall Hardy instinctively recognised the potential of the work.

He was so impressed that he hastily excused himself and left the room to step down the corridor and knock on the door of Walter Sandeman, then chairman of the company. The chairman needed little convincing, as he too acknowledged the self-evident appeal of the dual-nationality silhouette. A few minutes later the apprehensive artist was requested to join them, no-one seeming to have the slightest concern about his confusing identity. Less than an hour later, and considerably more

A 1931 print of George Massiot Brown's poster of the figure which was to become known as the Don, one of the most familiar trade logos in the world

relaxed by a little light lubrication, George Massiot Brown, or G. Massiot, as his signature would be read by future generations, emerged from the office, having been warmly congratulated by both men. They had agreed upon three basic and simple amendments to the sketch: a glass of port should be placed at one shoulder, the silhouette should be given a diffused green background to give the impression that it was standing above a misty vineyard, and the title SANDEMAN'S PORT should be printed below the picture in bold capitals. The agreed price was 50 guineas, a guinea being a gold coin worth £1 1s, the entire sum being worth in excess of $300 today. In 1928 it was as much as an artist could have hoped to earn in one year. In exchange, Sandeman would receive the copyright of what was to become one of the most familiar trade logos in the world.

The other version of the story suggests that rather than take the risk of any repercussions over his subterfuge, George Brown, as he was known in the office, avoided leaving the studio and involved a struggling sales representative, who was far from convinced of the drawing's quality, in his little scheme. According to this explanation, George had come to hear that Marshall Hardy, the Sandeman advertising manager, was a man who was always prepared to look at innovative ideas, and on this basis George decided to tailor-make a sketch to suit the house. It was therefore, perhaps, not George Brown, but the anonymous sales representative who called upon Sandeman, but whoever it was, the results were the same. The doubts harboured by the sales representative were quite groundless, as the figure George Brown had drawn had already won considerable public acclaim as a screen hero.

The cinema was one of George's few regular leisure pursuits; that is, apart from his daily lunchtime dip in Lambeth swimming pool. Along with many of his contemporaries, he probably enjoyed a dashing, swashbuckling Douglas Fairbanks adventure as an ideal form of escapism from the pressures and mundanities of everyday commercial life. It was this pastime that was to provide him with the basic inspiration for his sketch of the dark caped figure, so similar to that of the Zorro films. It was something he never admitted, but there seems little doubt that he was influenced by the daring Zorro and the publicity that promoted the films.

The Zorro stories were based on the escapades of Don Diego de la Vega, a legendary early-Californian hero, incorporating characteristics of Robin Hood and of the Scarlet Pimpernel. The films had been developed from a 1919 series, "The Curse of Capistrano", by Johnston McCulley, in *All-Story* magazine. In 1920, Londoners had seen Douglas

Fairbanks in the *Mark of Zorro,* and in March 1926 he had returned to the Stoll Picture Theatre in Holborn as *Don Q, Son of Zorro,* which was publicised on posters and in the London *Evening News* by a silhouette of Douglas Fairbanks as a dark, caped figure wearing a sombrero at a slant. Later, in October 1928, the very month George Brown drew the Don, *The Gaucho* was screened at the New Gallery Cinema in London's Regent Street. It was a sequel to the first two Zorro films, and once more starred Douglas Fairbanks as the shadowy cloaked hero. Again the posters and the London *Evening News* cinema page displayed the caped crusader dressed in black and wearing his sombrero at a slant, so George made an appropriate visit.

It suddenly crossed his mind that here, in front of him on the screen, was the basis of a new poster which might prove ideal for the House of Sandeman. The following morning, he arrived at the studio brimming over with enthusiasm at the prospect which lay before him. In less than an hour the germ of an idea blossomed into the original sketch of the caped figure the Don. Both the outline of the figure and its name had been gleaned from the film, and the whole affair fired his imagination and, he was certain, would fire the imagination of Mr Marshall Hardy, the advertising manager of Sandeman.

Whichever story is most accurate, there has always been an air of mystery surrounding the happenings, caused no doubt by the potential embarrassment of a minor artist who was anxious to conceal his one deceit in life, that of altering his name.

Initially the logo was referred to as "the Sandeman", and it was only in 1935 that the current name was used, when the new Dry Don label for Sandeman Fino Sherry was introduced. Then the logo's title was changed to the Don.

Strangely, a Don trademark was first registered in London by the House of Sandeman in 1888, apparently as something of an afterthought. The official register reveals an enlightening comment, "User since eight years before 13 August 1875", that being the commencement date for the UK Register of trademarks, and the note confirms that Sandeman had been using its Don trademark unofficially since 1867, but had not actually registered it until twenty-one years later. This would appear to justify the company's claim to possessing the earliest registered trademark in the wine trade. Ironically, that first trademark had little or no bearing at all upon the figure drawn by George Massiot Brown. In all probability the Scottish poster artist was not even aware of its existence. Strictly speaking, the only real connection between the two trade marks is the word DON, which was printed in capitals within a diamond-shaped outline. This trademark was used on branding irons to identify Sandeman pipes of port and butts of sherry, which in those days were being shipped to foreign markets for bottling.

The word Don at that time simply signified a gentleman in the old-fashioned sense of the word. As in England or the United States, a member of the gentry, unless otherwise titled, would expect anyone corresponding with him to append the word Esquire (later shortened to Esq.) to his name, so in Spain a man of similar standing would be addressed as Don. As the vast majority of the Sandeman wines were enjoyed by the gentry of the day, whether in Spain or Portugal, in Great Britain or the United States, the choice of trademark was entirely appropriate.

The first 1 000 Don posters, measuring 20 x 30 inches, were rushed out for the Christmas of 1928. They took the country by storm. The drawing had that remarkable quality, often found in simple art forms, of being instantly noticeable and virtually unforgettable. Walter Sandeman and Marshall Hardy came to the conclusion that they had in their hands one of the greatest promotional tools the wine trade had ever seen.

There was a great sense of excitement in the Sandeman head office once the Don had been purchased and the whole concept came under scrutiny. Marshall Hardy was confident that there would be a plethora of opportunities ahead for this simple but easily recognisable figure. The initial response to the posters was so overwhelming, and sales figures rose so sweetly, that he made immediate plans to have the poster reprinted in some eight or nine countries where the house had strong markets. In 1931 it was printed by the Parisian printer Draegar, with the wording beneath the figure being amended to suit the company's market in France. Now it read "Porto and Sherry" with "Sandeman" beneath. This was followed by Belgian, German, and even Japanese versions. Wherever Sandeman sherry, port or Madeira was drunk, the Don was certain to be conspicuous.

At the Sandeman wine lodge in Oporto, where all their ports are matured, and at their sherry bodegas in Jerez, the painters and carpenters set to work. Large cut-out silhouettes and murals of the Don began to appear in every possible location. Today it is impossible to visit Jerez without spotting that giant shadowy figure as you drive over the surrounding hillsides. And when you reach the Sandeman property, the Don dominates. In fact one enterprising employee, with a sense of humour, has placed a "Don" sign on the door of the gentleman's toilet, and similarly has created a

feminine "Doña" to make sure the ladies do not make any mistakes.

The possibilities for exploitation were endless. A completely new stock of company notepaper and envelopes was printed to display the Don, and even the accounts department used him on their invoices and statements. Don mirrors and ashtrays were manufactured, and since then the range of Don items has risen past 100, with even cigarette lighters, toys, T-shirts and radios included.

In 1931, Royal Doulton created a set of china Dons in black. The exercise was repeated in 1937 using five different colours. These figures have since become extremely valuable collectables. Later, in 1949, Royal Doulton produced some Don decanters, and in 1969 a large Wedgewood issue of 78 000 special Don decanters was provided to celebrate the investiture of Prince Charles as the Prince of Wales. There have been several other issues to mark significant occasions since.

Perhaps the most amusing of the stories surrounding the Don are two that could never be authenticated. One involves the recent Corgi collectable Thornycroft model London bus of 1919, which carries a Sandeman advertisement along the side of the vehicle, with the Don prominently displayed. It is a charming anachronism, as the Don was not produced until 1928, a little matter overlooked by another commercial artist nearly sixty years later. Of even more note is a book entitled *Ghost Stations*, by Bruce Barrymore Halpenny, which is clearly subtitled *True Ghost Stories*. The book is a record of alleged sightings of various ghosts at Great Britain's abandoned airfields. It includes, on page 91, the story of "Sandeman's Ghost", which reputedly appeared at RAF Aldergrove, in Northern Ireland, during World War II. It was sighted by a meteorological expert called Syd Frogley.

It was the practice of Frogley and some other colleagues to release hydrogen-filled balloons and follow them with radar up to 60 000 to 70 000 feet, tracking the wind and weather. One particular night they were encountering difficulty starting the diesel generator that powered their tracking equipment. Spotting a security patrol passing nearby, Frogley called to him to give them a hand in turning the engine. Frogley was a little surprised at the lack of response and so turned the ignition off and hurried after the patrol to ask his help in person.

"As I got nearer I saw that he was dressed in a cloak and a tall wide brimmed hat," said Frogley. "I halted for a few moments – then as I moved forward again he just disappeared."

The real Don will no doubt continue to be seen by millions worldwide for generations to come, and will be identified as the logo or trademark of the House of Sandeman. It brought George Massiot Brown considerable acclaim, and yet he was never able to produce a similar stroke of genius again. He did, however, continue drawing posters until World War II, but then returned, aged forty-nine, to his native Scotland, where he and two unmarried sisters designed miniature gardens. He eventually met his death as a result of an accident incurred when diving from a high board at a Scottish swimming pool. He will be remembered as the man who gave Sandeman and the world the Don, one of the most memorable advertising figures ever created. But the question will always remain as to whether the Don was his unique inspiration, or whether it was a concept borrowed from the Douglas Fairbanks film *Don Q, Son of Zorro*, itself a sequel to *The Mark of Zorro* or *The Gaucho*, which in turn were all based on a 1919 comic serial "The Curse of Capistrano". But that's another story!

HISTORY FOR ALL TO SEE
Martini & Rossi Vermouth, Italy

In some cases the foundation dates quoted by wine and drinks companies may appear questionable. Nevertheless, in my experience, the dates can almost always be substantiated. The foundation date 1847, published by the Martini & Rossi Company, is a fairly typical example. When I discovered that Alessandro Martini had been a trainee colleague of Gaspare Campari in Turin's prestigious Bass Bar, and afterwards owned a small trading company, and the dates of these activities coincided with the early years of the Martini & Rossi business, I admit that I was just a little suspicious, albeit erroneously.

Scrutiny of the Martini & Rossi records reveal that they in no way suggest Martini involvement in 1847. Indeed the company accurately describes Allessandro Martini as its agent from 1854, and relates that he did not become a partner until 1863, at which time the expanding business operated under the names of the four original partners, Michel, Re, Agnelli and Baudino. The Agnelli family later became widely known for their Fiat car company and their involvement in the Juventus soccer club.

In 1847 the original partnership had agreed upon the title Distilleria Nazionale di Spirito da Vino Company, but had not made use of it. Instead they had continued to use their individual names. In 1863, with added capital, they commenced the building of their futuristic new headquarters in the village of Pessione. Their competitors and the surrounding population were amazed when they installed a railway siding by paying for a branch line

to lead from the main railway onto their property. It is the earliest-known such utilisation of a public railway by any wine or drinks company in the world.

In the first sixteen years of the company's existence, the founding partners had organised matters on a very large scale, particularly for a drinks company of that era. Their principal activities were the production and sale of a range of vermouths and aperitifs, as well as an assortment of wines, liqueurs and other drinks. In the early days, many of these were made in a distillery in San Salvatore, from which they were shipped to different markets. Later, the partners realised the benefit of splitting some of their production among various corners of their growing empire. Soon they had strategically placed branches in Genoa and Cagliari, the foremost city of the island of Sardinia, which had been united with Piedmont under Victor Emmanuelle, and also at Béziers, in south-west France.

In 1860, Re died, and three years later Michel retired; new, influential and preferably wealthy blood was needed. The gap was filled by Alessandro Martini and Luigi Rossi, and by the end of the decade the organisation was trading as Martini, Sola et Cia, and was busily exporting to three continents. On 30 June 1879, following the death of Sola, whose shares were acquired by Luigi Rossi, the title of the company was officially changed to Martini & Rossi.

A *selection of ingredients at Martini & Rossi, Turin*

The Martini & Rossi vermouth label is a classic illustration of the great company's growing success as an international giant, and if it is examined studiously a colourful history unfolds. Apparently the 1863 labels were not dissimilar from the current version, but events from 1863 onwards added much decoration.

At the centre of the label, near the top, is a banner in recognition of more than forty medals won, a total that only covers the early days. Immediately below and to the left is a medal from the great American Centennial Exhibition at Philadelphia in 1876, and to the right is another medal from Alessandria, a province of Savoy, won in 1870. Beneath the Martini Rosso wording, some prominence is given to the gold medal won at the Paris Exhibition of 1878, which is reproduced twice, once on the left and once lower on the right. Centre right is a similar award from that era, from Dublin. Near the foot of the label is a picture of a large building, which is in fact the Pessione headquarters, showing the steam railway.

The reason for the name Martini being in such bold, large letters at the top of the label is that for some time the company sold two popular vermouths of differing styles, one called Martini and the other Rossi. The crowned figure in a yellow dress directly beneath the name Martini is the mythological Roman goddess Victoria. Trumpet in hand, she heralds the company's early achievements, or victories, in the international markets,

which are further emphasised by the flags of ten countries arranged to her right and left. On either side of Victoria, just under the banner, are two stout cherubs; the one on the left sits above the coat of arms of the kingdom of Savoy, an honour granted by King Umberto in 1893, and the one on the right is carousing behind the coat of arms of the city of Turin. The word Torino comes from *toro*, meaning "bull", hence the emblem on blue.

The arms of Savoy are repeated on a smaller shield, just below Victoria's left hand, and to the right of that is a shield of similar size, acknowledging Martini & Rossi's warrant as suppliers to the Portuguese royal family, a distinction gained in 1872. On either side of the label, about halfway down, are two somewhat mysterious allegorical figures about whom opinions are divided. One theory is that the queen enthroned on the left holds a map of the known world, representing their existing markets. Opposite her sits Columbus, who hailed from Genoa, later the principal port of Savoy during the foundation years of the company, and the first port used for shipping Martini vermouth to other countries. Records show that by the 1890s, Martini & Rossi were exporting 300 000 cases per annum from Genoa alone. Columbus's white-skinned European figure is curiously adorned with the feathers and quiver of a native American, and he also holds a palm leaf in one hand while resting the other hand on a map of the New World, displaying future markets to be conquered.

The label reproduced here is the one in regular use in Great Britain, but in other monarchies where royal warrants have been granted, labels are amended to display the warrant of that particular country. There are other slight variations, depending upon importation and bottling arrangements. The basic design is the same for each of the three Martini styles, Dry, Rosso and Bianco (launched in 1958), but the colours are varied to distinguish them. My description and explanation is based on the original Rosso label. It only remains to be seen what additions, if any, will be made to such a complex and colourful label in the future.

INSPIRATION BY PORTRAIT
Faustino Rioja, Spain

For several generations, three portraits on the label of three popular Rioja wines, produced by the house of Faustino Martinez, have had inquisitive wine drinkers debating their identities. From their traditional bodegas in the Rioja Alavesa region, in northern Spain, a constant supply of the three styles has been shipped to numerous international markets, where consumers have guessed at the names of the individuals portrayed on the labels, but few have

every three bottles of Rioja Gran Reserva exported, and one in every six Reservas.

The Gran Reserva Faustino I bears the portrait of the 17th-century Dutch master Rembrandt Van Rijn. Faustino V, their Reserva, carries a picture of Christopher Gluck, the 18th-century German composer, and the Faustino VII, which is a *sincrianza*, or non-aged wine, has the 16th-century Spanish artist El Greco on the label.

JUST "J"
Jordan Winery, USA

Those who have had the privilege of being entertained as overnight guests at the Jordan Winery, near Healdsburg, in California's Alexander Valley, relate their experience of sumptuous luxury to their friends for many months afterwards. Meticulous attention to detail is evident in both the delightful accommodation and the immaculate appearance of the winery cellars situated directly below the guest-suite window. Instead of waking up to sun, fog, or rain, one rises to the tranquil scene of Cabernet ageing in pristine surroundings.

The first Jordan Cabernet was launched with the 1976 vintage; that vintage and many subsequent ones have proved that multimillionaire Tom Jordan has invested wisely, not just in the marvellous facilities he has provided, but in his endeavours to follow the disciplines required to produce a wine of truly international standard. Indeed, the Denver oil magnate has given a relatively obscure valley a flagship wine and a property to match, one which is sadly, but understandably, at the disposal of trade and journalistic visitors only.

The Cabernet Sauvignon, fashioned in superb style by former André Tchelistcheff pupil Rob Davies, was the object of popular acclaim at an early stage. It was followed by a Chardonnay, which is well-known to countless thousands of international passengers on Northwest Airlines. In 1986, the prestige sparkling wine known simply as J arrived, launched by the Jordan Sparkling Wine Company, a new partnership formed between Tom and his daughter, Judy, who is herself a

been correct. Even a radio promotion in Britain, with tempting prizes of Faustino Rioja, was unable to find wine lovers with sufficient knowledge of the arts.

The labels were first brought into use during the third generation of the Faustino Martinez family's ownership, with the concept of inspiring their winemakers to attain the best possible standards. The concept appears to have succeeded since the company report that Faustino accounts for one in

The magnificent headquarters of Jordan Winery, near Healdsburg, California

longstanding senior member of the Jordan Vineyard and Winery team.

The J bottle, containing a blend of Pinot Noir and Chardonnay, was a sensational success, largely attributable to the unique bottle presentation. With one bold stroke of the brush, a large, elegant letter J, in a striking yellow, is painted directly onto the glass; there is no main label at all. The Jordans had seized upon the lack of label restrictions in California, an advantage their French rivals can never enjoy under the INAO appellation controls.

The Arbor Crest cameo; the winery's name was derived from the vines covering the lady's hair, and from the cameo crest

The sensationally successful J bottle, which contains a blend of Pinot Noir and Chardonnay

MORE THAN A CAMEO PERFORMANCE
Arbor Crest, USA

If you wish to produce a cameo wine that will stand out amid the star-name labels, what brighter idea could there be than to use an actual cameo. It was such a philosophy that led to the unique design of the Arbor Crest label from Spokane, in the east of Washington State.

In 1980, when the Meilke family, long-time Spokane Valley farmers and residents, were contemplating the development of their new winery, they searched for a label that would "represent the image of the winery", and selected an antique brooch as the model for its design. Hence the name Arbor Crest, which describes the vine arbor covering the lady's hair and the cameo crest itself. That a family ancestor should actually have owned such a design was plainly fortuitous,

and provided some heritage to a modern wine story.

The distinctive cameo was delivered to a Californian specialist in label designs, who then took painstaking care to develop an appropriate label of eye-catching appearance. An elaborate image was created using three types of foil: yellow for the lady, copper-gold for the lettering, and pearlised ivory for the background. This intricate work carried a clearly defined label message to those who saw it. The message has subsequently been endorsed by a host of medals and awards, and columns of journalistic praise for the Arbor Crest varietals, from those who have recognised the Spokane winery's cameo performances. Indeed it might be suggested that in such a short period of time the wines have received so many plaudits that it is necessary to declare the cameo label redundant and change it for a brightly shining star.

VIVID BLUE
Blue Pyrenees, Australia

It is generally accepted that beauty is in the eye of the beholder and I do not anticipate every reader agreeing with my choice of the Blue Pyrenees Estate label as the most eye-catching of all. For me the boldness of its vivid blue and the simplicity of its design epitomise the transformation of commercial art into a finer form.

The label, introduced in 1982, shows the view from the vineyard near the tranquil country town of Avoca, in the Pyrenees district of Victoria. Its panorama, encompassed in the south by a mountainous backdrop, forms a memorable image, which in some atmospheric conditions appears a dramatic blue, a natural phenomenon created by the forests of eucalyptus trees on the adjacent mountainsides. That dramatic blue, when first used on red wine bottles, caused certain traditionalists some dyspepsia, but a plethora of design awards and favourable compliments from consumers have since justified the daring selection. The label is based on an original oil painting by the gifted Lorrie Banks, a Victoria-based artist best-known for her highly individual representations of everyday objects, such as "teacups, biscuits or cappuccino", as well as her commercial work. Her commissions have included items as diverse as illustrations for *Traveller* magazine and *Penthouse*, to book covers for Penguin, Longman and McMillan, as well as limited-edition prints, posters and other wine labels.

The Pyrenees district of Victoria is now undergoing its second experience as a vineyard region. A grower called Mackeroth first planted vines there in 1848, which proved quite successful. At one stage he was reported to have cellar reserves of more than 10 000 litres and to own three wine stores in Avoca, which then had a slightly larger population. Tragically, in the latter part of the 19th century, Mackeroth sold his entire assets to a misguided clergyman named Dawson, who supported the then flourishing temperance movement. Dawson promptly ripped out all the vines, closed the winery and demolished the cellars.

In 1961, the French drinks group Remy Martin replanted vines in the Pyrenees district, initially concentrating on white varieties but also including small experimental plantings of two noble reds, Cabernet Sauvignon and Shiraz, to which they later added some Merlot and Pinot Noir. As the vines matured, the winemakers discerned differing characteristics at varying parts of the estate, and in one small western sector, at an altitude of about

2 000 feet, the juice of the grapes exhibited an unusual and attractive minty quality, which apparently originated from the surrounding eucalyptus trees. As this particularly beautiful location was shaded by the blue of the Pyrenees, it inspired the selection of the name for the vineyard, and hence the necessity of seeking an artist to reproduce that distinctive view on the label.

Today in this magical setting the young Bordelaise oenologist Vincent Gere strives to produce a blend of Bordeaux-style complexity and richness using Cabernet Sauvignon, Merlot and Shiraz. With his knowledge and skill, formed in Bordeaux and Montpellier, as well as during his childhood days, when his father was the manager of the highly rated Chateaux Malescasse and Pontet Canet, it is not surprising that the Blue Pyrenees Estate is beginning to make superb wines – wines to match its most beautiful label.

13. AFFAIRS OF THE HEART

BEAUTIFUL MIRACLE
Di Saronno Amaretto, Italy

The Saronno Madonna fresco by Bernardo Luini, in the Cathedral of Santa Maria delle Grazie

During the Renaissance, Bernardino Luini, a Milanese artist and follower of Leonardo da Vinci, began work on a commission to decorate the sanctuary of the Cathedral of Santa Maria delle Grazie at Saronno, with frescoes illustrating diverse biblical scenes.

When he started his work in 1525, Luini, who has since become famous for his Madonnas, selected faces from actual members of the congregation to represent the various characters depicted, a time-honoured practice. For the Virgin Mother he approached a beautiful young widow, who was especially honoured to be chosen. When the devout woman saw the magnificence of the finished work, she told the artist she must thank him for the privilege in some tangible manner.

She explained to Luini that she was an innkeeper of very restricted means and could not give him anything of value, but she did have a secret recipe for a drink called Amaretto, which had a mysterious bouquet of apricot kernels. This had been in her

family for many generations, but she would give it to him, even though it meant relinquishing ownership forever.

But, almost miraculously, that never occurred, for the artist and the young widow fell in love, and her family retained the secret recipe for what is today known as Di Saronno Amaretto.

CHAMPAGNE AND CAVIAR
Kattus, Austria

The Widow Clicquot, noted elsewhere in this book for her invention of the *remuage,* or riddling, process, at one time nearly lost her single status to the charms of an Austrian, who would regularly present her with the finest caviar known to man.

Johann Kattus had begun trading as a retail grocer in Vienna in 1857, but his business had steadily grown until he became a wholesaler specialising in gourmet foods and fine wines. He soon developed a special interest in caviar and, being a determined individual, he set off to find the best caviar of all, travelling east to Astrakhan.

Upon his arrival there, Johann immediately recognised the potential for a commercial venture and opened a trading centre in Astrakhan, where he purchased caviar for both the Russian and the international markets. He continued to divide his time between Vienna and Astrakhan, and from these bases found himself supplying both the Tsar of Russia and the Emperor of Austria.

At that time, Veuve Clicquot Champagne was enjoying notable popularity among the aristocracy of Russia and was a regular accompaniment to caviar. This combination gave Johann Kattus the idea of obtaining the agency for Veuve Clicquot in Austria, where he believed he could encourage a similar pattern of enjoying caviar with Champagne. Subsequently he travelled to Reims with ample stocks of caviar with which to tempt the Widow Clicquot, and thus began a personal relationship which not only resulted in Johann gaining the agency he desired, but also in his becoming over the years a regular visitor to the Chateau de Boursault, the Widow's private residence in the Marne Valley. The Widow even taught Johann the

Johann Kattus, the former grocer turned caviar trader and vintner who wooed the Widow Clicquot

The trading post operated by Johann Kattus in Astrakhan

intricacies of the *méthode champenoise* and, so it would seem, encouraged him to produce his own sparkling Austrian wine, a suggestion which he followed.

More than 130 years later, the house of Johann Kattus still represents the famous yellow label of the French Champagne and simultaneously sells its own more moderately priced but equally popular sparkling wine in Austria. The caviar business was lost with the Russian Revolution, but a painting of it hangs on the office wall, and it is said the directors still enjoy a little caviar with either bubbly when they toast the names of the Widow Clicquot and Johann Kattus together.

THE COURSE OF TRUE LOVE
Gratien et Meyer, France

The course of true love must surely be the daily toast at the much acclaimed sparkling Saumur house of Gratien et Meyer, producers of the attractive Gratien Brut *méthode champenoise* wine.

Without that course, none of today's four directors would exist, let alone enjoy their privileged positions. For behind the ownership of their Loire vineyards and famous 6 miles of caves on the Route de Chinon lies one of the most poignant tales of romance ever likely to be found; one that involves a war, four countries, a young widow, and a teenage sweetheart – sufficient ingredients, perhaps, to alter the path of anyone's life.

The majority of us can delve into our family histories and wonder just what might have happened if one of our ancestors had taken a different direction, chosen another lifestyle, or simply married someone else. But Alain and Gérard Seydoux, their octogenarian father, Eric, and their cousin Bernard de Bousquet know that if the romantic story of their ancestor-by-marriage had not occurred they would not own so much as a share in Saumur's leading house.

The ancestor in question was one Albert Meyer, and he was born in Gunsbach, in France's scenic Alsace region, in 1852. There, nurtured by some of the finest wines and gastronomy that his country could offer, he grew into a vigorous and healthy young man, who had every reason to anticipate a bright and happy future in his homeland.

In Albert's eighteenth year, Alsace, and indeed the whole of France, enjoyed the memorable summer of 1870, with day after day of warm sun and clear blue skies. As autumn approached, there was a great air of expectancy as the population realised that they were going to experience a truly great vintage. It was then that with a terrifying and shattering suddenness the Franco-Prussian War broke out, and Albert Meyer's dreams and plans were brought to an abrupt and dramatic halt. The peaceable young man found himself, on his eight-

eenth birthday, wearing a uniform amid the chaotic events that saw France's position declining daily. Almost as suddenly as the war began it ended, but the price of peace was high, and the prize for Germany the deepest cut of all to Albert. In their surrender, the French had agreed to Germany annexing Alsace-Lorraine.

In a land where Rouget de l'Isle had written the French national anthem, "*Les Enfants de la Patrie*", and where the vast majority used French as their mother tongue, there was mayhem. German forces and officials advised the inhabitants of Alsace, the vast majority of whom were French nationals and wished to retain that status, that they were being welcomed back and that their old language, an Alsacienne dialect, would be restored. It would be taught in all the schools and it would be an offence for anyone to be heard speaking French. Their "welcome" was extended to a land that had always been French, apart from a brief flirtation with the Austro-Hungarian empire 200 years previously. The people were stunned, and tens of thousands preferred to leave their homeland. They were French, French was their language and they wished to live only in France. Others, who were perhaps a little more adventurous, set out for the New World, among them Albert Meyer. His decision was destined to break two hearts. Albert cared deeply for a retiring young girl from his village, Marie-Dorothée Müller, who was just fifteen years old. She, like him, had been raised in the Protestant church in Gunsbach, and must have been greatly bewildered and distressed by the changing events which enveloped her. In less than a year the serene happy lives of two young people lay in ruins, as they lost both the freedom of their homeland and each other. Albert had made the decision to emigrate to the United States, where it seems likely he joined fellow countrymen somewhere in the vicinity of Detroit. He spoke little or no English and had never undertaken a long journey before, and must have felt as if he were in a dream from which he could not wake.

Gradually he adapted to a new way of life but he was never really at home. He had been accustomed to living in the Vosges mountains, in a quaint little old town where centuries-old wooden gabled houses leaned towards each other across the narrow streets. By contrast, he now found himself in a flat humid country, where the mosquitos could make conditions miserable and the dinner table offered little recompense. His mind was torn apart by his memories of Alsace and Marie-Dorothée. Before the Franco-Prussian War, everything had looked rosy and the future had been promising, but disaster had ruined all that. At times his heart longed for home and the quiet reserved girl he had

A*lbert Meyer (right) and friend at Niagara Falls, circa 1875*

adored, but he detested the thought of a homeland that was not free and he maintained his vow never to return while Alsace was occupied.

He began to travel, not great distances, but far enough to broaden his experience of life. On one occasion he even travelled through Canada to the Niagara Falls, where he had a picture painted of himself seated, looking across to America. During this period he happened to meet a young widow in her early twenties and just a few years older than himself. It seems likely she was Canadian, as a studio photograph of the couple, which was taken in Sarnia, Ontario, on the southern shores of Lake Huron, survives to this day. The relationship developed into a serious one and Albert considered proposing marriage, but somehow he could not bring himself to utter those words, for his heart was still in Alsace and the course of true love would not be thwarted.

One can only speculate on whether the correspondence between himself and Marie-Dorothée had reduced to a trickle, or even finally stopped, but one can imagine the reaction in her home town of Gunsbach when the young woman read his letter of proposal. He intended to return to France and after six years of separation he asked for her hand in marriage. His intention was to find another region of France where they could settle and where he could obtain work. They would search for a new Alsace. One thing he would not do, he reconfirmed, was return to his homeland while it was in German hands.

Marie-Dorothée agreed but with one exception. Yes, she did love him and would live with him wherever he wanted but she insisted on one condition – that their wedding must take place in Gunsbach so that both their families and all their friends could be present for the celebrations. It was her only request. If Albert loved her so deeply he would surely break his vow for one day and return to Alsace for that important occasion.

In 1877, Albert, then twenty-five years old, crossed the Atlantic Ocean for the second time in his life, but on this occasion to return to France in search of new territory. Perhaps he had heard from other French émigrés of the beautiful and fertile Loire Valley, but we can never be completely certain what led him to arrive in Saumur one day looking for work and a permanent home. There he found other settlers from Alsace and possibly it was through one of them that he came to learn of Alfred Gratien, who owned some remarkable wine caves on the Route de Chinon, a couple of miles east of the ancient chateau of Saumur. Alfred was seeking an assistant to help him in the management of his expanding sparkling wine business; it proved to be a suitable opportunity for Albert.

When Albert Meyer arrived to see Alfred Gratien, the latter had been trading for thirteen years. Albert could not promise that he had much real knowledge of management, but he did know a little about wine production from his upbringing in Alsace, and he did speak not only his native tongue, French, but also German and English with fluency. To add to this, he was a serious and diligent man who followed his Protestant faith with unerring discipline. It was more than enough, and Alfred, who was not the fittest and strongest of men, was delighted to hire his services. It was the beginning of a friendship which was to last just eight years, before Alfred Gratien died prematurely.

From the very beginning, Albert worked energetically and capably, and it was not long before Alfred Gratien gave him increasing responsibilities in the day-to-day running of the house. In due course, Albert moved into a comfortable three-storey residence by the main gateway to the winery and began to prepare for the time when Marie-Dorothée would join him there. He worked hard, saved carefully, involved himself in the Protestant church in Saumur, and in general established himself as a respected and model citizen.

When eventually he was able to provide a comfortable new home for Marie-Dorothée, he set out on the journey that was to break his vow. He returned to Alsace, and on a glorious spring day in May 1882 the young couple were married; Albert was now twenty-nine and Marie-Dorothée twenty-six. The ceremony was conducted in the Gunsbach Protestant Church by Pastor Louis Schweitzer, whose seven-year-old son Albert, of later Lambaréné fame, was to become one of Alsace's greatest heroes. Afterwards they undertook the 400-mile journey to Saumur, where they lived for the remainder of their lives. Coincidentally, some years later, they purchased a house of their own in the appropriately named rue d'Alsace, the selfsame road in which all three Seydoux directors live today.

In the early 1880s the Saumur business was still trading as Alfred Gratien, with Albert employed as manager. In addition to the expanding Saumur

Semi-abandoned Chateau Smith-Haut-Lafitte in 1985

house, Alfred Gratien had opened a small Champagne house in Epernay, which exists under his name to this day, and also remains under the same independent family ownership as the Saumur winery. For Alfred Gratien, his manager and his employees, a healthy and prosperous future seemed assured. But Alfred was a weak man physically, with serious respiratory problems, and his health began to decline alarmingly. In 1885 he died when just forty-five years old. Albert lost a man who was both his trusted friend and his employer. Alfred's widow, Nelly, had no experience of the business, and decided to take the only path which seemed open to her; she invited Albert to become her partner under the new title Gratien et Meyer, and they were to remain in joint charge for more than forty years. In due course, with the lack of any male heirs, marriage into the female line of the Meyer family by Eric Seydoux and Bernard de Bousquet led to their involvement and their families' ownership of the popular winery, which nowadays receives 70 000 visitors per year and exports to more than thirty countries. As the current four directors consider their prosperity, let us hope that they always remember not just to toast their ancestors and their own good fortune, but also the course of true love.

THE MOST COMMON NAME
Chateau Smith-Haut-Lafitte, France

Did you know that Smith, the most typical of British family names, is the most common surname in the Western world? Yet somehow this everyday name came to enjoy the elite status of being incorporated into the title of a celebrated Bordeaux chateau.

The story of Chateau Smith-Haut-Lafitte and how it obtained its identity has its origins in what, at the time, was something of a scandal. In 1720 a Scotsman called George Smith, who had already established himself as a successful wine merchant in the city of Bordeaux, decided to join the small but growing band of *négociants* who were investing in single chateaux which either possessed vineyards, or had suitable land for that purpose. He purchased a substantial vineyard known as Haut Lafitte in the *commune*, or parish, of Martillac, in the Graves region, which was so named because of its gravelly soil. Haut Lafitte simply meant the best part of the upper ground, and the energetic Scotsman merely added Smith to the estate's existing name.

For the first couple of years of his ownership George Smith continued to travel by pony and trap to the city of Bordeaux, on a trip of about an hour's duration, in much the same way as today's motorised commuters journey to and from their offices. He traded from premises on the famous Quai des Chartrons, on the left bank of the Garonne. This great road, whose once imposing architecture now appears somewhat faded, enjoyed for more than two centuries a prominent role as the thriving hub of the Bordeaux wine trade. In the tall buildings lining the Quai, offices and apartments for many of the *négociants* occupied the five or six storeys which rose above ground level. Below street level a further two or three floors were used as cellars. The lowest cellars usually had earthen floors, as it was believed that they provided the best atmosphere for the ageing of wines. All these great wine houses stood in one line on the city side of the Quai des Chartrons, while opposite was the dockside, with consignments of wine barrels piled high, awaiting their turn to be loaded aboard some high-masted schooner or barque, for shipment to some distant land.

The Chartrons was, in effect, a micro-society, with its own written and unwritten rules and codes of conduct, and as George Smith was one of its active members, it was presumed that he would conform. His status among his contemporaries certainly rose as a result of his purchase of the vineyard of Haut Lafitte, and it received a further boost when he completed the construction of a magnificent chateau on the estate, that served as a home for himself and his family, and also provided a *pressoir* and cellars for the predominantly red wines of Chateau Smith-Haut-Lafitte. Then a sudden twist in events caused a dramatic fall from grace, when his peers ostracised him for a moral crime that one cannot imagine was entirely alien to the France of his day.

It befell that in the peaceful village of Martillac, George chanced to meet a lovely young peasant girl named Elisabeth Louis — and fell headlong in love with her. Their passionate affair developed quickly into a deeper and more serious relationship and George Smith shocked Bordeaux society by leaving his wife and children in the magnificent new chateau, and moving into an old cottage on the other side of the vineyard with his new love. His fellow *négociants* on the Chartrons initially attempted to make George see sense, informing him that it was one thing for a man of his position to have a secret affair, or keep a mistress, but quite another to leave his wife and children. He was to return immediately to his matrimonial home or the consequences would be intolerable. Although the message was delivered in the plainest of terms, George failed to respond, and the reaction on the Quai des Chartrons was instant. An official Court of Morals was held, and George Smith was condemned to ostracism by the Bordeaux wine trade.

The Scotsman saw much of his life's work disappear, as everyone refused to deal with him, and so he put his assets on the Chartons into the hands of an *agent-fonçier* (an agent specialising in the sale of land, vineyards, cellars, and similar properties). He retired to his estate at Martillac, where he lived the rest of his life with Elisabeth Louis. In 1756, George Smith died, and in his will left Chateau Smith-Haut-Lafitte jointly to his son, George Jack Smith, and to his lover, Elisabeth Louis. George Jack vehemently denounced such a state of affairs and went to court to contest his father's decision. The court records show that the son had changed his name from its Scottish origin to the French, Georges Jacques, and finally to simple Jacques.

Jacques instigated a series of court actions against Elisabeth Louis in a bitter but unsuccessful attempt to have his father's will overridden so that he could claim the entire inheritance. Even Jacques' sudden and premature demise did nothing to prevent this acrimonious litigation from continuing. The pursuit was taken up by his elder brother, Christopher, who had never previously shown any interest in the property but had followed a completely different career.

For many years Christopher had been employed in the service of the royal court of King Louis XV, first as a counsellor and later as the monarch's private secretary. He was a fluent linguist and particularly able in the German tongue, something which influenced him to change his name also, but in an entirely different manner and for quite different reasons from his brother Jacques. In 1756, Great Britain had declared war on France, and France had signed the first Treaty of Versailles, which created an alliance with Austria. As Christopher was involved in these negotiations, he wished to pre-empt any suspicions that his Scottish background might influence his impartiality, and so he simply changed his "Smith" to the more Germanic "Smidt".

Christopher was a well-educated man and went to great lengths in preparing his case. He was utterly determined to rid his family of Elisabeth Louis once and for all. In the course of his research, it dawned upon him that he might be able to call on the support of the Carthusian order of monks, who, on the face of it, might appear an unlikely ally.

Chateau Smith-Haut-Lafitte was liable to a tiny fee farm rent, a relic that had survived several centuries since the Carthusians had originally owned much of the land in the region. Christopher carefully scrutinised the small print in the conditions of the title document concerned and discovered a clause which stated that the land owner must be a fit and proper person. Cunningly he went to the Carthusians and persuaded them to enter into the action against his late father's mistress. There were three separate cases, in 1759, 1761 and 1762, before the issue was exhausted, and in every instance the action against the peasant woman failed.

From 1762 onwards, Elisabeth Louis' name ceases to appear in the local records, and it is believed that in later life she must have sold her interest to Christopher Smidt as the property then acquired the revised title Chateau Smidt Haut Lafitte.

Between 1793 and 1856 the chateau changed hands five times; in the last of these years it was purchased by an eminent Bordeaux personality, Sadi Duffour-Dubergier. He was a former mayor of that great city and, more notably, was president of the famous committee which made the 1855 classification of Bordeaux Grand Cru Classés, which stands to this day. Apart from the obvious example of Chateau Haut-Brion, none of the other leading Graves chateaux had been included in the classification, yet M. Sadi Duffour-Dubergier realised that there were several properties on elevated ground in the area that had the potential to produce great wines. Hence, following some determined enquiries, he was able to make a successful bid for what he hoped would become one of the great wine-producing chateaux. Sadly he was not to see his dream come to fruition, as he died in 1860,

R*uins of farm buildings where George Smith lived with Elisabeth Louis*

when he left the chateau to his nephew, Martin Sadi Duffour-Dubergier.

Thus began a golden era for the chateau, with a steady succession of awards and plaudits, which were given to a property which once more had problems with its name, as it was referred to variously as Domaine de Smith Haut-Lafitte, Le Chateau de Schmith and Chateau Schmith-Duffour. In 1876, the estate was awarded La Grande Médaille d'Or de la Société d'Agriculture de la Gironde for the best-kept vineyard in the whole Gironde department. This award was followed by many gold medals and diplomas at numerous significant European wine exhibitions of the time.

Naturally the Germanic style of Smidt, followed by Schmith, attracted encouraging demand for the chateau's red and white wines in much of northern and eastern Europe. This led in 1902 to an agreement between Martin Sadi Duffour-Dubergier and the leading Bordeaux *négociant*, Louis Eschenauer, under which the merchant, who had strong representation in the German markets, assumed responsibility for all exportation and distribution of the wines. Three years later, in 1905, the elderly owner sold the estate to a German company. He had owned the chateau for forty-six years, during which time he had developed its reputation as a wine chateau of international class. The new owner had the bilingual title Société Commerciale de Bordeaux Handelsgesellschaft, and had its head office in Bremen.

The chateau's German ownership was to last the short span of thirteen years, before it was confiscated by the French government at the end of the World War I in 1918. Later, in 1921, it was sold to a new, aristocratic owner, Mme Mathilde Germaine de Fontenilliat, wife of the Comte de Labry. Immediately upon possession, she restored its earlier name, Chateau Smith-Haut-Lafitte, which had been out of favour for nearly 130 years.

The succeeding thirty-seven years brought four further changes of ownership, but at least the management of the vineyard remained consistently in the hands of the Louis Eschenauer company, who had held the reins since 1914. In 1953 the leading chateaux of the Graves region were classified for the first time, and Chateau Smith-Haut-Lafitte was granted the distinction of Grand Cru Classé. In 1958 the Eschenauer company finally purchased the chateau with fortuitous timing, as the following year, 1959, brought a reclassification of the Graves vineyards, with Chateau Smith-Haut-Lafitte being reconfirmed as one of the finest in the official Graves Appellation Contrôlée region.

Afterwards there followed a rather dull period, when for many the wines failed to inspire, until in 1982, Jacques Théo, the colourful Président-Directeur-Général of Louis Eschenauer, commissioned the services of the legendary Professor Emile Peynaud as a consultant. The famous oenologist immediately introduced a new regime of disciplines, insisting that only the best of the vineyard's grapes should be selected to make the wine which bore the name Chateau Smith-Haut-Lafitte and from that wine only the best should be selected for bottling. This fairly drastic but typical Peynaud action very quickly brought a reduction of about 20 per cent in volume, and an increase in quality which soon became apparent to all. By the 1985 vintage, Professor Peynaud had taken great strides to restore the wine to the standards it had enjoyed in its golden era, in the latter half of the last century. Once more, Chateau Smith-Haut-Lafitte, as it was originally named by George Smith on 29 June 1720, is being acknowledged as a chateau which provides wines of finesse and character that deserve to be remembered, not just because of their commonplace name, but also because of their ageing potential and drinking quality.

14. FOR ANIMAL LOVERS

THE CHERUB AND THE COCKEREL
Chianti, Italy

For half a century the two Chianti *consorzios,* or growers' organisations, the Chianti Classico Consorzio and the Chianti Putto Consorzio, have lived and worked harmoniously with each other in the very heart of Tuscany. When asked how people of allegedly fiery temperament, who even sound out of sorts when they share everyday conversations, succeed in sharing the land so well, the wise old men of the Chianti hills recall a local legend.

Once upon a time, as all the best tales begin, the sun rose over the enchanting country of Italy, its rays warming two quite different scenes, one set in a farmyard near Genoa and one in a church in Naples. In the farmyard, a proud black cockerel blinked his eyes before providing the local community with its daily alarm call, while at the very same time, a diminutive cherub, in a small parish church overlooking the broad sweep of the Bay of Naples, rubbed the sleep from his eyes as he began to sing his first morning psalm. The musical notes of both rose through the early morning air, rousing all living creatures to greet the new day. Both of them, entirely unaware of the other's existence, gazed up at the bright blue sky and declared it the finest day of his life, and vowed to use it in an attempt to fulfil his dearest wish. Both, so it fell out, were lovers of the ruby red, and dreamed of owning the finest vineyards in all Italy.

Unfolding his wings and declaring that it was too hot in the south to grow the best grapes, the cherub set off from Naples on the long and arduous journey north. A cherub's life has its advantages. He was not the least bit lonely on his journey, as he called in to visit other cherubs as he flew from church to church, alighting on their spires for a brief rest and to exchange ecclesiastical gossip. In this delightful manner he continued for some days, until one morning he awoke with that curious feeling that this was going to be the day when he discovered his vineyard paradise.

Simultaneously, in his farmyard in the north, the cockerel strutted to and fro, crowing to himself and complaining that it was too cold near Genoa to grow the finest vines and he was going to fly south. He set off, fluttering from farmyard to farmyard, calling on other cockerels and hens en route. He too experienced the strange feeling that one sunny dawn that this was going to be his lucky day. He liked the look of the rolling hills and shimmering olive groves that stretched before him in the distance. The day was full of promise.

Flying north the cherub looked ahead into the morning sun and smiled with joy at the sight of the

rich green farms below. Occasionally he passed close by some cypress trees, followed by rows of beans and potatoes, and then he spotted vines for the first time. There were just a few, growing wild amid the fertile profusion, and in his fascination he drifted down to look more closely. Little did he know that at that very moment the black cockerel was about to land on the selfsame spot, and they collided with a bump.

They picked themselves up, shaking off the dust.

"I was here first," claimed the cherub, his dignity and his white feathers a trifle ruffled. "Be off with you!"

"No you were not!" crowed the cockerel. "Anyone could see that I was here first," he declared, puffing out his chest.

Soon an argument developed, which escalated into a fight. First the cockerel was gaining the upper wing, and then the cherub, and so the advantage swung back and forth for some time. Eventually they both collapsed from exhaustion and, somewhat breathlessly, looked each other in the eye and agreed to parley rather than fight.

"This is a beautiful land," observed the cherub.

"It looks the perfect spot for a vineyard," commented the cockerel. "Just look at these vines, so abundant with grapes. But that hill over there looks an even better spot. Why don't you have that instead?"

"No, no, that's alright," replied the cherub. "You have it. I don't mind. I'm too tired to fly any further. I'll stay here."

In no time at all they were quarrelling again, and their exchanges became more and more heated, until they were on the point of resorting once more to fighting. As they struggled to their feet, they glanced at each other and roared with laughter at the sight of their bedraggled feathers.

"You know, there are enough rolling hills hereabouts for both of us to have all the vineyards we want," said the cherub, and the cockerel nodded his comb in agreement. Accordingly they decided to toss a coin to see who would have first choice. The cockerel won and chose the first vineyard site, the cherub chose the second, and so on, until they had divided all the best vineyards between them.

So says the story, and today, many of the best winegrowers in the beautiful Chianti hills in the ancient land of Tuscany belong either to the cherub or the cockerel. For the cherub, or *Putto*, is the symbol or seal of approval of one of the two large associations, the Chianti Putto Consorzio. The other, the Chianti Classico Consorzio, uses the black cockerel, or *Gallo Nero*, to identify it. They no longer fight but live in harmony, with the majority of the vineyards shared between them. They produce some of the most delightful, lively,

fruity, young red wines in the world, and also some very fine, older, oak-aged *riservas*. The characteristics of the cherub and the cockerel can still be seen in the wine producers of Chianti; peaceful and gentle or fiery and colourful, and in similar terms one can describe their tasty red wines.

So next time you enjoy a bottle of Chianti, examine the neck label and see if it displays the *Gallo Nero* or the *Putto*. If it does not, then you know the producer must be descended from an unknown intruder who somehow sneaked into that vineyard paradise when neither the cockerel or the cherub was looking.

EYE OF THE PARTRIDGE
Almadén, USA

In the heyday of the popular American winemaking giant Almadén Vineyards, a wide assortment of sparkling wines were offered, some of which were not considered worthy of serious attention by wine buffs in general, who dismissed the pioneer winery as a provider of mass-produced, low-quality wines.

It was a regrettable assumption, which led to many consumers missing the opportunity to taste a few especially attractive wines, such as Almadén's Eye of the Partridge. This curiously named wine was largely an imitation of a wine style that was once particularly common in the French Champagne region. Its origin arose when early Champagne makers left red grape skins in contact with white juice for a little too long, with the result that the wine acquired a pinkish tinge, akin to the bloodshot impression given by the eye of that eminently edible game bird.

HORSE BUSINESS
Garvey Sherry, Spain

The attraction of breeding horses was the magnet that drew a young Irishman, William Garvey, to the Jerez region in 1780. The second son of the wealthy owner of Castle Annagh, near New Ross in Wexford, he came from a noble house that could trace its descent directly from the English King Edward I. The breeding of fine horses had always been of paramount importance on the family's Irish estate, and it was therefore only natural that William should learn of the lively interest in early stud-farming that was spreading throughout the Spanish province of Andalusia.

With the advantage of family capital behind him, William Garvey sailed to Cádiz and settled in Sanlúcar. There he steadily built a business which developed three main trends: horse breeding was his first priority, next came trading in sherry, and finally some shipping of dry goods. As his experience in wine grew, he began to direct his attention chiefly towards that, but all his business ventures blossomed.

William, though, nearly did not arrive, for his ship capsized at Puerto Real, only a couple of miles from Cádiz. His life, fortunately, was saved by Captain Gomez, a kind and hospitable man who took the totally unknown and somewhat drenched youth to his own home, hence triggering a completely unexpected romance. William Garvey fell in love with the captain's daughter, Sebastiana, and later married her. Before he did, however, he insisted on building a secure business, and the patient young woman had to wait twelve long years before their wedding.

William was able to buy hundreds of butts of sherry from other merchants to begin his own *soleras*, and as his small sherry house expanded, the ambitious young Irishman decided to erect the largest aboveground cellar in the region. He named it the San Patricia Bodega, after the patron saint of his native land, Saint Patrick. Visitors were

Garvey Cellars, Jerez, Spain

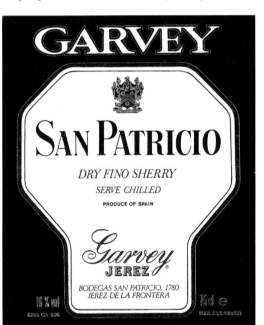

A cheque made out in 1791 in London as payment for a shipment of Garvey's Sherry

Vintage time in Garvey Vineyards, Jerez

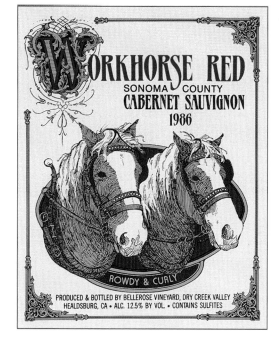

astounded at its size – 558 feet long by 126 feet wide – and some even compared it with a cathedral.

His religious beliefs and his Irish heritage resulted in his son being baptised Patrick. This son was the first sherry shipper to export a fino sherry, when in 1803 he shipped a wine called San Patricio which still maintains its early success.

IN MEMORIAM
Bellerose Vineyard, USA

When the *Washington Post* of 6 May 1988 reported the sudden and unexpected death of a beloved Californian wine figure, its obituary brought tears to the eyes of countless thousands who had either paid him a visit or who knew his proud figure from the wine labels of Bellerose Vineyard in Sonoma County. Ward Sinclair, an experienced staff writer

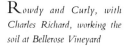

Rowdy and Curly, with Charles Richard, working the soil at Bellerose Vineyard

on the *Washington Post*, penned his account in an emotional yet factual style:

> There is no formal marker. Only a bare spot in the grass outside the corral indicates the grave where Curly, a muscular Belgian draughthorse, rests on this farm that gave him love and purpose. Curly died from injuries after he broke through a fence and tumbled down a hill into Dry Creek Road, where a passing neighbour found him in pain. Rowdy, the other Belgian in the farm work's tandem, cried all night, and Richard (his owner) moved a cot into the barn to sleep with him.

Usually the owner or winemaker is regarded as the star attraction at a Californian winery, but not at Charles and Nancy Richard's Bellerose Vineyard, where visitors see what are possibly the only full-time vineyard horses working in tandem in the USA. Since that sad equine tragedy, Rowdy has acquired a new partner called Chucky, and happiness has returned to the ploughing through the vines. Their regular tasks have changed little, as they tug mowers and other farm equipment, haul the freshly picked grapes to the crush house at the vintage, and even provide their manure for the soil. And there is a particular item that one hopes will never change – the label of Workhorse Red, a fruity bargain of a wine – for it still displays Curly's fine head in partnership with Rowdy, which is how his old friends will always remember him.

THE LIONS OF FONTAINEBLEAU
San Saba Vineyards, USA

The marriage of fine art and the wine label is one to be encouraged, and has received much stimulus

from the New World, and California in particular. Some paintings are commissioned, others purchased and a few reproduced by permission of their owners. The San Saba Cabernet Sauvignon label, from Soledas, in the Monterey region of California, is unusual in that it is the reproduction of a prized painting belonging to the winery owner.

The Lions, an 1865 work by Rosa Bonheur, was acquired by Mark Leonard Lemmon for two related reasons, both of them involving his names. In the first instance, the lion is the symbol of St Mark, and also, Lemmon's second name, Leonard, is derived from lion-hard, or possibly lion-heart. The painting is a classic example of animal art from one of the most successful women artists of the 19th century. History records Rosa Bonheur as one of the most sympathetic painters of live animals, and the first French woman to be granted the country's most distinguished award, the *Legion d'Honneur*.

Mademoiselle Bonheur, the daughter of a struggling Bordelaise art teacher, would no doubt have appreciated her painting being displayed on a Cabernet Sauvignon much more than she enjoyed the use of her feminine title. From an early age, she preferred to dress as a man, and spent much of her adult life living at Chateau de By, near the historic Chateau de Fontainebleau, which home she shared with her long-time companion, Nathalie Micas. There they maintained an unruly private zoo, which included everything from her favourite subject, horses, to the lions believed to be the subject of this label. The zoo also included wild boars, an otter which slept in one of the beds, an eagle, and numerous other birds of prey.

THE MAN ON A HORSE
Heggies Vineyard, Australia

Those who have enjoyed the Australian wine Heggies Vineyard will be familiar with the representation on the label of the shadowy figure of a

man on a horse. Behind that sketch lies the uncomplicated tale of a certain archetypal Australian, a rugged outdoors sort, a man who in his earlier years was a hardy adventurer and wanderer, but who later in life acquired some land and settled down to a more stable existence.

His name was Colin "Oscar" Heggie, and he was born at the turn of the century into a family of colourful characters, and developed into one of its most extrovert members. He was a man of decision and confirmed opinions and not one to suffer fools gladly, although on one occasion he may have done just that.

He originally earned his living by setting out on horseback into the Australian outback to visit a number of small towns and settlements. From these he would collect files of chained prisoners, who were tied to his horse by knotted rope, and take them down to Adelaide for sentencing. In the particular instance with which we are concerned, he camped overnight in the Flinders Range with a group of men who, throughout their three-week trek, had constantly protested their innocence. Gradually, Heggie had become convinced that these men were the victims of a major injustice and decided not to deliver them to the Adelaide court. To their amazement he set them all free, and afterwards, it seems, continued on his way to the state capital, where he reported that the prisoners had escaped. It was alleged, many years later, that he actually said that he considered that: "They were hard done by and deserved another chance." Whether he still received his pay remains unknown.

Later he settled down to a more peaceful life as a farmer, on land near Angaston, in the Eden Valley, and here he continued to virtually live in

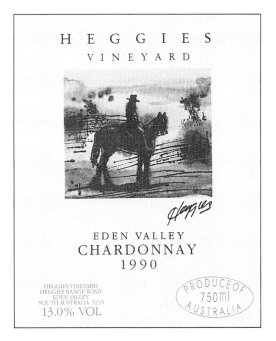

the saddle. In this manner he became a patron of the Valley Hotel in the little hillside town. On warm dusty evenings he would ride into town, seeking to quench his thirst. He did not just ride into town, however, but into the pub and into the bar, where he would often allow his horse one drink of beer only, while he indulged himself more liberally. His philosophy in adopting this eccentric behaviour was, it has been reported, that if he stayed in the saddle his horse would find the way home at closing time.

As he advanced in years, Heggie became even more eccentric, and was said to have always kept a twelve-bore shotgun to hand in case any intruders should break into his somewhat isolated home. On one evening during the run-up to the Australian general election of 1977, he turned on his television set to see the then Leader of the Opposition, Gough Whitlam, making a campaign speech. So intense was his hatred of Mr Whitlam and his politics that in a moment of fury Heggie picked up his shotgun and let the oblivious politician have both barrels flush in the face. The television instantly exploded, splattering fragments around the room and peppering the walls with buckshot. It was no doubt a sentiment that many of us have wished to express in a similar manner at some time in our lives but have never had the courage to commit.

When in the 1980s Heggie died, his successors sold some 300 acres of his land to the nearby Yalumba winery, who planted it as a vineyard. They decided, quite rightly, that the estate should continue to bear his name, and his memorable life should be recalled by the drawing on the label, depicting Colin Heggie astride his much-loved chestnut Jack. If as the vines mature they follow his unique character, we can be sure that they will be the embodiment of life and vigour, and will never be lacking in flavour.

THE TERROR OF TUCHAN
Terroir de Tuchan, France

The French word *terroir* is not simple to translate. Its meaning embraces more than just land; it includes the soil, the lie of the land, the atmosphere, the environment and locality. It is a word that has been adopted for the label of a particularly appealing Fitou from the highly successful coopera-

tive les Producteurs de Mont Tauch, in the Corbières region of southern France. The wine is a robust, mouth-filling red which has a substantial following in Great Britain. It is produced from an unusual blend of Syrah and Carignan Noir, and aged in new oak for twelve months, under the careful control of the ambitious cooperative director, Marc Guinebault.

The reason I refer to the wine as "terror" rather than *terroir* can be seen by carefully examining the top of the label. Beneath the single "T" is the head of a *sanglier*, or wild boar. This was brought to my attention during a 1993 visit to Fitou, when Marc Guinebault drove me to inspect various parts of the vineyard. At one point we left the car to walk among the vines, and as we approached one large parcel, he suddenly warned me not to advance any further because of what resembled a small tripwire.

"It is an electric fence to keep the *sangliers* out," he explained.

"Do they eat grapes?" I asked in all innocence.

"In that forest," he declared, pointing out an area that started less than 50 yards away, "is the largest natural reserve of *sangliers* in France, and the pigs so love the *terroir* of our vineyards that they like to come into them to have a roll in the earth. So we have this electric fence to protect the vines from them."

Being a clumsy individual, reluctant to tangle with anything electrical, especially when it is a bare wire, and also knowing of the vicious aggressiveness of the wild boar, I promptly turned back to the car, and indicated my readiness to accept a promised visit to a local restaurant where we could drink the "Terror of Tuchan" in peace.

15. FRAGMENTS OF HISTORY

THE BARON'S MISSING BODY
Offley Forrester, Portugal

The influence of gold in the histories of prominent wineries is not confined to California. In Portugal, a country where wine has been made for around 2 000 years, gold was the kiss of death to one major figure, a man who is rightly judged to be one of the most important personalities in the development of the port-wine trade. He was Baron Joseph James Forrester, a partner in the Porto house Offley Forrester, and one of the legendary names among the unique British community that became so powerful in Portugal during the 19th century.

The Baron's map-work, prepared while charting the length of the River Douro, brought him recognition as the leading expert on what was, in those days, an extremely treacherous waterway, a fact which made his dramatic end all the more ironic, for surprisingly the Baron met his death by drowning, in the river with which he was so familiar, on 12 May 1861, at the age of fifty-one.

Indeed, the circumstances surrounding his death were so strange that one only wishes that Agatha Christie's Miss Marple could have carried out an investigation. The Baron, who presumably knew and selected the most reliable of boatmen, had been partaking in a generous lunch at Quinta de Vesuvio as a guest of the legendary Doña Antonia Ferreira, head of the largest Portuguese-owned port house, and her husband, Francisco José da Silva Torres. It had long been rumoured that a relationship had developed between the Baron and Dona Antonia. She was a formidable lady who, through her own enterprise, had become the largest single landowner in the region. Her first husband had died many years previously and her second marriage appears not to have been harmonious, since Francisco José did not share her ambitious nature. On the other hand, the Baron

Forrester was a man of considerable talent, who displayed prowess in subjects as diverse as fine art, anthropology, the mastery of numerous languages, the commerce of the port-wine trade, and a great understanding of the wider Portuguese economy.

After luncheon the entire party of sixteen boarded a *barco rabelo*. This wooden boat was of a style unique to the Douro, specially designed with a high platform to allow the tillerman to see over the rapids and thus steer a safe course.

On this occasion, a few miles downstream, as the boat entered the Cachao rapids it hit some rocks and capsized, throwing its occupants into the river. How this came about is a mystery but, in my opinion, the account of an anonymous Douro farmer may well provide the answer. He relates that as the *barco rabelo* entered the Cachao rapids, a fight broke out between the Baron and da Silva Torres. Their struggle caused the tillerman to lose his balance, and the boat veered sideways and capsized. Three, including the Baron, were drowned. The ladies, thanks to their crinolines, floated gently away and survived to tell the tale, but the not-so-poor old Baron was said to have been dragged under the water by the combined weight of his mony belt and the high leather boots he sported. The money belt, which was strapped around his waist, was, according to popular theory, packed full of gold sovereigns, the payment due to some local farmers.

As the Cachao rapids are in an isolated position, some distance from the nearest road, it was some time before the alarm was raised, and when help finally arrived the light was already too dim for any proper search to be instigated. On the following day the bodies of a man and a woman were found, but of the Baron not a trace. Mysteriously, however, it was four days before news of the Baron's death was published in the national press, despite the proximity of telegraphic equipment in the little town of Pinhao. Presumably the search for him continued with the remote hope of his still being found alive.

Neither the Baron nor his treasure were ever recovered, and even today, if you dare enquire of local historians about the event, it is always dismissed as a greatly exaggerated piece of history. So what did happen to the Baron? All that can be reported is that a generation ago, when the angry river was converted, by means of damming, into a tranquil lake, no trace was found of the Baron's boat or that belt of gold, and more than one speculator has looked in hope.

The Douro farmer who relates the episode concerning the capsizing of the *barco rabelo* also has this intriguing information to impart. A troupe of gipsies were working on a new railway bridge in Pinhao at the time of the disaster, and quite by chance some of them happened upon the Baron's corpse. So much gold would be a temptation to most, so they removed the money belt and hid the Baron's body in the structure of the bridge, not a particularly dignified end, and perhaps one of the reasons for the deliberately vague accounts of Forrester's death circulated by the close-knit British community of Oporto at the time. He was recognised by them as their natural leader and any official recognition of impropriety on his behalf would have brought disrepute upon them all. To understand this premise, one has to realise that even today the British in Oporto have not only their own association, church and cemetery, and high society, but even their own cricket field, which is the most southerly grassed pitch of its kind in the Northern Hemisphere.

The railway bridge at Pinhao – burial place of Baron Forrester?

Whatever the truth surrounding the circumstances of the Baron's death, there will always be room for surmise. Visitors to the Douro valley may be curious to see the place where the Baron reputedly drowned and decide for themselves what might have happened. In any event, the Porto house of Offley Forrester continues to flourish, and the liquid refreshment offered there probably makes for a more rewarding visit.

CHURCHILL'S CHAMPAGNE
Pol Roger, France

In 1944, when the Allies were pushing north and Paris had been liberated, there was great cause for rejoicing, even if Parisian gourmet produce was in short supply. One can imagine the scene of excitement, tempered with consternation, at the British Embassy at 35 rue du Faubourg-Saint-Honoré, when the distinguished ambassador Sir Duff Cooper informed his recently returned staff that they were to receive a visit from the British Prime Minister. In four wartime years, Winston Churchill had become a living legend, and his coming now had the twofold purpose of showing gratitude to those who had performed historically and to boost morale. There would be the matter of the guest list for the official banquet dinner to be considered, and the pleasant but exacting task of which deserving individuals should be invited.

One of those who received an invitation was a beautiful blonde woman who had been risking her life as a courier in the French Resistance; her name was Odette Pol-Roger. Accompanied by her husband, Jacques Pol-Roger, she quickly caught the eye of the British premier, who was fascinated to learn of her daring exploits. His interest was heightened by the fact that he had long been a lover of the finest Champagne, and a customer of Champagne Pol Roger, among others. From that moment onwards, the other Champagnes faded into the background as he became a devotee of the house and a personal friend of its owners.

Thus began a warm relationship between the Churchill and Pol-Roger families, which continues to this day. Sir Winston, when in his prime, would amuse the Pol-Rogers by calling their cellars at 44 Avenue de Champagne, Epernay, "the most drinkable address" in the world.

One of the strangest anecdotes concerning the two families involves a medium – not a psychic medium, but an old bottle size of that name, which contained an amount halfway between a standard-size bottle and a half bottle. Churchill, as a *bon viveur*, had a remarkable capacity, which he even indulged at breakfast time, a custom which often worried his wife. This led to him changing his ordering habits with Pol Roger and, in response, to a query from them. Churchill is said to have explained that he wanted to have his Champagne in the old measure of medium or imperial pints, a bottle size no longer in use:

When I drink from a bottle, I'm happy, when I drink from a half-bottle, I'm not happy but Clementine is happy, but to make us both happy I will drink imperial pints.

The great statesman preferred the single-vintage style of Champagne, which is less seen these days. He was especially fond of the fullest of wines, and liked his Pol Roger with plenty of bottle age.

In 1952, Jacques Pol-Roger sent Winston Churchill, then serving as a peacetime prime minister for the very first time, a sample of the superb 1947 vintage, with the advice that it would age exceptionally well for many years. Churchill, who was then seventy-eight, was so impressed that he purchased sufficient to last him through the remaining thirteen years of his life.

Churchill even named one of his racehorses Pol Roger, and would always advise Odette Pol-Roger of its performances. This resulted in one of the most treasured Pol Roger souvenirs, a personal telegram sent to Odette at her private address in Paris. It was after the victory of the filly in the Black Prince Stakes Handicap at Kempton Park on 3 June 1953, the day of Queen Elizabeth's coronation. The telegram read:

> Pol Roger won splendidly today, so there is a small profit for you on both races, best love, Winston.

The great leader always placed a small sum for Odette on every appearance of Pol Roger, and the horse had succeeded in winning its last two races.

Possibly the most highly prized memento of Churchill owned by the Pol-Roger family is a volume of his war memoirs, which succeeded in winning him the Nobel Prize for Literature. A copy was sent to Odette Pol-Roger inscribed "Cuvée de Réserve/Mise en Bouteille/au Château Chartwell". It is fitting that Chartwell, Churchill's lovely country residence, is maintained by the National Trust, a British charity, and there, on display, is an imperial pint of Pol Roger 1928, one of his favourite vintages. Also, many visitors to London are curious to stroll through the Churchill War Rooms, immediately behind Whitehall, the site from which he would conduct operations when the capital was under attack. There, for all to see, are the 1928 and 1934 vintages, many examples of which he is believed to have consumed during Britain's darkest hours.

Churchill became such an enthusiast for Pol Roger Champagne that he often went to consider-

Winston Churchill, MP (left), and Christian Pol-Roger, Directeur Général of Pol Roger Champagne, toast the success of the Cuvée Sir Winston Churchill 1982 Vintage beneath a portrait of the great statesman at his former home, Chartwell

able lengths to ensure that his favourite wine was served. On one occasion, he was due to travel to the Council of Europe in Strasbourg, and felt that he should be seen only to drink Pol Roger in that historic French city. "Well ahead of time," Christian de Billy, joint Pol Roger managing director, said, "we got an order to have his Champagne on the table. He always liked to drink his Pol Roger when travelling."

In 1965, when Sir Winston Churchill died, aged ninety-one, he had completed the fullest of lives, with writer, journalist, artist, bricklayer, landscape gardener, historian, politician and gourmet being some of his most successful roles. No-one could be too sad at the passing of an extremely elderly Christian man at the end of such a span, but his friends at Champagne Pol Roger felt the need to make some gesture to salute their dearest customer. To mark their sentiments, Odette Pol-Roger, a widow herself by that time, gave instructions that the house should place a black border around its labels as a sign of mourning. That sign still remains on Pol Roger White Foil, the house's non-vintage style. Why, one may ask? Because perhaps there is a scant chance of ever having so great a man as a customer and friend again.

But that was not the only gesture that Pol Roger made of their respect and affection for Sir Winston. As recently as 1984, at Blenheim Palace, ancestral home of the Churchill family and the birthplace of Sir Winston, Pol Roger launched their new luxury style of Champagne – the Sir Winston Churchill Special Cuvée. It was served in magnums of the delicious 1975 vintage, and blended to provide the

fullness Churchill so much adored. It was a fitting tribute to his palate, and there to share it with a select gathering of British wine personalities was the courageous lady who had instigated this longstanding friendship by charming the British Prime Minister with the tales of her adventurous exploits in 1944 – none other than the elderly Madame Odette Pol-Roger.

NAPOLEON COGNAC: THE TRUTH
Courvoisier, France

One of the most amusing paradoxes of life is that the *nouveaux riches* are those in society who, above all, desire to impress. Some may regard a particular car as the essential status symbol, while for others, an overgenerous sprinkling of a celebrated brand of French perfume as the fragrance of this and every day is, they think, the hallmark of their wealth and style. Numerous examples of such easily recognisable characters and their just as recognisable behaviour will spring to the minds of readers everywhere.

But nowadays, make no mistake, there is in this society a growing substratum of people who cannot quite be identified as *nouveaux riches*, but can be considered apprentices, or even unfairly labelled as yuppies, although this is perhaps too general a term. I call these who are serving their apprenticeship for inclusion in the ranks of the *nouveaux riches*, the "napoleons". They are the advertising agent's dream, impressionable and determined to make an impression, often without a great deal of forethought. If the napoleons observe someone whom they consider the epitome of success displaying an item that bears a brand name, then they instantly presume that the brand demonstrates one's prosperity, and superior taste and judgement.

Sports clothing is an example which readily presents itself. A quick visit to any sports centre will confirm my theory; you will see napoleons arriving all the time. The bag has to be right, the shoes must bear a favoured name, and the shirts – they are almost a subculture in themselves.

Perhaps no item paints the picture more clearly than wine and drink, where snobbery and pretence can be painfully evident. Take Champagne, for instance, and one particular luxury brand immediately comes to mind. It is conceived by so many who know little or nothing about Champagne, but plenty about publicity and about motor-racing winners who spray the stuff liberally in all directions, that that is the brand one should be seen drinking. Yet it is notable that seldom in my experience have I noticed any expert drinking it by choice.

Posing with Champagne is one thing, but namedropping with brandy is another. This conduct

identifies a napoleon best of all, because a Napoleon Brandy or Cognac is seen by some of these characters as the ultimate status symbol of the drinks world, a perception which has encouraged the purchase of hundreds of thousands of bottles which somehow or other manage to bear the little emperor's name. Frequently the association of the name Napoleon is nothing short of a commercial lie, and in many cases is totally misleading. On the other hand, in some instances it is a generously named Cognac category that has developed over the last two centuries.

With one swift blow we can eliminate any Napoleon Brandy other than Cognac, since there is simply no evidence that the French emperor ever purchased, acquired or consumed any brandy other than Cognac itself. For any other product to borrow his name is utterly without justification. Yet an assortment of Napoleon brandies can be found on the silver trays and cocktail cabinets of those who aspire to good taste in countries all over the world.

Upon closer examination Napoleon Brandy can be seen to fall into three distinct categories:

1. Cognac produced during the reign of Napoleon and which occasionally reaches the auction rooms of Christie's and Sotheby's. One should be able to accept the word of these venerable houses that the dates concerned are authentic, and that the bottle contents are genuine Cognac. But careful observation will note that nothing further is claimed.

2. Many Cognac houses who cannot prove any connection with the little Corsican use the term Napoleon to describe a blend which is more mature and of better quality than their VSOP.

3. Quite alone stands the House of Courvoisier and its Napoleon style, for the Jarnac-based company is the factual source of the legend.

A Cognac cooper plying his trade for Courvoisier

The relationship between Emmanuel Courvoisier and Napoleon Bonaparte probably began in 1810, or even a year or two earlier. Courvoisier and his partner, Etienne Gallois, a minor politician, ran a substantial wine business at Bercy on the right bank of the River Seine and only a brief carriage ride from the Tuileries. From their 6 kilometres of underground caves, to this day the most extensive in Paris, they supplied the emperor with his wines.

For Napoleon, those caves became literally a treasure store, as he filled them with wagonloads of liquid bounty, the spoils of war seized by him, his relatives and his army as his power and empire expanded. As late as 1985, rare vintage sherries which had been seized in Spain remained in the Napoleon Cellar, for many years part of the main Paris cellars of the noted French wine merchants Nicolas.

The exact date on which Napoleon first moved his stock into these premises cannot be established, but the date on which a suitable and secure cellar became a pressing issue to him most certainly can. On 10 February 1811, he called upon his wine and Cognac supplier to request a favour. Naturally it was not difficult for the two men to reach an agreement. A pre-eminent condition of the arrangement was confidentiality and, as far as it is known, that has always been observed. After all, put yourself in Napoleon's place. Would you want all your leading supporters to know the exact whereabouts of your personal share of the spoils, when you were the first politician ever to inflict a liquor tax on the French people? The tax was introduced in 1804 and was not a popular move with the French public.

And so it came about that one section of the Courvoisier et Gallois cellars at Bercy was designated the emperor's cellar and, quite understandably, from that point onwards an intimacy between Emmanuel Courvoisier and the ambitious Corsican developed.

In the meantime, Courvoisier's partner, Etienne Gallois, began to devote an increasing amount of his time to Parisian politics, while Emmanuel Courvoisier decided to concentrate more on the developing market in Cognac. In due course he made his most important decision – to acquire some cellars in the little town of Jarnac, in the Cognac region, and take personal control of the new operation. Tirelessly, Emmanuel scoured the Charentes for fine, aged Cognacs that he could blend to carry the Courvoisier and Gallois name. It was not long before he realised the enormous potential market for Cognac and reached an agreement with Etienne Gallois, which allowed the latter to become a full-time politician while the

Napoleon Bonaparte, an early customer of Courvoisier

newly named house of Courvoisier maximised its trade in Cognac.

Matters moved as rapidly at this stage for Emmanuel Courvoisier as they did for Napoleon Bonaparte. In the short space of four years, Courvoisier had become well-established in Jarnac and his Cognac trade, in all likelihood, was exceeding even his greatest expectations. By contrast, the emperor, who had remained his most important customer, had suffered a series of major setbacks, including the infamous episode at Moscow, and had been subsequently exiled to Elba, with, it must be said, an annual pension of 2 million francs – more than enough to allow him a little of his favourite Cognac. The year 1815 was clearly the most significant in the story of Napoleon's downfall, and is the one which has the most bearing on the explanation of the truth behind the expressions "the Cognac of Napoleon" or "the brandy of Napoleon".

After his defeat by Wellington at Waterloo, Napoleon abdicated and Louis XVIII, France's last

George Wyndham (1801-1870), early Hunter Valley vintner who planted what were to become "the oldest wine-producing vines of all"

monarch, returned. With the knowledge that the Allies wanted to arrest him, the Corsican decided it was time to leave. Finally quitting Paris, he fled west to the little Aquitaine port of Fouras, which today lies within the official Appellation Contrôlée region for Cognac. In accordance with his advance instructions, his faithful supporters had been preparing two ships there, Napoleon's intention, which is well-recorded, being to slip quietly away to America. Among the cargo, he had arranged for the supply of two casks of the finest Cognac from his merchant, Emmanuel Courvoisier.

Unfortunately for Napoleon, his plans were discovered at the last minute and he was forced to surrender to the British officers of HMS *Bellerophon*. Understandably, they ransacked the provisions already stored on board his ships and helped themselves to the most attractive items. These included the two casks of Courvoisier Cognac, which they then used to celebrate in their officers' mess, where they were heard to boast of drinking the brandy of Napoleon, a story they were no doubt happy to repeat for the rest of their days. In the meantime, Napoleon was taken to his final exile in St Helena where, sadly, he was destined never to enjoy another drop of his favourite liquor.

In all probability, the exact expression used by the British officers was "the brandy of Napoleon" rather than "Cognac", as at that time the drink was not bottled and labelled as it is today, and the word Cognac was not in use with its current commercial impact. In fact, the advertising of the House of Courvoisier earlier this century referred to brandy rather than Cognac. On the other hand, it is perfectly fair and proper for them to use the expression "the Cognac of Napoleon", for that is what it was.

And so the next time you see a napoleon displaying his ignorance and crudely advertising his liquid money as he pontificates about Napoleon Cognac or Brandy, just take a quick glance to see if he has chosen the correct brand.

THE OLDEST VINES OF THEM ALL
Wyndham Estate, Australia

If there was a *Guinness Book of Records* entry for the oldest wine-producing vines, then pride of place would surely go to some Shiraz vines on the Wyndham Estate, in the Hunter Valley of New South Wales. In the late 1950s, some of these vines, believed to have been planted there in 1828, produced their last wine. They grew from 600 cuttings originally sold to George Wyndham by the Australian pioneer viticulturist James Busby. Busby, one of the earliest viticultural writers, had

planted the first Hunter Valley vineyard at his property, Kirkton, three years earlier, in 1825, and he was keen to encourage other growers. Unfortunately, Wyndham's first attempt to produce wine from the Busby vines, in 1831, proved disastrous, with the frustrated Englishman recording that they "promised to make good vinegar".

George Wyndham was a member of the English landed gentry, a refined British aristocrat of the type that was, and still is, bred in the shires. He was born "with a silver spoon in his mouth", the third son of William and Laetitia Wyndham, on their ample country estate, Dinton, near Salisbury, in the county of Wiltshire. If he had so desired, he need never have expended any energy. Yet he developed into a man of enterprise, individuality and determination. The family line descended from the an earlier Duke of Norfolk, and he spent the majority of his formative years screened from the real world by the upper-class society to which he belonged by birth. He was educated at Harrow and Cambridge, and there were plans for him to enter the Church of England, which may well not have been his own choice, for in 1824, when he was expected to take orders, he emigrated to Canada, where he travelled extensively with the novelist John Galt.

For reasons unknown, Wyndham failed to settle in Canada and made the return journey in the spring of the following year. Later, in 1825, he set out on the Grand Tour, a continental experience recommended at the time to all young gentlemen of sufficient standing and means, and which involved visiting the great and ancient cities of many European countries. George Wyndham took advantage of this journey to spend some time in certain French vineyard regions and, with his background, introductions to leading chateaux and *négociants* would not have posed any difficulty.

From France, he travelled south to observe the art and architecture of the various Italian states and dukedoms, and while there fell in love with Margaret Jay, a Dutch citizen of Huguenot descent, whom he married in her home city, Brussels, early in 1827. Their joint wanderlust was sufficiently powerful for George to decline an offer to settle in England in an official position with the British government, and the couple speedily but carefully planned their voyage to New South Wales, where George intended to farm. In fact, when they departed on board the 440-ton SS *George Horne* on 17 August of that same year, George even took his own Southdown sheep with him. Little further detail survives of their emigration, other than that they arrived in Sydney on Boxing Day.

After a perfunctory survey of the agricultural potential around Sydney, George and his young wife travelled inland to the newly developing area of the Hunter Valley, which was in its infancy as a wine-producing and coalmining region. In the latter half of 1828 he purchased a property of some 2 000 acres known as Annandale, which had been settled for a very few years by a man called David Maziere. George renamed it Dalwood, after a portion of his family's Wiltshire estate. He immediately hired labour and planted vines, bought from James Busby, in addition to peach, lemon, loquat, olive, fig, quince, and pomegranate trees. In 1830 he completed and moved into Dalwood House, and added a further 960 acres, called Terrace Hill, to his estate. Apart from the above-mentioned crops, he also planted maize, wheat, hemp, mustard, castor-oil plants, tobacco, millet, and Cape barley.

Yet, despite such an extensive list, his overriding interest still seemed to be his vines. In 1832 his second vintage was a success, and in 1836 he pressed some 7 425 litres of wine. His experience in the vineyards of France continued to be his guiding light, and he studied his vineyards and their problems with care. He transferred his allegiance from Busby to another noted Australian viticultural pioneer, John Macarthur, and purchased sufficient cuttings from the latter to extend his vineyard to some 65 acres.

Dalwood wines, as they were named, gradually earned both a national and international reputation. Cellars for their sale and distribution were opened in Macquarie Street in Sydney, not far from the current position of the imposing Ritz-Carlton Hotel. Wyndham also entered his wines in competitions in various countries, winning a cluster of medals, a tradition continued by his son (who won a much-admired gold in Paris in 1882), and by his successors. He was not the first man to plant vines in the Hunter Valley, an honour which the eminent Dr Norrie tells us belongs to James Busby. In spite of that, George Wyndham ranks as one of the ambitious founding fathers of the Hunter Valley, and as the man who planted the vines which became" the oldest wine producing vines of all", even if he will never be aware of the latter honour.

PRIEST'S PORT
Croft; UK and Portugal

The House of Croft is one of those classic English names that has been able to succeed jointly as a producer of port and of sherry. Indeed, its single-vintage ports have a long and healthy reputation, as does its more modern Late-Bottled Vintage style. In addition, its Pale Cream Sherry was the original of that type, as it correctly claims on its label. Essentially, Croft has a much longer-established history with port than with sherry, having commenced with the latter as late as 1970, hence my concentration on the house's dealings in Portugal.

In the early days of the first British-owned port houses, in the 17th and 18th centuries, the houses were not property owners, farmers or winemakers of any kind, but usually purchased their stocks from local producers and concentrated on shipping it. Normally the houses would operate as partnerships and, as new partners arrived and old partners left, there were frequent changes of trading titles. In the story of Croft, the original partnership, founded in 1678, was known as Phayre and Bradley, but by 1736, when the first John Croft joined the business, the title had changed to Tilden, Thompson and Croft, and there was little to record of any interest.

WYNDHAM ESTATE

BIN 222

SOUTH EASTERN AUSTRALIA
CHARDONNAY
1992

PRODUCED BY WYNDHAM ESTATE WINES, DALWOOD, HUNTER VALLEY, N.S.W. 2335 AUSTRALIA.

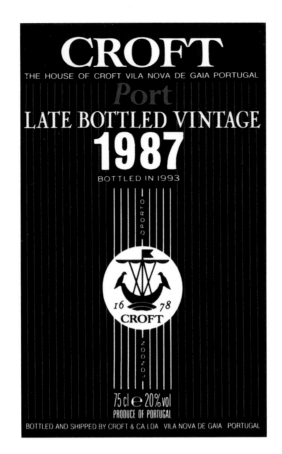

It was the birth of the second John Croft in 1732, in the medieval English city of York, that saw the arrival of the outstanding personality of the house. The Crofts were prosperous food and wine merchants who had a manifest interest in local affairs, and John Croft developed these qualities further. In his long life, the second John Croft demonstrated considerable stamina as he travelled back and forth between York and Oporto, following two or more occupations, as he continued his interests in York while pursuing his career as a shipper in Portugal. For quite some time he also held the office of Sheriff of York, which required his regular attendance at York Assizes. In addition, he became a noted collector of antiques and curios, of sufficient standing to be listed in the *Dictionary of National Biography*. He made two significant contributions to the story of port, namely the publication in 1788 of his *Treatise on the Wines of Portugal*, and his treasurership of the British Factors from 1786 to 1790, during the period when the historic Factory House was built. By a strange quirk of tradition the treasurer of that august organisation is also the presiding officer.

In his book, John Croft made one particularly illuminating remark, which will amuse any members of the clergy who happen to read this, but which may prove to have more bearing on the history of the development of port as a fortified wine. He referred to "Priest's Port", explaining that it was "stouter and stronger than common and very fashionable in England". His comments may have captured a turning point in the history of the wine.

When British shippers first started buying and selling port, it was not a fortified wine but a middleweight table wine that was probably no more than 11 per cent alcohol by volume. In fact it was another three years after the publication of Croft's book that the first vintage port was shipped by the first George Sandeman. Then gradually, and no-one has been able to pinpoint a specific date, port changed from being a table wine into one that was shipped as fortified wine. It appears likely that some of the monasteries in the Douro were the first to add brandy to the wine they sold, to help stabilise it for the fluctuating travelling conditions it would undertake. It may well be that the celebrated monastery at Lamego was the first to adopt this practice, though this is difficult to substantiate. In essence, Croft's first mention of "Priest's Port" may well indicate the origins of fortification rather than the partiality of the priesthood for a regular glass of port, as some have suggested.

For this reference, and for much else in his *Treatise*, we must thank John Croft, but he will be remembered chiefly for building the reputation of port in Britain, a reputation from which all port lovers and shippers have benefited.

REDMAN, RED SOIL, RED WINE
Coonawarra, Australia

Driving through Coonawarra reminds me oddly enough of driving down the Strip in Las Vegas. I am sure that analogy will bemuse most of the local wine fraternity unless they too have cruised down Nevada's fabled neon road. Las Vegas is brassy and vulgar, much busier and considerably noisier than Coonawarra, which by contrast is rural, a mere fraction of the size of Las Vegas, and more peaceful, as suits its aboriginal name meaning wild honeysuckle. Nevertheless, the two remind me of each other.

When you drive through Las Vegas, the dazzling names of the greedy casinos zip past your eyes on almost every corner, advertising some cut-price temptation to stop and enter their doors. Similarly, driving through Coonawarra, the road is virtually as straight, and the wooden winery signs flash past at regular intervals on either side, also tempting you with their tasty wares and inducing you to pay a visit and spend your hard-earned money. The one major difference is that every sensible investor is likely to leave Coonawarra with something material to show for the visit.

Coonawarra is also, in many ways, a micro-sized Australian version of the Médoc, where in the space of a couple of miles you can visit many of Australia's finest red wine growths. Heading south along the narrow road, you soon see those recognisable names that make a serious wine lover want to stop at every corner: Redman, Brands Laira, Rouge Homme, with a sign to Wynns tucked just behind it on your right, and Ridge, Mildara and Jamieson's Run on the left. Next you come to the names of the smaller properties that promise the region a great future, like Leconfield, Haselgrove, Hollick, and Bowen, and set back a little, the pretty Balnaves winery. Finally, as one approaches sleepy Penola, there is a small sign that bears the name that may yet attract most fame to Coonawarra – Parker.

The story of Coonawarra contains one peculiar coincidence, the recurrence of the letter R, which has appeared time and time again as the region's reputation has grown. Riddoch, Redman, red soil and red wine are the four best-known uses of that letter. Yet the history of Coonawarra as a wine region began with a W – William Wilson – and started in a large Scottish greenhouse. It was in the County of Fife, in the late 1830s, when a young gardener noticed the growth of a healthy grapevine which, when protected from the extremes of the weather, produced dessert grapes in abundance. It was a time when it was said that every mansion in Scotland worth its salt displayed the most impressive vine possible, and no doubt William Wilson saw similar vines and heard the comments of fellow gardeners about the normal cultivation of vines in suitable climates. Wilson, fortunately, was infected with a little wanderlust, and signed six years of his life away to the service of the Black Watch, the legendary Highland regiment. To his gratification, this commitment saw him pass the entire period in the Mediterranean and much of it in the Greek islands. There, with his horticultural background, he observed viticultural practices with considerable interest.

When his term with the regiment concluded he returned to Scotland briefly but, having become acclimatised to warmer weather, he decided to emigrate to Australia and seek his fortune, which he did a little later.

Arriving in South Australia in 1850, he quickly became engulfed in the gold-rush fever that gripped the continent in the following couple of years. After various trials and tribulations, he made £300 profit, with which he set out for Penola, one of the few established communities in South Australia, and purchased a 1-acre block just above the town. He selected a site upon a strip of rich red soil, known as *terra rossa*, which lay above a limestone strata, and there he planted his perfect garden, which included a small parcel of vines. William Wilson's acre became a beauty to behold and soon

enjoyed pride of place in the neighbourhood.

It was no coincidence that a newspaper account in 1890 described his pride and joy in glowing terms:

> In the town of Penola an old Scotsman, Mr Wilson, who told us he had been a resident of Penola for forty years, has an acre of orchard and garden which is worth a long journey to see. I do not think I have seen a more productive spot, not even in the irrigated gardens of Spain.

The success of William Wilson was well-known to John Riddoch, a fellow Scot who had become the self-styled Squire of Penola, and in that very same year the region's most prominent gentleman called upon the humble gardener for his advice.

Riddoch, who hailed from Banffshire, had also made his fortune in the goldfields, but as a merchant, not as prospector. With two of his brothers, he had established an extremely prosperous business transporting all kinds of merchandise from Melbourne to the Victorian goldfields. They then traded everything for gold, which they sold at an additional profit back in the city. As existing fields were exhausted and new strikes made, they moved on and repeated the exercise. With some of their newly gained assets, Riddoch and one of his brothers, Alexander, opened two large stores at Ballarat and Geelong, which were later sold in 1861, when they went their separate ways. Alexander travelled to Tasmania and John Riddoch headed for Penola. There he purchased a massive 35 000-acre estate called Yallum.

Twenty-nine years later, with a further career as a politician behind him, Riddoch decided to implement a dream project to keep him occupied in his retirement from public life. He called the enterprise the Coonawarra Fruit Colony, and offered the land for sale in blocks, for which he invented a word: comaum. Riddoch was aware from the successes on his own estate that the relatively cool climate was ideal for many fruit trees and also for vines, and his intention was to attract purchasers to part of his estate which he would sell in small, carefully allocated parcels. He promised to build a magnificent wine cellar and guaranteed to buy all

The Coonawarra soil profile, showing the rich, red terra rossa *strip at the surface*

the grapes grown. Proud man though he was, John Riddoch was wise enough to consult William Wilson, and it must have been an interesting conversation. Wilson, with the benefit of all his experience, advised Riddoch that the Coonawarra Fruit Colony should be staked out on the long strip of red soil that ran to the north of Penola, and which had proved so beneficial for his own garden. Apparently he also suggested to Riddoch that the growers should concentrate on red wine grapes, presumably based on the success he had enjoyed with his own tiny vineyard.

To put the relationship in some perspective it should be mentioned that at his peak, in the last twenty years of the 19th century, John Riddoch owned nearly 130 000 acres of freehold land, plus 112 square miles of leasehold, and more than 160 000 sheep. He was regarded very much as the local patriarch, and yet he was humble and wise enough to call upon his elderly neighbour, who possessed a mere 1 acre, to seek his counsel.

The word Coonawarra was not in general use at the time, but had been the name for the area north of Penola used by the Aborigines, of whom only one, nicknamed Yallum Jackie, remained in the region when the development of the fruit colony commenced. Even today Coonawarra is not a town, but a geographical district and an official wine region. In fact, at the time of writing, much debate is proceeding about the territorial restrictions of its proposed appellation. It is an extremely flat area, not a valley as some wine writers, who have not visited the region, have suggested.

Riddoch's dream project was quite well planned and in many ways deserved success. He believed the locality had much to offer in agricultural terms and wanted to see the community prosper. He planned to use his abundant wealth to support those who became involved , actually sharing the financial risks with them by agreeing to purchase the fruit and grapes harvested. As far as the grapes were concerned, it was his intention to produce and sell the wine, but he does not appear to have done much in advance to organise its marketing. Wilson showed him how the vines in his garden had developed more strength than the ones which Riddoch had planted at Yallum, where there was no *terra rossa*, and he advised Riddoch that his colony should be developed on the very same soil, which runs in a long strip for about 8 miles and which varies from between nearly 1 mile to 200 yards wide. Acting on that recommendation, Riddoch advertised an initial 1 147 acres at £10 an acre, which could be purchased by instalments over ten years with interest at 5 per cent. In due course he added a further 812 acres, bringing the total to 1 959 acres. His conditions limited each

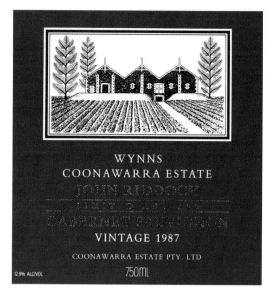

WYNNS
COONAWARRA ESTATE
JOHN RIDDOCH
CABERNET SAUVIGNON
VINTAGE 1987
COONAWARRA ESTATE PTY. LTD
12.9% ALC/VOL   750ML

purchaser to a maximum of 40 acres, but when insufficient interest was shown in the project he relaxed these stipulations. Eventually twenty-six families, who became known as blockers, acquired plots between 10 and 80 acres in size.

What Riddoch could not have prophesied was that in 1893 Australia was to suffer its great bank crash, which saw a succession of national banks fail and the sudden arrival of a depressing lack of economic confidence. In 1891 he had begun the construction of the classic cellars which are the home of Wynns Coonawarra Estate today, and which are so easily identified on the winery's distinctive labels. He told his neighbours that he had deliberately chosen the highest point for miles around, but in reality that only meant 5 feet higher than the township of Penola. He did, though, construct one of the finest cellars in South Australia, as can be seen to this day. The soil was excavated and a limestone basement built with a slightly raised ground floor above it. The beams used had been hewn from giant Oregon pines that had been carted overland from the nearby port of Robe. He also built a roof space above, suitable for storage. The cellars had a capacity of 75 000 gallons, which seemed optimistic at the time, but which soon turned out to be inadequate.

To encourage others, John Riddoch planted extensively, and by the end of 1891 had a total of 348 acres of vines. These comprised 181 acres of Hermitage (Shiraz), 110 of what was often termed Carbinet, and 57 acres split between Pinot Noir and Malbec. By 1896 the young vines of both the Yallum estate and the blockers were capable of providing wine with sufficient body to be sold with ease in the open market, and *Garden and Field* magazine wrote that Coonawarra "was capable of producing dry red wine of superior quality". Two years later, Riddoch, at his enthusiastic best, hired a second-generation Scot called Ewen McBain as his winemaker.

McBain was a graduate of the now famed Roseworthy College, where he had won the gold medal for the best student in his year. McBain had relinquished a respected position as the assistant viticulturist for the South Australian government because he was so attracted to Riddoch's scheme, which no doubt he believed would give him the opportunity to make great red wine.

In 1896, Riddoch paid £7 10s per ton for Carbinet and £4 10s for Shiraz, and spent a total of £170 on grapes. Demand was slightly down in 1897, and prices were £7 and £4 per ton. In 1898, Carbinet descended to £6 per ton, but Shiraz held at £4. Riddoch purchased 105 tons of grapes and produced 24 000 gallons of wine. There was a smaller harvest in 1899, with 18 000 gallons, and 1900 brought frost damage and only 7 450 gallons. For the blockers, very few of whom had grown vines before, it was proving an extremely inconsistent living, but then 1901 brought a bumper crop, with 53 250 gallons.

John Riddoch was by then seventy-five years of age and it was his last vintage, as he would die that July, but he did have the pleasure of watching over one great year when the volume was more than two-thirds of the cellar capacity, and by chance he was, for the first time, to share the experience with the second R, Bill Redman, who has left his name on two existing properties, Redman and Rouge Homme. Bill arrived at Coonawarra, aged fourteen, with his elder brother Dick, aged sixteen, to work the season as a fruit picker, including a spell in the vineyards. Bill fell in love with the area and remained, while Dick departed. By 1907, Bill Redman was head cellarman under the wing of the highly trained professional winemaker Ewen McBain, and in 1909 he became, at twenty-two years of age, the sole owner of a 40-acre block.

In the meantime, problems loomed ahead. Following his death, John Riddoch's family rejected his ambitious plan, and a large proportion of his estate was sold in parcels of varying sizes. His land at that time included around 350 acres of vines. Also, after the earliest years of inconsistent harvests, there was a run of bountiful vintages, with 1903, for example, providing 80 000 gallons, more than the cellar were designed to hold, and the following six vintages all exceeded 65 000 gallons. As a result, prices slumped, and many blockers simply abandoned their investments and left. Much of the red wine was intended to be sold as Coonawarra Claret, but there was no real sales organisation and it was naive to expect potentially interested parties to arrive in the somewhat isolated Coonawarra vineyards on a speculative basis. Subsequently most of

the wine went for distilling into brandy as Riddoch's dream disappeared in heady fumes. Bill Redman, however, knew the quality of the red wine they had been producing and was determined to continue the practice in his own small way. He had not received much education and had no experience of salesmanship, but he understood he had to sell his own wine to survive. He took his samples to Adelaide, where he found regular purchasers for Redman Coonawarra. For many years he was the sole producer to persist and keep the Coonawarra name in existence. That is not to say others did not continue to make wine, but it was generally sold for blending or distillation.

In 1919, Chateau Tanunda acquired the Riddoch Yallum Cellars to supplement their brandy stocks. Two years later they sold to another distiller, Milne & Co., who operated on the same basis until 1946, when the cellars were purchased by Woodleys, an Adelaide wholesaler, which hired Bill Redman and his son Owen. The arrangement was that the Bill and Owen would manage the vineyards and cellars, but were also free to continue producing their own wine at the Redman family property. They sold their wine in Adelaide, to Woodleys and to Tolley's. Much of it was red, largely Shiraz, for which there was some consistent demand, Cabernet Sauvignon being virtually nonexistent in the Coonawarra region.

Unfortunately, after a couple of years, a dispute arose between Tony Nelson, the head of Woodleys, and the Redmans, and the local men resigned to concentrate on their own winery. Feelings were running a little high, and the Redman family decided to try to sell their wines direct to those traders who had previously purchased from Woodleys. However, as the Adelaide wholesaler possessed stocks in the Redman name, Woodleys understandably prevented Bill and Owen Redman from using it on their labels. The wily Coonawarra pair racked their brains to find another suitable name, which eventually came to light in a French dictionary. This gave them Rouge Homme (meaning Red Man), a title which continues to this day as a winery within the Penfolds group. At this time, Bill and Owen Redman were the only true banner-wavers for Coonawarra red wine, and without their activity its production may well have ceased.

In 1951, acting on the advice of his son David, Samuel Wynn, formerly known as Weintraub, a Melbourne merchant who had immigrated from Russian-occupied Poland, purchased Chateau Comaum, as it was then called, using the strange name invented by John Riddoch for a block of land. David Wynn was placed in charge of the property, which still continued to produce some fairly undistinguished brandy. The name was changed to Wynns Coonawarra Estate and production of some serious wine was encouraged. David Wynn believed that Coonawarra could produce some fine red wine, and subsequently increased their Cabernet Sauvignon holdings to just 3 acres, which were planted on *terra rossa*. Some writers have erroneously suggested that the vineyard, at the time, was the largest planting of that grape variety in the Southern Hemisphere, but they seem to have totally overlooked extensive Cabernet Sauvignon plantings in Chile.

David Wynn had high hopes for his Coonawarra reds and intended to position his estate-bottled wines at premium prices. To do this, he knew that he had to develop an easily recognised label that would suggest a premium quality. In 1954 he commissioned the artist Richard Beck to complete a simple design showing the triple-gabled roof of the Riddoch-built winery. It was first seen with the launch of the 1950-vintage wines, actually made a year before the Wynns acquired the winery, but aged under their ownership. It was a label which was to attract considerable fame to Coonawarra, and was to become particularly familiar to knowledgeable consumers. It is perhaps a little strange that the silhouette of the winery is so recognisable on the label but that when driving through Coonawarra it is virtually impossible to see it from the road.

The story of Coonawarra red wine in the early 1950s is difficult to unravel. In general terms, to the Australian wine-buying public it was an utterly unknown product, but to medium and large companies that wanted to blend reds from several regions it was a boon. It provided colour, fruit and body, and could bring to life many a lesser and often duller wine. David Wynn proposed that the situation should change and he planned to be the person responsible. During the vintage of 1954 he told the local newspaper, the *Pennant*:

> My prime aim is an extensive advertising campaign in Melbourne to make Coonawarra famous. People, when thinking of claret would then naturally think of Coonawarra.

The first vintage of Wynns Coonawarra Estate Cabernet was 1954, which held much promise, but curiously it was the 1955 vintage which caused the greatest stir with an apparently unrepeatable wine, and it was not a Cabernet. It was Wynns Coonawarra Estate Michael Hermitage, which was made for the first time in that vintage. The year 1955 was good but not exceptional, but the Michael Hermitage was extraordinary, and more than thirty years later the few remaining bottles were still drinking extremely well. Only a tiny quantity was made, all 100 per cent Shiraz, and it was matured

for around eighteen months in one old fortified-wine cask. The end result was a wine of great power, immense character and delightful style, one that would be remembered for a very long time, which was especially fitting bearing in mind the story behind the wine's name.

Michael was David Wynn's infant son, who had died suddenly in 1955, and his father simply wanted to acknowledge the memory of his life. Wynns have apparently tried many similar experiments in an attempt to find that magic touch again, but while they have been able to provide some extremely good wines, mysteriously they have never been able to match the outstanding character and quality of the 1955 Michael. The wine is still produced in the finest vintages as one that needs cellar ageing and certainly rewards those who are patient.

Red-wine making, promoted by Wynns in the 1950s, attracted others, and various wine companies began to acknowledge that the red-wine torch, lit on red soil by John Riddoch, kept alight by the Redman family and fuelled by the Wynns, was one that all the nation's wine traders should bear. Thus a new generation emerged and Coonawarra was at last on the road to national recognition.

In 1968 a company called Hungerford Hill entered the market. It was operated by a highly successful former cotton farmer called John Parker. He was and is a modern entrepreneur, not a wine man by profession but by heart, yet one who possessed the financial acumen and discipline necessary to turn wine into a profitable commercial enterprise. Twenty years later, John Parker, tempted by his wife, Fay, was to show that even the toughest men can have their hearts melted by a love of wine. Encouraged by Fay, John became involved in Coonawarra's most daring exploit yet, a publicly declared aim to produce red wine that could match anything on earth. He, too, believed that the *terra rossa* strip could produce vinous miracles.

My introduction to the Parker wine came about when Adam Brett-Smith, the managing director of Corney & Barrow, one of Britain's only three retail wine merchants with a royal warrant, suggested I should feature it on my weekly LBC Radio spot. I had asked him to select from their stock any two samples of still wine that he felt typified the character of their business. Frankly, I anticipated the arrival of two bottles of traditional French wine, but not for a moment did I expect the surprise choice of the 1988 vintage of Parker Coonawarra Estate Terra Rossa First Growth. Adam sent detailed background notes which explained the name.

After reading a few pages I quickly realised that through the major problem of not having the time to read sufficient wine magazines, I had overlooked some excellent publicity the wine had received from the International Wine Challenge organised by the London-based *Wine* magazine. It had received one of only thirty gold medals awarded for red Bordeaux-style wines which, in that competition, had placed it on a par with such eminent names as Chateau Latour, Chateau Pavie and Opus One. Additionally, the American wine critic Robert Parker, writing in his *Wine Advocate* newsletter, had rated it with ninety-three points.

After some detailed research it became clear that the concept of Parker Coonawarra Estate was a meeting of minds. Ralph Fowler, the former Hungerford Hill winemaker, Doug Balnaves, that company's previous viticulturist, and John Parker, its past managing director, persuaded their families to merge some of their talents and assets into one partnership aimed at producing the Southern Hemisphere's greatest red wine. At last, in Australian terms alone, a determined challenge was going to be made to oust Penfold's Grange Hermitage from the top of the ladder.

But where should they start? Much debate ensued before the basic logistics involved were agreed. All the partners believed that Coonawarra's *terra rossa* strip was capable of growing a world-class wine with consistency, but they knew that to make it they would have to change the winemaking habits of a lifetime, for now a new tough word, "selection", confronted them. Using disciplines preached to so many Bordeaux chateaux by Professor Emile Peynaud, they planned to select only a tiny proportion of the finest grapes, and then to choose the best part of the wine produced for ageing in the most suitable assortment of small oak barrels. If the new partnership was going to succeed they would need to adopt the most beneficial practices from Bordeaux, California and Australia.

The three families, between them, owned 51 hectares of *terra rossa* vineyards, some of which had been acquired on the specific advice of old Bill Redman, who happened to have been Doug Balnaves's grandfather, and who seemed to know the soil better than anyone. He emphasised that having red soil was important, but to obtain the finest results it was essential that it had the limestone strata running through it. They also had to decide on the grape varieties, and elected to follow a traditional Bordeaux-style blend, these days called "meritage" in California. Shiraz, for so many the lifeblood of Australian red winemaking, was not to play a part. Cabernet Sauvignon was to be the major component, with a small percentage of Merlot and Cabernet Franc added. The proportions were to be determined by the needs of each individual vintage. While most winemakers preferred to use American oak for ageing Shiraz, Ralph Fowler decided to nominate an unusual trio of oaks, at least in Australian terms. He wanted Allier and Nevers from France, and Missouri from the United States. They even purchased matured staves to ensure they received the choicest grains and had them "made into new barrels". They simply intended to use nothing but the best.

Parker Coonawarra Estate first appeared with the 1988 vintage, with Doug Balnaves painstakingly searching out the finest 5 per cent of the crop from the entire 51 hectares. Their plan was and still is to limit each vintage to a mere 1 000 cases. John Parker had attracted the other partners to this venture with what he calls their "mutual aim to produce the finest of wines", which, through

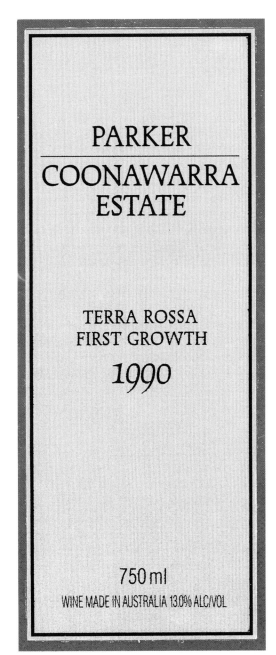

succeeding generations, would win a deserved reputation for unmatched excellence. If Bordeaux could provide first-growth wine, so could Australia, and Coonawarra was the place to do it. He stated: "We share the same belief and all contribute in our own different ways."

One night in Sydney he told me: "With Parker Estate Coonawarra First Growth we have the opportunity to produce a fine wine unconstrained by normal considerations."

With Ralph Fowler, who had already won a string of gold medals and awards for Coonawarra reds, and Doug Balnaves, John Parker would be in harness with two experienced campaigners. They were men with whom he had worked over a long period of time and who had Coonawarra in their blood. All three families firmly believed that their red strip of land could help them in their aim to make the greatest of wines.

Some viticultural neighbours must have thought the trio was a little unhinged when reports began to circulate in the community of the lengths to which the three men were prepared to go. In spite of that, none of their adopted procedures, viewed in isolation, was unique. Each one had been tried before, but not in such a combination, and the partners were prepared to learn from the greatest and follow the rules, however rigorous they might be. Coonawarra was generally regarded as a cool region, in Australian terms, for red wine production, with late budburst and flowering. Hence many locals had come to accept it as an area where the red grapes needed every hour of sun they could get. Balnaves and Fowler decided picking at night by hand was the only solution. They needed to have really cool juice to provide fruit and acidity with no risks from volatile acids that could cause problems in the fermentation. Ralph Fowler insisted they picked the grapes as late as possible. He warned that they must follow "the moon cycle", and this might mean some vintages waiting until ten or more days later than normal.

Fowler also had a precise plan for the oak ageing. They would mature the wine in twenty-seven casks from the previous vintage and thirty-three new barrels each year, providing they had sufficient volume. Obviously in the first year they had to use casks that had been aged by another wine. Their aim was a wine that would improve for a considerable time, and this meant the need for tannins, not just from oak, so Ralph stipulated that they must put the stems in with the berries for the pressing.

Corney and Barrow were so convinced by the 1988 vintage that they sent me two bottles, one to try in advance and one to be tasted live on LBC's "First Edition" program. Having read all the literature, I was prepared to find a big wine that was rather closed with plenty of tannin. Instead I found my palate and eyes being opened by a great red wine that was already showing fruit, but clearly had many years of growth ahead of it, and yet it was only five years old. It reminded me, in a way, of Chateau Cheval Blanc, the first-growth Saint-Emilion which is often so fruity and alive in its youth and then returns to sleep for a decade or more. Of course the blend of grape varieties and other components were largely different, but I wondered if the Terra Rossa First Growth would return to sleep. We will have to wait and all will be revealed.

When I leave my Kent home to travel to London for live broadcasts or prerecordings, the various samples are carefully tucked away in a thermal bag to maintain the best possible temperature, which in the case of reds is encouraged very carefully at home. Upon arrival at the studio, I often find the central heating too hot or the air conditioning too cold, so when for three years I was working with the fastidious but affable presenter Richard Dallyn, some careful planning was necessary. Otherwise there would be an on-air comment or two to the effect that he would would have preferred the wine a little cooler or nearer to room temperature, and of course he was right. So on the occasion in question, having taken such trouble and having allowed the wine to breathe for several hours, I poured the Parker Estate for Richard, knowing that he is lover of fine red wines.

His reaction was immediate: "This is quite simply the best red wine I've tasted in a long time, maybe the best ever on this program." Richard was not a wine professional, but a consumer who was prepared to pay a good price for a very fine wine. Parker Estate had passed test number one for me.

Test number two came in July 1993, when I visited Coonawarra and tasted the first four vintages. The 1988 confirmed my earlier opinion, the 1989 was good but not great, and the 1990 was quite simply astounding, a tremendous mouthful that matched the potential of any red wine I had previously tasted. Ralph Fowler was reported as having said:

> The 1990 Terra Rossa First Growth has the structure to live longer than 20 years. A more powerful wine, yet it has the greater finesse than the successful 1988 vintage.

His words could not be disputed. Finally I tasted the 1991, which was still at an early stage but showed all the signs of major promise.

The three families involved in the production of the Terra Rossa First Growth are well aware that the great Bordeaux first growths vary in character and quality from vintage to vintage, as will their future wines. I just hope that they will have the pleasure of drinking that wonderful 1988 and the remarkable 1990 when they both arrive at their peaks, and I hope I will have that privilege as well. Then in 2010, or whenever, we will be able to reflect on the men who discovered and nurtured Coonawarra. From John Riddoch with his fruit colony, influenced by William Wilson, the mantle was carried by Bill Redman and his family, on through the development of Wynns Coonawarra Estate, to the exciting emerging band of small growers. And finally there is the rising star, the Parker Estate First Growth. But all of them have one common factor, that rich red strip of *terra rossa* soil.

SURVEYING THE SCENE
Mitchelton, Australia

The painting of a river scene on one of the most attractive Australian wine labels is very clearly connected with the Mitchelton winery's name. The picture depicts Major Thomas Mitchell, the Surveyor-General for Australia, as he crossed the Goulburn River in 1836 at the exact spot where the Mitchelton winery at Mitchellstown, Victoria, would be constructed in 1969.

The wine is one of the most attractive examples of the Marsanne variety that one can find in any country, a comment that should be balanced against the knowledge that there are only two reasonably extensive plantings of the Marsanne grape in the world, one in the northern Rhône Valley of France and the other in the Goulburn Valley of Victoria. In the Rhône, Marsanne is best-known for the classic dry Hermitage Blanc, with wines such as Chevalier de Sterimberg setting fine

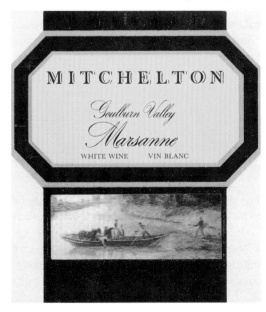

standards. In the Goulburn Valley, Marsanne is also produced as a dry white wine, but with more variation of style. Other than that, fairly small vineyard parcels are planted in California and Switzerland.

The Marsanne found its way to the Mitchelton Vineyards through a chain of events which began in the early 1860s, when the Yarra Valley, Victoria, pioneer, Hubert de Castella, imported cuttings from the French town of Hermitage. Hubert de Castella was a native of Switzerland, where he apparently knew of the variety both from the Swiss vineyards and from the Hermitage Blanc wines that were a popular import from the Rhône Valley, which is less than 100 miles from the Swiss border with France. Later in that decade, cuttings were taken to the infant vineyard of Chateau Tahbilk in the Goulburn Valley. Then, more thàn a century later, famed winemaker Colin Preece persuaded Mitchelton owner Ross Shelmerdine that they should plant Marsanne in the new vineyard at Mitchelton. It was a choice that was richly rewarded through wide public acclaim for the two contrasting versions of Marsanne that Mitchelton offer. These are a young non-oaked wine, ready for early drinking, and a reserve label that has been wood aged and which, it is claimed, will last for twenty years. The latter was considered good enough to be served by Paul Keating, the Australian prime minister, to George Bush, at a Parliament House dinner in honour of the US president in 1992.

TAX COLLECTOR'S WINE
Marchesi de Frescobaldi; Italy and UK

Many of the family-owned wine houses of Italy can trace their aristocratic ancestries over several centuries, but few can compare with the proud and talented Frescobaldi dynasty. They are best-known among wine *cognoscenti* for their eight estate properties set in the splendid Tuscan countryside. Names like Tenuta di Castelgiocondo, Tenuta di Pomino and the historic Castello di Nipozzano will evoke pleasurable memories for many a reader. The last of these comes from an estate which is not just a *castello*, but a village in its own right.

Castello di Nipozzano produces a most delicious and distinctive Chianti Riserva, and stands proudly on a rocky base from which it has overlooked the surrounding valley for more than 1 000 years. In the 11th century it became a possession of Count Guidi, and eventually was transferred to the ownership of the Frescobaldi family in the 13th century, when they had a useful supply of funds in cash.

In 1270 a contingent of bankers from the Frescobaldi family had travelled to England to rescue King Edward I from pecuniary disaster. The

Castello di Nipozzano, one of the eight estates of the noble winemaking Frescobaldi family

conditions they demanded were more stringent than any the International Monetary Fund could ever hope to impose on any current government or head of state. The Frescobaldis were appointed official bankers to the throne, and then "given the title of Inspectors and Receivers of Taxes", which ensured they collected and received all the taxes paid in England at that time. Berto Frescobaldi was appointed Crown Counsellor, and the family was awarded the contract to operate the royal silver mines in Devon. Then, to add gilt to the ginger-bread, they were given authority to mint and circulate England's coinage, as well as the pleasurable duty of supplying the royal court with its wine. The terms were almost too good to be true. The Frescobaldis profited bountifully from their banking and doubled it as purveyors of wine. This generous arrangement survived the reigns of Edward I and Edward II, but brought a hostile response from Edward III, who confiscated their entire English wealth. The Frescobaldis fled to their Tuscan base, having wisely returned much of their profit to their homeland, but, as a parting shot, they hit the English Royal court where it hurt most – in the palate! The Tuscan family sent agents to Bordeaux, still then an English possession, with instructions to spend a sizeable portion of their funds on purchasing every drop of wine they could find in the region. Simultaneously, supplies to England were halted, from Bordeaux and Italy, causing a rapid rise in the price of Bordeaux, as well as an almost complete lack of availability of good wine to the English nobility, who, to their chagrin, were obliged to drink the ale normally reserved for the peasants.

Other notable members of the family included Dino Frescobaldi, who was a friend of Dante Alighieri, and who is said to have hidden the first pages of *la Divina Commedia*, later called the *Divine Comedy*, for Dante when the poet was forced to flee Florence in January 1302. Leonardo Frescobaldi was a traveller and explorer, renowned for his Palestinian expedition of 1384 to 1385. Geralmo Frescobaldi was a noted composer and musician in the 17th century, and in this century, Lamberto Frescobaldi brought acclaim to the family name with his much-admired conversion of old Tuscan village properties.

Now, more than 1 000 years after the Frescobaldi story began, from their Castello di Nipozzano and their other seven estates, the noble family concentrate their talents on the production both of traditional and innovative wines. They love their castles, their farms, their vineyards and their wines. With their heritage they need no pretensions, and only desire to see their wines appreciated by those who are fond of the fermented grape and of the finest that their splendid Tuscan homeland can offer.

UNCLE JOE
Tio Pepe, Spain

The love and guidance given to a young Spaniard by his Tio Pepe, or Uncle Joe, gave rise to the name of the most popular of fino sherries.

When Manuel Gonzales Angel was a young child his father died, leaving his widow to raise five boys and two girls. All of them appeared to be healthy, active and intelligent, apart from Manuel, who was a sickly, spindly infant and was not expected to survive until adulthood.

During this time, his Tio Pepe watched over Manuel with care and affection. The boy lived with his family in Seville, while his uncle lived in the port of Sanlucar, where he traded in dry Manzanilla wines, and no doubt various childhood visits were paid to the coast for Manuel to benefit from the bracing sea air.

In due course, Manuel found a job as a bank clerk in Cadiz, close enough for his loving uncle to be on hand. By that stage his health was improving and he was becoming altogether more robust. After a few years he decided that banking was not his calling and began trading on his own account as a dealer and shipper of various fruits, vegetables and other commodities.

When he married in 1833, he transferred his business to the city of Jerez, where he intended concentrating on the export of sherries of all the differing styles. Early in his new career it seems his uncle paid him a call and asked to taste his personal preference in the drier fino sherries. Among the butts he tried was one that he singled out as his favourite, and on subsequent visits he always requested the same fino. Uncle Pepe was, it has

been reported, so impressed with this fino that he would bring some of his friends into Manuel Gonzales's bodega just to taste it.

Manuel's regard for his uncle was such that he was only too delighted for him to visit whenever he wished and to partake of his personal fino, and so he ordered the words Tio Pepe, or Uncle Joe, to be stencilled on the butt. The only snag was that this attracted the attention of other visitors to the bodega, and they naturally became curious as to the contents. As a result there were soon two butts of Tio Pepe. As word passed round Jerez of this delicate wine, the stream of enquirers grew, and Manuel had the butts placed in another section of the cellar, where he hoped it would escape the notice of visitors and where his uncle could bring his closest friends to while away a little time in bliss. But it was not to be; it was already too late. As the demand became never ending, Manuel realised that he must concentrate on increasing his production of Tio Pepe and offering it on his list. Today it is the biggest-selling fino sherry of all.

WHOEVER WAS THÉOPHILE?
Roederer, France

Lovers of Louis Roederer, one of the truly great Champagne houses, are occasionally bewildered when they find themselves stumbling across the odd bottle of Théophile Roederer, another Champagne of perfectly respectable quality, and which also states that it is produced in Reims.

Few have any notion that Théophile Roederer is actually produced in the same cellars as Louis Roederer, in the Rue de Savoye and Rue de la Justice, although it is not directly owned by that house. Fewer still will have noticed the name plate announcing Théophile Roederer, which, for many years, was attached to an unused back door in the little Rue Andrieux, at the rear of the Louis Roederer offices. These apparent anomalies can be resolved by the fact that the Théophile label was the result of a blatant piece of effrontery which dogged the name of Louis for forty years. It was the cunning connivance of two Remois brothers, Leon and Gustave Bousigues, which instigated a tortuous and bizarre train of events.

Early in 1864, Gustave and Louis were travelling through Strasbourg when they chanced to make the acquaintance of a local man of humble means, named Théophile Roederer. In the course of conversation the subject of the Louis Roederer Champagne house's success was raised, and Théophile reluctantly confessed that he was in no way related to the family and would never enjoy even a fraction of the wealth accrued by Louis Roederer.

Almost in fairy-godmother style, but with

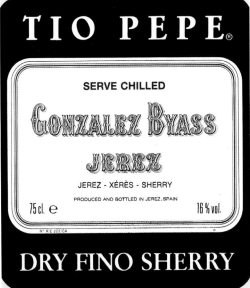

*Uncle Joe's cellar (*Tio Pepe Bodega*)*

wicked-uncle undertones, the Bousigues brothers suggested to Théophile that if he accompanied them to Reims, they would finance him in his own Champagne house, which would be able to challenge the supremacy of Louis Roederer and gain some of its finest business. The brothers had some capital and did not foresee any obstacles to setting up a small house overnight. It was perfectly legal to purchase bottles of mature Champagne from other producers *sur latte* (on their lees, with strung corks, prior to riddling), and then to apply their own disgorgement, labelling and packaging and to sell it under the Théophile Roederer name.

What the Bousigues brothers may not have enlightened Théophile about was the wicked simplicity of their plot to sell their wine as "Roederer Champagne", omitting the name Théophile, and in this manner attract custom from Louis' business, which was already nearly a century old.

Within three months of the Théophile Roederer house opening its doors, its partners found themselves appearing before the Tribunal of Justice in Reims, to defend an action brought about by Louis to prevent them selling Champagne under the Roederer name. After considerable deliberation, during which the chairman made it patently clear where his sympathies lay, all the tribunal could do was to make a halfway ruling. In future, all labels of the infant house had to print the Christian name Théophile before the Roederer surname, and also the words "Maison fondée en 1864" had to be added. But it had no power whatsoever to prevent a man using his family name.

The Bousigues brothers were furious at the decision and at the adverse publicity, which forced them to alter their devious strategy. They decided to attack Louis at long range, and that meant Russia, his premier market. There they could still find numerous potential customers who recognised the name Roederer, but would not appreciate the distinction between Louis and Théophile.

For the classic house, the problem envisaged was not so much a matter of serious confrontation as one of blatant deceit, which aroused much anger in the members of the Roederer family, who saw their proud and deserved reputation being abused by three would-be impostors. In round terms, the impersonating house never gained more than 12 per cent of the trade of its intended victim. It was simply that its very existence was offensive, and for thirty-two years little could be done to relieve the situation, until extraordinarily quickly and surprisingly, in 1896, the Théophile Roederer company was placed into liquidation and sold. Strange and suspicious circumstances surrounded the transaction in much the same way as they still surround some liquidations today. While records of the matter are very scanty, it seems odd that the liquidator sold the business in a matter of days to a Monsieur Aubert of Ay, whose house was somewhat smaller than that of Théophile Roederer. Also, no approach was made to the house of Louis Roederer, nor was the company placed on the open market.

Monsieur Aubert, of course, continued to compete by confusion, but not for long, as he died just four years later and was succeeded by his widow,

Roederer vintage, circa 1925

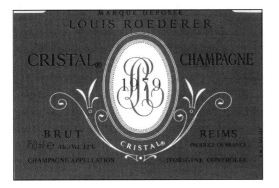

La Veuve Aubert. She persevered with the business until 1903, when she finally sold the Théophile Roederer Champagne house and all stocks to Léon Olry-Roederer, the grandson of Louis and, at that time, sole proprietor of the house that bore his grandfather's name. For reasons unknown Léon never merged the two houses, but continued to run them separately from the same premises, a situation which continues to this day.

In place of Léon Olry-Roederer, the little business of Théophile Roederer, with its entirely separate stocks, is owned by Dr Claude Rouzaud, husband of the current president of Champagne Louis Roederer, Madame Marcelle Rouzaud, and father of its Directeur-Général, Jean-Claude Rouzaud. The house produces around 150 000 bottles a year, about half of its last-century peak, and just enough to provide a humble pension for the retired man of medicine.

ZARA, LOST BUT NEVER FORGOTTEN
Luxardo, Italy

The Balkans is a term often used to denote a vague geographical area and so I would prefer to describe the chief location of this story as Dalmatia. There on the Adriatic coast, in and around the once lovely town of Zara, grows an indigenous fruit, which until the 20th century could not be found elsewhere. Called the marasca cherry, its unusually bitter taste made it ideal for distillation into the maraschino liqueur which for nearly one and a half centuries made Zara a landmark.

From time immemorial, local farmers had produced a rosewater, regarded by many as a drink of elegance and finesse. Its standing was first recorded in 1336, when the powerful Savoyan figure Count Verde, or the Green Knight as he was popularly known, was "regaled with rosewater" during a visit to Zara.

The production of rosewater was a minor industry of artisans but it was not an authentic liqueur; it was a maceration. It was not until the 18th century that farmers and merchants started to experiment with diverse liqueurs. Similar processes were under way in many parts of Europe and were not restricted to Zara. But at Zara, the development of maraschino was unique. As the owners of numerous pot stills experimented with various fruits and plants, they naturally tested the potential of the local marasca cherry. This gave a unique fragrance and flavour which distilled into a most pleasing liqueur.

In the *London Morning Post and Advertiser* of 17 June 1779, an interesting advertisement appeared from Johnson & Justerini (later Justerini & Brooks). It announced that the business "takes the liberty to inform the nobility and gentry that they have just imported a large quantity of Maraschino from Zara of the most exquisite flavour". The reputation of maraschino grew; by 1800 there were nine maraschino distilleries, and they were destined to attract fame on a scale they could not have foreseen.

Much of Europe was on the verge of the Napoleonic Wars, and as the liqueur at that time was made with a fairly high alcohol content, it found favour with the troops of the opposing forces, particularly those journeying to the Austrian Empire. It became a "shock drink", something along the lines of a strong schnapps, the consumption of which immediately revived the consumer and left a pleasing aftertaste.

In 1820, into this commercial environment came Girolamo Luxardo and his titled wife, the Marchioness Maria Canevari, both citizens of Santa Margherita Ligure. It would appear that the principal reason for their emigration to the already existing Italian enclave was Girolamo's intention of becoming a maraschino distiller, which he acheived in the following year. Within the next decade he had opened sales offices in Trieste, Venice and Genoa,

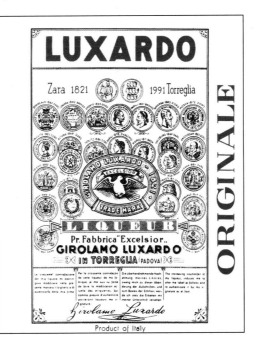

The Luxardo distillery (top) in Zara, 1940

The blending cellar (bottom) at the Luxardo distillery, 1940

and by 1833 a report by the local authority stated that:

> the distillery is the largest in Zara, that his shipments far exceed in bulk those of all the other factories and that he has correspondents all over the world.

It proceeded to name his markets, "from Constantinople to Rio de Janeiro, from Corfu to Calcutta, from Odessa to Madrid". He was also exporting to the USA, the colonial society in India, and the growing population in Australia. What had happened, as is true in so many similar stories of the evolution of a drink, is that Girolamo Luxardo had developed and patented an innovative and special method of production and distillation. Little is known of this, except that it involved a period of ageing over three years, using ash and larch barrels. In July 1829 he was granted a patent of privilege, as it was called, for his method of "manufacture and

distillation of Maraschino" and another drink, cinnamon rosilio. Girolamo Luxardo swiftly became an influential figure in his adopted community, of sufficient standing to be later appointed president of the Zara Chamber of Commerce.

When Girolamo died, aged eighty-one, in 1865, he was succeeded by his son, Niccolo, who further increased the prestige of maraschino, the Luxardo name and the town of Zara. In the space of ten years he was honoured with royal warrants to supply Luxardo Maraschino to the courts of Austria-Hungary, Denmark, Bavaria, Hesse, and Montenegro, and won gold medals at exhibitions in Oporto, Moscow, Lyons and London.

In 1882, Niccolo was followed by his two sons, Demetrio and Michelangelo. As Zara was still part of Austria, they wisely decided in 1888 to register a similar Italian patent, a move that was to prove of great value and consequence seventy-six years later. Demetrio died in 1906 leaving his brother in sole charge, and Michelangelo was still at the helm when World War I broke out. As it was Italian, the Luxardo family naturally supported its country, and Michelangelo's son, Nicolo, proved himself a most valiant man. As a cavalry officer he was twice promoted on the field, and was also awarded medals for gallantry. But the greatest reward came in 1919, when the Treaty of Versailles decided that Zara should be officially united with Italy.

World War I also brought major problems. Apart from the usual wartime dilemma of irregular supplies, Luxardo found their production capacity drastically reduced when part of their distillery and other property were requisitioned by the Austrian government. Furthermore, in the aftermath of the 1917 revolution in Russia, they learned that they had not only lost all their trade to the tsarist empire, but they had to write off 110 000 gold francs of debts.

Despite all these drawbacks, 1922 heralded a new era of peace and prosperity under Nicolo and his three brothers, Demetrio, Pietro and Giorgio. Further honours were won from the kings of Italy and Spain, and numerous awards accrued in a period when cocktails were a worldwide fashion. By 1939 the Luxardo plant covered more than 3 acres and employed more than 250 people in excellent working conditions, and for the Luxardo family and those members of their staff who had worked for them for many years, life seemed prosperous and secure. Less than a year later the peace of the Balkans was shattered again with the outbreak of World War II, and in 1940 Demetrio died unexpectedly. On 28 November 1943 the first of fifty-four successive and horrific air-raids fell on Zara and killed some 4 000 of the population of 20 000. Numerous bombs hit the Luxardo plant

Nicolo Luxardo (far left), drowned by Slav guerillas in 1945

Pietro Luxardo (left), allegedly deported during the World War II, but disappeared and was never seen again

and fire raged for four days, fuelled by 48 000 litres of alcohol.

Later, in 1947, prior to the formation of Yugoslavia, Zara and its vicinity were occupied by Slav forces. In due course, all Italian property was confiscated without compensation. Nicolo, a gentleman of honour, and his wife were drowned by a band of Tito's Slav guerillas, and Pietro was allegedly deported but was never seen or heard of again. Of the four brothers the only survivor was Giorgio. Fortunately the company had foreseen the potential risks and had transferred "a part of their activities to Italy", including branches in Trieste, Udine and Venice. A small production centre was established in Fiumicello, in Udine, and to guarantee supplies a 200-acre orchard of marasca cherries was planted in Torreglia in 1947.

With Pietro's young son, Niccolo, Giorgio made his way to Italy, where he began to pick up the threads of the business. In 1947 they centralised affairs in Torreglia, Padua, quite oblivious of an illegal attempt to rebuild the Zara, now renamed Zadar, distillery. The new operation called itself Maraska Zadar, and claimed to have been established in 1821. The seagull trademark they employed was very similar to the one registered by Luxardo, and the label displayed the numerous medals won around the world by the Luxardo company.

While sales of the illegal Maraska Zadar were restricted to Yugoslavia, there was little action that Luxardo could take, but when counterfeit bottles were seen on sale in Genoa in 1959 the authentic company struck. On 21 March 1960 they sued the imitator in the Genoa court and after many

frustrating delays won the case in October 1964. The result was confiscation of the counterfeit stock and the settlement of all other demands. The court described the bottles as "a Slavish imitation" and ordered the destruction of all that could be found, along with the labels. Shortly afterwards, similar cases were won in Germany and the United States. The family could be very grateful for the action of their ancestors Demetrio and Michelangelo when they registered their trademark in Italy in 1888.

Today the Luxardo company, under the direction of Franco Luxardo and his cousins Nicolo, Piero and Guido, operates peaceably from its Padua headquarters. The cocktail fashion has passed, and they no longer employ 250 people in their distillery, but they do still own the proud name which

The Luxardo Zara distillery after it was bombed during World War II

is synonymous with maraschino. As ever, they maintain their strict standards in their endeavour to produce a drink of fine quality as well as a wide range of other traditional Italian liqueurs.

One final thought comes drifting back to me from my teens. My father often kept a small bottle of maraschino; thank goodness the name on it was Luxardo.

16. A CURIOUS CASE

THE CALIFORNIAN WELSH

Trefethen Vineyards, USA

Like so many visitors to California's Napa Valley, when I met John and Janet Trefethen for the first time I found them pleasant and affable people. They were, understandably, extremely proud both of their historic winery, which they have restored to pristine condition, and of the wines they produce, especially their fruit-filled Cabernet Sauvignon, which has been described by some wine writers as having the flavour of blackberries. When I asked about their ancestry, John was particularly gratified to emphasise that he was one of the limited number of fourth-generation Californians, while Janet told me that she had an ancestor who was an old Welsh sea-dog who had shipped timber out of Eureka.

But it was only when I pressed for further details regarding the origins of John's fourth-generation Californian ancestor that we embarked on a most interesting and coincidental path. "We believe," Janet and John said almost in harmony, "that the earliest-known Trefethen ancestor was also a seafarer, who sailed along the east coast of Maine, and his family roots were in Cornwall, where there are a number of similar names."

A couple of months later I was fortunate enough to find myself in Portland, Maine, with a Saturday to spare, and so it occurred to me that it would be an amusing pastime to see what else I could discover about the Trefethen background. With the aid of the local Portland reference library it was not too difficult, and soon I found that it was true that the first Trefethen known in New England was a Henry Trefethen, who three centuries earlier had arrived from Britain, and who traded as a shipwright in New Castle, New Hampshire, as early as 1678. Two generations later another Henry Trefethen became a rich man by obtaining extensive real estate. He had substantial property on

Monhegan Island, and on Peaks Island in Casco Bay, just across the water from Portland, where a Trefethen homestead and Trefethen's Landing still survive. All seemed to fit in with the account I had been given; that is, apart from one thing. Nowhere had I come across any clear evidence that Captain Henry Trefethen had originally hailed from Cornwall. It is fairly widely known that the old Cornish and Welsh languages have a common Celtic source and that there exists both in Cornwall and Wales a good number of placenames that begin with the prefix Tre-. But by that time something was nagging my brain that Wales, not Cornwall, was his homeland, although I had no notion why.

Two weeks later, in the ancient Guildhall library in the City of London, I was able to have access to some of the oldest land records that exist in Britain, namely extracts from the Domesday Book and other documents from that period, dating back

over 900 years. Yet in none of them could I find any word or placename with reference to Cornwall which bore any real resemblance to Trefethen, and nothing that even came remotely near. When I began searching the records for Wales, it was not long before I alighted upon some startling evidence. There was a village near Pontypool, in the county of Gwent, today called Trevethin, which could be traced back to a Celtic foundation around 2 000 years ago, and which centuries earlier had been written as Trefethin. A man bearing that name would either be one who came from the village or whose ancestor was born there. The word referred to a gathering of people living inside a compound that was fortified by barbed hedges.

I could have kicked myself. How stupidly blind I had been. For ten years my wife and I had lived in an isolated rural community called Mamhilad, about 3 miles north of Pontypool, and there, just 2 miles away by footpath, on the other side of the hill, was that village of Trevethin, which ironically was still renowned locally for its spiky hawthorns and brambles that produced the ripest blackberries. Blackberries! Did some wine writer not say that they could recognise their flavour in Trefethen Vineyards Cabernet Sauvignon?

Y r Ywen (Yew Tree) – distinctively Welsh sign on a Trevethin pub, a suitable place for a glass of Cabernet Sauvignon

COS
Cos d'Estournel and Cos Labory, France

Strangely, the name Cos is restricted to just two wines in France, both of them celebrated Bordeaux growths from the St Estèphe appellation. Cos d'Estournel was rated as second growth in the 1855 classification of Grands Crus Classés, and its immediate neighbour, Cos Labory, as fifth growth. How the first part of their names evolved has long been a matter of conjecture and in all likelihood no proof will ever be conclusive enough to satisfy all interested parties.

Over the last hundred years or so, a number of experts have presented various explanations of the derivation of the word Cos, which while interesting in themselves have never been accepted as totally convincing. Now the time is opportune to proffer another reasoned argument and then invite the reader to judge for himself or herself which explanation seems most convincing.

To help the reader clarify the position, it is necessary to elucidate the historical background. With the French Revolution of 1789 came the secularisation of church property, and in this manner the wealthy d'Estournel family acquired an estate on the southern limits of St Estèphe, adjacent to its border with Pauillac. In the early part of the 19th century its ownership passed into the hands of Louis Gaspard d'Estournel, the last in the male line of the family.

Louis was a buccaneering, adventurous character, who was initially much more interested in trading in horses on an international scale than in making wine. This led him to tour the Arabian peninsula, the Indian subcontinent, and even China, as he searched for the strongest strains of livestock. Establishing Bordeaux as his base, he developed a substantial business in the buying and selling of Arab horses, and would trade them to aristocracy as far afield as Poland and Hungary. In fact, in 1811, the year of the much-acclaimed Comet Vintage, he sold his St Estèphe properties to concentrate on his other affairs, but repurchased them upon his return ten years later, in 1821. At this juncture he also enlarged the vineyard by more than three times its original size and gave part of the estate for Cos Labory.

Louis concentrated his efforts on developing Cos d'Estournel by improving its vineyards and by constructing the finest of oriental-style buildings in its grounds, based on designs he had encountered on his Far-Eastern travels. Many a visitor to St Estèphe comments on the much-admired and unusual architecture of Cos d'Estournel.

D'Estournel gleaned the word "Cos" from one of his visits to Hungary, where he had been intrigued to observe the trading habits of some Polish wine buyers who, like himself, were travelling from one small town to another. No doubt his involvement in wine stimulated his interest and inspired the idea which was to grow. He observed that the Poles always travelled in pairs and worked from cellar to cellar, trying to purchase the finest Magyar wines for their clientele. One man would act as taster and one as paymaster. As tasting was usually a much speedier exercise than the arrangement of financial matters, it was the usual practice for the taster to proceed at his own pace and if he approved of a wine to chalk on the side of the cask concerned the letters C.O.S., standing for the Latin words *colorem*, *odorem* and *saporem*, meaning colour, fragrance and flavour. Louis d' Estournel decided that a similar identification would be ideal for his own St Estèphe wines, and so introduced the names into the titles of his two properties.

The other explanations that have been forwarded are frankly uninspiring. The first claims that Cos is derived from the ancient Norman word *caux*, itself abbreviated from *cailloux*, for round pebbles, but there are none in the area. The second argues that it came from Oc, the ancient language, or *langue d'oc*, from the south of France, and meant a *côte*, or hillside. But if this is true, how is it that the name Cos is not used in the title of any other hillside properties elsewhere in France? Surely every reader will admit that both explanations are far too dull, especially for a man who was an adventurer, a horse-dealer and an oriental architect – a man who must surely have been well-versed in Latin.

CREAM NOT MILK
Harveys Bristol Cream, England

For centuries, Bristol, in the west of England, was one of the busiest ports in the world, a position it held until recent generations. Of prime importance among its trade was the shipping of wine, an occupation which has since reduced to a trickle. The most famous of its wine shippers has for two centuries been John Harvey & Sons, often known simply as Harveys of Bristol. They and others were responsible for developing substantial trade in

A bottle of fine, rich Bristol Cream Sherry at Harveys Wine Museum

sherry, and the quaysides in Bristol were, on occasions, said to be stacked with butts as far as the eye could see.

Most popular of the sherries was an oloroso of some character and elegance, which became known as Bristol Milk. It was not handled by any one shipper, but was a style which anyone could purchase and which became associated with Bristol. Understandably it was the most successful sherry in the Harvey cellars in Denmark Street, but one day in the 1880s a minor incident occurred which changed that dramatically. The exact date and record of the incident were unfortunately lost as a result of the bombing during World War II.

A French lady of aristocratic background was being conducted around the Harvey cellars by the company's elderly principal, the second John Harvey to head the business. He was being assisted by a cellarmaster, who was using a pipette to draw samples for the lady to taste. Having sipped the finest of the Bristol Milk, she expressed a certain curiosity about the contents of some other butts nearby. John Harvey instructed the cellarmaster to provide a fresh sample from one of those butts, which was not branded or stencilled with any name. The sherry was a fine, rich oloroso that was fuller in body than Bristol Milk. The French lady nosed her copita then sipped. With obvious gratification she turned and pointed to the Bristol Milk. "If that be the milk, then this is the cream," she is reported to have said, placing her order for the latter.

The next day, John Harvey gave instructions for the name Bristol Cream to be used for the style, and the rest of the story is history. Harvey's Bristol Cream gradually developed into the most successful of all sherries, and at its peak in the late 1970s was drunk by 37 per cent of the entire adult population of the United Kingdom.

Only one query remains. Is it not possible that the French lady actually said, "*Si celle-ci est le lait, celle-là est la crème,*" and if so should the name not have been *La Crème de Bristol?*

FIRST ENGINEER OF WINE
Lamborghini, Italy

When the late brilliant automotive designer and producer Feruccio Lamborghini finally sold his motor interests to a giant corporation, he felt the impulse to reinvest some of his money in a new hobby – wine production. His initial move was to purchase some 300 acres of land near Lake Trasimeno, in Umbria, where he had some success with his red Torgiano wine. Visitors to his estate, however, had to be beware of searching the vineyards for *Ingegnere* Lamborghini, for he preferred to leave the viticulture to his professional staff.

I ngegnere *Feruccio Lamborghini, the First Engineer of Wine, who felt more at home stripping down and servicing his tractors than practising viticulture*

Instead, a direct path had to be made towards the garage, where the great mechanical genius was usually found stripping down and servicing his tractors, the vehicles which originally came under his engineering skills. When asked why he preferred such apparently menial labour, he simply smiled and explained he felt happiest when he had oil on his hands.

THE HEART OF COGNAC
Otard, France

Baron Otard, founder of the house that bears that name, was so revered by his contemporaries in the town and region of Cognac that when he died in 1824 the mayor of Cognac and the officers of the prefecture requested that his heart should be donated to the town. It was duly cut out and placed in a tiny coffin, which was then buried in the parish church of Cognac, and a plaque was placed alongside it which reads: "Here lies the very heart of Cognac".

HER BEST DINING TABLE
Veuve Clicquot, France

One day the Widow Clicquot drew circles with chalk on her best mahogany dining table and then instructed her cellar carpenter to cut them out. The puzzled man obeyed her orders and watched in amazement as the widow placed a Champagne bottle upside down in each one.

It may seem as much of a riddle to you as it was to the carpenter, but that is precisely what the Widow, or *Veuve*, Clicquot is said to have invented; the practice of riddling, or *remuage*. Her dining-room experiment not only meant that her house sold crystal clear Champagne, but also all the other houses were soon copying her. Riddling simply threw the sediment, by turning and shaking the bottles, into the neck, where the wine could be frozen and the deposit removed.

KING OF WINES
Champagne, Tokay and Gumpoldskirchen; France, Hungary and Austria

Few academics would dispute that the Austro-Hungarians and the French have produced, during recent centuries, societies of great refinement and cultural achievement. Yet they have also experienced the occasional territorial skirmish, such as the time Napoleon Bonaparte's army attempted to intrude into the valley of the Danube.

Each has consistently demonstrated an appreciation of the most elegant architecture, the finest art, and the impressive creativity of their musical composers. Yet in that atmosphere of artistic

A *Tokay cellar with Gonci casks*

sympathy there has been one subject upon which the French and the Austro-Hungarians have failed to agree. It is the serious issue of which one is entitled to claim the accolade "King of Wines", an argument which continues to dog them even to this day.

The Champagne makers of France have no hesitation in supporting their claims by referring to the fact that when the Austrian Johann Strauss composed *Die Fledermaus*, he identified Champagne as "King of Wines, Wine of Kings". On the other hand, the older wine producers of Hungarian Tokay – that is, those who recall the days when they were free to be private producers and their legends were remembered with pride – have another interpretation of the expression. They tell of a traveller who, having returned from his sojourn in France, recounted to their wonderment the tale of his visit to the royal court of Louis XIV at the magnificent Palace of Versailles. There he had been granted an audience with the illustrious Sun King, who had sampled some of the Tokay Aszu the traveller had presented to his majesty. Among the court there had been a French writer, Voltaire, whose authority was acknowledged by all, and he had written in eulogistic terms of the properties of Tokay Aszu:

It contains such strength and sweetness that it renews one's vital energy. It brings new life to each brain cell and lights a firework of bliss in the depth of the soul.

Then he added (obviously with the idea of flattering his monarch in mind) that it was "The Wine of Kings and the King of Wines".

So who has the right to use this phrase? The Champagne houses, where I am fortunate to have several friends, or the producers of Tokay? The answer should perhaps come from the wine producers of another region which once was part of Austria-Hungary, Austria's Thermen region. They will tell you that the town of Gumpoldskirchen has always been known for its "King of Wines and Wine of Kings", and that it supplied the wine to their monarch centuries before the other two usurpers even laid claim to the title.

A LIKELY STORY
Godet Frères, France

For two centuries the vast majority of Cognac was shipped from the ancient and fortified harbour of La Rochelle, on France's Atlantic coast, as it was the nearest major port to the Cognac vineyards. Consequently, the quayside roads soon became home to a number of notable Cognac producers. This situation reversed dramatically with the arrival of commercial rail and road transport, until nowadays just one house remains active there. Called Godet Frères, it has some surprising but interesting claims to being the oldest surviving of all the Cognac houses, based on documentary evidence dating from 1583.

It is a family company which has always been in the control of successive generations, and its finest Cognacs are a match for any of its competitors, its Godet Gastronome blend being one of the most delicious VSOP Fine Champagne Cognacs one could ask to enjoy. It is a Cognac which strangely seems to have a dedicated following in Chicago, for reasons which just may have a history that evolves from the 1920s.

In true French tradition the late grandfather was Jean, the father Jacques and his son Jean-Jacques. In 1980, I think it was, I had the privilege of being a guest at the home of Jean Godet, then aged eighty-one. He thought he might have some interesting stories to tell me, which has always been an invitation I have accepted with eager and open ears.

As we sat and sipped a magnificent 1900 Godet Cognac, laid down by his father to celebrate the new century and the birth of his new son, Jean began to recall past trips across the oceans. Gradually he began to warm to the task and gave me little snippets of curious information that were well worth filing away. But it was when he reached the subject of the United States that his eyes began to light up, as he talked about the great cities he had visited in his younger days. "Perhaps the most astonishing [experience] was to find myself just 200 yards away from the St Valentine's Day Massacre when it actually took place."

"Really," I replied, recalling that 1929 date when the Al Capone mob murdered seven members of the rival Bugs Moran gang. "Whatever were you doing there? It was the middle of Prohibition, wasn't it?"

"Oh yes, I was just carrying out a little preparation in advance of the repeal!" was his jocular reply.

MURPHY'S WINE
Domecq, Spain

The Spanish house of Pedro Domecq has experienced a couple of notable name changes in its two and a half centuries. One point worth attention is that it was founded in 1730, not by a Domecq, but by an Irishman called Paddy Murphy. He was one of several Irish horse dealers and livestock farmers who were attracted to Andalucia by the region's superbly bred horses, and who eventually preferred to invest in the production of sherry.

Two generations later, Pedro Domecq, a French citizen of Basque lineage, inherited a share of the business, which he gradually increased until he gained overall control. Curiously, he chose to trade as Peter Domecq, and indeed the English writer John Ruskin wrote of him with his anglicised name: "Peter Domecq, a man of strictest honour." Yet it might have been more apt for Domecq to call himself Pierre, for he spent little time in the Jerez region and directed operations from Paris, where he had other significant investments.

THE PICTURE TELLS THE STORY
Chianti Ruffino, Italy

On the label of one of the most successful Chiantis, there is a picture of a wealthy hunter, halting his pursuits at a farm to refresh himself with a glass of wine. It is, in fact, an incident which occurred some 300 years ago and from which the wine Ruffino Chianti Classico Riserva Ducale took its name.

The powerful Duke of Mantova had been hunting in the Chianti hills, in the heart of the Tuscany vineyards, when he chanced to pass a farm belonging to the Ruffino family. As his exercise had left him with a great thirst, the Duke demanded that good wine should be brought for his refreshment. He was so delighted with the wine provided that he placed an order for several casks to be delivered to his castle.

The nobleman's approval helped spread the name Ruffino, and every year he would replenish his cellar with further stocks. After his death, the duke's memory lived on, as the Ruffino family, conscious of the influence his patronage had made on their fortunes, decided to show their gratitude by continuing to produce a blend in the very same style that their noble customer had enjoyed on that auspicious day's hunting.

RICHARD COEUR DE VIN
Anjou and Commandaria; France, Austria and Cyprus

The surface evidence would appear to justify Richard Coeur de Lions's title Lionheart, as he is represented as one of the great heroes of European medieval history and a man of supreme courage. Or so the military historians would have us believe.

A wine historian, on the other hand, might suspect that more of Richard's life was devoted to wine, women and song, thus entitling him rather more to the name Wine-heart, or in his native French, *Coeur de Vin*.

Richard was born in 1157, in Touraine, amid the vineyards of the Loire Valley, and was nurtured on the young red and white wines of that ancient kingdom. He spoke only French and Latin, and his early life included much feasting and celebrating, as his family's power extended across western Europe, and no doubt he enjoyed more than his fair share of the two most appreciated red wines of the Loire Valley, Chinon and Bourgeuil. He later became Richard I, King of England from 1189 to 1199, but he only made two brief visits to his kingdom, and they were not ones which enamoured the majority of the populace towards him. For despite the impression the Robin Hood legend might give, Richard taxed the nation severely to pay for his crusading army, and even threatened to sell London, if anyone would buy it.

With his army and a large party of minstrels and courtiers, he set off to free the Holy Land from the Saracens. Before reaching the Asian continent, however, he made a detour to visit Cyprus, where he married Berengeria of Navarre, celebrating his nuptials with ample supplies of Cyprus mana, known today as Commandaria. He repaid the inhabitants for their hospitality by conquering Cyprus and graciously adding it to his already extensive kingdom, and then set sail for Palestine, where he joined forces with the Austrians and the French to eject Saladin and his Saracens. There, instead of joining in the victory festivities with his allies, he fell to wrangling with them both. Initially he denied Duke Leopold of Austria's claim to have led a famous battle which brought the downfall of the Saracens. Then he brought the wrath of Philip of France upon his head by informing him of his marriage to Berengeria. Richard had been promised in marriage to Philip's sister, an arrangement made by Richard's father, Henri II.

Finding himself suddenly unpopular, Richard led his victorious army, his band of minstrels and his few remaining courtiers, back to Europe, continuing to enjoy the fruits of the vine wherever he rested en route. In the dukedoms of northern Italy many of his officers found the local wines so enticing that they left his company and married into the local society, bringing considerable spoils of war with them. There he received word that his person would not be safe in France. So, demonstrating a certain lack of wisdom, he journeyed with his still merry but rather depleted band through Austria to Vienna, where he was captured when one of his servants was recognised and followed to an inn where Richard had been enjoying a few glasses of wine. Duke Leopold held him prisoner secretly in the Castle of Durnstein, on the Bank of the river Danube, in the Wachau region.

During his incarceration, Richard found consolation in the local white wine, possibly a forerunner of the Grüner Veltliner produced in the area in modern times. It was in the Castle of Durnstein that Richard was discovered by his chief minstrel, Blondel, reputedly after they recognised each other's singing. Despite the discovery of his hitherto unknown whereabouts, Richard was not released until his mother, Queen Eleanor of Aquitaine, had paid a large ransom.

The Lionheart finally died at the early age of forty-two, as the result of an injury sustained in a somewhat trivial and unnecessary skirmish with a French baron. He was buried alongside other members of his family in the Abbey of Fontevrault, where he rests to this day in the midst of the Saumur vines.

During his lifetime, Richard possibly consumed more different wines than any other man of his generation. He was regarded as a gourmet and *bon viveur*. He loved music, sang well and played a variety of instruments with some skill. When he dined he feasted, and his court indulged in copious quantities of wine while enjoying the performances of his entertainers. So why he is remembered as the Lionheart and as a noble king of England remains a mystery. What we can be sure of is that his veins, if not his heart, were full of wine.

A TOUCH OF UNITY
Delaforce Porto, Portugal

The distinguished old Porto house of Delaforce, founded in 1868, is justifiably proud of its leading tawny-port brand, known as His Eminence's Choice. The label is a reproduction of a colourful painting of a Roman Catholic cardinal, in his vivid red surplice, enjoying a glass of port. A surprising choice of name and label it might seem for a strictly Protestant family, whose Huguenot ancestors fled in 1685 from persecution in France.

*T*he original oil painting of the cardinal was painted by B. Borione in Paris towards the end of last century. It was purchased by the House of Delaforce in the 1920s

WILLIE'S SECRET FIND
Singleton, UK

In the early 1970s the British-owned drinks group International Distillers and Vintners was scouring Scotland's Speyside for a suitable home for its new Singleton whisky distillery. In the course of its search it naturally took counsel of its local management. It already owned three distilleries, Strathmill, Glen Spey and Knockando, and senior staff there were the likeliest fund of helpful knowledge.

The entrance to Dorie's Well, now under Singleton lock and key

The prime requirement was a suitable source of water, on land available for purchase, and so one of the giant company's directors broached the subject with Willie Thompson, general manager of the Strathmill Distillery. He straightaway admitted that he might know the ideal spring, which he had been keeping quiet as his private water supply for special occasions.

Willie, in his leisure moments, enjoyed shooting and fishing, and he had one favourite spot, down by the banks of the Spey, where he could cast flies across the water in search of the occasional leaping salmon. Sometimes he would head into the woods, gun in hand, to bag the odd pheasant or partridge, and, being a whisky man, he would never embark on one of those solitary expeditions without having his flask of single malt and a tumbler in his bag.

He preferred to partake of this essential refreshment half and half with water, as is invariably the wont with distillers. Over the years, Willie had tried the various springs and streams along the hillside to add to his malt. In his search he chanced upon one freezing cascade, which he later learned was called the Auchroisk stream, and which came tumbling from a sandstone gulley and collected in a natural rocky well just below. He had never before found running water that was so cold, and when he used it to dilute his malt, it gave the most superb and restoring dram. He was rather vague as to why he had never thought to tell anyone else about it. He realised that a few others might know

of its existence but for many years he had enjoyed the privilege of being the only man on earth who watered his whisky directly from Dorie's Well.

Without further ado, it was arranged to analyse the water of Dorie's Well and attempt to ascertain just how reliable and long-lasting the supply might be. The company was planning a multimillion-pound investment which, like all single malt distilleries, would depend on its water source. In the event of it drying up the result would be ruinous.

As it turned out, the analysts were unable to offer much advice, and remarkably the decision to build a distillery had to be based on the memory of a local lady of nearly ninety years of age. She was the oldest person in the district, and recalled her great uncle telling her as a child that he had never known Dorie's Well to fail. She also could not remember it running dry, and so there was an oral tradition of the consistency of the water source stretching back to the first half of the 19th century.

Strangely, no-one in the surrounding district then or since has been able to explain who or what Dorie was. Of course it may simply be one of those names that has survived since time immemorial, or for as long as the water has flowed. The Singleton Distillery has even offered a substantial liquid reward for the information, but as yet no-one has proffered an explanation which is credible enough to claim the prize.

In the meantime, a slight problem has arisen, in that other single-malt enthusiasts have been tempted to partake of Willie's secret find. Attracted by the news that an icy spring has been discovered, which has established a reputation for itself as Scotland's

coldest freshwater source, they have created the need for security. The result is that the priceless supply is now housed and locked.

Twenty years on, Jimmy Logan, the master distiller at the Singleton, and a man with forty years experience in the whisky trade, says he is still taken aback by the quality of the water and its effect on the character of the whisky. He asserts that the single malt's gentle smoothness is due not only to its ageing in sherry casks, but also to the influence of Dorie's Well with its arctic chill.

LOCK, STOCK AND BARREL
Jim Beam, USA

Several postulations have been offered to explain the origin of the expression "lock, stock and barrel" but it is unlikely that any expert will be able to prove his or her theory irrefutable. One explanation regularly put forward in the past was that it was a legal term used to define the sale of a distillery with the entire contents of its warehouses, which in past days always came under the official lock and key of the customs and excise men.

Perhaps the most unfortunate use of the term made in the above context came from the lips of the legendary Kentucky whiskey producer James B. Beam in 1924. Jim Beam, as he is immortalised on labels today, was having his morning shave in a barbershop in the picturesque little Kentucky whiskey capital, Bardstown, and was not in the best of moods when the conversation turned to the disastrous effects Prohibition was having on the investments of the whiskey barons. Jim, who was experiencing cash-flow difficulties himself, blurted out that if any man there would give him $10 000, he would sell his Clear Spring Distillery, "lock, stock and barrel". It was an absurdly low price for a business which would have been valued in excess of $1 million just three years previously.

In a chair nearby, at the time of this statement, was a character whose standing in the local community was as low as the gentlemanly Jim Beam's honour was high. Will Styles was considered by many to be the most devious rascal in the area. He was a notorious gambler and a shady wheeler-dealer. Will leaned back and asked Jim to repeat what he had said.

"I'll sell everything at Clear Spring Distillery, lock, stock and barrel to the first man to give me $10 000," Jim reiterated.

Styles pulled the white towel from his neck, wiped his face clean of lather, looked towards Beam and said in front of the barbershop full of witnesses that he would accept the offer, and proceeded to amaze the assembled company by producing the $10 000 in cash. Will Styles smelt a

bargain and went in for the kill in front of an incredulous audience who, quite by chance, were watching a small step in Kentucky Whiskey history. Styles queried whether the popular distiller would honour his word. By this time, Jim Beam must have realised that he had made a foolish statement, as did all the observers. Styles, like the crafty poker player he was, had called the respected gentleman distiller's bluff, and Beam, who considered a man's word should be his bond, unflinchingly confirmed the deal and rose to instruct his lawyer to convey the Clear Spring Distillery, lock, stock and barrel. Legal records in Bardstown for 1924 show that Styles was given a power of attorney by Beam so that he could take control immediately, apparently while the necessary documentation was completed.

Will Styles, not too concerned about the niceties of the Volstead Act, spent the next twelve months selling the entire whiskey stocks, it was rumoured, to smartly dressed businessmen from Canada, who were later believed to have transferred their liquid assets to Chicago. In that time he received some $400 000 and still retained the mothballed Clear Spring property, which, after Prohibition, resumed trading as the Bardstown Distillery.

For Jim Beam, it was a long and hard path to recovery, and one which some might say he never conquered, for he never again achieved the asset level that he held before his unwise statement. Thanks to his successors, that honourable gentleman has been remembered in what many claim to be the best-known blend of Kentucky Bourbon. Much of its good name was gained in the current generation by the determined efforts of Beam's maternal grandson Booker Noe, a larger than life character who has helped Jim Beam become an international favourite in recent years. As for Will Styles, few outside of Bardstown, Kentucky, have ever heard his name.

17. CORNUCOPIA

CERTAINLY NOT JUST PLAIN SMITH
Hill-Smith Estate, Australia

Six generations after a former brewery manager from Dorset, England, planted his first vines in the Barossa Valley, his successors control Australia's largest and oldest family-owned wine company. Since his initial planting they have become the proud possessors of four major vineyards and have provided the South Australian wine trade with two of its most colourful characters. The Hill-Smith family own the Yalumba Vineyards, Pewsey Vale,

Samuel Smith, founder of a winemaking dynasty

SAMUEL SMITH
1849 - 1888

Heggies Vineyard and the Hill-Smith Estate, which was their latest addition, in 1979.

Samuel Smith, the founder, arrived from Wareham, in the English county of Dorset, in 1847. Aged thirty-five, he had worked for sixteen years as the manager of a small brewery belonging to his cousin. Local legend reports that he was a Congregationalist, deeply involved in church matters and strictly puritan in his lifestyle. When instructed to work on the Sabbath, he refused, gave in his notice and decided to emigrate with his wife, Mary, and four children. He sailed to Adelaide and temporarily stayed in the Prussian village of Klemzig, but probably encountered language problems there, and so set out for the Barossa Valley.

Naturally, any immigrant who arrives in a virtually undeveloped land, as most of South Australia was in 1847, is going to seek regular work at an early stage. Hence, to prevent his small savings being depleted, Smith was prepared to accept any reasonable offer of employment. He therefore loaded his family and possessions onto a bullock cart and headed for Angaston to take up a post as a gardener with John Howard Angas, son of George Fife Angas, who represented his father as agent for all of his land.

The entire population of Angaston then comprised only twelve households, it seems likely that he was offered work there on part of the Angas family estate, called Tarrawatta. Many writers have maintained that he was employed by the philanthropist and developer George Fife Angas, but this is inaccurate, as Angas did not arrive until January 1851, by which time Samuel Smith was already a prosperous man and was fully occupied with his new Yalumba vineyard.

In 1849, Samuel Smith purchased 30 acres of land just above the village of Angaston and named his property Yalumba, meaning "all the country around". Meanwhile, he continued in his position as gardener and tilled his land in the evenings and on Saturdays. He worked on the building of a small wooden cottage and on planting his vines. This situation probably lasted until 1850, when he was able to concentrate upon his own needs. In 1852, leaving his wife and five children behind, he headed for the Bendigo gold strike, and returned shortly afterwards a wealthy man, with £300 profit. With this he bought a further 80 acres, for £100, and allocated a similar sum for two horses and a harness, a plough and other items of equipment, and set aside sufficient to build a new and more extensive home.

Samuel Smith was in his element amid the giant red-gum trees and rolling Barossa hills, and though Angaston was growing, it was a peaceful town with deeply religious and industrious residents. In 1860, aided by his son Sidney, Smith made sixty hogsheads of wine, about 13 500 litres of Shiraz. By the time of his death in 1876, they had become active purchasers of grapes from other growers, in addition to pressing their own, and the volume they produced had multiplied by some 650 per cent.

Sixty-two years later, in an entirely different age, the second of the two illustrious Smith characters, Wyndham Hill-Smith, better-known as Windy, became the head of the family business. He had acquired the name Hill from his eldest brother, Sidney. Upon Sidney's arrival at St Peter's College in Adelaide, there had been some confusion caused by the existence of a multitude of boys called Smith. The headmaster, to aid identification, had instructed that each Smith must select a family name and attach it to their surname. Sidney chose Hill in honour of his maternal grandfather, John Hill, who was the first cricketer to score a century at the Adelaide Oval, and his uncle Clem Hill, a star of many Australian test-cricket teams.

Wyndham Hill-Smith took over the reins of the Yalumba operation when Sidney was tragically killed in the infamous crash of the airliner *Kyeema*, which overshot Essendon airport on 25 October 1938, killing all eighteen occupants, including Sidney's fellow wine men Tom Hardy and Hugo Gramp of Orlando. Wyndham, in his youth, was an especially talented sportsman, active at cricket, football and boxing, and he always had a passion for horseracing, which he had gained from his mother's father. He represented Western Australia at cricket with some regularity, and even played for an Australian XI against England and South Africa. As his business responsibilities increased, his participation in sport reduced, and he became more involved in horseracing. In 1983, he celebrated his 500th winner as a racehorse owner. In 1965 he had been a member of a small partnership that had purchased the 800 acres of the old Angas Estate

with the aim of creating Australia's foremost racing stud. Throughout his wine producing and sporting careers, he was one of those ebullient individuals who became a friend of many famous people, such as cricketers Sir Donald Bradman, Frank Worrell, Freddie Trueman and Keith Miller, gold-medallist swimmer Dawn Fraser, jockey Scobie Breasley, and many politicians, including the late Sir Robert Menzies.

Wyndham discovered in his middle years a fresh and unexpected talent which brought him and many others much pleasure. When he was recuperating from a serious illness in the early 1950s, he decided to try his hand at oil painting. He delights in telling a story about an early painting expedition with Hill-Smith vineyard manager Norman Hanchel. Upon seeing a quaint old farmhouse, he decided it would make an attractive subject, but painting it would necessitate going onto the owner's land. Spotting a young boy near the house, he asked, "Will it be OK for us to paint this place?"

The boy looked up and asked, "How much will it cost? I'll go and ask Mum."

Wyndam Hill-Smith's work can be seen on all the Hill-Smith Estate labels, including that of the Air-strip Block, named after a vineyard that was selected as a landing ground for crop-dusting planes as it was the highest place in the vicinity.

A new generation is now in charge, and wine and racehorses are still the order of the day. My ignorance of the latter led me into some trouble. When faxing the current managing director, Robert Hill-Smith, Wyndham's son, I addressed him as William Hill-Smith in error. The following day brought a stern reprimand, with the name Robert underlined twice, but I have subsequently been forgiven after explaining that William Hill is Britain's best-known bookmaking name.

THE CHANGING COLOUR OF
NOUVEAU MEDOC
Chateau Woltner, USA

In 1877, two eager young French vignerons headed for California's bustling Napa Valley, where they were far from alone in speaking their native tongue. They found themselves amid glorious, tree-lined countryside, in a region with a growing reputation, heralding a boom that was to bring prosperity to many. They had a clearly defined aim – to make great Bordeaux-style wines in America, combining the traditional skills and knowledge of France with the appealing climate of California.

They observed that most of the growers had chosen to plant their vineyards in or near the valley bottom, while the French tradition was quite the reverse. If possible they would seek slopes that ensured longer exposure to the sun and where there was more likely to be a rocky base at a limited depth. Guided by such a philosophy, they made their way towards Howell Mountain, to land at approximately 1 700 feet, where they founded their winery called Nouveau Medoc. In the course of time, they extended their planting and, as sales increased, reinvested their funds, until in 1866 they had sufficient capital to construct a three-storey cellar, which is still in use today.

Jean Adolphe Brun and Jean Chaix were first and foremost makers of red wine, and had quite correctly deduced that Howell Mountain was a prime location for Cabernet Sauvignon, a fact that has been confirmed in recent times by the outstanding results of other wine growers in the Napa Valley. The Frenchmen steadily built a reputation for excellent wines, and by the end of the 19th century had extensive sales in the New Orleans area, as well as to other French interests in New York. Later their property, like so many others, fell victim to Prohibition.

All was not lost, however. Nearly sixty years later the legend of the wines of Brun and Chaix reached the ears of the owners of a highly regarded Bordeaux chateau. In 1980, after two years spent scouring California for a property of great potential, the Nouveau Medoc site was purchased by Francis and Francoise De Wavrin-Woltner of the esteemed Chateau La Misson Haut Brion. To the bewilderment of their friends and neighbours, within the space of three years the Woltners sold their prized Graves Grand Cru Classé and decided to concentrate their efforts on Chateau Woltner, with the aim of developing it into one of the greatest of all vineyard properties.

The first surprising news was that Nouveau Medoc's soil was, so to speak, to change colour, for the Woltners, after receiving soil analysis reports,

Chateau Woltner, the reincarnation of Nouveau Medoc on Howell Mountain in California's Napa Valley

preferred to plant Chardonnay and make what they believed would be a white wine of distinction. They moved cautiously and were adamant that they would not be rushed, taking seven years before releasing their first vintage from an initial planting of 56 acres. It was, of course, not simply a change of direction for the soil, but also for the Woltners, who were famed for their Red Bordeaux and who had never worked with Chardonnay before arriving at Howell Mountain.

They have recently begun to achieve new success and attract professional praise, and so the Woltner family have not been dilatory in demonstrating a little tongue-in-cheek humour, which is evident in some of their labelling. Previously bound in the Graves region by the legal requirements imposed by the Bordeaux authorities and the EC, they have enjoyed the *laissez-faire* attitudes of Californian labelling. One section of land has been named St Thomas Vineyard to remind them of those doubting French colleagues who did not have the faith to believe that it was possible to make world-class wine in America. Another area is named Titus Vineyard after a much-loved family dog. Whether that acclaimed canine star is allowed to take a stroll through the vines for natural purposes, however, is dubious, for on the label he is represented as a tiny dot – not near any grapes but under a tree. In a more genteel manner, they called a third area

Frédérique Vineyard, after their daughter, Frédérique, and her great-grandfather, Frédéric.

From red to white, Nouveau Medoc has been reborn as Chateau Woltner, and the French language has been revived on Howell Mountain, where it was once in everyday use. Despite the change of colour, one can only presume that Brun and Chaix would approve of Napa's new Bordelaise adventure.

A DEGREE OF FORESIGHT
Seppelt, Australia

The world's largest stock of old fortified wines is owned by the South Australian Seppelt company and housed at its historic Seppeltsfield Winery, near Tanunda in the Barossa Valley. The winery business was founded by Joseph Seppelt, a Silesian from the town of Wustewaltersdorf, who owned a small factory for refining tobacco and snuff; he also produced a few liqueurs. He was of some influence in his locality, as borne out by records. When he emigrated to Australia he was the leader of a group he had organised, consisting of his wife, two sons and a daughter, thirteen entire families, and a group of bachelors.

His initial intention upon buying land in the Barossa Valley was to grow tobacco, but in due course this gave way to wheat and then wine. He died at the age of fifty-five in 1868, leaving the winery, which he had completed in 1867, under the control of his son Benno. Some time later, Benno decided to invest in the production of Australian port, and ten years later, in 1878, he opened the Seppelt Port Store, which still operates. That same year, he began a tradition that has been observed ever since. He laid down his best port for bottling when it was 100 years old, and in 1978 the Seppelt Company was able to release small quantities of 100-year-old Para Liqueur Port. Thanks to Benno's foresight, this has now become an annual practice.

AN EXCEPTIONAL TRIBUTE
Yalumba (Angas Brut), Australia

In January 1851, George Fife Angas, his wife Rosetta, and their youngest son sailed into Adelaide under exceptional circumstances. Angas was sixty-one years old and had lived all his life in England, apart from some brief business trips to Europe, yet he was to enjoy the remaining twenty-nine years of his life in South Australia. Yet before he even set foot on dry land, a reception party had organised a public celebration dinner to acknowledge his service to his new homeland.

Those who waited to congratulate him knew that without him the foundation of the colony

The Seppeltsfield Port Store, built in 1878, in the Barossa Valley of South Australia

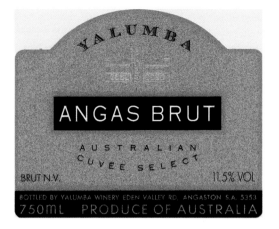

would have dissolved into chaos. They also realised that many Lutherans who had settled so satisfactorily into their new villages and homes would want to acknowledge the freedom he had provided for them.

His is the story of a man's faith, vision and unstinting use of his own wealth. Born in Newcastle-upon-Tyne on May Day, 1789, he was raised in an extremely prosperous Puritan family of shipowners and coachbuilders. At twenty years of age he was received into the Baptist Church, and seven years later he founded the first Sunday School Union in his home city. He became a director of the British and Foreign Bible Society and an activist for the complete emancipation of slaves on British-owned soil. Throughout his early years, his Christian philosophy broadened and he argued for religious tolerance and freedom, something he was able to put into practice in South Australia.

His interest in the birth of the new colony commenced in 1832, when he was first named a member of the committee of the South Australia Land Company. On that committee he fought for two totally new colonial conditions: first that there should be no penal labour and second that there should be religious liberty. When the British government made it clear they would not accept these conditions Angas resigned from the company, but a little later was appointed to the Government Colonization Commission. Its role was to sell £35 000 worth of land at 20 shillings per acre, a figure that was agreed in the absence of Angas, and which he considered excessive, particularly as it was four times the rate for land in New South Wales. Not surprisingly the proposed land sales foundered, but the plan was salvaged when Angas, with Henry Kingscote and Thomas Smith, purchased 13 770 acres at 12 shillings per acre and formed the South Australian Company, intent on playing a prime role in the development of the colony. He then provided a store ship, two whalers and a coastal trader, and supplies and funds for an initial company expedition.

Angas's involvement with the Lutherans came about after he was approached by Pastor Kavel, the leader of a group of Lutheran dissenters from Brandenburg, who were suffering persecution under the Prussian King Frederic Wilhelm III. Kavel had travelled alone to London, intent on finding a way to take his flock to a new land and freedom. These Lutherans came from an area which today lies just inside Poland, and they were mostly agricultural workers, though a good number of them had individual skills. They were likely to make good settlers and their needs appealed to Angas's sympathetic understanding of the right of religious freedom. In this spirit, he advanced £8 000 to cover the cost of their emigration. Afterwards, Kavel wrote to Angas in deepest gratitude, thanking him for his "generosity and Christian love". Many of the Brandenburg group agreed to buy land from Angas, who later reduced the price to help them, and then transferred some of it freely, once more demonstrating his philanthropy.

Angas built a substantial mansion at Lindsay Park in the Barossa Valley, near the small town of Angaston that proudly carried his name. Outside Angaston, the Yalumba Winery had opened its doors just two years previously. Nearly 150 years later, that winery provides a suitable home and pleasing wine, Angas Brut, for a name that South Australia should never forget, even if he was a lifelong member of the temperance movement.

FASTEST PLANTED
Richmond Grove Cowra Vineyard, Australia

The 1989 planting of Cowra Vineyard, owned by Richmond Grove, in the Hunter Valley of New South Wales, is believed to be something of a record. The owners claim it to have been the "fastest-planted vineyard of all". The 242 hectares were planted in fewer than twelve months, using the latest in laser technology. The task was executed with immaculate precision, with the most efficient lining of the vineyard rows, thus ensuring that the corridors between each row of vines were completely straight to allow for the most trouble-free pruning and harvesting.

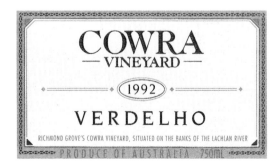

The "vineyard of the future", as some Australian experts are calling it, is irrigated by purified water, which is sprayed automatically by a computer-driven irrigation system. The fifty-six blocks and their individual rows are landscaped and scaled to precise size to encourage winds, thus reducing the threat of frosts and fungal disease.

FOR SCOTTISH LOVERS OF CHAMPAGNE
Champagne Piper Heidsieck, France

There is sadly no truth in the long-established rumour that Piper Heidsieck has Highland ancestry. The expression "The piper plays the tune" would probably have more bearing on the explanation of the Piper Heidsieck name if a little poetic licence were permitted in the form of a change to the past tense and some capitalisation; that is, "The Piper played the tune."

In 1834, Christian Heidsieck, a nephew of Florenz-Louis Heidsieck, who founded the original Heidsieck & Co. in 1785, decided to leave the house his late uncle had started and establish his own firm. He promptly hired three assistants, one of whom, Henri Piper, was a distant young relative who had also been employed at the original house for the previous few years. The others were Henri Piper's cousin Christian Walbaum, and a young Rhinelander called J.C. Kunkelmann.

Abruptly, just one year after founding his new house, Christian Heidsieck died and was succeeded by his widow, who two years later must have raised a few eyebrows by marrying Henri Piper, still a youthful assistant in the small house. M et Mme Piper changed the house's name straightaway to Piper and Co., and retained Heidsieck solely for the label of the finest cuvée. It is difficult to ascertain whether there was any resultant animosity, but it appears that a new working relationship was readily established. Piper remained in Reims to take charge of production, while Walbaum headed east to Russia to attempt to develop that market. Kunkelmann sailed in the opposite direction, to New York, with a similar aim. In that city he achieved great success, selling what he called Piper's Heidsieck Champagne, from which the name Piper Heidsieck is derived.

LOFTY THOUGHTS
Dominus Estate, USA

Many of us have experienced difficulty falling asleep when the rushing wheels of activity are whirring through our minds; this is especially true of those who travel extensively. One such gentleman must surely be Christian Moueix of Chateau Petrus and, more recently, Dominus Estate fame.

Arrangements were under way between him and Robin Daniel Lail and Marcia Daniel Smith of Napanook for a joint venture to produce a Californian wine of the highest possible standard, but somehow all parties had failed to agree on an ideal name. Then one night, thoroughly exhausted, Christian, the great Bordeaux wine man, lay down to sleep and just before he slipped into the unconscious the name Dominus came to his lips. A Latin word with a monastic background, *dominus* means

T*he Cellar Train at Champagne Piper Heidsieck*

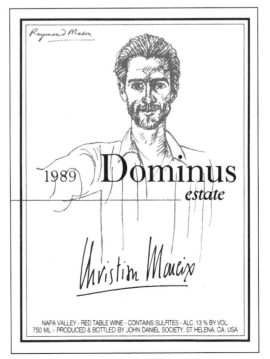

"lord" or "master", and no doubt it was a reflection on the supreme role which the French-American partnership desired their prestigious wine to play in the years to come.

Christian can be seen in the portrait on the label of the 1989 Dominus vintage, the seventh year of that wine to be released. The drawing was the work of the veteran Paris-based English artist Raymond Mason who, despite being better-known for his landscapes and sculpture, has produced a fine sketch. In it he shows the sensitive features of a far-seeing man who appears to be looking ahead with great confidence.

The great Bordeaux wine man Christian Mouiex (left), with a colleague at vintage time

A MATTER OF COMMITMENT
Niebaum-Coppola, USA

James Laube, the highly respected author of *California's Great Cabernets*, wrote: "It may be the greatest undiscovered wine in America today." Robert Parker, the eminent Baltimore-based wine critic, has described it as "outstanding". Frank Prial in the *New York Times* has identified it as "an exceptional wine, intense, concentrated and beautifully textured". Indeed many, if not most American wine journalists have pronounced in favour of

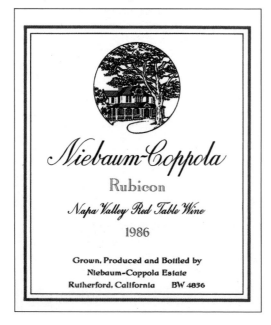

Niebaum-Coppola
Rubicon
Napa Valley Red Table Wine
1986

Grown, Produced and Bottled by
Niebaum-Coppola Estate
Rutherford, California   BW 4856

what is, in many ways, a most American wine, or to be more specific, a fine Napa red wine, which is likely to win many more plaudits with the coming generations, as it is a big wine which is meant to mature.

The wine is Niebaum-Coppola Rubicon, and the fact that its owner is a respected Hollywood film director has had more bearing on the wine's quality than many might assume. For when Francis Ford Coppola took control of the vineyard in 1975 and began producing a "serious" red wine in 1978, he was, in a manner of speaking, offering a true Bordeaux-style meritage blend in the Napa Valley before other meritage makers had fully comprehended the word. His concept of blending 70 per cent Cabernet Sauvignon, 23 per cent Cabernet Franc and 7 per cent Merlot resulted in a classic Bordeaux balance in the geographical context of the Napa Valley.

Francis Ford Coppola had bought the Rutherford estate and home, built in 1879 and founded by Captain Gustave Nybon, later known as Niebaum. Niebaum was one of the most successful of the early Napa winemaking pioneers. Initially, Coppola hired the indefatigable and extraordinarily talented André Tchelistcheff as his wine consultant, and later contracted Tony Soter of Spottswode and Etude fame. The film director chose for his wine a name that would give the educated a clear indication of his ambition. He called his star wine Rubicon, and then attached his name to that of the original Finnish sea-captain owner, hence Niebaum-Coppola Rubicon. The word Rubicon underlined his determination to persist with his self-imposed standards and disciplines.

His first and foremost rule was to use only the best 20 per cent of the estate vineyard's crop. His second rule was that his wine would always spend a minimum of thirty months ageing in Nevers oak, and his third was that he would never permit Rubicon to be released for sale until a minimum of six years after its vintage date. In this respect it is probably the latest released of all American wines. Just as Julius Caesar publicly marked the commencement of his campaign in Gaul by crossing the little Rubicon stream, thereby irreversibly committing himself, so too Francis Ford Coppola crossed his Rubicon when, at the outset, he publicly laid down his self-imposed rules, as he strove to make the greatest possible red wine from his property.

Coppola, evidently a man of determination and achievement, has received the widest acclaim in his much publicised field, in which he has dedicated himself to pursuing the highest standards. His films have included the three *Godfather* epics, *Finian's Rainbow*, *Peggy Sue Got Married*, *The Cotton Club* and *Bram Stoker's Dracula*. His name is sufficient to attract his fellow professionals and the general public to his work. In a similar vein, it will, as his first decade of wines reach full maturity, attract wine professionals and enthusiasts to his Rubicon.

It is enlightening to examine the greatest of his films and note how well they stand the test of time. Anyone who happens to see the original *Godfather* will surely discover that its pace remains lively, its themes timeless and its ripeness undiminished. These are qualities that the Niebaum-Coppola Rubicon possesses and will undoubtedly continue to possess in parallel with the finest of his films for many years to come.

A MATTER OF RAINFALL
Oxford Landing, Australia

Oxford Landing, the peaceful stretch of the Murray River at Waikerie, South Australia, has not always been a scene of tranquillity. In the second half of the 19th century it was the site of ceaseless activity, as drovers with endless flocks of sheep headed from the northern pastures for the markets of Adelaide. The river bank at Oxford Landing was a convenient and readily accessible watering hole for the weary flocks on their long journey. As the 20th century progressed, South Australia's extensive network of roads began to develop. With the simultaneous advent of motorised transport and steam railways, Oxford Landing's time of busy activity ground to a halt and tranquillity was restored.

It was not until 1958 that the clamour of men's voices was again heard there , as they hammered vineyard posts into the hard-baked soil, sweltering in the sunny microclimate, which is reputedly warmer that Queensland's much-vaunted Gold Coast. The planting marked the birth of a 580-acre project by the Hill-Smith family of Yalumba fame.

At the time, fortified wines were still the most profitable style in Australia, and Wyndham Hill-Smith proposed using the land to cultivate grapes for that purpose. He ordered a selection of Sultana, Muscat, Gordo Blanco, Crouchen, Palomino and Doradillo grape varieties, some of which could also be used for brandy. As the demand for fortified wines diminished in favour of fresh, fruity table wines, the Yalumba managing director, to the amusement of many neighbouring growers, began planting some Cabernet Sauvignon, to which he later added Chardonnay. Wyndham Hill-Smith, one of the most colourful Australian wine person-alities of his generation, had realised that if the Oxford Landing water had been accessible to drovers then it was also available for the benefit of the new vineyard. In an area that normally saw 10 inches rainfall per annum, Hill-Smith increased that figure to the equivalent of 29 inches by

pumping and spraying, and thereby transformed a fairly ordinary piece of land into a prolific and profitable major vineyard.

MONSIEUR ARNAUD'S CHRISTIAN NAME
Chateau Petrus, France

Christian Moueix, the controlling force behind the rapid rise in recent years of Chateau Petrus to the status of the world's highest-priced wine, might well feel a little peeved at the title of this story. But he has no cause to be, nor for any complaint at my recognition of the 19th-century developer of the imposing Pomerol chateau, who gave his Christian name to the property. For Christian Moueix is renowned for saying that great wine is made in the vineyard, not in the chais, and at least the first part of that maxim was a dearly held belief of Monsieur Arnaud.

With that philosophy, Christian should indeed toast the memory of Petrus Arnaud, who planted the vineyard in the middle of the 19th century on land his family had probably owned for generations. It was he who first believed that the soil was likely to produce superlative wine.

Early records of Petrus are difficult to unearth, and most wine writers begin their accounts with the 1868 Cocks et Feret directory, which wrote unofficially of "*premiers artisans*", and listed Chateau Petrus as number 3. This must have been an encouragement to M Petrus Arnaud, and the vineyard he founded went on to win gold medals at les Expositions Universelles de Paris of 1878 and 1889. In fact the 1900 Chateau Petrus label boldly announced the wine as "*ler des Grands Crus*", clearly indicating that Monsieur Arnaud's successors were in no doubt as to the exceptional quality of the wine.

At the time, Pomerol was not generally regarded as a wine region in its own right, but rather as a vague subdivision of Saint-Emilion. Also, wine writing was a practically nonexistent profession and so there was little chance of a potential star gaining all the credit to which it might be entitled. Good wine continued to be made at Petrus but,

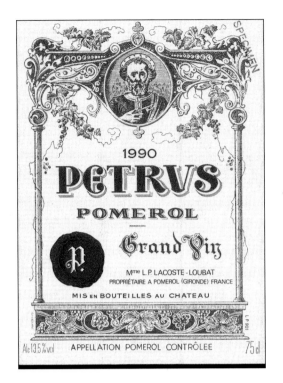

1990
PETRVS
POMEROL
Grand Vin
P.
Mme L. P. LACOSTE - LOUBAT
PROPRIÉTAIRE A POMEROL (GIRONDE) FRANCE
MIS EN BOUTEILLES AU CHATEAU
Alc 13.5 % vol   APPELLATION POMEROL CONTRÔLEE   75 cl

fetching around £90, an increase of some 700 per cent. I bought a case of 1969 Petrus at Christie's South Kensington "End of Bin" sale in 1980 at the price of £13 a bottle, and while 1969 was a fairly *ordinaire* Bordeaux vintage, Chateau Petrus did not disappoint. The veteran English wine journalist Edmund Penning-Rowsell wrote of that vintage that he "could award points to 7 wines including Petrus, with Petrus probably the most fruity".

Many an American, the occasional Australian, and more than a few French and Italians have dreamed of aspiring to the giddy heights of Petrus. Of these, most would consider the winemaker the most important factor in a wine's production, and that is where the Petrus philosophy differs. The Moueix family are adamant that it is not necessarily a matter of a star winemaker, but adhere to Jean-Pierre Moueix's saying that "great wine is made in the vineyard, not in the *chais*", a sentiment with which one of Burgundy's greatest influences, Aubert de Villaine, at Domaine de la Romanée-Conti, wholeheartedly concurs.

To begin to understand Petrus, it is wise to assimilate a few statistics. The vineyard these days still only covers a mere 28.4 hectares. From that small estate, some 4 000 to 5 000 cases maximum are produced per annum. The vines are 95 per cent Merlot and 5 per cent Cabernet Franc, and their average age is more than forty-five years. A small number are believed to be around ninety years old. Perhaps that last figure is the most revealing, for in Bordeaux terms it is undoubtedly high. The reason for such old vines has its origins in a near disaster.

In 1956, before the Moueix family acquired their interest in Petrus, the most biting and de-structive frost that the vineyards of Bordeaux had known swirled in to settle on Pomerol and Saint-Emilion. The result for the majority of vines was catastrophic, and in the minds of owners the only possible policy to adopt was complete replanting. At Chateau Petrus the decision was to bide their time and await the outcome. The vineyard was left to lie "fallow for 2-3 years to see whether the hardiest vines would recover – and they did". This explains why the average age of vines at Chateau

possibly due to its then restricted size of around 6 hectares, few Bordeaux *négociants* regarded it seriously, particularly when many much larger chateaux from the highly acclaimed Médoc, Graves and Saint-Emilion regions were readily available. In this climate, little occurred in the story of Chateau Petrus until after World War I, when it became a limited company. Between 1925 and 1945 all the shares were acquired by the colourful Madame Loubat, whose husband owned the Hotel-Restaurant Loubat in neighbouring Libourne, as well as several other vineyard properties. It was Mme Loubat, it appears, who was responsible for dropping the name Arnaud and placing the drawing of St Peter on the label. She realised, as did Petrus Arnaud, that a major influence on the character of the wine was the *crasse de fer*, or rocky iron soil, beneath the vineyard's blue-tinted clay. As St Peter had been called "the Rock" by Christ, his annex-ation would be eminently fitting.

Many believed that the historic blockbuster vintage of 1945 demonstrated the greatness of Chateau Petrus, and coincidentally that was also the first year in which Jean-Pierre Moueix became involved in the production and sale of the wine. The Moueix family then became part-owners in 1961, together with Mme Lilly Lacoste, the niece of Mme Loubat.

If one considers four principal ingredients of a wine – the grapes, the winemaker, the soil, and the microclimate – one must ask why it was possible, as late as 1980, to buy a bottle of mature Chateau Petrus 1969 for just £13 (US$31) a bottle, and yet a decade later the astounding 1990 vintage was

The Chateau Petrus helicopter, as much a horticultural tool as a form of transport

Petrus is so high, an advantage inherited by the new owners in 1961.

Because the Petrus vineyard is so small, picking takes only three days, which means a decision can be made instantaneously on the exact time to start. The *vendange*, or grape harvest, never begins until late morning or early afternoon; in other words, when the morning dew has evaporated and will not dilute the precious grape juice. The picking is always carried out by the Moueix team of family and employees, which totals around 180 pickers.

One of the more revealing facets of modern Petrus must be its ability to produce giant wines in what other Bordeaux producers consider light-weight vintages. There are, of course, sound reasons, some of which would be outside the financial budgets or logistic scope of many top vineyards because of the sheer size of the estates. For example, in the rain-diluted 1987 vintage in Pomerol, Christian Moueix performed at Chateau Petrus what might be termed "vinobatics", as he seared across the vineyard in his helicopter, using the down draught from the rotor blades to dry the excess moisture from the grapes immediately prior to picking. It was an aeronautical feat that had previously been applied elsewhere, but probably not in such a dramatic manner or on so small or prestigious a site. That aviation was successful, and the 1987 Chateau Petrus surprised even the most pessimistic doubter with its body and character.

Four years later, in 1991, the use of the helicopter, for other purposes, failed. On this occasion Christian Moueix developed another viticultural engineering technique when the foe was not moisture but frost. He instructed his staff to light braziers throughout the vineyard, and again employed the helicopter in an attempt to spread warm air across the vines to protect the grapes. However, he and his key staff were not satisfied with the result, and consequently Chateau Petrus 1991 does not exist.

Mme Lily Lacoste and the Moueix family are aware that they possess the jewel in the crown of the wine world, at least where red wine is concerned. They realise that while there are four main factors and several lesser ones in the production of a wine, it is the *terroir* – the soil, the rock and the situation – that is the key to the greatest result. After all, is a key not what Saint Peter is holding in his hand? Or is that key a subtle hint that Chateau Petrus, which has never been officially rated, has the highest classification of them all?

MONTES NOT MOUNTAINS
Montes, Chile

Being ignorant of the Spanish language, when I received some samples of a new Chilean wine

P R O D U C E   O F   C H I L E

MONTES

Merlot

CURICO VALLEY
CHILEAN RED WINE

PRODUCED AND BOTTLED BY
DISCOVER WINE LTDA.
CURICO, CHILE

IMPORTED   BY   H.W.   &   CO.   CM23   3YT
75 cl.   12% vol.

called Montes, I drew the wrong conclusion regarding the translation of the winery's name. The labels of the Montes Chardonnay and Merlot showed the snow-capped Andes range towering over the vineyards and so I presumed the name referred to the mountains; that *montes* meant mountains seemed a natural deduction. A little research into the wines of the Curico Valley revealed that snow from the

*S*now irrigation in the Montes vineyards, Chile

Andes was used to irrigate the vines, and this served to compound my error.

A little later some background literature on the winery arrived and my misguided attempts at translation were exposed. Montes did not refer to the mountains but to Aurelio Montes, a Chilean oenologist, who in his forties has developed his own 20-hectare estate called Villa Montes, where he is making some very attractive wines with fresh, fruity flavours. The literature asserted that the character of the wines was influenced by the use of the melted snows from the Andes for irrigation; water was taken from the glacial streams and snow was dug into the soil between the vines.

Aurelio Montes is also involved in a unique winemaking partnership with the English inter-national winemaker Hugh Ryman. I use the word "unique" loosely, as Hugh has several such partner-ships which are unique to the countries concerned. Hugh was born in England, raised and educated in France, trained in oenology in Australia, and has participated in joint wine-production initiatives in Hungary, Moldova, France and, of course, Chile. Their Cuvée Montes-Ryman Sauvignon Blanc has found much favour in the United Kingdom as a young, fresh, dry white wine and, like Aurelio's other wines, shows one has to be thankful for the Andes Mountains and the ideal climate they create.

The couple are generous patrons of fine art. This led them to commission the Florentine artist Marco Sassone to provide his painting *Tramino* for the label of the first vintage of Ferrari-Carano Reserve, which was a 1988 blend, predominantly Cabernet Sauvignon with a little Petit Verdot and Cabernet Franc. The painting was commissioned to reflect the "depth, vibrancy and richness of the wine", which it does with authority.

NO GAMBLING ALLOWED
Ferrari-Carano, USA

Winemaker George Bursick and Vineyard Director Barney Fernandez are under no illusions about their roles at the exciting Ferrri-Carano Winery at Healdsburg, in California's Sonoma Valley. Their skills and experience are greatly appreciated and their opinions valued in the development of the winery's production, but one thing they are not expected to do is gamble with the end results.

For the owners of the Ferrari-Carano vineyards and winery are the husband and wife team of Don and Rhonda Carano, directors of the prestigious Eldorado Hotel and Casino in Reno, Nevada. The Caranos are all in favour of a little fun in the relaxed atmosphere of Reno, but when it comes to the winery it is time for serious business, a philosophy that took them, in just ten years, from their first Alexander Valley vineyard purchase in 1981 to finding their wines on sale in all fifty US states and in eight international markets.

The Caranos originally intended using Rhonda's maiden name, Beviluga, on their labels, but Bevi-luga-Carano would not have been suitable for a wine, since *beviluga* is Italian for "drink water". They therefore adopted Don Carano's grand-mother's name, Ferrari.

NO. 4 BUBBLY
Chateau Remy, Australia

In the last century the Avoca area, in the Pyrenees region of Victoria, was the scene of intensive goldmining activity, but all that remains now of that chapter in history are a few museum relics. Today the only gold for miles around is found in the *méthode champenoise* sparkling wine at Chateau Remy. Yet proud as its winemakers are of its numerous awards, they have to accept that within the Remy group it is only the number-four bubbly. That does not imply inferiority, but honours Chateau Remy by bracketing it with three of the most prestigious French Champagne houses – Charles Heidsieck, Piper-Heidsieck and Krug – all of which are owned by the Remy group.

The development of Chateau Remy began in the early 1960s, and since then it has consistently maintained the time-honoured style that has proven so successful in France. It ferments its wine from the three traditional Champagne varieties, Pinot Noir, Pinot Meunier and Chardonnay. It also practises the two-century-old technique of blending its current vintage with mature, still wines which have been allowed to age in their cellars. The addition of these reserve wines, which always

comprise at least 30 per cent of the final blend, adds more character and complexity. Other than that, little seems to differ from the Champagne region, except the Australian sun and Chateau Remy's harsh soil, which includes a high proportion of gravel and stone, in contrast with the white chalk its three French brothers call home.

THE OLDEST WHISKY ROCK OF ALL
Bowmore, Scotland

The variations in the styles of single malt whiskies are as great as those of Bordeaux wine chateaux and, with both whisky and wine, explanations of these differences are abundant. Yet one wonders if there is not a direct link between the individual streams that provide the water source and their

geology, and the pungency and flavour of the single malt involved. By regulation, a single malt Scotch whisky must be distilled from 100 per cent malted barley, at one distillery, which must have its own water source. It is arguably the latter which contributes many of the distinguishing characteristics that form the flavour and style of a single malt.

For example, the island of Islay, off the west coast of Scotland, is home to seven distilleries, all producing single malts with what many experts describe as a peaty flavour, which varies in weight from the lightest, perhaps at Bruichladdich, to the fullest, at Lagavulin, while somewhere in between lies the superb Bowmore, whose results, in recent times, have been gaining it a noteworthy succession of medals and awards.

Bowmore, coming from the Gaelic for big reef, distils and matures a dram that is a delightful balance between the elegance and power of the contrasting Islay malts, and which seems to be beginning to enjoy its deserved heyday. The Big Reef is not what it claims to be, but is a small run of dark grey rocks that shelter the 1779-dated distillery's position on the very edge of the water. This geographical location is subject to the high tide, which twice a day rises up the northern wall of the ageing warehouse, providing unique moist and salty conditions which no doubt exert a significant influence on the malt whisky that matures immediately behind that wall.

The key ingredient, however, must be the narrow River Laggan, which runs down the mountainside to Bowmore over a bed of Caledonian quartz, assessed as being 700 million years old. As it approaches the peaceful town of Bowmore, the river then tumbles over Torridonian rock, which, at 900 million years old, must be the oldest whisky rock of all. The water is so highly regarded by the local inhabitants that, after being used in the

Bowmore Distillery's unique ageing warehouse

Bowmore distillery, it is recycled to supply the swimming pool next door, where all the swimmers apparently have smiles on their faces.

POET'S CORNER
Montrose, Australia

More than seventy years after Henry Lawson's death, lovers of Australian poetry still argue over his merits as poet and writer, and yet his work has achieved national status. Certainly his poems convey the harsh realities of the life and times he experienced and observed.

In many ways it was not surprising that a child born in a Grenfell goldfield tent on a bleak winter's day in 1867, and whose formative years were always those of economic struggle, should regularly return to such themes in his literary work.

Lawson, a name derived from his father's Norwegian family name, Larsen, grew up in one of those unusual families where the parents' talents were quite divergent. His father, who owned a small plot at Pipeclay on the outskirts of Mudgee,

was a carpenter by trade, who desperately needed to use those skills to subsidise his inadequate income as a smallholder. To obtain carpentry work he frequently travelled to other towns and regions, while his wife, Louisa, immortalised by a charming Mudgee restaurant of that name, was an intellectual, a minor writer and, later in life, publisher of the *Republican* and an emerging feminist. The combination of such parental talents were reflected in Henry's working life, in which he varied periods of working on building sites with more artistically creative ones, during which he used his pen to demonstrate his ability.

Some of his poetry and many of his short stories are based on his experience of life in the Eurunderee district, just north of Mudgee, where he spent most of his childhood. Local legend relates that he would sometimes wander daydreaming through the very piece of land which today is called Poet's Corner Vineyard. Visitors to Montrose Wines, owners of that literary soil, are invited to taste a glass or two in the Eurunderee Room, where, if they are fortunate, they will hear Australia's only part-Aboriginal winemaker, Robert Paul, recall the words of Henry Lawson in such verses as:

> The faithful dog a moment
> Sits panting on the bank,,
> And then swims through the current
> To where his master sank.
> And round and round in circles
> He fights with failing strength,
> Till, borne down by the waters,
> The old dog sinks at length.

As one who has visited the Montrose cellars at Mudgee and sampled a glass or two of their soothing nectar while listening to the articulate Mr Paul relate that colourful verse, I can assure the reader that the experience gradually makes it easier to understand how Lawson's work has attracted such affection. Recognition of Lawson's work has been acknowledged by his country, with his face having been printed on its former $10 notes.

"A ROSE BY ANY OTHER NAME WOULD SMELL AS SWEET"
Johannisberg Riesling, Burgundy and Chablis; Germany and USA

The millions of European immigrants who poured into America during the last century took with them their drinking habits, and quite understandably identified early American wines by using the European names with which they were familiar. In this way, terms like Johannisberg Riesling, Burgundy and Chablis came into popular use. Of these, the first description, Johannisberg Riesling, is still used to name wines that are quite similar in style to the original German wines from the River Rhine, while the use of the words Burgundy, for the cheapest red jug wines, and Chablis, for many of the most basic semi-dry and semi-sweet whites and the occasional sugary pink, have strayed great distances from their classic French origins.

The background to the modern Johannisberg Riesling is one of the more confusing stories of varietal evolution that has occurred in California, where the vast majority of wine of that name has been and still is produced. When the earliest Prussian immigrants arrived in the infant Golden State, some brought with them a real hotchpotch of vine cuttings, often not appreciating their differences. Many simply called these Johannisberg Riesling to associate them with the highly rated Riesling wines produced in the *Bereich*, or district, around the town of Johannisberg in the Rheingau. Here the celebrated Schloss Johannisberg had attracted worldwide acclaim and was sold at a higher price than the first-growth Bordeaux such as Chateau Lafite, Latour and Margaux. It deliberately only used the finest Riesling vines and encouraged the surrounding vineyard owners to adopt the same practice, advice that was especially necessary in this case.

The problem was that all the vines in the locality were trained on single poles and crowded together in steep hillside vineyards, where all too often the growers were not too fussy about the identity of their vines. As far as they were concerned they made wine in a village style and the grape variety was not of prime importance. In fairness, it must be emphasised that generally wine was sold in casks under the one-word name Johannisberger, merely

indicating that it came from the vineyards of Johannisberg. So the Californian Prussians in their new American vineyards often planted vine cuttings such as Elbling, Sylvaner, Traminer, and no doubt others, among the White Riesling which is the true noble Riesling of Germany today.

From the dawn of the Californian winemaking era, a few, perhaps better-educated producers identified White Riesling correctly and called it by its proper name. Then, both before and after Prohibition, confusion really set in, as the terms Riesling, White Riesling, Johannisberg Riesling, and later Grey Riesling, were all in use, whether applied correctly or not. Eventually a little German influence helped untangle the knot, resulting in the term Johannisberg Riesling, which nowadays requires that the wine should be made from at least 75 per cent White Riesling, compared with 100 per cent in the wine that comes from Germany.

A little less erratic is the application of the word Burgundy to American wines. Originally, the old dukedom of Burgundy in France won itself a praiseworthy name for many of its fine white and red wines, which for centuries have enjoyed the highest international acclaim. Despite that, it is not difficult to understand how the name Burgundy came to be used in America, particularly for inexpensive, robust red wines. During the middle of last century, as millions sailed west from Europe, the pattern of selling true Burgundies, in France and its export markets, became firmly established, with the acknowledged wines from the leading vineyards and villages such as Aloxe-Corton, Puligny-Montrachet and Clos de Vougeot being named after their specific places of origin. Alongside these great names was the humblest wine to carry the name Burgundy, Bourgogne Ordinaire, which was made using the grapes from lesser vineyards, but which was normally strengthened in colour, flavour and alcohol by the addition of full-bodied wines from Algeria. These latter wines were relatively inexpensive and could fairly have been described as beefy or hearty, words that are still used to describe some American Burgundies.

As for Chablis, its name seems to have suffered most of all, as its recognition as an extremely inexpensive American wine with no pretensions to elegance or finesse has made it difficult and sometimes impossible for the French producers of the real Chablis to sell their fine, bone-dry white wines in the great consumer markets of the United States. This state of affairs is not only a considerable loss for the vignerons of Chablis in the Yonne department of France, but also for those American wine buffs who love classic, dry white wines, and in particular for those among them who enjoy the most satisfying Chardonnays, for this distinguished

French wine must by 100 per cent Chardonnay by law.

The very name Chablis has a confused and slightly misty past, with several etymological explanations. Of these expositions, the most likely harks back to pre-Roman days, when it would appear that a small Celtic settlement existed on the site of modern Chablis. At this point the problem of proof arises, because Celtic buildings of that time were constructed entirely of wood, the result being no remaining archaeological evidence. The sole witness to their occupation appears to be the name Chablis, which can be proven to have developed from the Roman name for the town – Cableia. It is suggested that the Romans simply adapted the Celtic word *chable*, or *shable*, meaning a kind of rope, from which we obtain the English word cable. This term was used to identify the town because it was the crossing-point on the River Serein. A flat-bottomed boat was used here as a ferry, being pulled from one side of the river to the other by means of a rope stretched between the opposite banks.

SECRET REVEALED, SECRET REMAINS
Chartreuse, France

There is a much-related anecdote concerning the visit of the playwright Oscar Wilde to the Abbey of La Grande Chartreuse late in the 19th century. Before departing he asked the almoner one last question: why the monks always wore benign smiles on their faces.

"Oh, that's easy Monsieur," came the reply. "Two-thirds yellow to one-third green."

The story is true but it is not simply a piece of light-hearted banter. It possibly sheds some light on why the monks still greet those few outsiders

The magnificent Abbe de la Grande Chartreuse

privileged to meet them with the same benign smile. That smile might be interpreted as a response to enquiries for the origin and secret of their nearly 400-year-old recipe for the Elixir of Long Life (*l'Elixir de la Longue Vie*), which constitutes the basis of their classic liqueurs. On this matter, I write with the benefit of some experience, gained in 1983 while making a television program, "The Masters and the Monks". A rare exception to the secrecy was made when Brother Marie-Bernard, the monk then in charge of the preparation of the liqueurs, was allowed to confer with me to ensure that I understood the various practices entailed in the production. Filming might then proceed in the correct sequence. It seems to me that the monks are all too well aware that some visitors are simply bursting to ask them about their illustrious secret recipe, and the now famous benign smile supplies an answer, an escape route, as the monks simply smile and walk on briskly, leaving no opening for a second challenge.

Their desire for isolation and peace must be respected and is their right. Indeed, that smile, in some instances, is a polite façade behind which their contemplation continues uninterrupted.

Throughout four centuries, the Carthusians have treated their recipe with a strange inconsequentiality bordering at times on indifference. Or maybe they feel that the possession of what amounts to a material good should not interfere with their spiritual lives. Whatever the reason, they have consistently maintained two secrets: the original source of their recipe, and its analytical details. Quite why they have attempted to shroud the first in mystery one may never know, as the answer is quite simple and can now be revealed.

Documents issued by the Chartreuse Diffusion Company, with the approval of the monks, state: "The recipe came into the hands of Marshal d'Estrées." These refer to François Hannibal d'Estrées, a companion of King Henry IV of France, who in 1605 presented the Carthusian Abbey of Vauvert, near Paris, with the original formula. D'Estrées was an interesting and highly talented man who had been consecrated as a bishop at twenty-one years of age, but later rejected the cloth to become a marshal of the French artillery. He is accredited with delivering the formula into Carthusian hands, but in essence he was its creator, for the original work was handwritten by him and bears his signature. That he should be the creator of the Elixir of Long Life is further substantiated by the fact that he lived to a grand ninety-seven years of age, truly exceptional at that time. I am confident that there will be no denial of this revelation either by the Carthusians or their Chartreuse Diffusion Company, as to contradict it would require public

production of the original recipe. That document would, of course, show the creator's name as Monsieur François d'Estrées.

In the meantime, the content of the recipe remains a closely guarded secret, despite several attempts to steal it and one noteworthy endeavour to copy the production. Fortunately the elixir remains the exclusive possession of the Carthusians, who in the 18th and 19th centuries put it to exemplary use as a medicine and comfort for passing travellers, and for the sick and undernourished of towns and villages for miles around. Upon examination it would appear that the generation of monks who received the original manuscript

at Vauvert were too preoccupied with their spiritual calling to demonstrate any interest in such an earthly matter. It was another 132 years before there was any activity, and then one of their order took it to their father house, the Abbey of La Grande Chartreuse, in the French Alps near Grenoble, and gave it to Brother Jerome Maubec, who was the herbalist and chemist there. From 1737, another twenty-seven years of research on Brother Jerome's part were needed to solve the formula and trace the 130 herb and plant ingredients it demanded. On the brink of completing the preparations, Brother Jerome fell mortally ill and, on his deathbed, revealed the entire secret to his assistant, Brother Antoine.

The various infusions and distillations were soon completed by Brother Antoine and *l'Elixir de la Longue Vie* was produced. Brother Antoine modified the elixir, however, with its extremely strong level of 71% (or 142° US proof), to create the Green Chartreuse liqueur, at 55%, which became very popular. Seventy-four years later, in 1838, Brother Bruno Jacquet created a third drink, the sweeter Yellow Chartreuse liqueur, which is lower in alcohol again, at 40%. The signature, L. Garnier, which appears on the Chartreuse labels is that of the monk responsible for the official registration of the trademark in 1869.

The rise in popularity of the elixir and of the Green Chartreuse liqueur aroused intense curiosity in the secret recipe, which brought the monks more than a little trouble. The first major problem

A *monk takes a cask sample at the Distillerie de la Grande Chartreuse, Voiron*

The Distillerie de la Grande Chartreuse

the Carthusian document, but it was indecipherable and was sent back to the pharmacist with the comment that it was "inadmissible". Eventually the manuscript was returned to the ownership of the monks, after their reinstatement in the abbey was authorised in 1816. Since that date several further attempts have been made to steal and decipher the recipe. In one instance a servant acting as an assistant tried to trick the brothers into granting him access, and in another a young clerk in the laboratory office managed to steal the formula and conceal it on his person. But when he tried to run out of the distillery he dropped the priceless documents on the floor.

The most underhanded incident was an attempt to copy all three drinks following the expulsion of the Carthusians from France in 1903. Owing to increasing demands for their liqueurs between 1860 and 1884, the monks had constructed a large distillery at Fourvoirie, in the valley below the abbey, and when they were expelled they removed all their documents, records and key equipment from Fourvoirie and took them to the Carthusian monastery in Tarragona, in Spain. At Tarragona they maintained production until their emotional return to the Alpine mountainside in 1940. Connections with Tarragona, however, have continued, and distillation is still carried out there for three months every year. The same team of three monks responsible for distillation and production in France set out by car for their annual journey to Tarragona and repeat the processes there, led by Brother Paul, the monk now in charge of the liqueurs' manufacture.

During the time of the Carthusians exile, from 1903 to 1940, the abbey and the Fourvoirie distillery were placed in receivership, under the control of two Isère men of dubious reputation called Schuerer and Lecoutrier. Both "had schemed without success for years, to buy, steal, copy or otherwise ruin the Carthusian Industry". Lecoutrier had been successfully sued by the Carthusian order "for violating the Chartreuse trademark", but now, with the Carthusians expelled, the men were free to establish the Compagnie Fermière de la Grande Chartreuse at the distillery in Fourvoirie.

The two men's attempts to copy the liqueurs made little profit and finished in disaster. In the last year of the monks' occupation, the monthly production had averaged 50 000 bottles. The pretenders never passed 3 000 in the same period, and the quality of their liqueurs was regularly criticised. In 1929 the Compagnie Fermière de la Grande Chartreuse went bankrupt. Without the necessary income to maintain a major distillery, the property fell into disrepair, and in 1935 a landslide destroyed the main building. Some have speculated that this

arose in 1789 with the French Revolution, when the monks abandoned the abbey, fearing the decimation of their order, and sought refuge in various other chapterhouses across Europe. A copy of the precious manuscript was made and kept by the one courageous brother left behind to observe the fate of the abbey. The original was entrusted to another Father, "who kept the papers on his person at all times". On one occasion that monk was arrested and imprisoned in Bordeaux, but somehow he managed to slip the recipe to another monk, Dom Basile Nantas, who had taken refuge near their fatherhouse. Dom Basile brought shame upon his tradition by giving the papers to a Grenoble pharmacist, M Liotard, in exchange for some bread.

It was now 1811, and the government of Napoleon Bonaparte had issued a decree that all secret formulae in the possession of French nationals should be forwarded to Paris for investigation and registration. From Grenoble, M Liotard submitted was "an act of God", but most reports suggest otherwise. In an area where rock falls are common, the land drains had not received any attention and had become blocked. In 1983, with some members of the "Masters and the Monks" crew, I went exploring on the site of the Fourvoirie distillery and we quickly unearthed some empty miniature bottles from that era.

Today the monks continue to reside peacefully in their formidable abbey, secluded from the busy secular world, while for some years the distillation and infusions have been carried out in cellars in Voiron, near Grenoble. The details of the formula remain a secret, but that is no longer true of its origin, for which we must thank the memory of a gentleman variously described as Monsieur, Marshal and Bishop. Perhaps Inventor would have been more accurate.

THE SLEEPING SISTERS OF LAFITE
Chateau Lafite, France

I was discovered in 1967, in a magnum in the cellars of Queen Elizabeth the Queen Mother's Scottish home, Glamis Castle. There I was, one of some forty forgotten vinous sisters, resting peacefully in that stone bastion once favoured by Shakespeare's Macbeth. It was as if we had been rudely awakened from a 100-year sleep.

Our life had begun at Chateau Lafite, in the village of Pauillac, in the Haut-Médoc region of France, in the memorable autumn of 1870. At that time, we were born into what appeared to be a wonderfully warm and comfortable world. Initially we were all nursed together in one apparently giant oak cask, but when we were no longer babies, at the age of two, we were each given our own double-sized bottles, or magnums, to wear. They were a very pretty shade of green which allowed the occasional glimmer of light to shine through and reveal our ruddy colour. The kind men in the cellars said we would grow bigger and more beautiful in our separate magnums. The French language we heard the men use was quite different from the language we have become accustomed to since. They would speak about the Franco-Prussian war and how glad they were that it had ended. They only wanted to enjoy peace for the rest of their lives – a sentiment we shared.

Later, after a seemingly endless journey by road and sea, we arrived at a place called Leith, where the native Scotsmen used such a strange language that we had to strain very hard to understand the words they spoke. When we eventually reached our final destination, Glamis Castle, all we desired was rest. We were, after all, mere children, and had learned from a few old bottles in Lafite that we had

no cause for anxiety, as we would not be disturbed for years. It would be a long, long time before our purpose would be revealed. And rest we did.

We were laid down in the dark, cool cellar alongside one another, and there we remained peaceful and content as the decades passed and the dust settled. The long silence was occasionally broken by distant tones speaking of wars, coronations and great sporting events. But for us the world appeared changeless until suddenly, before we were fully aware of anyone's presence, a bright light shone down upon us and excited voices disturbed our slumbers.

The next few weeks were the busiest we had ever known. The turmoil was both exciting and bewildering, as practically every day someone would enter the cellar and turn on a gas lamp to peer down at us and mumble as if addressing a nursery full of infants. It is quite startling to hear what adults will say when they think that no-one can understand. Occasionally men would lift one or other of my sisters out of our bin, dust her shoulders, peer at her neck and make, what were to us, incomprehensible comments to themselves about having a marvellous level. Afterwards they would gently and reverently replace the magnum in its previous position. All these goings-on appeared rather odd to us.

From that time onwards, life never regained its previous calm and peaceful tenor. Our existence became a curious combination of excitement and apprehension. Gradually the recollection of those words of wisdom imparted to us by the older bottles at Lafite began to take on a new significance. They had urged us not to be concerned about what and who was going to handle us and for what purpose, but a deepening sense of suspicion grew in my mind as I queried this new interest which had ruffled the smooth stillness of our untroubled lives. Doubts and questions raised themselves, which would not be answered until four years later, by which time it would be too late – I would never be able to forewarn any younger members of my family.

It was in the spring of 1971 that I experienced my final long journey of 600 miles to London, where I was separated from my sisters and taken in a small wooden box to a part of that giant city known as St James's. Here I was carried into a fine old building in King Street; I remember the name because the man made some joke about me being "fit for a king". At this juncture I suffered one of the few indignities of my life, when a young, fair-haired assistant actually wrote a number on a ticket and tied it around my neck. He evidently had little respect for my station in society, as without a single word he picked me up, carried me into another room and placed me on the floor among a group of wine bottles of all kinds and descriptions. There were, to be just, some near neighbours of mine from the villages of the Gironde, and even a couple from our highly reputed village of Pauillac, but none of them, not a single one, was from my generation. Most of them were mere striplings.

Communication was a problem. Could I remember my childhood French? At first, I admit, it was slow, and I became a little confused, as it seemed to me that some of the words had been changed a little, or was my memory playing me false? The other wine bottles kept telling me that I was going to be the star of the show, which made me even more puzzled and uncertain. I thought I overheard some of the others mentioning a sale and that I was going to be tasted the day before. Tasted? Whatever was that? I felt deeply perturbed by all this chatter and began to tremble. But then I tried to compose myself. Was this my *raison d'être*, my purpose, the whole reason for my existence? Was this to be my great individual performance? After all, I had not been created to be yet another bottle on a shop shelf. I had been privileged to be born into the very aristocracy of the wine world. I had not been quietly developing for 101 years to disappoint. I was determined to give a virtuoso performance and have the critics extolling the most lavish praise upon my name.

At last the day arrived and I was carried carefully into a spacious, airy room, where I was placed by a tall, silver-haired man on what I imagined to be a large wooden table, but which was covered by a white damask tablecloth. He beckoned to a small group of other men. It was strange and unfamiliar; there were no other women present and suddenly I felt a little alone.

The tall man leaned over me in a threatening posture. It flashed across my mind that he was going to strike me, but then I noticed him putting his hand into his pocket and removing something which resembled a small piece of twisted wire. Holding me gently but firmly around the neck, he cut my foil with a small knife. I flinched, anticipating pain, but it did not hurt at all, and I suppose the foil was rather battered and it was quite pleasant to be relieved of it.

Taking the piece of twisted wire, the man threaded it carefully into my cork, which was particularly long. The threading stopped and I waited eagerly but nervously to discover what would happen next. Placing his left hand on my shoulders, the man pulled firmly at my cork. At first I felt a little rumbling in my neck, succeeded by a feeling of light-headedness. With a final tug my cork popped out. I was free! My bouquet welled up, creeping up my neck, and drifted, expanding, until it filled the room.

I had always expected it to be a shock when the time came, but it was not. Here I was, enjoying the climax of my life, achieving my sole purpose on a wonderful occasion. I was being revealed in all my glory in the assembled tasting room of Christie's, the greatest wine auctioneers in the world, and assembled there were some of the most reputed wine writers in Europe, not merely to gaze at me and admire my bouquet, but to taste. These were to be the last glorious moments of my existence. I was determined to produce the most elegant and classic display. Already I could hear the tall man telling the others that I was the most magnificent wine he had ever been privileged to taste.

I steadied myself in the magnum, balanced all my mouth-filling flavours and concerted my efforts towards delighting the entire gathering. My thoughts returned fleetingly to my sisters and their fate. I began to wonder what had happened to them and to my cousins from Chateau Latour, not so far away. And then, with startling clarity, I recalled the time of my conception. What a wonderful year 1870 had been. After a cold winter the sap began to rise in the vine which gave birth to me. In midsummer, the sun baked down on so many long, hot days, but we still had plenty of water to quench our thirst, from those occasional nights of rain and the early-morning dew ... and the early-morning dew ... and the morning dew ... the dew ...

18. BIBLIOGRAPHY

ANDREWS, ALLEN. 1977. *The Whisky Barons.* London: Jupiter Books.

ANDRIEU, PIERRE. 1945. *Petite Histoire de l'Etiquette.* Paris: Maurice Ponsot.

ANNELY, AEUCKENS, GEOFFREY BISHOP, GEORGE BELL, KATE MCDOUGALL AND GORDON YOUNG. 1988. *Vineyard of the Empire, Early Barossa Vignerons 1842-1939.* Underdale: Australian Industrial Publishers.

ARLOTT, JOHN, AND CHRISTOPHER FIELDEN. 1978. *Burgundy Vines and Wines.* Revised edition. London: Quartet Books.

BAKER, TONY. 1987. *The Orlando Way, A Celebration of 150 Years 1837-1987.* Adelaide: G. Gramp and Sons.

————. 1991. *Wolf Blass, A Journey in Wine.* Adelaide: Wolf Blass.

BALZER, ROBERT LAWRENCE. 1978. *Wines of California.* New York: Harry N. Abrams.

BARIGAZZI, G. n.d. *Cento Anni in Galleria.* Milan: Industrie Grafiche Italiane Stucchi.

BAUCH, HERMANN. 1990. *Mein Kindheitstraum Wurde Wahr.* Vienna: Verlag Niederösterreiches Presshaus.

BEGG, CHARLES A., AND NEIL C. BEGG. n.d. *James Cook and New Zealand.* n.p.

BIERMANN, BARRIE. 1971. *Red Wine in South Africa.* Cape Town: Buren Publishers.

BELFRAGE, NICOLAS. 1985. *Life Beyond Lambrusco.* London: Sidgwick and Jackson.

BENSON, JEFFREY, AND ALISTAIR MACKENZIE. 1979. *Sauternes.* London: Sotheby's, Parke Bennet and Philip Wilson.

BIERMAN, BARRIE. 1971. *Red Wine in South Africa.* Cape Town: Buren Publishers.

BOLSMANN, ERIC H. n.d. *Bertrams Guide to South African Wines of Origin.* Bertrams Wines.

BROOK, STEPHEN. 1987. *Liquid Gold.* New York: William Morrow.

BURDEN, ROSEMARY. 1978. *A Family Tradition in Wine Making.* Adelaide: Thomas Hardy & Sons.

CHARLWOOD, DON. 1993. *The Long Farewell.* Ringwood: Penguin Books Australia.

CHISHOLM, JANE. 1987. *World History Dates.* London: Usborne.

CLARK, CORBET. 1989. *American Wines of the Northwest.* New York: William Morrow & Co.

COATES, CLIVE. 1982. *Claret.* London: Century Publishing.

COBBAN, ALFRED. 1971. *A History of Modern France.* Vols. I-III. London: Penguin Books.

COOK, CHRISTOPHER (ed.). 1982. *Pears Cyclopaedia.* 91st edition. London: Pelham Books.

COSSART, NOEL. 1984. *Madeira and the Island Vineyard.* London: Christie's Wine Publications.

DELAFORCE, JOHN. 1979. *The Factory House at Oporto.* London: Christie's Wine Publications.

DUNSTAN, DAVID. 1989. *Morris of Rutherglen.* Adelaide: Morris.

ENGLISH, SARAH JANE. 1989. *The Wines of Texas.* Austin, Texas: Eakin Press.

FAITH, NICHOLAS. 1978. *The Winemasters.* London: Hamish Hamilton.

FARMER, DAVID HUGH. 1992. *The Oxford Dictionary of Saints.* Oxford: Oxford University Press.

FERET ET FILS. 1986. *Bordeaux and its Wines.* Bordeaux: Editions Feret.

FORBES, PATRICK. 1967. *Champagne; the Wine, the Land and the People.* 4th edition. London: Victor Gallancz.

FORESTER, J.J. 1856. *Portugal and its Capabilities.* London: John Weale.

FRANCIS, A.D. 1972. *The Wine Trade.* London: Adam and Charles Black.

GENTILE, ROGER. 1991. *Discovering Ohio Wines.* Columbus, Ohio: Enthea Press.

GEORGE, ROSEMARY. 1989. *The Wine Dictionary.* Harlow: Longman Group UK.

GETZ, OSCAR. 1978. *Whiskey.* New York: David Mackay Company.

GRAMP, COLIN RAYMOND. n.d. Various family papers. Barossa Valley, South Australia.

GRASBY, W. COTTON. 1990. *Coonawarra Fruit Colony*. Penola, New South Wales: G & G Clifford.

GRUN, BERNER. 1975. *The Timetables of History*. 3rd edition. New York: Simon & Schuster/Touchstone.

HALLIDAY, JAMES. 1985. *The Australian Wine Compendium*. London: Angus & Robertson.

———. 1992. *Pocket Guide to the Wines of Australia and New Zealand*. London: Harper Collins.

HENRIOT, JOSEPH. 1982. *Champagne Charlie*. Paris: Editions Albin Michel.

HOLDEN, R., AND GLENDA HOLDEN. 1986. *Northwest Wine Country*. 2nd edition. Seattle: Holden Pacific.

HOWKINS, BEN. 1982. *Rich, Rare and Red*. London: Heinemann.

IRWIN, C., A.D. ADAMS AND S.A. WATERS (eds). 1964. *Crudence Complete Concordance to the Old and New Testaments*. Revised edition. London: Littleworth Press.

JACQUELIN, LOUIS, AND RENÉ POULAIN. 1965. *The Wines and Vineyards of France Bookplan*. London: Hamlyn.

JAMIESON, IAN. 1984. *The Mitchell Beazley Pocket Guide to German Wine*. London: Mitchell Beazley.

JEFFS, JULIAN. 1982. *Sherry*. London: Faber & Faber.

JOHNSON, HUGH. 1971. *The World Atlas of Wine*. 10th edition. London: Mitchell Beazley.

JOHNSON, TOM. n.d. The Story of Berry Bros and Rudd. In-house publication.

LAMBERT-GÓCS, MILES. 1990. *The Wines of Greece*. London: Faber and Faber.

LAUBE, JAMES. 1989. *California's Greatest Cabernets*. 2nd edition. San Francisco: Wine Spectator Press.

LAURENT, ANDRÉ. 1988. *La Grande Guerre en Champagne*. Le Coteau: Editions Horvath.

LICHINE, ALEXIS. 1967. *Alexis Lichine's Encyclopaedia of Wines and Spirits*. 4th edition. London: Cassell.

LINKLATER, ERIC. 1965. *The Prince in the Heather*. London: Hodder and Stoughton.

MACDONAGH, GILES. 1992. *The Wine and Food of Austria*. n.p.

MAYO, OLIVER. 1986. *The Wines of Australia*. 2nd edition. London: Faber and Faber.

MEINHARD, HEINRICH. 1976. *The Wines of Germany*. International Wine and Food Society, USA.

MILDE. n.d. Family History of Wilhelm and Elisabeth Milde and Descendants, 1837-1984. Private family documents.

MUNCHENBERG, PROEVE & PARTNERS. 1991. *The Barossa, A Vision Realised*. Barossa Valley Archives and Historical Trust.

MUSCATINE, D., M. AMERINE AND B. THOMPSON (eds). 1984. *The Book of Californian Wine*. Berkeley, California: University of California.

NOLAN, FREDERICK. 1981. *White Knights, Red Dawn*. London: Hutchinson.

NORRIE, DR PHILIP. 1990. *Vineyards of Sydney*. Sydney: Horwitz Grahame.

———. 1993. *Lindeman, Australia's Classic Winemaker*. Sydney: Apollo Books.

PALMER, A.W. 1964. *A Dictionary of Modern History 1789-1945*. 2nd edition. Harmondsworth: Penguin Books.

PASCOE, L.C. 1981. *Encyclopaedia of Dates and Events*. London: Hodder and Stoughton.

PELLUS, DANIEL. 1987. *La Marne dans la Guerre 1939/45*. Le Coteau: Editions Horvath.

PENNING-ROWSELL, EDMUND. 1969. *The Wines of Bordeaux*. 4th edition. Harmondsworth: Penguin Books.

PLATTER, JOHN. n.d. *Book of South African Wines*. n.p.

PLUMB, J.H. 1972. *The First Four Georges*. London: Fontana & Collins.

RAY, CYRIL. 1973. *Cognac*. London: Peter Davies.

READ, JAN. 1978. *Guide to the Wines of Spain and Portugal*. London: Pitman.

ROBERTSON, GEORGE. 1982. *Port*. London: Faber and Faber.

ROBINSON, JANCIS. 1986. *Vines, Grapes and Wines*. London: Mitchell Beazley.

———. 1989. *Vintage Time Charts*. London: Mitchell Beazley.

ROBY, NORMAN, AND CHARLES OLKEN. 1991. *The New Connoisseur's Handbook of Californian Wine*. New York: Alfred A. Knopf.

RONDELLO, ANTONIO. 1967. *La Galleria Vittorio Emmanuele II*. Milan.

RORSCHACH, KIMERLY. 1985. *Eighteenth-Century French Book Illustrations*. Philadelphia: The Rosenbach Museum and Library.

SAINTSBURY, GEORGE. 1927. *Notes on a Cellar-Book*. London: Macmillan & Co.

SCHOONMAKER, FRANK. 1967. *Encyclopedia of Wine*. London: Nelson.

SEELY, JAMES. 1986. *Great Bordeaux Wines*. London: Secker and Warburg.

SHEARER, MURIEL. 1982. *Quakers in Liverpool*. Liverpool: Religious Society of Friends.

SIMMONS, DOUGLAS A. 1983. *Schweppes, The First 200 Years*. London: Springwood Books.

SIMMS, PETER, AND SANDRA SIMMS. 1991. *The Wines of Corbières and Fitou*. Toulouse: Cristal/Privat.

SULLIVAN, CHARLES L. 1982. *Like Modern Edens*. Cupertino, California: California History Center.

TEUSNER, ROGER. n.d. Family history of Wilhelm Friedrich Kleeman. Private.

TREVILLE, R. (ed.). 1989. *Jefferson and Wine*. 2nd edition. Virginia, USA: The Vinifera Wine

Growers Association.

VANDYKE PRICE, PAMELA. 1984. *Alsace Wines.* London: Sotheby's Publications.

VERGANI, GUIDO. 1990. *Thirty Years and a Century of the Campari Company.* Milan: Campari.

WAIT, FRONA EUNICE. 1973. *Wines of Vines of California.* Berkeley: Howell-North Books.

WHEATLEY, DENNIS. 1965. *The Eight Ages of Justerini's.* Aylesbury: The Dolphin Publishing Co.

PHOTOGRAPHIC
ACKNOWLEDGEMENTS

The author would like to express his sincere gratitude to all of the many individuals, institutions, and members of the wine and drinks industries who provided the images which have helped bring this this book to life. In particular, the author would like to acknowledge those who provided the following photographs:

Champagne Mercier: pp. 1, 2
Alain Bouhier: top p. 5, p. 6
The British Museum: p. 8
The Berners Place Consultancy: pp. 23, 131, 132
Hans de Lijser: pp. 25, 26
Florio Marsala: p. 38
Sandeman: bottom p. 43
Babich Wines Ltd: pp. 55, 56, 57
Berry Bros & Rudd Ltd: p. 58
Cutty Sark Whisky Library: p. 59, bottom p. 61
Woodmansterne Ltd: p. 60, top p. 61
Service Photo Pernod Ricard: pp. 78, 79
The National Museum of Wales: photo and label, p. 81
Helicolor France: p. 88
A.H. Wines Ltd: p. 93
Peel Estate Wines: p. 97
Campari: pp. 100, 101, 102, 103
Cousino Macul: p. 104
Caymus Vineyards (J. Patrick Forden): p. 105

Asbach GmbH & Co.: p. 123
Drambuiè Liqueur Co. Ltd: p. 124
Justerini & Brooks: p. 129, top p. 172
McWilliam's Wines Pty Ltd: p. 133
Musée Bartholdi, Colmar, France: p. 137
Guenoc Winery: p. 147
Adler Fells: p. 148
Peter Thomson Agencies: p. 167
Westbay Distributors: pp. 168, 169
Studio Guérin Publicité Épernay: p. 179
Champagne Perrier-Jouët: pp. 180, 181
Martini & Rossi: p. 187
Arbor Crest Wine Cellars: top right p. 190
Chudeau: p. 194
Washington Post: p. 202
Dent & Reuss: p. 207
Annette Balnaves, Coonawarra: p. 213
Geoffrey Roberts Agencies: p. 220
Gonzales Byass SA: p. 221
Champagne Louis Roederer: p. 222
Ford Robinson Photographic: p. 229
Michael Harrison Wines: p. 231
Delaforce Sons & Co. (London Ltd): p. 233
S. Smith & Son Yalumba Winery: p. 236
Woltner Estates Ltd: p. 238
Intercontact: p. 239
Janet Price: p. 245
Image Library, State Library of New South Wales: p. 248

INDEX

X

Y

Z